McNae's Essential Law for Journalists

McNae's
essential law
for journalists

Twenty-second edition

Mike Dodd   Mark Hanna

OXFORD

UNIVERSITY PRESS

Great Clarendon Street, Oxford, OX2 6DP,
United Kingdom

Oxford University Press is a department of the University of Oxford.
It furthers the University's objective of excellence in research, scholarship,
and education by publishing worldwide. Oxford is a registered trade mark of
Oxford University Press in the UK and in certain other countries

Nineteenth edition 2007
Twentieth edition 2009
Twenty-first edition 2012

Impression: 2

Published in the United States of America by Oxford University Press
198 Madison Avenue, New York, NY 10016, United States of America

British Library Cataloguing in Publication Data
Data available

Library of Congress Control Number: 2014930462

ISBN 978–0–19–967910–2

Printed in Italy
by L.E.G.O. S.p.A.—Lavis TN

In Memory of mein guter freund Robert 'Jeff' Jeffery
M.P.D.

To my wife Linda, my son Rory, my mother Mary and my father Michael
M.H.

Preface to the 60th anniversary edition

There's a tendency for journalists to think that the law brings them nothing but responsibilities, so it is a great thing when they understand that the law also gives them power. All of us who believe in a free press and its role in our democracy take pride in watching a journalist, armed with the relevant law, take on an obstructive local council, an unhelpful clerk to the magistrates or an overbearing police officer.

Typically, the journalist does so with the confidence that comes from having a copy of McNae to hand, a resource that remains as invaluable to the experienced editor as to the young trainee. From its first edition, 60 years ago, it has been written with a desire to help journalists put information into the public domain, rather than intimidate them into keeping it out. Here's a book that guides rather than lectures, a desktop companion that has helped generations of its readers keep out of trouble or – when circumstances demand – encouraged them to stir up some. A much-creased 21st edition sits by the computer in front of me: it's reassuring to know its successor is about to publish.

Of course, McNae and the NCTJ are of a similar generation. We've grown up - but never old - together. We were established in 1951, three years before the first edition of this great book, with a remit to train and qualify competent and confident journalists. It is a task that would be hard to fulfil without McNae at our side. And if our joint purpose has remained constant, we've both moved fast to embrace radical changes in the world of media. Who, five years ago, would have imagined that British judges would allow us to report from their courtrooms using Twitter? Come to that, if we go back 10 years, who would have imagined Twitter?

McNae has faced too the considerable task of keeping abreast of a constantly changing body of law. Some authors deliver a final manuscript and rest on their laurels: McNae authors deliver a manuscript and begin on the next. We are hugely indebted to them for their tireless work and immensely grateful to the Oxford University Press for taking on publication with such enthusiasm. It is wonderful to work with writers and publishers who demonstrate such passion for the subject.

We have a first edition of McNae in the NCTJ library. The style of Leonard McNae's preface is of the period, but his point is timeless: "The journalist is best able to exercise his craft and uphold the traditions of his profession who knows both his rights and his privileges."

Kim Fletcher
Chairman of the National Council for
the Training of Journalists
April 2014

Preface

This 2014 edition of *McNae* marks the book's 60th anniversary. The world of journalism has, of course, been transformed in many ways since the first edition was printed in 1954. Indeed, since the edition published in 2012, journalism in the United Kingdom and media law in England and Wales has undergone almost revolutionary change.

The report of the Leveson Inquiry into the culture, practice and ethics of the UK press led to legislation and a Royal Charter intended to establish a new 'Leveson-compliant' self-regulatory body for the newspaper and magazine industry. But if the government hoped its actions – which critics say introduce the real danger of political interference in press regulation – would lead to the establishment of one 'recognised' regulator, it has so far been sadly disappointed. Almost all the nation's press, national, regional and local, have refused to join any body recognised under the Royal Charter, and have instead opted to sign up with Ipso, the Independent Press Standards Organisation established by the press industry, which was scheduled to start work in May 2014 and replace the Press Complaints Commission (PCC). Another entrant into the regulatory field is Impress, the Independent Monitor for the Press, which says it is Leveson-compliant but appeared, at the time of writing, to have attracted little support from the press.

In the meantime, the fall-out from the *News of the World* phone-hacking scandal continues, with journalists, police officers and public servants having been convicted of offences, others on trial on a variety of charges, and more being arrested or charged as police inquiries continue on a number of fronts. This edition of the book contains a new chapter to focus on charges used in those prosecutions.

The Defamation Act 2013 came into effect on 1 January 2014, reforming libel law in England and Wales. It introduced new defences, particularly for website operators, and a single publication rule, ending the anomaly that material in online archives was in effect never subject to the one-year limitation period for bringing a libel action.

In the criminal justice system reform has abolished committal hearings, replacing them with a new process under which magistrates simply 'send' either-way cases due for jury trial to a Crown court, in the same way that indictable-only cases are 'sent', with no consideration by magistrates of the strength of prosecution evidence. Sending hearings are no longer covered by the well-known reporting restrictions in section 8 of the Magistrates' Courts Act 1980, and are instead subject to those in section 52A of the Crime and Disorder Act 1998.

All this has meant a considerable amount of re-working and updating material for this, the twenty-second edition of *McNae*, which seems to be a suitable way of marking the 60th anniversary of the appearance of the first – and considerably shorter – edition. The attention rightly being paid to press practices and ethics means we have kept coverage of the regulatory systems for both the print and broadcasting industries at the front of the book. For the time being we have concentrated on the Editors' Code of Practice which was overseen by the PCC, on the basis that it is likely at the very least to form the foundation of any code to be overseen by Ipso.

Coverage of defamation has also been widely re-cast, to take account of the reforms in the Defamation Act 2013, although at the time of writing no cases had emerged to give guidance on how the courts will handle the legislation. We have also analysed changes in court rules which should allow journalists greater access to case material, to aid reporting of trials and other hearings. We have also explained changes in the rules governing reporting local government and access to information about it.

This edition follows the practice in previous editions of using the term 'media organisations' to encompass the publishers of newspapers, magazines, websites and broadcasters. The term is not wholly satisfactory, especially where the point being made also applies to freelance journalists or to any individual 'blogger' or 'tweeter', but we felt it remains the most practical option to reflect the technological convergence in how journalism is published.

The amount of law affecting UK journalism continues to grow, and we are using www.mcnaes.com to provide content for which there was no space in the book. For example, www.mcnaes.com supplements the explanation in ch. 13 of the complex law governing reporting of family courts. The site will also be used for updates, such as on legislation arising from the government's review of defamation law.

We are keen to hear what you think of this edition and of the www.mcnaes.com site. We particularly hope that both project the fact that journalism remains an exciting, varied career, that most of its practitioners pride themselves on being ethical and law-abiding, and that they can and do 'make a difference', not least in their watchdog role of exposing wrongdoing and reporting on and examining the workings of society. It is worth noting that the extent of phone-hacking by some journalists, or private investigators working for them, was revealed to the public by other journalists, not by the original police investigation.

If you wish to contact us, our email addresses are given at the end of the preface.

This book covers the law in England, Wales and Northern Ireland which it is essential for journalists to know. A chapter on www.mcnaes.com provides an introduction to Scottish law most relevant to journalists.

Walter Greenwood and Tom Welsh

We also have the sad duty of commemorating the contribution to *McNae*, and to journalism training generally, made by media law gurus Walter Greenwood and Tom Welsh.

Walter died at the age of 87 on 1 October 2013 and Tom died on 10 April 2014 at the age of 85, as this edition was being finalised. For more than 40 years both were major forces in journalism training and law, and for more than 30 of those years Walter and Tom were co-authors of a total of 13 editions of *McNae*, covering an increasingly complex media law field during decades of wide-ranging change. Together, in their work for the NCTJ and in *McNae*, they fostered the idea that reporters and their editors should, armed with this book, feel confident to make challenges in courts to invalid or unnecessary restrictions on what could be published about cases.

Even after stepping down as co-editors both maintained close links with the book as honorary consultants. Walter wrote the chapter on media law in Northern Ireland for the twenty-first edition, and earlier editions as well. Only his final illness stopped him contributing to this edition. In addition to his work in the Thomson Regional Newspapers training scheme, including in its Newcastle centre now run by Press Association Training, Walter made a huge contribution to the work of the National Council for the Training of Journalists' media law examinations board, helping for more than 40 years – including in spells as its chair – to set the standards of legal competence expected of all trainee journalists.

Tom too was involved with the NCTJ for much of his career, and chaired its media law examinations board for five years. His achievements included becoming the first director of Journalism Studies at City University, London in 1976, editing the North-Western Evening Mail in Cumbria for seven years, launching Media Lawyer in 1996, and editing it for 10 years.

As the book's current authors we owe a great debt to Walter and Tom for their kindly advice and generosity in sharing their knowledge.

Acknowledgements

As authors we are grateful to the NCTJ's chief executive Joanne Butcher, its media law examinations board and NCTJ staff for support and suggestions as we wrote this edition. We owe a great debt to Abbey Nelms, senior publishing editor at the Higher Education Department of Oxford University Press for her ideas, guidance and patience and to Fiona Tatham for her care in the editing process.

We also owe thanks to the following people who helped us by making suggestions for content, including those who read drafts of chapters or responded to our queries when we sought to draw on their expertise: Amanda Ball, the NCTJ's chief examiner, a senior lecturer at Nottingham Trent University; Jackie Errigo, who has been chief examiner of the NCTJ media law examinations board, a senior lecturer at Brighton University; Keith Mathieson, a partner at law firm RPC, and his colleague Robert Johnson, an associate solicitor with the firm; Heather Rogers QC, of Doughty Street Chambers; Hugh Tomlinson QC, of Matrix Chambers; and Simon Westrop, Head of Legal, Newsquest Media Group.

We also thank the Judicial College for permitting use of diagram material, the Press Standards Board of Finance (Pressbof) for permitting reproduction of the Editors' Code of Practice and Ofcom for allowing us to cite extracts from its Broadcasting Code.

We owe thanks too to our employers – in Mark's case, the Department of Journalism Studies, Sheffield University, and in Mike's the Press Association – for their support and encouragement.

The main body of the text of this edition was completed in November 2013, but it was possible to add some late news until early March 2014.

Mike Dodd, Legal Editor, Press Association, and member of the NCTJ media law examinations board
Email: m_dodd@msn.com

Mark Hanna, chair of the NCTJ media law examinations board
Email: M.Hanna@sheffield.ac.uk

This book bears the name of its first author, the late Leonard McNae, who was Editor of the Press Association's Special Reporting Service.

Summary Contents

Detailed Contents

Late News

Star gains harassment injunctions

One Direction popstar Harry Styles won permanent High Court injunctions against four paparazzi photographers in his legal battle to end the 'crazy pursuit' of him. The singer's barrister said that four individuals had so far been identified as being among the paparazzi since harassment proceedings were launched last year (*Media Lawyer*, 10 March, 2014).

Ch. 27 explains harassment law

Ofcom censures BBC over bodies

Broadcasting regulator Ofcom censured the BBC for screening images of naked corpses and testimonies about being tortured with hot metal rods, when children could have been viewing. The documentary, 'Our World - Sri Lanka's Unfinished War', was shown at 5.30am on the BBC News Channel and broadcast simultaneously on BBC1. Ofcom said this breached rules 1.3 and 2.3 of its Broadcasting Code. The BBC admitted the 'significant scheduling error' (*Ofcom Broadcasting Bulletin*, issue 249, 3 March 2014).

Ch. 3 explains the Code

Newspaper breached juvenile's anonymity

The *North Devon Journal* breached an anonymity order made under section 39 of the Children and Young Persons Act 1933. The newspaper's owner Local World Ltd was fined £750 after it admitted the offence at a hearing at Taunton magistrates court.

A Crown Prosecution Service spokesman said that the newspaper's website carried a report of a magistrates court case which named the victim of an alleged offence of assault causing grievous bodily. The victim was aged under 18. The court subsequently made a section 39 order. 'The *North Devon Journal* removed the victim's name from its website, but the report without this amendment appeared in the printed edition of the newspaper a few days later,' the CPS spokesman said.

Mark Sainsbury, managing director of Devon and Cornwall Media, the group which includes the newspaper, said: 'This was a one-off incident which arose through human error' (*Holdthefrontpage* and *Media Lawyer*, 28 February 2014).

Ch. 9 explains section 39 anonymity

Data law guide for journalists

The Information Commissioner's Office issued a draft guide for the media on data protection law. This followed Lord Justice Leveson's recommendation that the Commissioner should develop specific and comprehensive guidance on the application of the Data Protection Act to the press (ICO press release, 23 January 2014).

See http://ico.org.uk/~/media/documents/library/Data_Protection/Research_and_reports/data-protection-and-journalism-a-guide-for-the-media-draft.pdf

Ch. 2 outlines the Leveson Report and ch. 28 covers data protection

PACE hearings must not be secret

Courts must allow media organisations access to all the evidence when dealing with police requests for orders under PACE and that such organisations or their journalists should hand over journalistic material, the Supreme Court ruled in March 2014. It rejected an appeal by the Metropolitan Police Commissioner against the decision of the High Court to overturn a production order against broadcaster BSkyB. It had been made by a judge at the Old Bailey after a hearing in which he heard evidence from a police officer in secret, denying BSkyB representatives access to it. The case arose after the Metropolitan Police, in a criminal investigation under the Official Secrets Act 1989, sought disclosure of various documents, including copies of all emails between Sky journalist Sam Kiley and two officers in the armed forces. BSkyB's arguments against the production order included that Mr Kiley was very experienced and that there was no risk that information damaging to national security would be published. The investigation did not lead to any charges (*R (on the application of British Sky Broadcasting Ltd) v The Commissioner of Police of the Metropolis* [2014] UKSC 17).

Ch. 33 explains the 1989 Act and ch. 34 explains PACE

Court of Appeal upholds FOI rights

Attorney General Dominic Grieve's use of a ministerial veto to stop the public seeing letters the Prince of Wales wrote to government ministers was unlawful, the Court of Appeal ruled.

Guardian journalist Rob Evans had accused Mr Grieve, as the Government's principal legal adviser, of failing to show 'reasonable grounds' for blocking disclosure.

The Upper Tribunal, headed by a High Court judge, declared in September 2012 that Mr Evans was a requestor of information, and therefore the public had rights to see the letters under the Freedom of Information Act 2000 and under the Environmental Information Regulations 2004. But a month later Mr Grieve issued a certificate to use his ministerial veto to prevent disclosure.

The Court of Appeal ruled that the certificate should be quashed because Mr Grieve had 'no good reason' for overriding the Upper Tribunal's decision and had acted in a manner incompatible with European law (*The Queen on the application of Evans v HM Attorney General and the Information Commissioner* [2014] EWCA Civ 254).

A spokesman for Mr Grieve said he would appeal to the Supreme Court (*Media Lawyer*, 12 March 2014).

Ch. 30 explains FOI law and earlier stages of this case

Journalists' access to family case documents

A judge in the Family Division of the High Court said that journalists should be given copies of written skeleton arguments when hearings are held in open court, unless they contained 'very confidential' material. Mr Justice Holman was dealing with a case involving a dispute between a Moroccan man and his English ex-partner over the future of their five-year-old son. Nothing could be reported which might identify the boy (*Media Lawyer*, 10 March, 2014).

The President of the Family Division Sir James Munby said he would shortly issue further draft Practice Guidance, dealing with disclosure to the media of certain categories of document, subject to appropriate restrictions (*View from the President's Chamber*, 3 March 2014).

Ch. 13 explains family courts

Same-day searches reinstated for decrees

Journalists who visit the Principal Registry of the Family Division in London to inspect information from divorce decrees absolute can once more see it on the same day they request this. A Registry reorganisation meant journalists faced a wait of up to 10 working days for the information. But after representations by the Newspaper Society, the Registry restored same-day searches for journalists (Newspaper Society press release, 13 February 2014).

Ch. 13 explains inspection rights for such decrees

Northern Ireland and Defamation Act 2013

The refusal of the Northern Ireland Executive to enact the Defamation Act 2013 meant that the province is becoming 'an anarchic force in UK media law', Lord Black of Brentwood told the House of Lords during a debate.
Lord Black, an executive director of the Telegraph Media Group, said Northern Ireland's 'opting out' of the new defamation laws will punish ordinary people, and that it 'is clinging to an oppressive, outdated regime' (*Hansard*, 25 February 2014).

Chs. 19–22 cover the 2013 Act and ch. 37 outlines Northern Ireland's defamation law

Anger at anti-terrorism ruling

Human rights campaigners reacted angrily to a High Court ruling rejecting David Miranda's claim that he was unlawfully detained under anti-terrorism laws.

Home Secretary Theresa May said the judgment supported the action taken by police at Heathrow Airport last year. Scotland Yard rejected suggestions that detaining Mr Miranda, partner of investigative journalist Glenn Greenwald, who with *The Guardian* newspaper exposed secret information on US surveillance leaked by whistle-blower Edward Snowden, was an attack on press freedom (*Media Lawyer*, 20 February 2014).

See www.mcnaes.com ch. 40 on how counter-terrorism law affects journalists

Council permits filming of meetings

A hyperlocal news website has persuaded a council to end a ban on the filming of its meetings. Wrexham.com was then able to publish what it thinks is the first ever video of a Wrexham Council meeting. The council had in recent years rejected several previous requests that it permit filming (*holdthefrontpage*, 5 March 2014).

Ch. 31 covers access to council meetings

New contempt law on archives

The Criminal Justice and Courts Bill contains proposals which if, as expected, become law, would give the Attorney General the power to warn news organisations that material in their online archives could breach the Contempt of Court Act 1981 in relation to specified court proceedings, and therefore should be taken down while those proceedings are going on. The Bill also confirms the power of the Crown courts to issue injunctions ordering that material should be removed from websites while criminal proceedings are taking place, because of the risk of contempt. The Bill confirms this by providing that appeals against such orders may be made by way of section 159 of the Criminal Justice Act 1988 (*Media Lawyer*, 24 February, 2013).

Ch. 18 covers contempt of court and ch. 15 explains section 159 of the 1988 Act

McNae's at a glance

McNae's Essential Law for Journalists contains a range of features to help you find the information you need quickly – in class and on the job. This short guide outlines these features and how they can help you.

→glossary Glossary terms are highlighted in the text and defined in the glossary at the back of the book and on www.mcnaes.com.

Chapter summaries introduce each chapter and outline the content – and why it matters to a journalist.

Cross-references point out related information in other chapters, helping you navigate key areas and understand the full picture.

Case studies appear throughout the text to provide context and examples of how the law and ethical codes have been applied to real-life situations.

! Advice from the authors on applying media law and ethical codes on the job, and reminders about relevant content elsewhere in the book.

The website that accompanies this book, www.mcnaes.com, contains regular updates from the authors as well as self-test resources, writing tips and additional chapters and information on a range of key topics.

➡ Each chapter features a summary of the essential points – ideal for revision and as an at-a-glance reminder.

((•)) A list of useful websites is included at the end of each chapter to help students and journalists find information quickly

www.mcnaes.com

McNae's Essential Law for Journalists is accompanied by a free-to-use website – www.mcnaes.com – that features extra resources for both students and journalists.

Updates

Whether you are studying or a working journalist, keep your knowledge up-to-date at www.mcnaes.com with regular updates from the authors on key changes affecting media law and ethics.

Online-only chapters

Access additional online chapters on: The Official Secrets Act
Scottish media law
Terrorism and the effect of counter-terrorism law as well as extended chapters on family law and the incitement of hatred.

Additional material

Find additional detail and resources on a range of topics, including media coverage before trial, reporting on juveniles, challenging the courts and privacy.

Self-test questions

Test your media law know-how and get instant feedback with chapter-related questions – ideal preparation for exams or to refresh your knowledge.

Glossary

Need to check a key term at court or on the way to class? Download the *McNae's* glossary for on-the-go access to essential legal terms. The glossary is also available to download as flashcards for ready-made exam preparation.

Extra resources

Writing tips – including how to avoid clichés and advice on commonly confused words – from the experts at Oxford University Press.

www.mcnaes.com also features regular discussion pieces and information on the history of *McNae*, as well as key news from OUP and the authors.

Part 1

The landscape of law, ethics and regulation

Introduction

Chapter summary

The UK media enjoy freedoms which are the envy of journalists in oppressed societies. Nevertheless, the UK has more laws affecting journalism than is the case in some other democracies, and so a sound, thorough knowledge of legal matters is especially important for UK journalists, particularly in their role as 'watchdogs' acting on the public's behalf. This chapter explains how the UK's laws are made, and how the European Convention on Human Rights helps safeguard freedom of expression. It also outlines the distinction between criminal and civil law, and between solicitors and barristers.

▌ Free but with restrictions

Although the UK has a 'free press' in comparison to the authoritarian censorship which stifles liberty in some other nations, the description must be qualified, because of the many and growing restrictions on what can be published. This book covers the increasing number of laws affecting journalism.

The importance of freedom of expression, and of the journalist's position as a public watchdog ensuring a properly informed populace in a democratic society, have been stressed by both the UK courts and the European Court of Human Rights in Strasbourg.

The senior law lord, Lord Bingham said in 2000 in a case in the House of Lords (now replaced by the Supreme Court):

> " In a modern, developed society it is only a small minority of citizens who can participate directly in the discussions and decisions which shape the public life of that society. The majority can participate only indirectly, by exercising their

ch. 21, p. 270, The nature of press confer- ences, explains this case

rights as citizens to vote, express their opinions, make representations to the authorities, form pressure groups and so on. But the majority cannot partici- pate in the public life of their society in these ways if they are not alerted to and informed about matters which call or may call for consideration and action. It is very largely through the media, including of course the press, that they will be so alerted and informed. The proper functioning of a modern participatory democracy requires that the media be free, active, professional and enquiring (*McCartan Turkington Breen v Times Newspapers Ltd* [2001] 2 AC 277). 〃

It is the journalist's job to help safeguard freedom of expression and a free media, by accurate reporting and ensuring that people are properly informed about what is being done in their name by those who claim to govern them. It is also the job of journalists to safeguard the principle of an independent judiciary by reporting what is going on in the courts which apply the laws intended to safe- guard the interests of all.

To do all this, journalists must know the law – where it comes from, what it says, and what it allows them to do or stops them from doing.

The UK has a vibrant and wide-ranging media – newspapers, magazines, radio and television stations and of course the ever-growing internet, with the myriad text and audio-visual sites it offers – and the law applies to all of them. Many are also subject to regulatory systems. This book explains how report- ing restrictions, libel and privacy laws limit what may be published – and the financial consequences of mistakes or recklessness in journalism. But it also emphasises the freedoms which exist to publish and investigate. Only by know- ing what is and is not possible, and what may or may not be done can journal- ists, broadcasters, website operators and those who work with them keep the freedoms and variety of platforms they have now, campaign for greater free- dom—and ensure that their work is not discredited or curtailed by some foolish but expensive error.

chs. 2 and 3 focus on codes of ethics

Journalists' ethics are under increasing scrutiny. The observance of ethi- cal codes should be an integral part of how journalists operate, to help produce respected, fair journalism and preserve freedoms. The risk is that if some jour- nalists do not respect these codes, new and punitive law will be created in attempts to curb malpractices, and limit everyone's freedoms.

▌ Sources of law

 →glossary The main sources of the law have traditionally been custom, precedent and **statute**.

Custom

When the English legal system began to take shape in the Middle Ages, royal judges were appointed to administer the 'law and custom of the realm'. This devel-
 →glossary oped into the **common law**.

Precedent

As judges applied the common law to the cases before them, their decisions were recorded by lawyers. This process continues. Records of leading cases give the facts considered by a court, and the reasons for its decision. The UK has a hierarchy of courts, so a decision made by a lower court can be challenged by appeal to a higher court. The decisions made by the higher courts – precedents – are then binding on all lower courts, thus shaping their future rulings. Precedents evolve and develop the common law.

Figure 1 is a diagram of the hierarchy of the courts in England and Wales. The nature and role of these courts is explained further in later chapters.

 Ch. 37 explains Northern Ireland's courts, and the www.mcnaes.com chapter on Scotland outlines that nation's courts system.

A **Supreme Court** judgment binds all other UK courts, apart from – in most respects – Scottish criminal courts. Supreme Court Justices can refuse to follow their earlier decisions, which otherwise can only be overturned or reversed by legislation.

 →glossary

ch. 8 explains these courts' roles

Figure 1 Hierarchy of the courts.

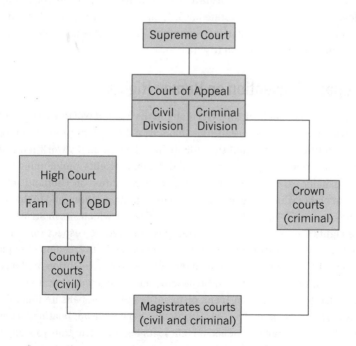

Fam = Family (civil); Ch = Chancery (civil); QBD = Queen's Bench (civil and criminal). See chs. 8, 12 and 13 for these High Court roles.

Below the Supreme Court, the Court of Appeal's decisions bind the High Court and the lower courts, and High Court decisions bind all lower courts.

Statutes and statutory instruments

Common law can be modified or replaced by statutes – Acts of Parliament, which are primary legislation. But UK governments have made increasing use of secondary legislation known as **statutory instruments**. Parliament frequently uses Acts to enshrine broad principles in legislation, but delegates the detailed framing of the new law to the departmental Minister concerned, who sets its detail out in statutory instruments in the form of regulations or rules. Statutory instruments must be approved by Parliament.

→ glossary

European regulations and directives

As the UK is part of the European Union, EU treaties and other EU law are part of UK law. The EU's Council and its Parliament agree regulations and directives which are binding on member states as part of the EU's *raison d'etre* of encouraging trade between member states by harmonising laws throughout its area. EU Regulations apply in the form in which they are drawn up, but member states decide how directives should be implemented, through their own legislation.

The European Court of Justice, based in Luxembourg, clarifies – for the national courts of EU member states – interpretation of EU legislation. It can, for example, rule on allegations that a member state has infringed EU law to gain advantage in trade, and penalise a state for such infringement. This court is not to be confused with the European Court of Human Rights.

The European Convention on Human Rights

The repression and genocide of Nazi Germany in the Second World War prompted western European nations to create the Council of Europe to promote individual freedom, political liberty and the rule of law. The Council's work led to the European Convention for the Protection of Human Rights and Fundamental Freedoms – usually referred to as the European Convention on Human Rights – which sets out rights which must be protected by signatory states, and to the foundation of the European Court of Human Rights (ECtHR), which sits in Strasbourg. Among the rights the Convention guarantees are the right to respect for privacy and family life, in Article 8 of the Convention, and the right to freedom of expression, in Article 10. Forty-seven nations have adopted the Convention, and any of their citizens can take a case to the Strasbourg court to argue that a signatory nation has failed to protect them from, or to sufficiently compensate them for, a breach of a Convention right. The Convention has very wide application, because a nation will be held to have breached a right if its legal system fails to stop or to offer an adequate remedy for a violation of an individual's rights by a private body or individual as well as by a state authority or body.

The Human Rights Act 1998

The Human Rights Act 1998, which came into force on 2 October 2000, put the Convention into UK law, greatly increasing its influence on UK courts. Individuals can require any UK court to consider their rights under the Convention in the context of any case.

The Act requires any UK court determining a question in connection with a Convention right to take account of the ECtHR's decisions. It also says that new UK legislation must be compatible with Convention rights, and that old and new legislation must be construed so far as possible to conform with them.

It is unlawful for UK public authorities to act in any way that is incompatible with the Convention.

Convention rights

Adopting the Convention directly into UK law has required judges systematically to consider Convention rights, which conflict in many cases.

For journalists, the most important part of the Convention is Article 10, which says in part: 'Everyone has the right to freedom of expression. This right shall include freedom to hold opinions and to receive and impart information and ideas without interference by public authority.'

Article 10 makes clear that restrictions on this right have to be justified, necessary in a democratic society and 'prescribed by law'.

Journalists wanting to exercise their rights under Article 10 may find themselves facing a claim under Article 8, protecting the right to respect for privacy and family life, such as someone seeking an injunction to stop publication of a story about his/her personal life, or seeking damages if the material has been published.

Weighing competing rights

The methodology a court should use to decide in any particular case whether one Convention right should prevail over another was detailed in *Re S (A Child) (Identification: Restrictions on Publication)* [2004] UKHL 47. In that House of Lords judgment, Lord Steyn said:

> First, neither article has as such precedence over the other. Secondly, where the values under the two articles are in conflict, an intense focus on the comparative importance of the specific rights being claimed in the individual case is necessary. Thirdly, the justifications for interfering with or restricting each right must be taken into account. Finally, the proportionality test must be applied to each. For convenience I will call this the ultimate balancing test.

Lord Steyn was emphasising that the particular circumstances of each case must be intensely considered to decide which Convention right – and therefore which party to the argument – prevails in each matter to be decided.

In some judgments relevant to the media, Article 2 (the right to life) and Article 3 (the prohibition of torture and inhuman or degrading treatment or punishment)

www. mcnaes. com ch. 13 has more detail of the *Re S* judgment

are cited and, by their very nature, can have great weight – for example, if it is argued with justification that someone's name or address should not be published to protect them from violent criminals or vigilantes.

 Articles 2, 3, 6, 8 and 10 are set out in Appendix 1, pp. 441–442

Divisions of the law

There are two main divisions of law – criminal and civil.

Criminal law deals with offences which harm the whole community and thus are considered to be an offence against the sovereign. A Crown court case in which John Smith is accused of an offence is listed as R v Smith. 'R' stands for Regina (the Queen) or Rex (the King), depending on who is reigning at the time, and 'v' for 'versus'.

A lawyer talking about this case would generally refer to it as 'The Queen (or the King) against Smith'.

 See chs. 4–10 for more detail about the criminal justice system, a huge source of news for journalists.

 glossary

Civil law concerns disputes between individuals and organisations, and includes the redress of **torts** – that is, wrongs suffered. Medical negligence, defamation and breach of copyright are all torts. A case in which Mary Brown sues John Smith will be known in writing as Brown versus Smith. Lawyers will speak of the case as 'Brown *and* Smith' (our italics).

In practice, the two divisions overlap – many acts or omissions are criminal offences for which an individual may be prosecuted and punished as well as being civil 'wrongs' for which an injured party may recover compensation. For example, a motorist in a road accident may be prosecuted for dangerous driving and sued by someone who was injured in the crash.

Civil and criminal law cases have different terminologies. In criminal courts a defendant is prosecuted, pleads guilty or not guilty, and will be acquitted or convicted, and if convicted, fined or jailed. In civil courts a claimant sues a defendant or respondent, who admits or denies liability, and is found either to be liable or not liable, and, if liable, ordered to pay damages.

Civil courts also resolve disputes between couples such as divorce actions.

 Chs. 12 and 13 explain the civil courts, which have newsworthy cases. Other chapters cover civil laws, such as privacy and copyright, which journalists can be accused of infringing.

The legal profession

Lawyers are either solicitors or barristers.

By tradition and practice, solicitors deal directly with the client – a defendant in a criminal case or someone seeking advice or representation in a civil case. Solicitors advise, prepare the client's case and take advice, when necessary, from a barrister specialising in a particular area of the law. Solicitors may represent their clients in court, and solicitor-advocates may appear in the higher courts.

Barristers are known, singly or collectively, as '*counsel*'. A barrister wears a wig and gown in the higher courts, the Crown courts and county courts, but not in magistrates courts. Barristers who have been practising for at least 10 years may apply to the Lord Chancellor for appointment as a Queen's Counsel, and, if successful, use the letters QC after their names.

▶ High offices in law

The constitutional position in the UK and other democracies is that the nation's 'executive' (the government) is separate from the judiciary (the judges), to help ensure that the judiciary is independent of political influence, and that the government is subject to the rule of law, just as other organisations and citizens are.

The head of the judiciary is the Lord Chief Justice.

The UK government is advised on law by the Attorney General, which is a political role, with some holders being of Cabinet rank. The Attorney General also has a role to prosecute, in that he/she approves the instigation of, and may personally conduct in court, prosecutions in certain important types of cases. These include, as ch. 18 explains, proceedings against media organisations for contempt of court.

➡ Recap of major points

- The media are the eyes and ears of the general public, and free media are an essential element in maintaining Parliamentary democracy.

- The European Convention on Human Rights has codified fundamental freedoms, including that of freedom of expression.

- Sources of UK law include custom, precedent, statutes and statutory instruments, and European Union regulations.

- The two main divisions of the law are criminal law and civil law, and journalists need to use correctly the legal terms appropriate for the type of court they are reporting.

((•)) Useful Websites

www.parliament.uk/about/how/laws/
UK Parliament – 'Making Laws'

www.echr.coe.int/
European Court of Human Rights: the 'Official Texts' link leads to the Convention

www.judiciary.gov.uk/
Judiciary of England and Wales – information on judges and courts system

www.lawsociety.org.uk/becomingasolicitor/careerinlaw/difference.law
Law Society information on solicitors

www.barcouncil.org.uk/about-the-bar/about-barristers/
Bar Council site – 'About barristers'

www.attorneygeneral.gov.uk
Attorney General's Office

Press regulation

Chapter summary

People aggrieved by what newspapers or magazines and their websites publish about them, or by how journalists have treated them may want a watchdog body to intervene or adjudicate on their complaint. A new watchdog – the Independent Press Standards Organisation (Ipso) – is due to begin operating in 2014. This replaces the Press Complaints Commission (PCC), which will cease to exist. Ipso will, at least initially, use the Editors' Code of Practice overseen by the PCC to adjudicate on complaints. This chapter introduces and outlines the code.

▶ Introduction

There are no state controls in the UK on who can own or run newspapers, magazines, their online versions or any kind of website. Anyone with the resources can launch a new publication. These liberties help keep the UK's media relatively free from state influence. Newspapers, magazines and websites are free to be partisan about social issues, and can support a political party. Editors may use leader columns, news stories and features to campaign on any issue, from environmental law or tax reform to local hospital closures. They and their journalists can also publish, subject to the restraints of libel and other laws, their own fierce criticisms of those in the news, or anyone else. The lack of any requirement for these media sectors to be impartial contrasts with the position of the broadcasting industry, as the next chapter explains.

But newspaper and magazine owners recognise that irresponsible journalism could lead Parliament to introduce a statutory system of regulation, specifying standards of accuracy, fairness, and so on, or even establish an official tribunal to hear complaints against publications, impose financial penalties or compel editors to publish corrections or replies.

The UK broadcasting sector has such a statutory system, as explained in the next chapter but – as also outlined there – that arguably produces journalism which, in general, is tamer.

The newspaper and magazine industry established the PCC in 1991 to keep the threat of statutory regulation at bay. It helped the industry regulate the conduct of journalists and editors, and operated a free and relatively fast service to deal with complaints against newspapers, magazines, their websites and 'online-only' publications.

But disclosures by *The Guardian* in 2011 about the huge scale of the phone-hacking by the *News of the World* sounded the death knell for the PCC, which critics saw as ineffectual, and led Prime Minister David Cameron to appoint senior judge, Lord Justice Leveson, to hold a public inquiry into 'the culture, practices, and ethics of the press'.

Controversy after Leveson reported

((•))

see Useful
Websites
at the end
of this
chapter
for
Leveson's
report

The Leveson Report, published in 2012, called for a new regulator which should be more independent of the industry than the PCC was, and should have investigatory powers and the power to fine the newspapers, magazines and websites it regulated if they were found to have seriously or systemically breached its code of ethics.

The industry had already accepted that a new regulator should be able to impose fines of up to £1 million for the worst cases of breach. But some of Leveson's main recommendations proved unacceptable to most editors and major groups in the press.

One of the deep concerns was that Leveson's proposed regulatory system included statutory underpinning for an overseeing 'recognition body', offering potential for future governments to interfere with press freedom.

In addition, legislation went through Parliament to impose a legal framework which would penalise media organisations which did not sign up for the regulatory model Leveson advocated by making them pay 'exemplary' (punitive) damages in privacy and libel cases they lost in the courts, and depriving them of the right to recover their costs from the losing parties in cases they won. These provisions were not yet in force at the time of writing.

By late 2013 the government, with cross-party support in the House of Commons, had also put in place a Royal Charter creating a legal framework for a model of regulation close to that proposed by Leveson.

However as this edition of *McNae's* was completed there seemed little prospect of that model becoming operative as mainstream newspaper and magazine publishers were refusing to sign up to it. Instead, most of the major newspaper and magazine groups agreed to establish and fund the Independent Press Standards Organisation (Ipso) – a system with no statutory element. This was due to begin operating in 2014, at which point the PCC would cease to exist.

See www.mcnaes.com ch. 2 for a detailed explanation of why Leveson's recommendations were so fiercely opposed.

▌The Independent Press Standards Organisation

Members of the public aggrieved by what a journalist has done or what an editor has published can use Ipso's complaints process, which is explained later in the chapter and which is free to use but offers no financial redress. But in addition the Ipso system will pilot an independent arbitration scheme – Leveson called for a low-cost arbitration system. The scheme will, for suitable cases, enable a complainant to seek financial redress from a signed-up media organisation through arbitration, rather than risk an expensive lawsuit when alleging, for example, defamation or breach of privacy. The media organisation must also agree to arbitration.

 ch. 19 explains defamation and ch. 26 explains privacy lawsuits

Ipso will adopt some other elements of the regulatory model proposed by the Leveson report. Ipso will have the contractual power to 'fine', to a maximum of £1 million, a newspaper or magazine or website which, having signed up to its system, seriously or systemically breaches its code. Also, people from outside the industry and editors will be on a committee which draws up its code of ethics, whereas a committee comprised only of editors drew up the Editors' Code of Practice overseen by the PCC.

 See www.mcnaes.com ch. 2 for more detail of the Ipso system, the extent of its independence from the media organisations which fund it, and who will run it.

Fragmentation

But the Ipso era is likely, at least at the start, to be one of fragmentation for self-regulation of the UK press. The PCC was supported by all major newspaper and magazine groups, but several newspapers – *The Guardian*, *Observer*, *Financial Times* and *London Standard* – have said they will not join the Ipso system, because their owners and editors do not agree with some aspects of it. Consequently, people unhappy with how any of these papers have treated them cannot turn to Ipso and so will have to be satisfied with the paper's response to their complaint, or to sue in the courts if they are confident they have a legal case. In addition, the legislation and Royal Charter intended by the government to underpin a regulator closely modelled on the Leveson proposals apply only to England and Wales, meaning media groups in Scotland, Northern Ireland, the Channel Islands and the Isle of Man may not sign up to it even if any media groups in England and Wales do.

▌ The Ipso complaints process

In cases where the complainant does not seek financial redress through the arbitration system, or does not want to pay the fee for it, Ipso will offer what the PCC did – a free process involving mediation and if necessary an adjudication on the complaint. When adjudicating, Ipso will consider if the conduct of any journalist or editor, or any failure to act, has breached its code of ethics. Ipso indicated in 2013 that, initially at least, it would adopt the Editors' Code of Practice. As it seems likely that the code used by Ipso will be, or be based in some respects on, the Editors' Code of Practice, and because the PCC's jurisprudence will continue to be valuable guidance for journalists and Ipso, this chapter explains the Editors' Code of Practice and uses PCC adjudications in case examples, as other chapters do.

 See www.mcnaes.com for updates on Ipso and explanation of its structure.

The complaints process

Under the Ipso system, as was the case with the PCC, an aggrieved person or organisation should complain first to the relevant editor. A complainant who remains dissatisfied can then contact Ipso. It may rule that a complaint was not justified or that an editor's response, such as a private or published apology or an offer to publish a correction, was enough to resolve an issue. It may negotiate resolutions to problems, and intervene before material is published, as the PCC did – for example, in cases in which people want the press to leave them alone. But if Ipso needs to proceed to a formal adjudication, it will require an editor to publish any adverse adjudication, which it can also publish on its website. This public acknowledgement that the code of ethics was breached will be the redress for those whose complaint was upheld in the adjudication. This was the redress under the PCC system. In any case where Ipso imposes a financial penalty on the media organisation for the breach, the complainant will have the additional satisfaction of knowing that has occurred.

Under the PCC system no editor failed to publish an adverse adjudication, not least because, broadly speaking, they and media organisations supported the PCC system. Ipso, because of its contractual powers to impose financial penalties, will have the clout, if needed, to insist that a signed-up organisation publishes an adverse adjudication with suitable prominence.

Ipso may – again, following the practice of the PCC – itself publish adjudications which do not uphold a complaint in high profile cases or to illustrate how it interprets the code.

▌ The scope of the Editors' Code

The Editors' Code – reproduced in full in Appendix 2 – has 16 clauses setting out ethical standards on: accuracy, opportunity for people to reply to inaccuracies, privacy, harassment, intrusion into grief and shock, excessive detail in covering suicides, the welfare of children who become the subject of journalism, anonymity for children in sex cases as well as all victims of sexual assault, making inquiries at hospitals, crime reporting, and secret filming and recording and using subterfuge or misrepresentation.

see Appendix 2, pp. 443–447

In this book most of the code's clauses are featured with case studies in relevant chapters – for example, clause 3 (Privacy) is featured in chs. 26 and 27. Ch. 27 covers clause 6 on children's welfare and clause 5 (intrusion into grief and shock). This book's index entry for the Editors' Code lists pages featuring each clause.

see Useful Websites at the end of this chapter for the Codebook and PCC site

This chapter deals with some clauses of wide application or relevancy for comparatively rare practices or specialist work in journalism.

The Editors' Codebook, produced by the Editors' Code of Practice Committee, offers guidance on the code and PCC rulings. It is also useful to browse the PCC's online archive of cases.

The code does not deal with issues of taste and decency – the industry's position has been that as these are subjective matters, rulings on them could compromise freedom of expression.

! Remember

Breaching the Editors' Code is not a criminal offence or a civil **tort** But observing its requirements is ethical conduct and can help journalists avoid legal problems. Judges ruling on claims of media intrusion into privacy must take relevant codes into account.

→ glossary

Public interest exceptions in the Editors' Code

Some clauses or sub-clauses in the code are marked with an asterisk, which indicates that breaches of these parts can be justified if an editor can demonstrate that what was done was 'in the **public interest**'.

→ glossary

see ch. 25, p. 311, Relevance of ethical codes, on judges and the code

The code says 'the public interest' includes, but is not confined to

- detecting or exposing crime or serious impropriety
- protecting public health and safety
- preventing the public from being misled by an action or statement of an individual or organisation.

The code says editors seeking to rely on public interest exceptions must 'demonstrate fully that they reasonably believed that publication, or journalistic activity undertaken with a view to publication, would be in the public interest'.

As can be seen, this use of the term 'in the public interest' denotes that the journalism has a particularly high potential to be beneficial to society. But the code also says: 'There is a public interest in freedom of expression itself.'

An adjudication, even in these categories of stories, is also likely to consider whether what was done in research and what was published was 'proportionate' – that is, not excessive.

The code makes clear that when a story involves children under 16, editors seeking to justify breach of a relevant clause 'must demonstrate an exceptional public interest to over-ride the normally paramount interest of the child'.

 The code's clause 6, covering the interviewing and photographing of children, and clause 7, covering children in sexual offence cases, are explained in ch. 27, pp. 332–334, Protecting children's privacy and welfare, and ch. 10, p. 111, Ethical considerations.

Accuracy and opportunity to reply

Clause 1 of the code says: 'The Press must take care not to publish inaccurate, misleading or distorted information, including pictures.' A 'significant' inaccuracy, misleading statement or distortion must be corrected promptly, and any correction or apology must be given 'due prominence'. It adds that the press can be 'partisan' but must 'distinguish clearly between comment, conjecture and fact'.

Clause 2 says: 'A fair opportunity for reply to inaccuracies must be given when reasonably called for.'

The majority – usually nearly 90 per cent each year – of complaints to the PCC alleged breaches of clause 1 and/or 2. Neither clause is subject to the public interest exception – there is no public interest in inaccuracy.

👁 Case study

In 2010 the PCC upheld a complaint of inaccuracy against the *Daily Star* over a front-page report that a Rochdale shopping centre had installed 'Muslim-only squat-hole loos' on which the local council had wasted 'YOUR money'. The PCC said the toilets were not paid for by the local council and could not be described as 'Muslim only'. It was particularly concerned at the newspaper's lack of care in its presentation of the story (*Adam Sheppard v Daily Star*, adjudication issued 27 September 2010).

see also ch. 16, p. 197, Ethical considerations when covering deaths, on reporting about suicides

Coverage of suicides

Research has found that news of suicides may prompt others to take their own lives in the same way. To minimise this risk, clause 5 of the code says reports of suicides should avoid giving excessive detail about the method used. In 2012 the PCC ruled that a report of an inquest into a suicide breached the clause because it named the gas a man had fatally inhaled, how he obtained it and how he inhaled it (*A woman v Wiltshire Gazette and Herald*, adjudication issued 1 November 2012).

Deception (subterfuge and misrepresentation)

Clause 10 of the code says:

" i) The press must not seek to obtain or publish material acquired by using hidden cameras or clandestine listening devices; or by intercepting private or mobile telephone calls, messages or emails; or by the unauthorised removal of documents or photographs; or by accessing digitally-held private information without consent. "

ch. 28 explains data protection law and ch. 35 hacking offences

" ii) Engaging in misrepresentation or subterfuge, including by agents or interme-diaries, can generally be justified only in the public interest and then only when the material cannot be obtained by other means. "

It makes clear that journalists should normally be open and transparent when seeking information or comment, making clear from the outset to anyone unfamil-iar with them that they are journalists.

It also means that normally photography or filming must be done openly, and that eavesdropping by using 'bugs' or audio-recording by hidden microphones will breach the code because the activity is 'clandestine'. Irrespective of the code, using hidden cameras or microphones could be a breach of privacy law, as chs. 26 and 27 explain.

see also p. 18, Recording phone calls

But this clause is subject to the public interest exceptions, so that if the story or journalistic activity is justified by a sufficient public interest, a journalist may pose as someone else or use other kinds of subterfuge, including hidden cameras or microphones, without breaching the code. Such methods are common in inves-tigative journalism. But the code says they should only be used when an open approach would not work, even when a public interest exception applies.

👁 Case study

In 2009 the PCC rejected a complaint by the mother of murderer Levi Bellfield after a *Daily Mirror* reporter used subterfuge to interview him in prison by phone. Bellfield had already been convicted of murdering two young women, and his relatives helped arrange the interview after the reporter falsely offered to help his appeal. The reporter's true objective was to ask Bellfield about events relevant to a third murder of which he was suspected – that of schoolgirl Millie Dowler. The PCC said the reporter had not misrepresented his identity and when interviewing Bellfield had obtained significant and new information about Millie's murder. The subterfuge was fully justified by this objective (*Mrs Jean Bellfield v Daily Mirror*, adjudication issued 23 July 2009 and *Press Gazette*, August 2011). In 2011 Bellfield was convicted of Millie's murder.

'Fishing expeditions'

The PCC adjudications make clear that it will not condone subterfuge or misrepre-sentation – including using hidden cameras or recording devices – or infringement

of privacy, in 'fishing expeditions'. A 'fishing expedition' is an investigation
→ glossary launched without sufficient, **prima facie** grounds to justify such methods. An editor who authorises their use needs to be able to demonstrate there is a specific allegation serious enough to justify them – for example, that the investigation's target was committing crime, or was guilty of serious impropriety, or misleading the public or putting people's health or safety at risk. An editor will also need to be able to demonstrate that using these methods was proportionate and necessary.

👁 Case study

In 2011 the PCC upheld a complaint by the Liberal Democrats about a *Daily Telegraph* undercover investigation in which reporters posed as constituents to talk to Lib Dem Ministers during constituency surgeries, secretly recording the comments. The object was to gather evidence that the Ministers were misleading the public by making official statements in support of the Lib Dem-Conservative coalition government while privately expressing views at odds with coalition policies. The PCC said the reporters' misrepresentations breached clause 10. The *Telegraph* did not appear to have had, before launching the investigation, any specific information that the target Ministers had expressed such views, it said. The PCC added that what information the newspaper did have in advance was not sufficient to warrant the undercover taping of the MPs as they did their constituency work, even though the newspaper had pointed out that during the surgeries most of them had voiced opinions about the coalition which were at odds with their public positions (*Liberal Democrat Party v the Daily Telegraph*, adjudication issued 10 May 2011).

Recording phone calls

Journalists, particularly those involved in investigations, may decide to record their own telephone calls, for example when they are interviewing the target of their inquiries. The recording may be needed as proof if the subject sues for defamation over what is published. In the UK it is legal for one party in a phone conversation to record it, even if the other is unaware this is being done.

The PCC has made it clear that journalists who record calls they make or legitimately receive are not regarded as using a clandestine recording device under clause 10, even if they do not tell the other person the call is being recorded (*Messrs Lewis Silkin on behalf of Mrs Isobel Stone*, Report 49, 2000), so do not require a 'public interest' exception to justify this conduct.

But a journalist who fails to declare in such a call that he/she is a journalist may breach the code's ban on subterfuge and misrepresentation, unless the 'public interest' exception applies and it seems reasonable to conclude there is no other way to obtain the information.

But *intercepting* a phone call – using external technology to hack directly or 'tap' into a phone system to listen to or record other people's conversations or messages – is illegal in most circumstances, as demonstrated by the scandal which closed the *News of the World* in July 2011.

Discriminatory material

Clause 12 of the code bans publication of pejorative material which discriminates on grounds of race, religion, sexual orientation, gender, disability or illness. It is subject to the public interest exceptions – for example, racist material could be aired if the purpose was to criticise it.

👁 Case study

In 2010 the PCC ruled that reviewer A.A. Gill's reference to TV journalist Clare Balding as 'a dyke on a bike' in a *Sunday Times* article on her programme 'Britain by Bike' breached clause 12. It said Gill's use of the word 'dyke' – whether or not it was intended to be humorous – was pejorative, demeaning and gratuitous, and the newspaper should have apologised at the first possible opportunity (*Clare Balding v the Sunday Times*, adjudication 17 September 2010).

Financial journalism

Clause 13 of the code seeks to prevent journalists making personal profit by anticipating movements in share prices on the basis of information leaked to them by business contacts. It says journalists 'must not use for their own profit financial information they receive in advance of its general publication, nor should they pass such information to others'. It also bans journalists from dealing in shares or securities about which they have recently written, or intend to write, as what they publish might affect market prices, and it would be unethical for them to take financial advantage of this power. It says journalists must tell their editors about shares or securities in which they or close relatives have a significant financial interest.

Payments to witnesses

Media organisations covering high-profile stories may pay people, including the victims of notorious crimes, for the exclusive right to publish their accounts of events. In the case of crime victims, those accounts would be more than the evidence they can give in court, which would not have exclusive value. An account could, for example, include descriptions not limited by court rules on evidence. Clause 15 of the code aims to prevent these 'chequebook journalism' deals interfering with the process of justice. The risk of contempt of court which can arise from these deals, or from a reporter interviewing anyone due to testify in a trial, is explained in ch. 18.

ch. 35 explains the law on hacking and interception

((•))

see Useful Websites at the end of this chapter for guidance on reporting mental illness

((•))

see also Useful Websites at the end of this chapter for guidance issued by the PCC on financial journalism

The first part of clause 15 says: 'No payment or offer of payment to a witness – or any person who may reasonably be expected to be called as a witness – should be made in any case once proceedings are active as defined by the Contempt of Court Act 1981.' The ban applies until a case ceases to be active or the suspect pleads guilty.

The second part says that:

> where proceedings are not yet active but are likely and foreseeable, editors must not make or offer payment to any person who may reasonably be expected to be called as a witness, unless the information concerned ought demonstrably to be published in the public interest and there is an over-riding need to make or promise payment for this to be done; and all reasonable steps have been taken to ensure that no financial dealings influence the evidence those witnesses give. In no circumstances should such payment be conditional on the outcome of a trial.

It says a payment or an offer of payment made to a person who is later called to testify in proceedings must be disclosed to the prosecution and defence.

Payments to criminals

Clause 16 of the code says: 'Payment or offers of payment for stories, pictures or information, which seek to exploit a particular crime or to glorify or glamorise crime in general, must not be made directly or via agents to convicted or confessed criminals or to their associates – who may include family, friends and colleagues.' This recognises that people, particularly crime victims, are likely to condemn a deal under which criminals or those close to them profit from tales of wrongdoing. But the clause also recognises that press payment to a criminal may be justified by the code's public interest exceptions.

➡ Recap of major points

- The Editors' Code of Practice sets standards for journalists working for newspapers, magazine and free-standing editorial websites.
- It has clauses to uphold accuracy and to protect people's privacy.
- It permits undercover reporting, but only if justified by special, 'public interest' factors.
- The Independent Press Standards Organisation, which adjudicates on complaints against editors and journalists in member organisations in newspaper, magazine and online sectors, requires editors to publish adverse adjudications.

((•)) Useful Websites

www.ipso.co.uk/
   Ipso

www.pcc.org.uk
   PCC website

www.editorscode.org.uk/
   Editors' Codebook

www.pcc.org.uk/advice/editorials-detail.html?article=NDIwMA==
   PCC guidance on the reporting of mental health issues

www.pcc.org.uk/advice/editorials-detail.html?article=OTM=
   PCC guidance on best practice in financial journalism

www.levesoninquiry.org.uk/about/the-report/
   Lord Justice Leveson's report

3

Broadcast regulation

Chapter summary

Television and radio journalism in the UK is regulated by statute. The Office of Communications (Ofcom), the independent regulator, adjudicates on complaints against broadcast journalists. Ofcom's Broadcasting Code says commercial broadcast organisations must be impartial when covering politics and social issues, and must be accurate, treat people fairly, respect privacy and avoid causing harm and offence. Ofcom can impose substantial fines for breaches of the code. The BBC is also required to be impartial and ethical. It is subject to the Ofcom code in some respects, but also has a system of self-regulation involving the BBC Trust.

▌ Introduction

In the UK commercial broadcasters – those funded by advertising revenue – are regulated in terms of ownership and journalistic output. As the previous chapter explains, newspaper, magazine and online-only publishers are free to be politically partisan. But broadcasters and their journalists must when reporting news be impartial about politics and social issues, although they are free to cover them in depth. The regulatory system also requires broadcasters to observe 'due accuracy' in news and other ethical norms. The regulator, the Office of Communications (Ofcom) can levy substantial fines on any broadcast organisation which seriously breaches journalistic standards.

▌ Why regulate broadcasters?

Historically, broadcast media have been seen as having particular potential to influence, offend or harm their audiences. The emotional impact of moving images and sound can be greater than that of printed text and still pictures, while the ability of television and radio to air material instantaneously means they have great potential to provoke immediate public disorder or violence.

A further rationale is that television is seen as having great potential – because moving images and sound can often portray intimate or harrowing experiences more vividly than photographs or text – to intrude into privacy, or to harm children because it can project unsuitable portrayals of sex or violence or other disturbing material directly into their homes.

Politicians also decided that broadcasting must be regulated because for decades transmission was only possible on analogue wavelengths. These are relatively scarce, so a regulator was needed to decide who could broadcast, and on which frequency. The consensus was that the regulator should specify requirements for quality in programmes and diversity in output.

These rationales for regulating broadcast media have lost some force as technological advances mean that newspaper, magazine and other publishers can 'broadcast' audio-visual material on websites, so the power is no longer exclusive to TV and radio. Digital transmission also allows many more channels, giving the public greater freedom of choice.

There is also an argument that regulating broadcast journalism is a socially-beneficial counterbalance to the unregulated, partisan journalism of newspaper, magazine and website-only publishers, although it could also be said that regulation means broadcast journalism tends to have less 'bite' and impact than newspapers.

▌ Ofcom – its role and sanctions

Commercial broadcasters cannot transmit without a licence from Ofcom, which began operating in 2003, replacing previous regulators. It is structurally independent of the government, although Ministers appoint members of its main board. Ofcom, which for 2012/13 had a budget of £121.4 million, is funded mainly by licence fees paid by broadcasters, other charges it imposes and government funds. It has a range of duties, including regulating phone services. The Communications Act 2003 gives Ofcom roles which include ensuring the existence of a wide range of TV and radio services of high quality and wide appeal, and maintaining plurality in broadcasting. When deciding on applications for national, regional or local broadcast licences, it considers what programming is being proposed and whether the applicant is 'fit and proper'. Ofcom monitors whether TV and radio broadcasters comply with the conditions of their licences, for instance, by meeting a 'public service' obligation to provide news. Licences are granted for set durations, for example 12 years, and can be renewed.

The 2003 Act and the Broadcasting Act 1996 require Ofcom to draw up standards for programme content. These are detailed in the **Ofcom Broadcasting Code**. →glossary Anyone aggrieved by a programme's content or by how they were treated when it was made can – as long as the programme has been broadcast – complain to Ofcom, which assesses complaints against the standards set in the Code. Ofcom does not regulate all aspects of the BBC's output. Web content, even on sites run by broadcasters, is not subject to the code as it is not 'broadcast' material.

If Ofcom upholds a complaint it can direct that a programme should not be repeated, or that the broadcaster must air a correction or a statement of its findings in a specified form.

It can impose a fine if it considers breach of the code serious or reckless. If broadcasters consistently breach the code it can shorten or suspend their licences or, in the worst cases, revoke them, closing the station. Ofcom used this power in 2012 to close Press TV, the controversial news channel broadcasting in English from the UK, funded by the Iranian government. Press TV failed to respond to concerns that it had breached its licence because it did not control its own editorial content, which, it had indicated, was controlled from Tehran. Press TV had also failed to pay a £100,000 fine imposed by Ofcom after it breached fairness and privacy sections of the Broadcasting Code by screening an 'interview' it conducted with a *Newsweek* journalist without his consent and when he was under duress and being held in an Iranian prison.

Ofcom cannot shorten, suspend or revoke the licences of the BBC, S4C or Channel 4 – they are public service broadcasters. But it can fine the BBC or S4C up to £250,000 for a code breach. For other broadcasters, the maximum fine is £250,000 or 5 per cent of the broadcaster's 'qualifying revenue'. In 2008 Ofcom fined ITV plc a total of £5,675,000 for multiple breaches which involved the misleading of viewers in phone-in competitions.

👁 Case study

The highest regulatory fine imposed for unethical broadcast journalism is £2 million paid by Central Independent Television, part of the ITV network, after a 1998 Independent Television Commission ruling that scenes in The Connection – a documentary which claimed to show a new heroin smuggling route from Columbia to the UK – were fabricated. The ITC said this was 'a wholesale breach' of the trust viewers placed in programme-makers. The Connection had won awards before its authenticity was questioned in an investigation published by The Guardian newspaper, which led to the ITC's findings (ITC press release and The Guardian, 18 December 1998).

▌ The scope of the Ofcom code

The Ofcom Broadcasting code has rules on: protecting under-18s (section 1); avoiding harm and offence (section 2); covering crime (section 3); covering religion (section 4); due impartiality and due accuracy and undue prominence of views and opinions (section 5); covering elections and referendums (section 6); fairness (section 7); protecting privacy (section 8); commercial references in television programming (section 9); and commercial communications in radio programming (section 10).

With appendices and index, the code runs to 135 pages. It covers all broadcast output.

see Useful Websites at the end of this chapter for the code's full text

Protecting under-eighteens

Section 1 of the code says: 'Material that might seriously impair the physical, mental or moral development of people under 18 must not be broadcast' (rule 1.1). Broadcasters must take all reasonable steps to protect those under 18 (rule 1.2), it says, adding: 'Children must also be protected by appropriate scheduling from material that is unsuitable for them' (rule 1.3). 'Children' means those under 15.

see also p. 26, Imitation of harmful behaviour

The TV watershed

Rule 1.4 says television broadcasters must observe the 9pm 'watershed' marking the transition for free-to-air TV channels between the times of day – from 5.30am to 9pm – when children are most likely to be watching, and later slots for which the audience is assumed to be more adult. Material unsuitable for children must not, in general, be broadcast pre-watershed, and the transition to post-watershed material must not be unduly abrupt (rule 1.6).

For pre-watershed broadcasts clear information should, if appropriate, be given about content which might distress children (rule 1.7). For example, news anchors can warn if footage about to be shown portrays violence. Violence or its after-effects must be 'appropriately limited' in pre-watershed broadcasts, and be justified by context (rule 1.11).

Rules also limit the pre-watershed televising of offensive language (rules 1.14–1.16), and portrayal or discussion of sexual behaviour (rule 1.20).

Times when children are likely to be listening to radio

The term 'watershed' is not used for radio. But the code says radio broadcasters must have particular regard to what is aired when 'children are particularly likely to be listening' (rules 1.5–1.6). Rules on content involving violence, offensive language, sexual material and so on apply to radio at such times – for example, breakfast time.

Protecting children

Ofcom code rule 1.28 says broadcasters must take due care over the physical and emotional 'welfare and the dignity' of children under 18 who take part or are involved in programmes, irrespective of any consent they, their parents or guardians give. Rule 1.29 says they must not be caused unnecessary distress or anxiety.

Other elements of the code's protection of children are dealt with elsewhere in this book.

See p. 30, Informed consent; ch. 10, p. 111, Ethical considerations, on children in sex offence cases; ch. 27, pp. 332–334, Protecting children's privacy and welfare, on privacy.

 See also www.mcnaes.com ch. 4 on children and teenagers involved in pre-trial investigations into crime.

Harm and offence

Section 2 of the Ofcom code says in rule 2.1 that 'generally accepted standards' must be applied to the content of television and radio broadcasts to avoid including harmful or offensive material. Material which may cause offence includes pictures or sounds of distress, humiliation or violation of human dignity; offensive language; violence; sex; and discriminatory treatment or language. Material likely to cause offence must be justified by context, and appropriate information should be broadcast where it would help avoid or minimise offence (rule 2.3).

Section 2 says context includes the programme's editorial content, the time of the broadcast and the likely size and composition of the potential audience.

👁 Case study

In 2006 Ofcom ruled that the GMTV channel breached section 2:3 in the way it showed CCTV images of an unprovoked knife attack by three men on two students, one of whom – Daniel Pollen – was killed. Police released the footage, with the students' families' permission, after a murder trial. Ofcom said the violent images were already being seen on screen by the time the newsreader completed an introductory sentence, and the tone of the introduction did not convey any sense of warning about the shocking images broadcast. Also, the wording left the *impression* that viewers were watching the actual murder when in fact the images ended just before the fatal blow. Ofcom said this casual use of exceptionally violent material added to the potential for causing offence to viewers (*Ofcom Broadcast Bulletin*, No. 68, 4 September 2006).

The code says demonstrations of exorcism, the occult, the paranormal, divination, or related practices which purport to be real (as opposed to entertainment) must be treated with due objectivity and, if they are for entertainment, this must be made clear (rules 2.6 and 2.7).

There is also a general rule (2.2) that factual programmes or items or portrayals of factual matters must not materially mislead the audience (though accuracy in news output is regulated under the code's section 5: see p. 28, Due impartiality and due accuracy).

Imitation of harmful behaviour

Programmes should not include material which, taking into account the context, condones or glamorises violent, dangerous or seriously anti-social behaviour and is likely to encourage others to copy it (rule 2.4). Violence, verbal or physical, which children can easily imitate in a harmful or dangerous manner, or easily-imitable dangerous behaviour of any kind, must not, without editorial justification, be broadcast pre-watershed on television, or on radio when children are particularly likely to be listening (rules 1.12 and 1.13).

Methods of suicide and self-harm must not be included in programmes except when justified editorially and by context, to avoid people imitating them (rule 2.5).

 For the rationale of the rule on reporting suicide methods, see ch. 2, p. 16, Coverage of suicides, for similar provision in the PCC code.

Photosensitive epilepsy

Broadcasters must take precautions to maintain a low level of risk to viewers who have photosensitive epilepsy (rule 2.12), who can be affected by broadcasts of flashing lights, including news footage of photographers using flash equipment.

Crime

Section 3 of the code says material likely to encourage or incite the commission of crime or to lead to disorder must not be included in television or radio services (rule 3.1). Descriptions or demonstrations of criminal techniques which contain essential details which could enable the commission of crime must not be broadcast unless editorially justified (rule 3.2).

Broadcasters must use their best endeavours not to broadcast material which could endanger lives or prejudice the success of attempts to deal with a hijack or kidnapping (rule 3.6).

! Remember

Police dealing with kidnaps may ask news media to observe a news 'blackout' to help preserve the victim's life. Also, coverage of an anti-terrorist or hostage recovery operation should not include broadcasts of live material which might alert the terrorists to armed police or special forces launching a rescue operation.

Payments to criminals

Section 3 forbids making any payment or promise of payment, directly or indirectly, to 'convicted or confessed criminals' for a programme contribution by the criminal relating to his/her crime, unless doing so is in the public interest (rule 3.3). As with similar provision in the Editor's Code of Practice, see ch. 2, p. 20, Payments to criminals, this is to avoid distressing victims of crime and outraging the public.

see p. 31, Public interest exceptions

Payments to witnesses

Section 3 also prohibits broadcasters making or offering payments to witnesses in 'active' criminal cases, or to anyone who might reasonably be expected to be called as a witness, though they can be paid expenses (rule 3.4). If a criminal case is not 'active', but is likely and foreseeable, payment should not be made to anyone who might reasonably be expected to be a witness unless there is a clear public interest. Any payment should be disclosed to the defence and prosecution if the person becomes a witness (rule 3.5).

ch.18 explains contempt law and 'active'

These rules are to ensure broadcasters do not jeopardise the administration of justice or commit contempt of court.

Religion

Section 4 of the Ofcom code says the views and beliefs of those belonging to a particular religion or religious denomination must not be subject to abusive treatment. Rule 4.7 says religious programmes containing claims that a living person (or group) has special powers or abilities must treat such claims with due objectivity. They must not be broadcast when significant numbers of children may be expected to be watching or listening.

Due impartiality and due accuracy

see p. 34, The BBC

Section 5 of the Ofcom code sets out impartiality and accuracy requirements for broadcasters other than the BBC, which has its own regulatory requirements on these matters.

Rule 5.1 says: 'News, in whatever form, must be reported with due accuracy and presented with due impartiality'.

It says impartiality means not favouring one side over another, and the qualification 'due' means adequate or appropriate to the programme's subject and nature. 'So "due impartiality" does not mean an equal division of time has to be given to every view, or that every argument and every facet of every argument has to be represented. The approach to due impartiality may vary according to the nature of the subject, the type of programme and channel, the likely expectation of the audience as to content, and the extent to which the content and approach is signalled to the audience'.

Politicians may not be used as newsreaders, interviewers or reporters in any news programme unless, exceptionally, this is editorially justified and the individual's political allegiance is made clear (rule 5.3).

Owners of broadcast organisations may not use them to project their own views on 'matters of political or industrial controversy and matters relating to current public policy'. The code offers a general definition of such matters in this section.

Rules 5.5 to 5.12 require the providers of television programme services, teletext services, national radio and national digital sound programme services to preserve due impartiality on such matters in their output. This may be achieved over a series of programmes 'taken as a whole' rather than in a single programme.

The code seeks to ensure the presentation of a diversity of opinion in respect of major political and industrial controversy and major matters of current public policy, saying 'an appropriately wide range of significant views must be included and given due weight in each programme or in clearly linked and timely programmes' (rule 5.12).

👁 Case study

In 2008 Ofcom ruled that Channel 4 breached impartiality requirements in part of *The Great Global Warming Swindle*, a programme challenging the mainstream scientific view that human activity is a major cause of climate change. When the programme referred to policies espoused by Western nations – that industrial production must be restrained worldwide to limit global warming – the narration suggested that a consequence of these policies was a lack of electricity in many parts of the developing world, and resultant higher rates of mortality and respiratory disease. Ofcom said the programme had not presented an appropriately wide range of views on these policies (*Ofcom Broadcast Bulletin*, No. 114, 21 July 2008).

Any personal interest of a reporter or presenter which would call the due impartiality of the programme into question must be made clear (rule 5.8).

'Personal view' and 'authored' programmes

Rule 5.9 says: 'Presenters and reporters (with the exception of news presenters and reporters in news programmes), presenters of "personal view" or "authored" programmes or items, and chairs of discussion programmes may express their own views on matters of political or industrial controversy or matters relating to current public policy. But alternative viewpoints must be adequately represented either in the programme, or in a series, taken as a whole. Presenters must not use the advantage of regular appearances to promote their views in a way which compromises the requirement for due impartiality. Presenter phone-ins must encourage and must not exclude alternative views.'

'Personal view' programmes are defined as those presenting a particular view or perspective. These could involve a person who is a member of a lobby group and is campaigning on a subject expressing highly partial views, or 'the considered "authored" opinion of a journalist, commentator or academic, with expertise or a specialism in an area which enables her or him to express opinions which are not necessarily mainstream.' The code says a personal view or authored programme or item must be clearly signalled as such at the outset.

Accuracy considerations

Ofcom guidance says that the clarification of the term 'due' in respect of impartiality, see earlier in the chapter, also applies to the accuracy requirement.

Significant mistakes in news should normally be acknowledged and corrected on air quickly, with corrections appropriately scheduled (rule 5.2). Views and facts must not be misrepresented (rules 5.7 and 2.2).

((•))

see Useful
Websites
at the end
of this
chapter
for this
guidance

! Remember

A journalist who, to produce a dramatic effect, edits news or documentary footage or an audio recording in a way which, when it is broadcast, misrepresents a sequence of events would breach the code. The code would also be breached if a broadcaster stages and airs a reconstruction of a news event while failing to make clear to the audience that it was not the real event.

Undue prominence of views and opinions

Rule 5.13, which applies to local radio services and local digital sound programme services, including those at community level, says their broadcasters 'should not give undue prominence to the views and opinions of particular persons or bodies on matters of political or industrial controversy and matters relating to current public policy' in programming when 'taken as a whole', by which it means programming 'dealing with the same or related issues within an appropriate period'.

It defines 'undue prominence of views and opinions' as a significant imbalance of views.

 Section 6 of the Ofcom code sets out specific requirements for broadcasters to maintain impartiality during election and referendum periods – see ch. 32.

Fairness

Section 7 of the Ofcom code sets out general principles on how programme-makers should treat people or organisations participating or featured in programmes.

Rule 7.1 says 'Broadcasters must avoid unjust or unfair treatment of individuals or organisations in programmes'.

The section details 'Practices to be followed'. A failure to follow these which leads to unjust or unfair treatment will be a breach of the code.

Practice 7.2 says broadcasters and programme-makers should be fair in dealings with potential contributors to programmes unless doing otherwise is justified.

Informed consent

Practice 7.3 says people or organisations who agree to take part in programmes should do so on the basis of 'informed consent', which requires that a person invited to contribute to a programme should normally be told:

- its nature and purpose, and what it is about, and be given a clear explanation of why they were asked to contribute and when and where it is likely to be broadcast;
- the kind of contribution they are expected to make – live, pre-recorded, interview, discussion, edited, unedited, etc.;
- the areas of questioning and, wherever possible, the nature of other likely contributions.

The public interest or other provisions may justify withholding all or some of this information.

 This chapter explains that public interest exceptions may justify deception. But see www.mcnaes.com ch. 3 for the case study on The Toughest Seaside Resorts in Britain, a programme ruled by Ofcom to have breached its fairness rule about 'informed consent'.

The code says that guarantees given to contributors, for example about the content of a programme, confidentiality or anonymity should normally be honoured (practice 7.7).

 See ch. 34 for cases in which journalists ethically kept secret the identities of their sources.

Informed consent in the case of children

If a contributor is under 16, the parent or guardian's consent should normally be obtained. Those under 16 should not be asked for views on matters likely to be beyond their capacity to answer properly without such consent (practice 7.4).

Getting and airing the other side of the story

Practice 7.11 says that if a programme alleges wrongdoing or incompetence or makes other significant allegations, those concerned should normally be given an appropriate and timely opportunity to respond. Where a person approached to contribute to a programme chooses to make no comment or refuses to appear, the broadcast should make this clear – and give their explanation if it would be unfair not to do so (practice 7.12).

Public interest exceptions

Ofcom accepts that programme-makers may be justified in breaching some of the code's provisions 'in the public interest'. It uses the term **warranted** to indicate when there must be a public interest, or some other exceptional justification to merit breaching the usual rules.

- Section 8 says that examples of public interest include:
  - revealing or detecting crime
  - protecting public health or safety
  - exposing misleading claims made by individuals or organisations or
  - disclosing incompetence that affects the public.

 There are similar public interest exceptions in the Editors' Code of Practice, see ch. 2, p. 15, Public interest exceptions in the Editors' Code.

Deception and misrepresentation

The Ofcom code says in practice 7.14 that

> broadcasters or programme makers should not normally obtain or seek infor-
> mation, audio, pictures or an agreement to contribute through misrepresenta-
> tion or deception

But the code adds that it may be warranted to use material gained by such tactics if it is in the public interest *and* the material cannot reasonably be obtained by other means.

A journalist who lies about the nature of a programme in order to trick a crimi-nal into taking part will not breach the code if the programme's purpose is to expose sufficiently serious offences. Similarly, giving a false reason to a public institution when seeking consent to film its activities will not be a breach if the public interest is sufficient, such as exposing incompetence affecting the public. The public interest can justify journalists misrepresenting themselves, for exam-ple by posing as members of another profession or an uninformed citizen. But in all such instances, if a complaint is made, Ofcom will consider whether what was done was proportionate (not excessive) and whether there was any other way the material could reasonably have been obtained.

Secret filming and recording — deception and privacy

The Ofcom code says in practice 7.14 that 'surreptitious' – secret or undercover – filming or recording is a type of deception. Under the code material gained in this way should not normally be broadcast unless the person filmed or recorded consents.

Surreptitious filming or recording includes using long lenses or recording devices, and leaving an unattended camera or recording device on private prop-erty without full and informed consent of the occupiers, or deliberately continu-ing a recording when the other party thinks it has ended (section 8).

- But practice 7.14 says that it may be warranted to use, without consent, film or audio gained surreptitiously, if it is in the public interest and the mate-rial could not have reasonably been obtained in another way.

Practice 7.14 adds that if an individual or organisation filmed or recorded sur-reptitiously is not identifiable in the programme as broadcast, their consent to be included in it is not required (though their right to privacy would need to be taken into account).

Surreptitious filming or recording can violate privacy, for example by record-ing private conversations without consent, even if the person is not identified in, or the conversations included in what is broadcast.

Section 8 of the code, covering protecting privacy, says any infringement of privacy in programmes, or in connection with obtaining material included in pro-grammes, must, unless broadcast with consent, be warranted by the public inter-est or some other exceptional reason (rule 8.1 and practice 8.5). Ofcom will deem a failure by programme-makers to observe the 'practices to be followed' in section 8 as breaching the code if it leads to an unwarranted infringement of privacy.

Practices 8.13 and 8.14 say surreptitious filming or recording should only be done when warranted and that normally, it will only be warranted if:

- there is **prima facie** evidence of a story in the public interest; and → glossary
- reasonable grounds to suspect that further material evidence could be obtained; and
- it is necessary to the programme's credibility and authenticity.

The requirement for prima facie evidence is to prevent arbitrary 'fishing expeditions'.

Case study

Ms Rachel Gray, a worker at Gillman Funeral Services, South London, owned by Funeral Partners Ltd (FPL), complained to Ofcom that she was treated unfairly and that her privacy was infringed by an edition of ITV's *Exposure* programme entitled *The British Way of Death*. It showed that a lack of refrigeration facilities at Gillman's led to some bodies decomposing. Footage shot by an undercover reporter showed Ms Gray placing, as a joke, a shopping bag over one body's head, singing 'Big Spender' – a song associated with striptease – as she undressed another body to amuse a colleague, and referring to another body as 'Chelsea scum'. FPL's chief executive described some of Ms Gray's behaviour in the footage as totally unacceptable. ITV said it filmed covertly after gathering prima facie evidence of callous treatment at Gillman's of the deceased, and that the programme's commentary recognised that some 'gallows humour' there was understandable. Ofcom ruled that Ms Gray had not been treated unfairly, and that ITV's right to freedom of expression and the public interest in the programme's subject matter outweighed her expectation of privacy (*Ofcom Broadcast Bulletin*, No. 236, 27 August 2013).

for explanation of this term, see ch. 2, p. 17, 'Fishing expeditions'

Ofcom guidance says broadcasters should take care not to infringe the privacy of bystanders who may inadvertently be caught in the recording – for example, it might be necessary to obscure the identities of those recorded incidentally.

Recording phone conversations

Practice 8.12 of the Ofcom code says broadcasters can record telephone calls if they have, from the outset of the call, identified themselves, explained to the other person the call's purpose and that it is being recorded for possible broadcast (if that is the case) unless it is warranted not to identify themselves or give such explanation. 'Warranted' means that failing to tell the person that the call is being recorded for broadcast, failing to explain its purpose or broadcasting a recording of it without consent can be justified if the journalism is 'in the public interest'.

Ofcom might class recording a phone call without the other person's knowledge as a surreptitious recording, and therefore – if the intention is to broadcast it – practices 7.14 and 8.13 apply. But it is acceptable for journalists to record their own calls for note-taking purposes.

 See ch. 35 p. 419, Regulation of Investigatory Powers Act (RIPA) 2000, as regards the illegality of the interception of phone calls.

Privacy in general

Section 8 of the Ofcom code includes general provisions for protecting people's privacy in relation to journalists openly filming or audio-recording. These are explained in ch. 27, which also explains the code's use of the term 'legitimate expectation of privacy' and its restrictions on 'doorstepping'.

Practice 8.2 says the location of a person's home or family should not be disclosed without permission, unless it is warranted.

Financial journalism

Appendix 4 of the code sets out 'binding guidance' on how commercial broadcasters must operate to comply with legislation prohibiting financial promotions and setting standards for investment recommendations. People working on programmes who make an investment recommendation must disclose any financial interest they have that 'may reasonably be expected to impair the objectivity of that recommendation'.

Other parts of the Ofcom code

Parts of the code regulate commercial references in television programming (section 9) and commercial communications in radio programming (section 10). These sections have over-arching rules to ensure there is a distinction between editorial and advertising content, and set out specific principles of editorial independence as regards television. News and current affairs programmes on television must not be sponsored (rule 9.15). No commercial reference is permitted in or around radio news bulletins (rule 10.2). There are also rules on the broadcasting of charity appeals. With the exception of relevant 'product placement' rules for television, these sections do not apply to BBC services funded by the TV licence fee as they do not carry advertising.

▶ The BBC

The BBC, the biggest broadcasting organisation in the world, has 10 national TV channels plus regional programming, 10 national radio stations, more than 40 regional and local radio stations, plus its website.

The legal basis for the BBC's existence is its Royal Charter, and the Agreement with Parliament which is renewed every 10 years. The Agreement says the BBC must do all it can to ensure that controversial subjects are treated with due accuracy and due impartiality in all relevant output. These aspects of its output, including its journalism, are regulated by the BBC Trust, the corporation's governing body. This means that complaints about inaccuracy or lack of impartiality in BBC output cannot be considered by Ofcom, only by the BBC itself. Also, Ofcom does not regulate the BBC's online output or its World Service.

The BBC has an Editorial Complaints Unit. Complainants unhappy with its decisions can appeal to the Trust, which publishes its appeal findings online

In other respects – for example, if it is alleged that material broadcast was unfair or offensive – Ofcom regulates the BBC, which is therefore subject to relevant parts of the Ofcom code. So, while the BBC will consider complaints about all such matters, complainants can contact Ofcom directly, either initially or if they are dissatisfied with the corporation's response.

The BBC's Editorial Guidelines set out standards for its journalism, including undercover investigations. The BBC's online College of Journalism, which helps train its journalists in law and ethics, is accessible to everyone.

((•))

see Useful Websites at the end of this chapter

➡ Recap of major points

- Broadcast journalism is regulated by the Office of Communications (Ofcom).
- Broadcast organisations must comply with the Ofcom Broadcasting Code, which requires them to avoid harm and offence, to be fair and to protect people's privacy.
- Ofcom has statutory power to compel broadcasters to air its adjudications on complaints against them.
- It can fine them for the worst transgressions of the code, and can close a commercial broadcaster which persistently or recklessly flouts the code.
- There must be 'due accuracy' and 'due impartiality' in all broadcast news.
- The BBC is not regulated by Ofcom as regards accuracy and impartiality. The BBC Trust is the ultimate adjudicator on complaints against the BBC in these respects.

((•)) Useful Websites

www.ofcom.org.uk/about/what-is-ofcom/
   What is Ofcom?

http://stakeholders.ofcom.org.uk/broadcasting/broadcast-codes/broadcast-code/
   The Ofcom Broadcasting Code

http://stakeholders.ofcom.org.uk/broadcasting/guidance/programme-guidance/bguidance/
   Ofcom's guidance on the code

www.bbc.co.uk/aboutthebbc/
About the BBC

www.bbc.co.uk/guidelines/editorialguidelines/
BBC Editorial Guidelines and Guidance

www.bbc.co.uk/guidelines/editorialguidelines/news/news-2011-09-13/
BBC revised guidance on investigations and secret recording

www.bbc.co.uk/complaints/
BBC complaints system

www.bbc.co.uk/bbctrust/
BBC Trust

www.bbc.co.uk/journalism/
BBC College of Journalism

Part 2

Crime, courts and tribunals

Crime: media coverage prior to any court case

Chapter summary

This chapter explains how police investigations are driven by the standard of proof needed to convict someone of a crime. Reporters should understand police powers to arrest and to detain. There is a strong public interest in media reporting of crime and police investigations, but the media need to be wary of contempt of court law, made 'active' when a crime suspect is arrested and in other circumstances. There may also be libel risks if media reports identify a suspect before he/she is charged.

▋ Standard of proof in criminal law

Those accused of crime enjoy 'the presumption of innocence'. This legal principle means that those charged with criminal offences are not required to prove themselves innocent. The onus is on the prosecution to prove guilt 'beyond reasonable doubt', the standard of proof necessary in law for a conviction. Police and other agencies which investigate crime need clear evidence to meet this standard.

▋ Arrests

Police have wide powers of arrest. Under the Police and Criminal Evidence Act 1984 a police officer can arrest a person who has committed, is committing or is about to commit an offence (however minor), or anyone about whom there are reasonable grounds for suspicion. But the officer must also have reasonable grounds for believing the arrest is necessary to achieve one of the purposes specified in the Act – for example, that the arrest is necessary to allow 'prompt and effective investigation' of a crime, or to stop a person from obstructing the highway. Police can use 'reasonable force' to make an arrest. An arrest automatically makes the case 'active' under the Contempt of Court Act 1981, affecting what can be published about it.

! Remember

The 1981 Act, explained in ch. 18, safeguards the fairness of trials. That chapter explains what types of material, if published about an active case, can breach the Act. A breach is a contempt offence, for which a media organisation can be heavily fined.

Police questioning of suspects

An arrested person is usually taken to a police station. A suspect who goes to a police station voluntarily may be arrested there. Police sometimes tell the media that someone is 'helping with inquiries'.

- Journalists should check whether the suspect is helping police voluntarily or is under arrest, because newsrooms need to know if the case is 'active'. If it is 'active', contempt law affects what can be published.

Limits to detention by police, prior to any charge

To protect civil liberties, no-one should normally be held under arrest for more than 24 hours, and if they have not been charged within that period they must be released. This period runs from the time of arrest or from when the suspect was brought into the police station, depending on circumstances. A police superintendent can authorise the detention of someone suspected of an **indictable offence** (→glossary) for a further 12 hours. Police can then ask a magistrates court to authorise the person's detention for another 36 hours. If a further application is made, the court cannot extend this detention beyond a maximum period of 96 hours – that is, 96 hours since detention began. The exception is that people suspected of terrorism can be detained 14 days without charge.

False imprisonment

If an arrested person later decides to sue the police for damages, alleging 'false arrest' or 'false imprisonment', he/she must prove that the police grounds for detaining him/her were unreasonable.

www.mcnaes.com ch. 4 explains the *habeas corpus* procedure in which the police and other official agencies can be required to justify to the High Court why a person is being detained.

Ch. 36 explains that photo-journalists covering tense incidents may be threatened with arrest.

▌ The Crown Prosecution Service

((•))

see Useful Websites at the end of this chapter for the CPS site

Most prosecutions are the responsibility of the Crown Prosecution Service (CPS), a government department. It has bases serving each of the 43 police areas in England and Wales. The head of the CPS is the Director of Public Prosecutions.

It is independent of police, but has the duty to advise and direct them in investigations, except those into the most minor crimes. The CPS decides, in all major cases involving police investigation, whether a suspect should be prosecuted, and if so, on what charge(s).

- A charge is a formal accusation, giving the alleged offender basic details of the crime allegedly committed. It includes, for example, what property was allegedly stolen and the name of the alleged victim of the crime. It means the case will be prosecuted, and go to court.

Usually a suspect is charged at a police station. He/she should be given the charge in written form, but may already have been charged orally, before that document was ready. The charge makes the case 'active' under the Contempt of Court Act 1981, if it is not active already because of an arrest.

The case ceases to be 'active' if an arrested person is released without charge, unless he/she is released on **police bail** because officers want more time to complete investigations. A suspect on bail must return to a police station on a specified date. Then the suspect may be charged, or released without charge.

→ glossary

 The www.mcnaes.com chapter on Scotland provides an outline of its prosecution system.

Decisions on whether to prosecute

When considering whether a suspect should be prosecuted, CPS lawyers assess whether there is 'a realistic prospect of conviction'. If the case passes that test, they consider if it is in the public interest to prosecute. In almost all serious cases, consideration of the public interest leads to a decision to prosecute.

Limits to detention by police, after any charge

Once someone has been charged police questioning of him/her must stop, except in limited circumstances. The person, if under arrest, must by law be taken before a magistrates court on the day he/she is charged or on the following day, excepting Sundays, Christmas Day or Good Friday. Alternatively, after being charged the person may be released on police bail to attend court.

In all major cases lawyers employed by the CPS conduct the prosecution in the courts, but police have power to prosecute in some cases.

▍ Other prosecution agencies in the public sector

Various other governmental agencies investigate and prosecute offences. For example: local authorities can investigate and prosecute property landlords for breach of tenants' rights; the Serious Fraud Office, a government department, investigates and prosecutes serious and complex fraud.

▍ Laying or presenting of information; summonses; requisitions

The decision whether to prosecute may be taken quickly – for example, soon after an arrest. But it might not be taken for months if time is needed to gather evidence. A prosecution can begin with a charge. It can also begin by the 'laying' or 'presenting' – both terms are used – 'of information' before a magistrate. In this procedure an allegation that a crime has been committed is made orally or in writing to a magistrate. He/she will, without at that stage full consideration of evidence, issue a summons to be served on the alleged perpetrator.

- A summons is a formal document, issued by a magistrates court, setting out one or more crime allegations in similar detail to a charge. It requires attendance at court on a specified date to respond to the allegation(s).

The summons makes the case active under the Contempt of Court Act 1981, as ch. 18 explains.

ch. 6,
p. 63,
Many
cases
dealt with
by post,
explains
fixed
penalty
offences

For public prosecutors – including the CPS – the 'laying/presenting of information' has been replaced with a streamlined procedure called 'written charge and requisition' in which the prosecuting agency issues a written charge to the accused person. The requisition served with it is formal notification of the date for him/her to appear at the magistrates court. Service of the charge makes a case 'active' under the 1981 Act.

Summonses and requisitions are used routinely for minor offences if these cannot be resolved by a 'fixed penalty'.

▍ Arrest warrants

→ glossary

Magistrates can issue an arrest warrant if sworn, written information is laid before them that a person has committed an indictable offence, or any **summary offence** punishable by imprisonment, or as regards any offence if that person's address is not sufficiently established for a requisition or summons to be served. These offence categories are explained in the next chapter.

- An arrest warrant is a formal document in which a magistrate empowers any police officer to arrest the suspect wherever he/she is located in England or Wales to be brought to the magistrates court.

It can be used for a suspect 'on the run'. The terms of an arrest warrant may allow for a person, after being arrested and having completed formalities at the police station, to be released on **bail** to attend the magistrates court at a future date.

→ glossary

The issue of an arrest warrant makes the case 'active' under the 1981 Act, if it has not already become active because of the issue of a summons or service of a written charge.

▶ 'Private prosecutions'

Any citizen can, by laying information before a magistrate, start a prosecution, seeking to prove that an accused individual is guilty of a specified crime. The police and the CPS may have been aware of the allegation but concluded there was no or insufficient evidence. The capacity for any citizen to start a 'private prosecution' is seen as a fundamental right to counter-balance any inertia or partiality by police or other official agencies. But a magistrate can refuse to issue a summons if the allegation is deemed frivolous. A private prosecution may quickly become unsustainable because, for example, an individual citizen lacks the investigatory powers of the police. The CPS can take over a 'private prosecution', and therefore also withdraw the case, and the Attorney General can also stop private prosecutions.

ch. 1, p. 9, High offices in law, explains the Attorney General's role

The Royal Society for the Prevention of Cruelty to Animals regularly conducts private prosecutions for cruelty to or neglect of animals.

▶ The risk of libel in media identification of crime suspects

The media may discover that someone is being investigated by the police or another agency – for example, that the person is under arrest. A media report which includes the suspect's name, or other detail identifying him/her in this context, could allow that individual successfully to sue the publisher for libel if the investigation does not lead to a prosecution. Publishing a statement that someone is under investigation, even when this is factually correct, may be defamatory because it creates an inference that he/she is guilty.

chs. 19 and 20 explain defamation dangers

Case study

In 2011 Bristol landlord Chris Jefferies won 'very substantial' settlements in libel actions against eight national newspapers for articles published after one of his tenants, the landscape architect Joanna Yeates was found dead. Mr Jefferies had been arrested at one stage by police but was later released. The newspapers published defamatory material about him. But then another man was charged with murdering Joanna and was subsequently convicted of this. Louis Charalambous, Mr Jefferies' solicitor, said of the libellous coverage: 'Christopher Jefferies is the latest victim of the regular witch hunts and character assassination conducted by the worst elements of the British tabloid media' (*Media Lawyer*, 29 July 2011).

As ch. 18 explains, what was published about Mr Jefferies also led to two newspapers being convicted of contempt of court.

If the media are officially given the name of a person under investigation or arrest by a spokesperson for a governmental agency, for example, the police, CPS or a local council, it can safely be published because the report will be protected by the libel defence of qualified privilege if its requirements are met. Ch. 21 explains this.

In reality, when reporting high-profile investigations, especially if a celebrity or public figure is a suspect, media organisations may choose – within the fierce competition to break news – to publish the suspect's name before it is known if he/she will be charged, and without any qualified privilege. News organisations might decide that the person is unlikely to sue for libel because, for example, a celebrity or politician may not wish to alienate the media or stir up more publicity. Or the media may take the risk of naming the person because police leaks indicate that a charge is sure to follow. If the person is charged, a libel action over pre-charge publicity becomes less likely, because any damage this caused to the person's reputation will usually be outweighed by, or indistinguishable from, damage caused by reports of the consequent court case, which the media can safely publish.

▶ ACPO guidelines on police naming of suspects and victims

Guidelines issued to police forces in 2010 by the Association of Chief Police Officers (ACPO) state that generally police do not give to the media the name of a person under investigation prior to any charge but that some details – for example, that the person is 'a 27 year old Brighton man' – may be released. Some forces will confirm the name of such a person if put to them by the media.

((•))

see Useful
Websites
at the end
of this
chapter
for the
ACPO
guidelines

These guidelines state that most forces will, if a person is charged, tell the media his/her name, age, and occupation and may, unless there is an operational reason not to, give his/her home address, plus detail of the charge and forthcoming court appearance. The guidelines add that forces will generally confirm investigations into companies.

The guidelines warn that police usually consider the names of witnesses and crime victims to be confidential, but that dead crime victims will usually be identified to the media after immediate relatives are informed.

See www.mcnaes.com ch. 4 for law banning the disclosure of identities of police informants, including 'investigation anonymity orders'; ethical considerations when journalists accompany police 'raids' to arrest or search; ethical considerations in media coverage of crime and of juveniles involved in 'pre-trial investigations'.

▌ Teachers given anonymity

The Education Act 2011 gives **automatic** lifelong anonymity to teachers in respect of any allegation that they have or may have committed an offence against a pupil at their school.   →glossary

The ban makes it illegal to publish any detail likely to lead members of the public to identify the teacher as being the subject of such an allegation. But the anonymity ends if he or she is charged with an offence, or a court agrees to an application that it should be lifted in the interests of justice.

The anonymity also ends if the Education Secretary publishes information about the individual in connection with an investigation or decision relating to the allegation, or if the General Teaching Council for Wales publishes information about the individual in connection with an investigation, hearing or decision on the allegation.

This law was created because teachers complained that they were vulnerable to false allegations. But it is controversial in that it made them the first – and so far the only – group of people in UK legal history to be given anonymity by law in respect of an allegation.

A teacher may waive his/her anonymity, by giving written consent – for example, to a media organisation – to being identified. But the consent is not valid if it is proved that it was obtained by unreasonable interference with his/her peace or comfort.

The anonymity provisions are in section 13 of the Act, which amended part of the Education Act 2002. The section makes it unlawful, for example, to identify a teacher who has been accused of assaulting or sexually abusing a child at his or her school if that teacher has not been charged with a criminal offence – even if the accusation is referred to in public, for example at an employment tribunal hearing at which the teacher claims unfair dismissal.

 ch. 17 explains employment tribunals

Publication of anything which breaches the anonymity is punishable on summary conviction by a fine of up to £5,000.

But it is a defence for anyone accused of publishing such information to show that at the time he or she was not aware, and did not suspect or have reason to suspect, that the publication included the information in question, or that he or she was not aware, and did not suspect or have reason to suspect that the allegation had been made.

 this maximum fine may be increased, see ch. 6, p. 62, Fining power to be without limit

➡ Recap of major points

- Covering crime stories presents contempt of court dangers for the media, because an arrest, an oral charge, service of a written charge, or the issue of a summons or an arrest warrant makes a case 'active' under the Contempt of Court Act 1981.

- There could well be libel risks if a suggestion is published, prior to any charge, that a suspect is guilty of a crime, if what is published identifies the suspect.

- But if the police or another governmental agency, in an official statement, identifies a person as a suspect, it is safe to report the statement.

- Some police informants are protected by anonymity orders. Teachers accused of an offence against a pupil have anonymity unless they are charged.

- Teachers accused of an offence against a pupil have anonymity unless they are charged.

((•)) Useful Websites

www.cps.gov.uk/
   Crown Prosecution Service

www.cps.gov.uk/about/principles.html
   Code for Crown Prosecutors

www.acpo.presscentre.com/content/default.aspx?NewsAreaID=19
   Association of Chief Police Officers (ACPO) Communication Advisory
   Group – Guidance 2010

www.acpo.police.uk/documents/reports/2013/201305-cop-media-rels.pdf
   College of Policing 'Guidance on Relationships with the Media' 2013

Crimes: categories and definitions

Chapter summary

All criminal cases begin in the magistrates courts. The most serious cases – for example, charges of murder, rape or robbery – progress to a Crown court. Journalists must know the different categories of crimes, to understand when reporting restrictions affect what can be published in court stories. They also need to know the legal definitions of some crimes to avoid libel problems when referring to offences.

▌ Categories of criminal offences

Criminal charges – and therefore the offences they allege – are grouped into three categories: indictable-only, either-way and summary.

(1) *Indictable-only offences* are the most serious crimes, punishable by the longest prison terms – for example, murder, rape, **robbery**. Such a case is processed initially by a magistrates court, but cannot be dealt with there because the maximum jail sentence which magistrates can impose (six months) would be too lenient for a defendant convicted of a serious offence. So, indictable-only cases progress quickly to a Crown court, as explained in ch. 7. If the defendant admits the charge there, or a jury finds him/her guilty, the judge will sentence. The term 'indictable-only' derives from 'the indictment', the document used at a Crown court to record the charge(s).

→glossary
→glossary

ch. 8 explains Crown courts

(2) *Either-way offences* include **theft**, sexual assault and assault causing grievous bodily harm. These charges can be dealt with either at a Crown court or by magistrates, hence the term 'either-way'. For this category,

→glossary
→glossary

magistrates may – after hearing an outline of the case – decide it is so serious that only a Crown court can deal with it. As ch. 7 explains, if magistrates decide they can deal with the case, the defendant may nevertheless exercise the legal right of those charged with either-way offences to choose trial by jury at Crown court. Either-way offences are regarded as being less serious than indictable-only offences, but nevertheless include distressing, harmful crimes.

! Remember

Confusingly, indictable-only and either-way charges are sometimes referred to collectively as 'indictable' charges, because both categories share the possibility of jury trial at Crown court. But, as stated earlier, magistrates can decide to deal with an either-way case in their summary proceedings – that is, as if it were a summary offence.

→ glossary

(3) *Summary offences* These are comparatively minor offences, and include common assault, drunkenness and speeding offences. Summary charges are dealt with in magistrates courts, except in some cases in which a defendant faces both summary and either-way or indictable charges arising from the same event, in which instance a Crown court may deal with all of them. But people charged with a summary offence have no right for it to be tried by jury. So, 'summary proceedings' means 'proceedings in a magistrates court', with the term 'summary' indicating the relative speed of the process.

▌ Defining criminality

There are two elements in most crimes:

- an act which is potentially criminal – which lawyers refer to as the *actus reus* (which they pronounce, in lawyers' Latin, 'actus reeus'); and
- a guilty mind – referred to as the *mens rea* ('menz reeah'), which means that such an act was carried out, or planned or attempted, with guilty intention – that the perpetrator knew he/she was acting, or intending to act, in a way which is unlawful.

Generally, the prosecution must prove both elements. In the crime of murder, the *actus reus* is that of unlawfully killing someone, and the *mens rea* is that the act was done with intent to kill or cause grievous bodily harm. If there is no such intent, a killing may be a lesser crime – for example, manslaughter.

Strict liability

Some offences are of 'strict liability'. Strict liability, when it applies in law, removes or strictly limits the defences to the charge. Strict liability means that a motorist who exceeds the speed limit commits an offence, even if he/she did not realise how fast he/she was driving. A motorist who drives with too much alcohol in his/her blood commits an offence, even if he/she did not intend to breach the alcohol limit. Strict liability can be seen as a practical, societal solution to deter dangerous or anti-social conduct for which, in many cases, it would be impossible to prove that *mens rea* – a guilty mind – existed.

Journalists must understand this concept, not least because some criminal offences arising from publishing material are strict liability offences, meaning it is not a defence to say 'Sorry, I didn't intend to. ...' – for example, if matter is published which breaches the Contempt of Court Act 1981.

see ch. 18, p. 215, Contempt of Court Act 1981– strict liability

▌Definitions of crimes

A victim of theft may tell friends he/she has been 'robbed'. If a journalist makes this colloquial error when reporting a court case he/she seems foolish and – worse – the error could lead to a libel action.

chs. 19–20 explain libel

If a defendant is guilty of a minor theft, but is wrongly reported as guilty of robbery, the mistake suggests to the public that he/she committed a much worse crime, in that robbery – because it involves violence or threatened violence – is generally regarded as worse than theft.

The crime definitions in the following list are simplified. For fuller definitions, see the Crown Prosecution Service's Legal Guidance section, listed at the end of this chapter under Useful Websites.

Crimes against people

Murder The unlawful killing of a human being with the intention of killing or causing grievous bodily harm. An adult convicted of murder must be sentenced to life imprisonment. Indictable-only.

Manslaughter The unlawful killing of another person, but without the intention to kill or cause grievous bodily harm. Manslaughter can be a charge in its own right, or a jury in a murder trial, if it finds the defendant not guilty of murder, can in some circumstances convict him/her of manslaughter as an alternative. Indictable-only.

Corporate manslaughter An offence for which the senior managers of an organi-sation, including a company, a government department or a police force, can be convicted if it causes a person's death in the circumstance of a gross breach of a duty of care owed to that person, if the way in which its activities were managed or organised by its senior management was a substantial element in that breach. Indictable-only.

Causing or allowing the death of a child or vulnerable adult An offence intro-duced in 2004 to close a legal loophole through which, for example, a couple whose child died because of physical abuse could escape justice by blaming each other, making it impossible to prove which was the killer. This offence enables both to be successfully prosecuted. Indictable-only.

Infanticide The killing of an infant under 12 months old by its mother, when her mind is disturbed as a result of the birth. Indictable-only.

→ glossary *Assault, common assault, battery, assault by beating* The way these offences evolved in case law led their definitions to overlap. These charges are likely to be used in cases in which no, or only transient or trifling, bodily injury is alleg-edly caused. 'Assault' and 'common assault' can mean an unlawful infliction of force/violence, or a hostile act – for example, a threatening gesture – which put another person in fear of immediate violence. Journalists should not assume that an assault charge necessarily alleges that a physical attack occurred. Either type of act must be proved as intentional or reckless. A push can be a common assault. Battery can also be expressed as a charge of 'assault by beating'. They are sum-mary offences, unless the assault involved allegedly racial or religious motives, in which event they are either-way.

Assault occasioning actual bodily harm (ABH) An assault – that is, a threat and/or attack, see earlier – which caused harm more than transient and trifling. The harm could be psychiatric illness. Either-way.

Wounding or inflicting grievous body harm (GBH) These charges are in section 20 of the Offences Against the Person Act 1861, and overlap in their definitions. It must be proved that the defendant intended or foresaw causing some harm, and – depending on which charge the prosecution chooses – that the harm caused was a wound or grievous (that is, serious) harm which was not or not only a wound. Either charge, in full form, includes the term 'malicious' – for example, 'malicious wounding'. A 'wound' is the slicing-through or breakage of skin, and can be a mere cut. But a wounding charge tends to be used only if the wound is serious. A GBH charge tends to be used, for example, if the harm includes broken bone, or led to substantial loss of blood, and/or extended medical treatment and/or permanent disfigurement and/or permanent disability. These charges are either-way.

Wounding 'with intent'/inflicting grievous body harm 'with intent' Under section 18 of the 1861 Act, the wounding or GBH is deemed to have been 'with intent' if there is intent to cause GBH or to resist 'lawful apprehension'. Such a charge is indictable-only. It carries a maximum penalty of life imprisonment.

Rape Indictable-only. See definitions of sexual offences in ch. 10, which also explains that victims of these offences must have anonymity in media reports.

Crimes against property or involving gain

Theft Dishonest appropriation of property belonging to another with the intention of permanently depriving the other of it (Theft Act 1968). Either-way. The act of theft is stealing. Do not refer to this offence as robbery.

Robbery Theft by force (that is, violence), or by threat of force. Indictable-only.

Handling Dishonestly receiving goods, knowing or believing them to be stolen; or dishonestly helping in the retention, removal, disposal or sale of such goods. Either-way.

Burglary Entering a building as a trespasser, and then

- stealing or attempting to steal from it; or
- inflicting or attempting to inflict grievous bodily harm to anyone in it; or
- making trespassing entry to a building with:
  - intent to steal; or
  - intent to inflict GBH; or
  - intent to do unlawful damage.

Generally, burglary is an either-way charge, though in some circumstances it is indictable-only.

Aggravated burglary Burglary while armed with a firearm, imitation firearm, or any other weapon or explosive. Indictable-only.

Fraud Under the Fraud Act 2006, there are now general offences of fraud, defined as conduct 'with a view to gain or with intent to cause loss or expose to a risk of loss' involving either:

- a dishonest making of a false representation (for example, using a credit card dishonestly, or using a false identity to open a bank account); or
- a dishonest failure to disclose information when under a legal duty to disclose (for example, failure when applying for health insurance to disclose a heart condition);
- dishonest abuse of a position (for example, an employee swindling money from his/her employer).

The Act also includes a fraud offence of obtaining services dishonestly. Fraud charges, such as obtaining property by deception, created by earlier legislation, survive transitionally, their use dependent on when the alleged offences occurred. These statutory fraud offences are either-way, but if deemed to be of sufficient 'seriousness or complexity', are treated procedurally as indictable-only (procedure explained in ch. 7). Conspiracy to defraud is indictable-only.

Blackmail Making an unwarranted demand with menaces with a view to gain. This offence could be a threat to disclose embarrassing secrets or photos involving the victim, unless money is paid. But it could also be another type of extortion such as a threat to contaminate goods on a supermarket company's shelves unless money is paid. Indictable-only.

Taking a vehicle without authority – sometimes referred to as TWOC (taking without owner's consent). It can cover conduct known as 'twocking' or 'joy-riding' in which perpetrators abandon a car after using it. This offence does not involve an intention to deprive the owner permanently of the vehicle, and so should not be described as theft. Summary.

Aggravated vehicle taking When a vehicle has been taken (as above) and, because of how it was driven, someone is injured or the vehicle or other property is damaged. Either-way.

Motoring crimes

Driving under the influence of drink or drugs Driving a motor vehicle when the ability to do so being thus impaired. Summary.

Driving with excess alcohol When alcohol in the driver's body exceeds the prescribed limit; that is, 80 milligrammes of alcohol in 100 millilitres of blood, 35 microgrammes of alcohol in 100 millilitres of breath, or 107 milligrammes of alcohol in 100 millilitres of urine. Summary.

Causing death by careless driving when under the influence of drink or drugs The driver must be unfit to drive through drink or drugs; or must have consumed excess alcohol or failed to provide a specimen. Indictable-only.

! Remember

It may not be fair or accurate (and therefore could be a libel problem) to describe a driver with more than the prescribed limit of alcohol as 'drunk'. He/she may only be marginally over the limit. It is safe to use the term 'drunk' if and as it is expressed in evidence or if – in the case of a convicted defendant – the evidence clearly supports this.

Other noteworthy crimes

Perjury Knowingly giving false evidence after taking an oath as a witness to tell the truth in court, or in an **affidavit**, or to a tribunal. Indictable-only.

→ glossary

Perverting the course of justice Concealing evidence, or giving false information to police. Indictable-only.

Wasting police time A lesser offence than the two above. It is committed by a person knowingly making a false report that a crime has occurred or falsely claiming to have information material to an investigation. Summary.

Kerb-crawling/soliciting The colloquial term for the offence, usually committed by men in streets frequented by prostitutes, of 'soliciting' (which, in this context, means seeking the services of a prostitute) from a motor vehicle in such a manner as to cause annoyance to the person approached (who may be a local resident, not a prostitute) or to others in the neighbourhood. Summary.

It is not an offence to be a prostitute, but is an offence for a prostitute to loiter in a public place, or to 'solicit' there (which means, in this context, to offer sex in return for money).

➡ Recap of major points

- There are three main categories of criminal offences:
  - Indictable-only, which can only be dealt with by a Crown court;
  - Either-way, dealt with by a Crown court or a magistrates court – see ch. 7;
  - Summary – almost all such cases are dealt with by magistrates.
- If an offence is of 'strict liability', the defendant can be convicted even if he/she had no clear 'intention' to do wrong.
- A media organisation which fails to report an offence or charge accurately might be successfully sued for libel by the defendant.

((•)) Useful Websites

www.cps.gov.uk/legal/
    Crown Prosecution Service 'Legal Guidance'

6

Magistrates courts: summary cases

Chapter summary

Magistrates courts deal with about 95 per cent of all criminal cases, and send the rest – the most serious – to Crown courts. Hearings in which magistrates try or sentence defendants are called summary proceedings. Offences with which they deal include burglaries, sexual assault and dangerous driving. Magistrates can jail convicted defendants for up to six months for a single offence. This chapter also explains bail, and details the automatic reporting bans restricting what the media can publish from pre-trial hearings at magistrates courts.

▌ Who are magistrates?

The role of magistrates originates in the twelfth century. They still use the ancient title of 'justice of the peace'. Almost all are volunteers and part time – that, is lay magistrates. There are about 23,500 lay magistrates, who are trained and paid expenses. There were more than 200 magistrates courthouses in England and Wales.

If lay magistrates try a criminal case, there must be at least two of them. A trial in a magistrates court is known as a **summary trial**, reflecting the fact that magistrates dispense quick and relatively informal justice whereas the higher courts, having more serious and complex cases, have slower processes.

One magistrate is sufficient for some court duties. When a court hearing has more than one magistrate, one acts as chair and announces decisions. Magistrates are advised on law by a justices' clerk or one of his/her staff of qualified lawyers, who sits in front of the magistrate(s) in court.

→ glossary

@

see www. mcnaes. com ch. 6: 'More about magis- trates'

District judges

There are also about 140 professional magistrates (that is, they get a wage) referred to as district judges, appointed after at least five years' experience as a lawyer or legal executive. Most are in city districts with high caseloads. District judges used to be officially known as stipendiary magistrates (from the Latin term stipend, meaning a wage) – colloquially, 'a stipe'. A district judge tries cases on his/her own. For convenience, this book refers to 'magistrates' (that is, plural) sitting in court, because two or three lay magistrates sit in many hearings.

▌ The taking of pleas

Defendants facing summary charges are asked, usually during their first appearance in the magistrates court, how they plead. If they plead guilty to a charge, this means they are convicted of it. Sentencing usually takes place at a later date, to enable preparation of a 'pre-sentence report'.

A contested case will in most instances be adjourned for summary trial. When it is first adjourned, the magistrates must decide, unless the charge is a minor one, whether to grant bail.

Defendants who deny **either-way** charges can ask magistrates to try them. The **allocation (mode of trial)** procedure is outlined in the next chapter, which explains that a denied either-way charge is tried at a Crown court if the defendant wishes, or if magistrates decide it is too serious for them to try.

ch. 4 explains categories of charges and pp. 60–61, Sentencing by magistrates

→ glossary
→ glossary

▌ Bail

Bail is the system by which a court grants a defendant his/her liberty until the case's next hearing.

The court may impose conditions – for example, that the defendant should live at his/her home address.

The Bail Act 1976 has a general rule that a defendant must be granted bail unless:

- the court is satisfied there are substantial grounds for believing that if bail is granted
  - he/she will abscond, or
  - commit another offence, or
  - obstruct the course of justice (for example, by interfering with witnesses);
- the court decides the defendant should be kept in prison for his/her own protection, (for instance, if the alleged crime has so angered the local community that a mob may attack him/her);

- the defendant is alleged to have committed an offence when he/she was on bail granted in an earlier case;
- the defendant is already serving a jail sentence;
- there is insufficient information to decide on bail.

A court must give reasons for refusing bail.

A defendant charged with murder can only be given bail by a Crown court judge.

Evidence and previous convictions aired

When deciding on bail, the court is told of the defendant's relevant previous conviction(s), and some details of prosecution evidence about the charge(s) faced. A defence lawyer arguing for bail may outline defence evidence.

Surety

In some cases, a court will insist that the defendant has a surety before bail is granted.

A surety is someone, for example a relative or friend of the defendant, who guarantees that the defendant will 'surrender' to bail – that is, turn up at court as required. The surety agrees to forfeit a sum of money, fixed by the court, if the defendant absconds.

If the defendant absconds, a surety who fails to pay the sum can be jailed.

Failure to surrender

It is a criminal offence for a defendant to fail to surrender to bail, and will probably result in the court issuing an arrest warrant authorising the police to bring him/her to court.

Appeals

If magistrates refuse bail, a defendant can apply for bail to a Crown court judge. The prosecution, if the alleged offence is serious, can appeal to a Crown court judge to challenge a decision by magistrates to grant bail.

▶ Reporting restrictions for pre-trial hearings

When a denied charge is heading for a summary trial, magistrates may hold at least one pre-trial hearing to consider any dispute between prosecution and defence on admissibility of evidence or about other questions of law, to make rulings about such matters, and to decide on bail.

Section 8C of the Magistrates' Courts Act 1980 has **automatic** restrictions which limit contemporaneous reporting of these pre-trial hearings.

 →glossary

The restrictions are intended to prevent the risk of prejudice should a case originally due to be tried by magistrates end up being tried by a Crown court jury. Parliament anticipated that, because of changes to integrate the courts system, a case – even if a magistrates court started preparing to try it – could end up being tried at a Crown court with a 'related' either-way or indictable-only case. Also, a magistrates court could initially agree in the allocation procedure to try an either-way case but later in a pre-trial hearing decide that a Crown court should try it after all because the alleged offence was more serious than it first appeared.

see ch. 7, pp. 72–74, Allocation procedure in either-way cases

The type of material aired in a pre-trial hearing which could, if published contemporaneously by the media, subsequently prejudice a jury's verdict at Crown court is outlined in the next chapter. It includes evidence ruled to be inadmissible.

- The section 8C reporting restrictions ban media reports from referring to evidential matters aired in pre-trial hearings at magistrates courts, so that if the case is later sent to Crown court for trial, people who later become jurors will not have read or heard about evidence which may not be presented during the trial.

The scope of the section 8C reporting restrictions

The section 8C reporting restrictions automatically apply for pre-trial hearings at magistrates courts in cases due to have a summary trial.

They ban publication of:

- any ruling by magistrates on admissibility of evidence and other questions of law, and of any order to discharge or vary such a ruling;
- applications for such rulings and for such orders, including legal argument and discussion about whether such a ruling or order should be made.

The Act defines a pre-trial hearing as one relating to a charge due to be tried by magistrates to which the defendant has pleaded not guilty; and which takes place before magistrates start hearing prosecution evidence at the trial. So section 8C could cover a defendant's first appearance at court, as well as any other pre-trial hearing, but does not prevent contemporaneous reporting of the plea.

While the restrictions are in force, the media can only report seven categories of information from pre-trial hearings about admissibility of evidence or other questions of law. These are (in simplified form):

- the name of the court and the magistrates' names;
- the names, ages, home addresses and occupations of the defendant(s) and witnesses;
- the charge(s) in full or summarised;
- the names of solicitors and barristers in the proceedings;

- if the case is adjourned, the date and place to which it is adjourned;
- any arrangements as to bail;
- whether legal aid was granted.

It is also safe to publish that reporting restrictions are in force – this is not prejudicial.

The effect of the restrictions is to ban publication of any reference to evidence, except as it is encapsulated in the wording of the charge(s), or to other prejudicial matter.

As regards 'arrangements as to bail', it will be safe to report, unless the court orders otherwise, whether bail was granted, and, if it was granted, any bail conditions and **surety** arrangement.

But the media should *not* report in most instances if or why the prosecution opposed bail, or the reasons the magistrates gave for refusing it, as doing so could be prejudicial.

It would be safe to report that someone was remanded in custody for their own protection, because it was feared, for example, that their life would be at risk if they were to be released.

The home addresses which may be published are those current when the report is published and former addresses which were current during events which gave rise to the charge(s).

→ glossary

see also
ch. 7,
p. 66,
Types of
prejudicial
matter

! Remember

If a report refers to a defendant's former address or includes a picture or footage of it, it should make clear that he/she no longer lives there. Failing to do so could cause the current occupants to sue for libel because people think they are linked to the court case.

The explicit ban in section 8C on publishing pre-trial argument and rulings about admissibility of evidence and other questions of law is a 'belt and braces' approach, since its limitation of reports to the seven categories cited earlier has the same effect.

A media report of a pre-trial hearing can safely include neutral descriptions of the court scene and neutral background information.

see ch. 7,
pp. 66–67,
The scope
of the sec-
tion 52A
restric-
tions,
about
such
neutral
material

When do the section 8C restrictions cease to apply?

The magistrates can lift the section 8C reporting restrictions, wholly or in part, to allow the media to publish contemporaneously fuller reports of these pre-trial applications, and of any ruling or order made in them.

If any defendant objects, the court can lift them only if satisfied that doing so is in the interests of justice. If there are objections, they and any representations made to the court about them (that is, argument in court about whether the restrictions should be lifted) cannot be reported until the case is 'disposed of', even if restrictions are lifted earlier in other respects.

The section 8C restrictions automatically lapse when the case is 'disposed of', which happens when all defendants in the case are acquitted or convicted of all charges in the case, or if the court dismisses the case, or the prosecution decides not to proceed with it.

So, at the end of the trial, a media organisation could publish a report of evidence ruled inadmissible some weeks or months previously in a pre-trial hearing, or of any ruling made in it.

Liability for breach of the section 8C restrictions

A proprietor, editor or publisher can be prosecuted for breaching these restrictions. The maximum fine is currently £5,000, but see p. 62, Fining power to be without limit.

▶ Procedure in summary trials

Though reporting restrictions cover pre-trial hearings, what is said in a trial at a magistrates court can usually be reported fully as it occurs.

No restrictions under the 1980 Act apply, but they could apply under other law, explained in chs. 9, 10 and 11.

The usual summary trial procedure is:

- The prosecutor makes an opening speech, describing the alleged crime.

- Witnesses testify, after swearing an oath or affirming that their evidence is true.

- Prosecution witnesses are called first. Each is asked questions by the prosecutor to elicit their evidence-in-chief (that is, evidence given during questioning by the side which called them). The defence can cross-examine them. The prosecution may then re-examine them.

see also
ch. 4,
p. 39,
Standard
of proof in
criminal
law

- When prosecution evidence ends, the defence may submit, for any or all charges faced, that there is no case to answer – that is, that the prosecution cannot meet the standard of proof required.

- If the magistrates agree with this submission, they dismiss the charge. Otherwise, or if there is no such submission, the trial continues.

- Defence witnesses are called. These may include the defendant, though he/she cannot be compelled to testify.

- Defence witnesses are questioned to elicit their evidence-in-chief. They can be cross-examined by the prosecutor, and then re-examined by the defence.

- When the court has heard all witnesses, the defence may address the court in a closing speech, arguing how facts and law should be interpreted. Either side can address the court twice in total, in opening or closing speeches. The defence has the right to make the last speech.

- If the magistrates feel a charge is not proved, they acquit the defendant
- If they find him/her guilty on any charge, he/she is convicted of it, and the magistrates sentence the defendant, or adjourn to sentence at a later date.

! Remember

There are court rules on what case material journalists can see to help them report a trial, and a national protocol on what prosecution material can be released to them to help coverage of cases – see ch.14, pp. 158–161, Journalists' access to case material in court proceedings.

Hostile witnesses and leading questions

Normally, to ensure witnesses tell of events in their own words, leading questions are not allowed to be put to them when they give evidence-in-chief, but:

- a witness who refuses to testify or retracts a statement made to investigators can be ruled by the court to be 'a hostile witness' – that is, someone who can be asked leading questions by the side which calls him/her.
- A leading question is one which suggests what answer is expected. 'Did anything happen after that?' is not a leading question. 'Did you then see a man with a knife?' is.

ch. 4, p. 39, Standard of proof in criminal law, explains this principle

'Bad character'

As a general rule, prosecutors in trials cannot refer to a defendant's previous 'bad character' because – to comply with the principle of the presumption of innocence – the focus is on evidence for the charge(s) being tried, not any past crime.

But evidence of previous offences and other reprehensible behaviour can be introduced to correct a false impression given by the defendant, or as evidence that he/she follows a distinctive method when committing offences of the kind with which he/she is charged, or if the defendant's evidence has attacked another person's character.

▶ Sentencing by magistrates

In sentencing hearings for an admitted charge, the prosecution gives magistrates details of the crime. If there is dispute about the facts of an admitted offence the magistrates must accept the defence version unless the prosecution proves its version in a **Newton hearing**.

Otherwise, defendants who admit an offence and those convicted at trial are sentenced in the same way:

The court will consider any written statement the victim of the crime provides. Before sentence is passed, the defendant's lawyer can make a speech in mitigation, citing any extenuating circumstances while asking for leniency.

A defendant may ask for other offences to be 'taken into consideration'.

- Offences to be 'taken into consideration', which should not be confused with previous convictions, are crimes which the defendant admits although he/she has not been charged with them.

The defendant brings these to the court's attention to be sentenced for them as well as for the charged offence(s). By admitting uncharged crimes – for example, burglaries – the defendant removes the possibility of being prosecuted for them in future, giving the opportunity of a fresh start.

Magistrates may also consider a 'pre-sentence report' about the defendant's background, prepared by a probation officer.

((•))

see Useful Websites at the end of this chapter for details about the probation service

Jail sentences

Magistrates can jail a defendant for up to six months for a single offence, and for up to 12 months for more than one offence if they decide that jail terms should run consecutively, depending on penalties specified for an offence.

- Consecutive sentences are two or more jail terms ordered by the court to run one after the other, imposed when the defendant is convicted of more than one crime. If a sentence of six months is made consecutive to one of three months, the defendant is sentenced overall to nine months.
- *Concurrent sentences* are those where the defendant is sentenced overall only for the length of the longest sentence imposed. In the example just given, this would be six months.

Courts can give a suspended sentence to a defendant deserving leniency.

- A defendant given a suspended sentence does not have go to jail unless he/she commits a further offence or breaches a requirement of the suspended sentence – for example, doing unpaid community work – during the period for which the sentence is suspended.

So, a jail term of six months can be suspended for two years. If the defendant commits no other offence in that time, and does not breach any requirement, the suspended sentence lapses.

! Remember

A report which inaccurately portrays a suspended sentence as an immediate jail term could create a libel problem. In some circumstances, the defendant could sue for the inference that the crime was worse than it was.

see ch. 21 for libel considerations in court reporting

Committal for sentence

Magistrates who convict a defendant of an either-way charge can commit him/her for **sentence** to the Crown court if they believe, because of what they are told of the case, and/or about any previous conviction(s), their punishment powers are insufficient. A Crown court judge can impose longer jail terms.

Fines

For years it has been the case that, broadly speaking, the maximum fine which magistrates can impose is £5,000, where law specifies this. Most fines are much lower. But an employer can be fined up to £20,000 for a health and safety breach. Failure to pay a fine could lead to a jail sentence

Fining power to be without limit

The Legal Aid, Sentencing and Punishment Act 2012 empowers the Secretary of State for Justice to abolish the general £5,000 limit on magistrates' fining power. The Secretary will have discretion to decide which offences this change affects.

 This law could remove the £5,000 cap on fines which apply for some breaches of reporting restrictions, making such breaches much more costly for the media. Check www.mcnaes.com for updates.

Other types of sentences

- A community order – the court orders a defendant to obey one or more requirements, which could include:
  - unpaid work in the community under a probation officer's direction;
  - a curfew, with a requirement that the defendant wears an electronic 'tag' to monitor whether he/she obeys it;
  - receiving treatment for drug or alcohol dependency.
- A conditional discharge – meaning that the court has not immediately imposed or specified punishment, but states that if the defendant commits any other offence within a period specified by the court, such as a year, he/she is liable to be punished for the first offence as well as for the subsequent conviction.
- An absolute discharge – meaning that the court feels that no punishment, other than the fact of the conviction, is necessary.

A court can order a defendant to pay compensation to a crime victim.

Binding over and restraining orders

Since the fourteenth century, courts have had power to 'bind over' a person 'to keep the peace'. This can be used to resolve, without trial, minor allegations of assault, threatening behaviour, or public disorder, in that the prosecution may drop a charge if the defendant agrees to be 'bound over'. A binding over can also follow a conviction. A witness can also be bound over, if, for example, he/she seems to have been involved in a fracas. When binding over, the court specifies a sum of money which the person must pay if he/she breaches the peace – for example, by violent or threatening conduct – within a period specified by the court. The order is a preventative, civil law measure, not a punishment, and is *not* a conviction, and should not be reported as such.

A court may impose a restraining order on a defendant, even one acquitted at trial, to protect another person – for example, an ex-partner – from harassment. The order may ban the defendant from any contact with that person.

Section 70 committal

Magistrates can make an order under section 70 of the Proceeds of Crime Act 2002 committing the case of a convicted defendant to a Crown court hearing to assess what money or property he/she has gained from crime and, if necessary, to make a confiscation order. No automatic reporting restrictions apply to the committal hearing or the Crown court hearing.

▌ Many cases dealt with by post

Magistrates courts also deal with minor, 'fixed penalty' offences – for example, speeding. A defendant does not need to appear at court if he/she, having received written notice of the charge, returns a form admitting guilt and pays the fine.

▌ Appeal routes from magistrates courts

The defence or prosecution may contest a ruling by magistrates by appealing to the High Court by means of the 'case stated' procedure. In other types of challenge, the defence can ask the High Court for a **judicial review**.

→ glossary

A defendant appealing against a conviction by magistrates or the severity of the sentence imposed appeals to a Crown court.

These High Court and Crown court roles are explained in ch. 8.

➡ Recap of major points

- Trials and sentencing at magistrates courts are known as summary proceedings.
- Automatic reporting restrictions, under section 8C of the Magistrates' Courts Act limit what the media can report from pre-trial hearings.
- Trials at a magistrates court can usually be reported fully and contemporaneously.
- Magistrates can jail a convicted defendant for up to six months for one offence, and for up to 12 months for two or more offences

((•)) Useful Websites

www.magistrates-association.org.uk/
Magistrates Association

www.justice.gov.uk/about/probation
National Probation Service

Magistrates courts: the most serious criminal cases

Chapter summary

Those charged with the most serious crimes – such as murder and robbery – make their first court appearance in a magistrates court, usually having been held since arrest in police cells. Journalists may be on the court's press bench. But automatic reporting restrictions are in force in these preliminary hearings, to safeguard the defendant's right to fair trial by jury, because the case is bound for the Crown court. It is illegal for the media to breach the restrictions, but some newsworthy facts can be reported immediately from the magistrates court. The restrictions apply too in preliminary hearings for either-way charges, such as sexual assault. Magistrates try some either-way cases.

▌ Indictable-only and either-way charges – 'Sending for trial'

Defendants charged with the most serious crimes cannot be tried by magistrates. These cases are, as ch. 4 explains, **indictable-only**. They have an initial phase in the magistrates court, where decisions on **bail** and case management may be made, but are quickly 'sent for trial' to a Crown court where, if the defendant denies the offence, a jury trial will take place. For most indictable-only cases magistrates can decide on bail. But only a Crown court judge can decide on bail if the charge is murder (when it is exceptional for bail to be given).

So, when a defendant on an indictable-only charge appears in a magistrates court, this is only a preliminary hearing, known as a 'sending' hearing. Yet it will be of news interest locally and nationally if the alleged crime is already notorious.

→ glossary

→ glossary

see ch. 6,
pp. 55–56,
Bail

The formality of sending for trial may occur during the defendant's first appearance before magistrates.

→ glossary   Some **either-way cases** are also sent to the Crown court for trial, if in the 'allocation' procedure – explained later in this chapter – magistrates do not offer the defendant the option of being tried in the magistrates court or if the defendant chooses to be tried by a jury.

▶ Section 52A automatic reporting restrictions

→ glossary   Automatic reporting restrictions tightly limit what the media can publish contemporaneously from any **preliminary hearing** at a magistrates court if the case has potential for jury trial. These restrictions are in now in section 52A of the Crime and Disorder Act 1998, having replaced similar restrictions in section 8 of the Magistrates' Courts Act 1980. Their scope is set out in the next section. Unless lifted, they cover all indictable-only cases processed at these courts, and – as this chapter explains – some either-way cases. They prevent media reports of these 'sending' and 'allocation' hearings disclosing information which could create a risk of prejudice to jury trials – and cover *any* hearing of the case at the magistrates courts which occurs before its 'sending'.

the jury
system is
explained
in ch. 8   The concern is that people who read or hear information given at preliminary hearings may include some who months later will be called to be jurors in these cases. Justice demands that they try it only on the evidence presented at the trial, and should not be influenced by what they remember from pre-trial coverage.

Types of prejudicial matter

The section 52A restrictions are designed to prevent publication from preliminary hearings of:

- any reference to evidence in the case, apart from what is encapsulated in the wording of the charge(s);
- a defendant's previous conviction(s);
- any other material with potential to create prejudice.

Evidence Some evidence might be referred to in detail in a sending or allocation hearing – for example, magistrates may need to hear it to assess the risk of a defendant re-offending if given bail or, in an either-way case, to assess if the defendant should be offered the option of summary trial. But some evidence raised by the prosecution or defence might not figure in the trial. When the case reaches the Crown court a judge may rule, before the trial, that some evidence is inadmissible. For example, evidence that a defendant confessed the crime could be ruled inadmissible if the judge accepted that the confession was made under duress. Yet if journalists covering a preliminary hearing at a magistrates court could immediately report such evidence, a juror might remember reading about that 'confession' or some other detail of evidence aired then, and not understand why it does not figure in the Crown court trial. That recollection could contaminate the jury's consideration of the case, and a defendant could be wrongly convicted.

Previous convictions Generally, in accordance with the principle of the 'presumption of innocence' a Crown court jury will not be told if a defendant has previous conviction(s). But a defendant's criminal record may be disclosed in a 'sending' hearing – for example, to help magistrates decide on bail. Magistrates will also be told about a defendant's criminal record in the allocation procedure, which will precede any 'sending' in an either-way case. If a juror could remember a media report of these preliminary proceedings which disclosed that criminal record he/she could be prejudiced against the defendant.

Other material with potential to create prejudice could include suggestion by the prosecution in a 'sending' hearing that a defendant is guilty of more offences than the crime he/she is charged with. For example, in a rape case police may be checking other unsolved rapes if they suspect that the defendant is a serial rapist, and magistrates might be told of these inquiries by a prosecutor opposing bail. The inquiries might come to nothing, but if the media could immediately report these unfounded suspicions a juror may remember this at the trial and tell other jurors that the defendant might be a serial offender.

ch. 4, p. 39, Standard of proof in criminal law, explains this principle

The scope of the section 52A restrictions

The section 52A restrictions function by listing categories of information which can be published from such preliminary hearings at a magistrates court. The list is expressed here in simplified format (with explanation in italics):

- the name of the court (*for example, Doncaster magistrates court*) and the magistrates' names;
- the name, age, home address and occupation of the accused;
- in the case of an accused charged with a 'serious or complex' fraud, any 'relevant business information' – see later;
- the charge(s) in full or summarised;
- the names of counsel and solicitors engaged in the proceedings;
- if proceedings are adjourned, the date and place to which they are adjourned;
- 'arrangements as to *bail*' – that is whether bail was granted or refused, and, if it was granted, any bail conditions and surety arrangement.
  - When bail is refused, the usual interpretation of the restrictions is that in most instances the media should not report why the prosecution opposed bail or any reason the magistrates gave for refusing it – because such matter could be prejudicial. But it would be safe to report that someone was remanded in custody for his/her own protection;
- whether legal aid was granted.

→glossary

→glossary

The fact that reporting restrictions are in force can be reported. The 1998 Act does not specify this, but it cannot be prejudicial to publish this fact.

The 'relevant business information' which the media can report from a preliminary hearing at a magistrates court in a case of 'serious or complex' fraud is the same as that which can be reported from Crown court hearings dealing with applications for such charges to be dismissed.

 For 'serious or complex' fraud, see p. 74, Committal hearings and 'transfer' abolished and ch. 8, pp. 78–79, 'Relevant business information'.

The scope given in section 52A to report the place to which the case has been adjourned permits, on any logical interpretation, reporting that a case has been 'sent for trial' to the Crown court specified.

If, in a hearing in which there is more than one defendant, one unsuccessfully asks for the section 52A reporting restrictions to be lifted, see later, section 52A permits the reporting of the bare fact that the court declined to lift them.

 www.mcnaes.com ch. 7 has more advice on the section 52A reporting restrictions.

Reporting denials of guilt and choice of jury trial

When reporting preliminary hearings covered by section 52A the media routinely publish:

- *basic protestations of innocence* made by the defendant from the dock or through a solicitor. In an indictable-only case no formal plea is taken at the magistrates court, but it may be made clear there that the charge is denied. In either-way cases defendants are asked to indicate how they will plead;
- *that a defendant, in an either-way case, has chosen trial by jury.*

Although publication of protestations of innocence and choice of jury trial is beyond what strict application of section 52A would permit, the media are safe in reporting these facts, because:

- it seems only fair to the defendant to quote his/her denial of guilt – if made in relation to the only charge faced, or to all charges – and choice of jury trial, which too indicates denial of the charge(s);
- publishing such matter cannot be prejudicial – a jury, obviously, will know if a charge is denied.

But the media should be wary, when the restrictions apply, of reporting anything suggesting that a defendant will later enter a mixture of pleas – for example, quotes suggesting he/she will admit one charge while denying another. This could be prejudicial if at trial jurors are not told of the admission but remember it from pre-trial coverage.

Describing the courtroom scene

The media routinely report, even when section 52A restrictions apply, scene-setting information; that the hearing lasted 10 minutes, what the defendant wore, that he/she 'spoke only to confirm their name and address', that guards stood on either side of him/her. Such bland material will not cause prejudice.

Background material

Media organisations publishing reports of preliminary hearings usually add some background material about the defendant and/or the alleged crime. Background material, from sources other than the court hearing, is not itself a report of those proceedings and so does not contravene section 52A. But the Contempt of Court Act 1981 would cover such material, so nothing should be published which creates a substantial risk of serious prejudice or impediment – see ch. 18. Mingling background material into a court report without sufficient care could create such a risk – for example, potential jurors who see/hear the report could draw wrong inferences about the evidence.

An option for the media, when they want to report on an alleged crime incident which has occurred, say, in the previous 24 hours and that the alleged perpetrator has already appeared in court in a preliminary hearing, is to publish items segregated by page design or separate narrative. Each item could have its own headline/introduction – a story on the alleged incident, conforming to contempt law, not citing matter from the court hearing, and then a separate report solely of the preliminary hearing, conforming to the section 52A restrictions.

Liability for breach of the section 52A restrictions

Section 52B of the 1998 Act says that 'any proprietor, editor or publisher' of a newspaper or periodical can be prosecuted if it breaches the section 52A restrictions. If the breach is published in any other type of written report – for example, on a website not linked to a newspaper – 'the person who publishes it' can be prosecuted.

In the case of a TV or radio programme, 'the body corporate which provides the service' and any person 'having functions in relation to the programme corresponding to those of an editor of a newspaper' can be prosecuted. The maximum fine is currently £5,000.

see also
ch. 6,
p. 62,
Fining
power to
be without
limit

👁 **Case study**

In 2012 *The Sun* newspaper was fined £3,350 after it admitted breaching the section 52A restrictions in its report of the hearing in which Oldham magistrates court sent the case of Andrew Partington, charged with manslaughter and criminal damage, to Manchester Crown court for trial. The report – including its headline 'Gas pipe's cut, boom...you bitch' – quoted evidence from texts, described as the crux of the prosecution case, in which Partington threatened his girlfriend. Fining *The Sun*, district judge

Jonathan Taaffe said at Manchester magistrates court that this was 'shoddy' journalism. He endorsed the view that it went way beyond what was permitted, and that its content and tone created a substantial risk of prejudice. At Crown court Partington, 28, of Buckley Street, Oldham, was jailed for 10 years after admitting causing the gas blast which destroyed houses and killed a neighbour's child

(Judiciary of England and Wales press release, *The Independent* and BBC online news, 5 April 2013). See Useful Websites at the end of this chapter.

! Remember

If a breach of the section 52A restrictions occurs after a trial has begun, and is serious enough – because of what is published – to cause the trial to be aborted, a media organisation may also become liable for huge costs under section 93 of the Courts Act 2003. See ch. 18, p. 227, Media could face huge costs if 'serious misconduct' affects a case.

When do the section 52A restrictions cease to apply?

see
*Express
and Star*
report in
Useful
Websites
at the end
of this
chapter
→ glossary

These restrictions cease to apply in three circumstances.

(1) *If the section 52A restrictions are lifted by the magistrates court.* These courts have a discretionary power to lift the restrictions, including at the request of a defendant. If any defendant objects, the restrictions may only be lifted if the magistrates decide that doing so is in the interests of justice. A defendant may want restrictions lifted so his/her solicitor can publicise, by means of a full media report of the hearing, an appeal for witnesses. For example, the defence solicitor may be seeking witnesses to help corroborate the defendant's **alibi** – 'My client was at the funfair, not the crime scene. Did anyone see him at the fair?'

- Even if the restrictions are lifted at a defendant's request, the media should not, for as long as the case has potential of jury trial, publish details of any defendant's previous convictions, even if these were disclosed in the preliminary proceedings.

Pre-trial publication of previous convictions is so foreseeably prejudicial that, arguably, the section 4 defence in the Contempt of Court Act 1981, which normally protects fair and accurate reports of court hearings, might not apply.

ch. 18,
p. 227,
Court
report-
ing – the
section 4
defence

Section 52A says that if a defendant, whether a sole defendant or a co-accused, objects to the restrictions being lifted, their representations to magistrates on this issue, even if a lifting order is then made, should not be reported – that is, while the case retains potential for jury trial. But the fact that such a lifting order was made or not made can be reported.

Once this type of reporting restrictions have been lifted they cannot be re-imposed (*R v Blackpool Justices, ex p Beaverbrook Newspapers Ltd* [1972] 1 All ER 388; [1972] 1 WLR 95). If magistrates decide, after a request from one defendant, to lift the restrictions this means they are lifted in respect of all defendants in the hearing – even if any objected (*Leeds Justices, ex p Sykes* [1983] 1 WLR 132).

(2) *The section 52A restrictions automatically cease to apply if and when, for an either-way charge, it becomes clear as a result of the allocation procedure that the defendant is to be dealt with summarily.* This means that the restrictions no longer apply to an either-way charge if a defendant pleads guilty to it at a magistrates court. But other reporting restrictions begin to apply to pre-trial hearings there if he/she denies the charge and chooses to be tried by magistrates, see later.

(3) *The section 52A restrictions automatically expire when the proceedings against all defendants in the case have been concluded* – that is, no jury trial remains pending for any defendant in the case.

After such conclusion, evidence aired or submissions made at any preliminary hearing at a magistrates court weeks or months earlier can be fully reported. The media may wish to highlight evidence which, for legal reasons, the jury did not hear, which might give a fuller picture of the defendant or throw light on how the crime was investigated.

 See www.mcnaes.com ch. 7 for an example of a newspaper reporting evidence aired at a preliminary hearing months after it occurred.

Libel considerations

A report of preliminary proceedings published as soon as practicable after the section 52A restrictions are lifted or expire will be regarded as a contemporaneous report and so can enjoy the protection of absolute privilege in libel law, explained in ch. 21.

▌ Section 52A also applies to either-way cases

An either-way case will have at least one preliminary hearing in a magistrates court, and if the defendant denies the charge the allocation procedure will occur. Either-way cases include theft, burglary and sexual assault charges. A defendant in an either-way case has a right of jury trial, but may choose not to exercise it. An allocation hearing determines, for the defendant who intends to deny the charge, whether he or she will be tried by magistrates or by a jury. For as long as an either-way case retains potential for jury trial, the section 52A restrictions apply to reports of its preliminary hearings, including the allocation procedure and the process of 'sending' the case to a Crown court. To recognise if this potential for jury trial continues to exist, journalists must understand that procedure. See also Figure 2 which shows how an either-way case is processed.

Allocation procedure in either-way cases

In an either-way case, the defendant is asked, usually in its first hearing in the magistrates court, to indicate how he/she intends to plead.

Figure 2 Processing of either-way cases in magistrates courts

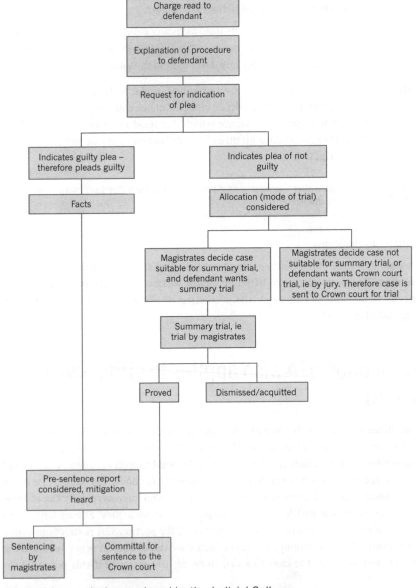

Adapted from a design produced by the Judicial College

- *If the defendant indicates an intention to plead guilty,* this is automatically treated as a formal plea of guilty, convicting him/her of that offence. The section 52A restrictions automatically lapse in respect of that charge, because there will be no trial. The magistrates will sentence the defendant at that hearing or a later one. But they may decide, after hearing more detail of the offence and of the defendant's previous conviction(s) that their powers of punishment are insufficient, and that the case should be **committed for sentence** to the Crown court for the defendant to be sentenced there. ➔glossary Magistrates' sentencing powers are explained in ch. 6.

- *If the defendant indicates he/she will plead 'not guilty',* magistrates then decide if he or she should be offered the option of trial by magistrates. This 'allocation' decision is based primarily on whether the magistrates consider that their court has sufficient power to punish the defendant, should he or she be convicted there. The maximum sentence which a magistrates court can impose is six months for one offence and 12 months for more than one offence. In the allocation procedure, the magistrates are told some detail of the evidence which gave rise to the charge, so they can now assess the seriousness of the allegation – for example, what effect the crime had on the alleged victim – and are also told if a defendant has any previous conviction(s), as a defendant who already has a criminal record may well deserve a punishment more severe than a first time offender would receive. If the magistrates decide that either or both of these factors make the case too serious for them to try, they will send it to Crown court for trial. If this is their decision, the section 52A restrictions continue to apply, limiting what can be reported from the allocation and sending proceedings.

If magistrates agree to try the case – known as the magistrates 'accepting jurisdiction' – the defendant is then asked if he or she wants that or jury trial.

Magistrates may indicate to the defendant whether he or she could be jailed if convicted by their court. If the defendant's choice is jury trial, magistrates will send the case to Crown court for that trial, and the section 52A reporting restrictions continue to apply.

If the defendant chooses to be tried by the magistrates court – that is, summary trial – he or she is asked to enter a formal plea of not guilty, and if he or she does, the trial will take place in that court, most likely after adjournment to permit preparations.

The section 52A restrictions cease to apply to a charge as soon as the choice of summary trial is made. But little changes for the media, because as soon as the defendant pleads not guilty other reporting restrictions, under section 8C of the Magistrates' Courts Act 1980 Act automatically come into force to cover subsequent pre-trial proceedings, now classed as summary proceedings. These section 8C restrictions, similar in format to those of the 1998 Act's section 52A, are explained in ch. 6. They do not affect media reports of the summary trial itself.

Committal hearings and 'transfer' abolished

In 2012 and 2013 changes in the law abolished committal hearings in England and Wales in either-way cases. In these hearings magistrates considered the strength of prosecution evidence in such cases to decide whether they should be sent for trial to a Crown court. But that decision is now made solely in the allocation procedure which does not consider the strength of prosecution evidence, only what it indicates about the seriousness of the alleged offence. The same reform also abolished 'transfer' procedure for either-way cases alleging 'serious or complex' fraud or sexual and/or violent offences in which a child is due to be a witness. 'Transfer' was a procedure which, to help ensure such cases reached Crown court quickly, removed the defendant's right to a committal hearing. Such cases are now 'sent for trial' to a Crown court by a process in which a notice served by the prosecution on a magistrates court means there is no allocation procedure, just the 'sending' – a hearing normally covered by the section 52A reporting restrictions.

➡ Recap of major points

- An indictable-only case will be 'sent for trial' to the Crown court.
- A denied either-way case can be tried by magistrates or by a jury. The defendant can choose trial by jury.
- Reporting restrictions in section 52A of the Crime and Disorder Act 1998 automatically apply to media reports of all preliminary hearings in the magistrates court if the case retains potential for jury trial.

((•)) Useful Websites

www.expressandstar.com/news/crime/2013/02/08/halesowen-murder-suspect-acted-in-self-defence-claim/

    An *Express and Star* newspaper report of a preliminary hearing in which reporting restrictions were lifted

www.judiciary.gov.uk/Resources/JCO/Documents/Judgments/sentencing-remarks-dj-taaffe-r-v-news-grp-newspapers-ltd.pdf

    District Judge Jonathan Taaffe's remarks when fining *The Sun* for breach of the section 52A restrictions in Andrew Partington case

www.independent.co.uk/news/media/press/sun-fined-3000-for-oldham-gas-explosion-reporting-breach-8562354.html

    The Independent's report of *The Sun* being fined

www.bbc.co.uk/news/uk-england-21499501

    BBC report of Partington being sentenced

Crown courts and appeal courts

Chapter summary

Crown courts deal with the most serious criminal cases, including murder. Their trials lead to the tense moment when the jury announces the verdict, with the press bench full for major cases. This chapter details the work of Crown courts, and explains the jury's role. It explains how reporting restrictions ban the media from publishing full reports of pre-trial hearings. It outlines the work of the High Court, Court of Appeal and Supreme Court.

▶ Roles at Crown courts

There are Crown courts at 77 locations in England and Wales, in administrative regions referred to as 'circuits'. The most famous is the Central Criminal Court in London – known as the Old Bailey.

In Crown court trials:

- juries decide if each charge is proved;
- judges rule on law, and sentence convicted defendants.

In very rare circumstances – for example, if there is a real risk that criminals could intimidate jurors to acquit a defendant – a Crown court trial can proceed with no jury, leaving the judge to decide the verdict(s).

▶ Who are jurors?

A Crown court jury consists of 12 people, aged between 18 and 70 (with the upper age limit due to be raised in 2014 to 75) selected randomly from electoral rolls for the local districts, who are sent a summons to turn up for jury service. Some categories of people, such as anyone jailed in the previous 10 years, are barred from being jurors.

▌ Types of Crown court judges

Three types of judges sit in Crown courts:

- High Court judges – that is, those who can sit in the High Court and Crown courts. They are referred to as, for instance, Mr Justice Smith or Mrs Justice Smith. They wear red robes for criminal cases. Only they can try the most serious offences, such as murder, as they are the most experienced judges.

- Circuit judges, referred to as Judge John Smith or Judge Mary Smith. They are barristers of at least 10 years' standing or solicitors who have been Recorders.

- Recorders, who are part-time judges. They are barristers or solicitors who have held 'right of audience' (that is, the right to represent clients) at Crown court. Recorders are usually referred to as the Recorder, Mr John Smith or Mrs Mary Smith.

! Remember

Some cities have bestowed the title of 'Honorary Recorder of –' on the senior circuit judge, who carries out ceremonial duties.

▌ Lawyers at Crown court

see also
ch. 1, p. 9,
The legal
profes-
sion, on
solicitors
and
barristers

Prosecutions at Crown court are conducted by barristers. Barristers also usually appear for the defence. Barristers are referred to as counsel. Solicitors have 'right of audience' in some circumstances. A court clerk sits in each Crown court in front of the judge, to assist in procedures.

▌ Routes to Crown court

A case yet to be tried reaches a Crown court because it has been sent for trial by the magistrates court or youth court – see ch. 7, pp. 65–66, Indictable-only and either-way charges – 'sending for trial'; ch. 9, p. 90, 'Sending for trial' for homicide, 'grave' and other cases – or by a High Court judge by means of a voluntary bill of indictment, see www.mcnaes.com ch. 7.

A case can also be heard by the Crown court if the case has been committed for sentence or been subject to 'section 70' committal – see ch. 6. pp. 61–62, Committal for sentence and p. 63. Section 70 committal – or is an appeal, see pp. 85–86, The Crown court as an appeal court.

▶ Arraignment

A defendant whose case is sent to a Crown court for trial is asked there to plead guilty or not guilty to each charge on the indictment, so formal pleas can be recorded. This process is known as arraignment. At Crown court charges are referred to as 'counts'. See also 'Reporting the arraignment' later in this chapter.

▶ Hearings prior to jury involvement: automatic reporting restrictions

In cases in which a defendant denies guilt, there will be at least one hearing at Crown court before the jury is involved. Statutes have applied **automatic** →glossary
reporting restrictions to media coverage of certain types of these hearings. The hearings are for the judge to make rulings, some of which may determine what the jury, if the case proceeds to trial, will be told, and may include **bail** →glossary
decisions.

The reporting restrictions are to prevent publication of information which
could prejudice a trial. The principle is that potential jurors should not learn
bail deci-
about information discussed in hearings before the trial, because it could relate
sions are
to a case which they might try. Material which could prejudice a jury's verdict,
explained
and which could be discussed in these hearings, includes a defendant's previous
in ch. 6,
conviction(s), or evidence ruled inadmissible. For examples of what can cause
pp. 55–56,
prejudice if published, see ch. 7, p. 66–67, Types of prejudicial matter, where
Bail
explanation is given in relation to similar restrictions in section 52A of the Crime and Disorder Act 1998 which apply – for the same reason – to media coverage of preliminary hearings in magistrates courts.

The scope of the automatic reporting restrictions

The automatic restrictions which limit media reports of some types of pre-trial hearings at Crown courts are in various statutes, but of the same format. They restrict these reports to seven categories of information:

- the name of the Crown court and the judge's name;
- the names, ages, home addresses, and occupations of the defendant(s) and witness(es);

- the charge(s), or a summary of it/them;
- the names of solicitors or barristers in the case;
- if proceedings are adjourned, the date and place to which they are adjourned;
- arrangements as to bail – that is, whether bail was granted or refused, and, if it was granted, any bail conditions and **surety** arrangement.
- whether **legal aid** was granted.

→ glossary

→ glossary

see chs.
9, 10 and
11 for
anonym-
ity law

Witnesses are unlikely to take part in a hearing prior to trial. But if they do, or are mentioned in court, under these restrictions they can be named in reports, unless other law gives them anonymity.

In cases in which bail is refused, the usual interpretation of the restrictions is that the media should not report why the prosecution opposed bail or reasons the judge gave for refusing it, as such information could be prejudicial.

Home addresses can include past addresses in events which gave rise to the charges – see ch. 6, p. 58, The scope of the section 8C reporting restrictions, on care needed in references to former addresses.

Which types of hearings?

The types of hearings for which the above format of restrictions apply are:

Unsuccessful applications for a case to be dismissed, prior to arraignment A defendant whose case is sent for trial to Crown court may apply to a judge, before arraignment, for it to be dismissed because of insufficient evidence. The reporting restrictions on such hearings are detailed in schedule 3 of the Crime and Disorder Act 1998.

see p. 82,
Selection
of the jury
and the
giving of
evidence,
for mean-
ing of
'sworn'

'Preparatory hearings' A Crown court may hold a 'preparatory hearing' in cases involving a serious offence or which will involve a complex or lengthy trial. A pre-paratory hearing must be held in a terrorism case. The hearings are so the judge can rule on case matters. Such a hearing, if held, marks the start of the trial, and takes place shortly before the jury is sworn. If the arraignment has not yet been held, it must take place at the start of the preparatory hearing. The reporting restrictions – again, in the format set out earlier – are in section 11 of the Criminal Justice Act 1987 for preparatory hearings in 'serious or complex fraud' cases, and in section 37 of the Criminal Procedure and Investigations Act 1996 in respect of preparatory hearings in other types of case.

The same restrictions apply, generally under section 37 of the 1996 Act and – for such fraud cases – under section 11 of the 1987 Act to media reports of any application to a Crown court judge for leave to appeal against rulings made at a 'preparatory hearing', and to any such appeal in a higher court.

'Relevant business information'

Section 11 of the Criminal Justice Act 1987 allows journalists covering an unsuc-cessful application for a 'serious or complex' fraud case to be dismissed, or a preparatory hearing in such a case, to include 'relevant business information' in reports of the hearing, even when the automatic restrictions are in place. This means the media can report:

- any address used by the defendant for carrying on business on his/her own account;
- the name of the business at 'any relevant time' – that is, when events which gave rise to the charge(s) occurred;
- the name and address of any firm in which he/she was a partner, or by which he/she was engaged, at any such time;
- the name of any company of which he/she was a director, or by which he/she was otherwise engaged, at any such time, and the address of its registered or principal office;
- any working address of the defendant in his/her capacity as a person engaged by any such company.

'Engaged' means under a contract of service or a contract for services.

What else can be reported?

In addition to the information which the format of restrictions lists as safe to publish, it is safe to include in reports of pre-trial, Crown court hearings neutral descriptions of the court scene, and non-prejudicial background facts of the type outlined in ch. 7 in relation to preliminary hearings before magistrates, see p. 69, The scope of the section 52A restrictions.

'Pre-trial' hearings – automatic reporting restrictions

The Criminal Procedure and Investigations Act 1996 defines a pre-trial hearing as any hearing at a Crown court before a guilty plea is accepted (that is, before it becomes clear there will be no trial) or – in cases which remain contested – all hearings which occur before a jury is sworn or before the beginning of a 'preparatory' hearing in the case. Reporting restrictions in section 41 of the Act automatically ban publication, before the conclusion of all proceedings in the case, of what is said in a 'pre-trial hearing' in:

- applications for rulings on the admissibility of evidence or any other question of law, including any rulings made by the judge;
- applications for such a ruling to be varied or discharged, including any order made.

The safest course to obey the restrictions

As can be gleaned from the earlier passages, the law enshrining these various sets of restrictions developed piecemeal. Their definitions of hearings held at Crown court before a trial overlap, and the extent to which the restrictions apply to all types of these hearings is unclear.

- A journalist's safest course, to avoid any illegal publication, is to include in a contemporaneous report of *any* Crown court hearing held before a jury becomes involved – that is, a contested case - only the categories of information listed under the heading 'The scope of the automatic reporting restrictions' plus in fraud cases 'relevant business information', and non-prejudicial background information.

See also 'Reporting the arraignment' later in this chapter.

When do the automatic reporting restrictions cease to apply?

A Crown court judge can lift the restrictions, or lift them in part, to allow the media to publish contemporaneously fuller reports of such hearings.

If any defendant objects to this, the judge may lift them only if satisfied that doing so is in the interests of justice. Argument in court about whether the restrictions should be lifted cannot be reported until the 'conclusion' of all relevant trials, even if restrictions are lifted in other respects.

If the judge leaves the restrictions in place, they automatically cease to apply at the 'conclusion' of relevant proceedings. The statutes state that this is, or it can safely be construed to be, the acquittal or conviction of a sole defendant or, for multiple defendants of all defendants in respect of all charges in all trials in the case, or when it becomes clear that, for some other reason, no relevant trial remains pending, which might be when the prosecutor decides not to proceed with the case, or when all charges are dismissed for lack of evidence. But reporting restrictions under other law may still apply – see chs. 9, 10 and 11.

👁 Case study

In 2010 the media successfully argued that reporting restrictions covering a pre-trial appeal should be lifted. The case concerned three MPs and a Peer charged with fiddling Parliamentary expenses. A pre-trial issue was whether 'Parliamentary privilege' protected them from prosecution. The Crown court judge ruled it did not, and allowed this pre-trial ruling to be published contemporaneously. The defendants appealed against the ruling to the Court of Appeal, which agreed – at the media's request – to lift the reporting restrictions in section 37 of the Criminal Procedure and Investigations Act 1996 to allow contemporaneous publication of submissions made in the appeal, and of the court's decision upholding the Crown court ruling. Explaining the decision to lift the restrictions, the then Lord Chief Justice, Lord Judge, said the appeal had nothing to do with whether the defendants were dishonest but was 'confined to a narrow but important issue of constitutional law'. Thus there was no realistic prospect that the defendants' trial might be prejudiced by the lifting of the reporting restrictions (*R v Chaytor and others* [2010] EWCA Crim 1910).

Liability for breach of the automatic reporting restrictions

Liability and penalty, for breach of the reporting restrictions under the Acts cited earlier, are the same as for breach of restrictions in section 52A of the Crime and Disorder Act – see ch. 7, p. 69, Liability for breach of the section 52A restrictions. If a breach occurs after a trial has begun, and is serious enough – because of what is published – to cause it to be aborted, a media organisation may also become liable for huge costs under section 93 of the Courts Act 2003 – see ch. 18, p. 227, Media could face huge costs if 'serious misconduct' affects a case'

▌ Appeals against rulings by judge: reporting restrictions

The Criminal Justice Act 2003 gives the prosecution the right to appeal against a ruling made by a Crown court judge which would terminate all or part of the case – for example, that there is no case to answer – no matter what stage the case has reached when the ruling is made. Section 71 of the Act, intended to prevent prejudice to the trial, or to any linked trial, automatically bans reporting of any Crown court discussion (which, if the trial has begun, would be in the jury's absence) about such an appeal. It also restricts reports of the Court of Appeal hearing, and of any further appeal made to the Supreme Court, to the same seven categories of information listed earlier under the heading: 'The scope of the automatic reporting restrictions'. These restrictions apply, unless lifted earlier, until the conclusion of all trials in the case.

▌ Reporting the arraignment

If defendants in a case plead guilty at the arraignment to each charge, they are convicted of each charge, in which case the restrictions detailed earlier in this chapter cease to apply, as there will be no trial.

If a sole defendant or all defendants deny the charge or charges at the arraignment, the media can safely report those pleas contemporaneously if there will be just one trial in the case.

But if a defendant or co-defendants enter a mixture of guilty and not guilty pleas, or if denied charges are to be dealt with in more than one trial, a judge may – to avoid what he/she considers a substantial risk of prejudice – make an order under section 4(2) of the Contempt of Court Act 1981 postponing publication of some of that information. A judge could do this, for example, to ban media reports of an arraignment from mentioning, until the trial ends, any charge which has been admitted (if the jury is not to be told about it) or – if the case will involve more than one trial – any charge not due to be dealt with in the first trial. Or the judge could use section 4(2) to ban any reporting of the arraignment, and of the first trial, until any further trial in the case is concluded.

For detail on section 4(2) orders, and for considerations to be borne in mind even if a judge does not make such an order, see ch. 18, pp. 228–230, Section 4(2) orders.

▶ Procedure in Crown court trials

see chs. 9, 10 and 11 for such law.

The media may publish contemporaneous, full reports of what the jury is told at a Crown court trial once it has started, as long as they comply with any discretionary reporting restriction or any automatic anonymity for a complainant of a sexual offence

! Remember

Until the jury has returned all verdicts, no report of a trial should include – unless the judge says otherwise – any ruling, discussion or argument which takes place in the jury's absence. This is explained in ch. 18. To avoid libel dangers, reporting must be fair and accurate, as explained in ch. 21.

Selection of the jury and the giving of evidence

A Crown court trial can be regarded as under way when the jury is 'empanelled' – a group of potential jurors is brought into the courtroom, and the court clerk selects 12 at random. These will be 'sworn' – required to swear a legal oath that they will try the case according to the evidence.

Soon after this the prosecution counsel 'opens the case' by outlining it. Prosecution witnesses then testify. A Crown court trial usually follows the same sequence used in magistrates' trials, as regards the giving of evidence, including cross-examination, and speeches by lawyers.

ch. 6, pp. 59–60, Procedure in summary trials, explains trial procedure in magistrates courts

At Crown court defence counsel may choose to make a speech 'opening' the defence case prior to calling the defence witnesses. After all these have been heard, prosecuting counsel in most cases makes a closing speech to the jury, which is followed by the defence's closing speech.

The judge then sums up the case, to remind jurors of evidence and direct them on law. The judge will, if he/she decides that evidence is not sufficient to support a charge, direct the jury to bring in a verdict of not guilty on that charge.

Otherwise, and to consider any other charge, the jury 'retires' to a jury room to decide the verdict(s). A jury bailiff escorts jurors to and from it and is the only official allowed contact with them in it. The jury will have been directed to elect a foreman or forewoman to be its spokesperson.

Majority verdicts

A judge initially asks a jury to reach a unanimous verdict on each charge – that is, a unanimous decision to acquit or convict.

- But if a jury has 'retired' to discuss the case for at least two hours and ten minutes and has failed to reach a verdict, the judge can recall it to the courtroom to tell it that a majority verdict is acceptable (for each charge).

- For a full jury of 12, majority verdicts of the ratios 11–1 or 10–2 are acceptable.

- If a jury is reduced in number for any reason, for example, because one or two jurors have fallen ill during the trial, a majority of 10–1 or 9–1 is allowed.

- If a defendant is convicted by a majority, rather than unanimously, the media should report the fact that it was by a majority decision, as this indicates that one or two people in the jury disagreed with the 'guilty' verdict.

ch. 11 explains the legal ban on interviewing jurors about verdicts

If the verdict is an acquittal, the court asks no questions of the jury about the ratio of the vote – so no indication is usually given of how many jurors concurred in the verdict. But if the foreman/woman volunteers in court the fact that acquittal was by a majority it is by convention regarded as unfair to publish this fact, because stating that one or two jurors voted against acquittal could leave a stain on the defendant's character even though he/she is cleared of the charge.

A jury which cannot reach a verdict by a sufficient majority is known as a 'hung jury'. The prosecution then has to decide if it wants to seek a re-trial.

▌ Sentencing at Crown court

If a defendant pleads guilty at a Crown court to all charges, the judge will pass sentence, often after an adjournment. First, the judge will hear the prosecution's summary of the case facts, and be told if the defendant has previous convictions, and of any offences to be **taken into consideration**. The judge will also consider any statement from the victim(s) about the impact of a crime or – in a homicide case – a statement by bereaved relatives on the crime's effect on them. The judge will also hear **mitigation**.

➔glossary

➔glossary

Sentencing after a Crown court trial follows a similar pattern, though the judge, having presided in it, will not normally need to hear again detail of the offence(s).

The same sentencing procedure is used for a defendant who, after conviction in the magistrates court, has been **committed for sentence** to the Crown court.

➔glossary

Crown courts frequently impose jail terms, but have the same range of other sentencing options as magistrates – see ch. 6.

If no other factors apply – for example, the defendant is not sentenced to life or deemed 'dangerous', see later in this chapter – he/she can expect, if he/she behaves well in prison, to be released half-way through the term imposed by the court, and if the sentence was of a year or more he/she will be 'on licence' if released before its full term. This means he/she will monitored by a probation officer and could be returned to prison to serve the remainder of the jail term if a licence condition is broken.

Life sentences and extended sentences

Life sentences may be imposed for murder and other serious offences. The judge will state, when sentencing, a minimum term of the life sentence which the defendant should serve, and may pass 'a whole life order' meaning the sentence will actually be for life.

A defendant convicted of a sexual or violent offence can be categorised as a 'dangerous offender'. This law is complex, but in summary: An offender can be categorised as 'dangerous' if a Crown court judge considers there is significant risk of him/her committing further offences which might cause serious harm to members of the public. The offender could incur a life sentence. Other categories of 'dangerous offender' receive 'extended' sentences, meaning they will not be considered for release from prison until they have served two-thirds of their sentence. Any early release after that depends on the Parole Board deeming that the level of risk he/she poses to the public is manageable in the community.

 For the Parole Board's work and information from the Sentencing Council about different types of sentence, see Useful Websites at the end of this chapter.

Figure 1 in ch. 1, p. 5 shows the hierarchy of the court system

▌ The Court of Appeal

A defendant who wishes to appeal against a conviction or the severity of the sentence imposed by a Crown court can seek permission to appeal to the Court of Appeal Criminal Division, based in London. Permission to appeal can be granted by the Crown court trial judge or the Court of Appeal itself.

The Court of Appeal may, if it allows the appeal, quash a conviction. It may decide there must be a re-trial of the case, by another Crown court jury.

Appeals are usually heard by three judges. A reporter covering a Court of Appeal hearing in which its judgment is delivered may, in cases decided by a majority rather than a unanimous decision, have to wait until each of the three judges has announced his/her own decision for that majority, and therefore the appeal result, to be revealed.

The Court has a similar procedure in appeals in civil cases. Appeals beyond the Court of Appeal go to the Supreme Court.

see also 'Visiting prisoners', www. mcnaes. com ch. 8

▌ Journalists can visit prisoners

The right of a convicted prisoner to be visited in jail by a journalist investigating whether there had been a miscarriage of justice was upheld in *R v Secretary of State for the Home Department, ex p Simms* [1999] 3 All ER 400.

The Supreme Court

The Supreme Court has replaced the appellate committee of the House of Lords (a committee also known as the Law Lords) as the highest court in criminal and civil law. Its judges are referred to as Justices of the Supreme Court. It only hears appeals of high significance, usually no more than 40 to 50 each year. Appeals are heard by several Justices, with a majority decision being binding. It sits in the former Middlesex Guildhall.

Retrials after 'tainted acquittal' or after compelling new evidence emerges: reporting restrictions

Under what is known as the 'double jeopardy rule', the law usually – as a protection of civil liberties – prevents someone who has been acquitted of an offence being tried for it again. But there are two major exceptions:

- If a Crown court trial convicts a person of interference with or intimidation of a juror, witness or potential witness in an earlier trial in which the same or another defendant has been acquitted, the prosecution can apply to the High Court for an order quashing that acquittal, to allow a retrial.
- Under the Criminal Justice Act 2003, if 'new and compelling evidence' emerges after a defendant has been acquitted at Crown court of a serious charge as defined by the Act, the prosecution can apply to the Court of Appeal for the acquittal to be quashed and a new trial to be held.

The Court of Appeal can make an order under section 82 of the Act imposing reporting restrictions which make it an offence to publish anything which would create a substantial risk of prejudice to a retrial. This can ban the media from reporting the application to quash the acquittal, or anything relating to it – for example, from reporting that there are ongoing police investigations about the new evidence. The restrictions can be in force until the end of any retrial, or until the matter is otherwise dropped.

The Crown court as an appeal court

Defendants can appeal to a Crown court judge against refusal by magistrates to grant bail.

Defendants can appeal to the Crown court against conviction by magistrates, including in youth courts. In the appeal there is no jury – a judge will sit normally with two lay magistrates. The Crown court also hears appeals against the severity of sentences imposed by magistrates, and may confirm a sentence, substitute a lesser penalty, or increase it, but not to more than the highest sentence magistrates could have imposed.

▌ The High Court

The High Court Queen's Bench Division, which deals with criminal and other matters, has about 70 judges, and hears cases in London and Cardiff and major regional cities.

for the High Court's role in civil law, see ch. 12

A defendant convicted by magistrates, or who has appealed unsuccessfully to the Crown court, may appeal to the Queen's Bench Division on the grounds that a decision was wrong in law. This procedure is known as appeal by way of 'case stated', because no evidence is given verbally to the High Court, which considers a written record of the case. The prosecution can also use this procedure to challenge an acquittal by magistrates. The High Court has wide powers to reverse, affirm or amend magistrates' decisions, including those of youth courts. It can order the case to be retried summarily.

Judicial reviews

ch. 15 covers media challenges to court decisions

Part of the High Court's work involves judicial reviews, hearings which can consider other types of challenges to decisions made by magistrates. The media can use the judicial review procedure, to challenge discretionary reporting restrictions imposed by magistrates.

▌ Courts martial

People in the armed forces are subject to UK law in the courts martial system, even if the alleged offence was committed in another country. These military courts are usually open to the public and media – for example, when in 2013 a Royal Marine was convicted of murdering an insurgent in Afghanistan.

 For more information on courts martial, see Useful Websites at the end of this chapter, and www. mcnaes.com ch. 8.

➡ **Recap of major points**

- Crown courts deal with the most serious criminal cases.
- Crown court judges rule on law and decide on punishment, and in trials juries decide whether each charge is proved.

- Automatic reporting restrictions limit what the media can report from most Crown court hearings held prior to trial.

- A defendant convicted in a Crown court can seek to appeal to the Court of Appeal, and thereafter to the Supreme Court.

- Crown courts hear appeals from magistrates courts against conviction or sentence.

- The High Court is also an appeal court for certain matters.

((•)) Useful Websites

www.gov.uk/jury-service
  Government guidance on jury service

http://justice.gov.uk/about/probation
  National Probation Service

www.justice.gov.uk/about/parole-board
  Parole Board

http://sentencingcouncil.judiciary.gov.uk/
  Sentencing Council

www.supremecourt.gov.uk/
  Supreme Court

www.judiciary.gov.uk/about-the-judiciary/the-judiciary-in-detail/jurisdictions/military-jurisdiction
  Courts martial

9

Juveniles in criminal and anti-social behaviour cases

Chapter summary

Juveniles charged with crimes are dealt with in youth courts by magistrates. The public cannot attend these courts, but journalists can. Reporting restrictions automatically ban reports from identifying the juveniles involved to protect their welfare. The term 'juvenile' covers those aged under 18. Adult courts can also ban media reports from identifying a juvenile involved in a case. An order can be imposed on a juvenile to ban anti-social behaviour. A media report of this may be able to name him/her.

▌ Juveniles and the age of criminal responsibility

ch. 13 explains family law cases

Children under the age of 10 have not reached 'the age of criminal responsibility', and so cannot be prosecuted for a crime as they are considered too young to distinguish between right and wrong. But they may be placed under the supervision of social workers.

The distinction between a 'child' (a person aged under 14) and a 'young person' (a person aged 14 to 17) is not important for journalists reporting court cases, although both terms survive in the relevant statute. Lawyers, courts and this chapter use the term 'juvenile' broadly to describe defendants aged from 10 up to, but not including, the age of 18, and witnesses under 18.

▌ Juveniles in youth courts

Most juveniles who are prosecuted are dealt with by youth courts, presided over by magistrates or a district judge. But youth courts – though usually in the same building as magistrates courts (where adult defendants appear) – have smaller courtrooms to make juveniles feel less nervous than they might be in an adult court.

Magistrates who sit in youth courts receive special training. Procedures there, including trials, are similar to those in adult magistrates courts, described in chs. 6 and 7.

A juvenile denied **bail** may be sent to non-secure accommodation run by the local authority, or – if the alleged offending is persistent or serious – to custody, as explained later in this chapter.   → glossary

Youth courts' powers

Most offences dealt with by youth courts are minor. Because youth courts' sentencing powers are limited they cannot try extremely serious cases, such as homicide and must send such cases to a Crown court, in a procedure discussed later. But a youth court has discretion, if it considers its punishment powers sufficient in a particular case, to try other offences – such as rape or robbery – which, had the defendant been adult, could only be tried by a Crown court.

Sentencing

A youth court can impose **community punishment**, **absolute** and **conditional discharges** – sentences explained in ch. 6, p. 62, Other types of sentences – and can fine. A parent must pay this fine if the offender is aged under 16. A youth court can also make a 'youth rehabilitation order', which can involve community punishment and other requirements, such as a curfew.   → glossary → glossary

Many young offenders who admit a first offence are merely made subject to an order which means they must cooperate with a referral to a youth offender panel, comprising of trained youth workers. This includes agreeing to do unpaid community work. An offender who fails to cooperate can be given a more severe punishment.

Youth courts can make 'a detention and training order' in a serious case. This can be imposed for between four months to two years. Normally this means that the juvenile spends half the period in custody with training, and the other half supervised in the community.

The court can make 'a parenting order' requiring, for example, a parent to attend counselling and guidance sessions.

Juveniles in custody

A juvenile refused bail by a youth court or sentenced there to detention and training can be held on **remand** or for that sentence in a secure children's home, a secure training centre or a young offenders' institution.   → glossary

'Sending for trial' for homicide, 'grave' and other cases

A juvenile charged with a homicide offence, such as murder, or one of a range of firearms offences cannot be tried or sentenced by a youth court because of the seriousness of the charge. In these cases defendants make initial appearances there for decisions on bail and procedure but are then sent for trial to a Crown court.

Grave offences

→ glossary

The law relating to juvenile defendants classifies some crimes as 'grave'. These are those for which an adult offender could be jailed for 14 years or more (apart from the homicide and firearms offences referred to earlier) and certain sexual offences. In a 'grave' case the youth court considers whether its maximum power of punishment – a two-year detention and training order – would be sufficient if it convicted the defendant. This is similar to the **allocation** procedure for either-way charges in an adult magistrates court – it determines which court is the venue for the trial. If the youth court considers its sentencing power would be insufficient, the case is sent to a Crown court for trial.

'Dangerous offenders' and co-accused with an adult

The youth court will also send a case for Crown court trial if it considers that the defendant would, if convicted, meet the 'dangerous' offender criteria, explained in ch. 8, p. 84, Life sentences and extended sentences, or because the juvenile is to be tried there co-accused with an adult defendant.

Section 52A reporting restrictions

→ glossary

A youth court case which must or may be sent for trial to the Crown court has the potential of being tried by jury, so the **automatic** reporting restrictions of section 52A of the Crime and Disorder Act 1998 apply to all preliminary hearings of such a case in the youth court for as long as that potential exists. For a case sent for trial, these restrictions normally continue in force, as regards reports of preliminary hearings, until the Crown court finishes dealing with it.

> See ch. 7, pp. 66–73, Section 52A automatic reporting restrictions, for detail of the section 52A restrictions and how on rare occasions they may be lifted. They are explained in relation to cases in the (adult) magistrates courts – but apply identically in respect of such preliminary hearings at the youth court.

ch 6, pp. 56–59, Reporting restrictions for pre-trial hearings, explains section 8C

Section 8C restrictions

Pre-trial hearings of a case to be tried by a youth court are covered by the automatic reporting restrictions in the 1980 Act's section 8C.

! Remember

Other reporting restrictions normally apply automatically to cases at youth courts, as explained later in this chapter, preventing the media from identifying juveniles involved. So, for some hearings, section 52A of the 1998 Act or section 8C of the 1980 Act *and* anonymity will apply.

Committal for sentence – 'dangerous offenders'

A youth court which convicts a juvenile of a serious crime can also at this stage consider whether he/she should be regarded as 'dangerous offender'. If the answer is Yes, there will be a **committal for sentence** – that is, the youth court can commit →glossary him/her to Crown court for a judge there to decide the sentence.

! Remember

The reporting restrictions in section 52A of the 1998 Act or section 8C of the 1980 Act do not apply in respect of a trial at a youth court, or a hearing which decides whether to commit for sentence. These restrictions only apply to preliminary/pre-trial hearings.

▌ Admission to youth courts

Parliament has decided that the public should not be allowed inside any youth court, to avoid juveniles being stigmatised in their communities by allegations of or convictions for immature law-breaking. Exceptions can be made – a victim may be allowed to see an offender being sentenced.

- Journalists can cover youth court cases because section 47 of the Children and Young Persons Act 1933 gives 'bona fide representatives of newspapers or news agencies' the right to attend.

▌ Section 49 automatic restrictions on identifying juveniles

Parliament decided – again, to stop juveniles being stigmatised – that defendants in youth courts should not usually be identified in media reports of their cases. This anonymity also applies in such cases to juvenile witnesses and juvenile victims. The anonymity protects the reputation of juvenile witnesses if their character is scrutinised in cross-examination.

All juveniles involved in youth court cases are given this **automatic** anonymity →glossary by section 49 of the Children and Young Persons Act 1933.

Section 49 says that a report of youth court proceedings must not reveal:

- the name;
- or address;
- or school;
- or any particulars likely to lead to the identification of any person aged under 18 'concerned in the proceedings' – which means as a defendant, witness or a victim/alleged victim;
- or include any picture or television footage of, or including, any such juvenile.

In the Act, the definition 'concerned in the proceedings' includes a juvenile 'in respect of whom the proceedings are taken', which means that:

- section 49 anonymity applies to a juvenile who is the victim/alleged victim in the case even if he/she is not a witness, for example because he/she is too young to give evidence.

But a juvenile victim/alleged victim who is dead *can* be identified by the media, as explained in ch. 15, p. 182, A section 39 order cannot validly be made in respect of a dead juvenile. A dead juvenile is not 'concerned in the proceedings'.

No identifying detail should be published

see www. mcnaes. com ch 4 on the Ofcom rule against identifying juveniles pre-trial

The section 49 restrictions mean that normally media reports of youth court cases should not include any detail which could identify a juvenile concerned in the proceedings. Describing a defendant as 'a 14-year-old Bristol boy' would not identify him because Bristol is large. But naming a small village as a defendant's home could well identify him to people who know he lives there. Including a juvenile's nickname or an unusual physical characteristic in a report might identify him/her to some people. Another example: Saying in a report that a juvenile is the 12-year-old twin son of a policeman may identify him to anyone who knows of such twins. The test is always whether, as a result of the report, any member of the public could realise who the juvenile is. Adults who figure in youth court cases as witnesses or are mentioned in evidence can be named in reports, as long as doing so does not identify a juvenile (or breach any discretionary restriction imposed by the court in respect of the adult). But a journalist may need to leave a name and detail identifying an adult out of a report to avoid identifying a juvenile – for example, a father who gives evidence about his son, the defendant, cannot be named. See 'Example of section 49 anonymity' in www.mcnaes.com ch. 9.

Section 49 is a blanket ban on identifying the juvenile's school, however large, unless the youth court permits this. It may do, for example, to let the media highlight a problem of drug-dealing at a particular school.

Appeal proceedings – anonymity retained

- Section 49 anonymity also applies to reports of Crown court hearings of appeals from the youth court against conviction or severity of sentence, and to reports of High Court hearings of appeals from the youth court (or from the Crown court appeal hearings) on a point of law. The anonymity also applies to proceedings in a magistrates court for breach, revocation or amendment of youth rehabilitation orders.

ch. 8, explains these Crown court and High Court appeal routes

- The section 49 restrictions do *not* apply to reports of the Crown court proceedings involving a juvenile sent there for trial or committed there for sentence. But the Crown court may make a discretionary order giving him/her anonymity under section 39 of the 1933 Act, as explained later.

Breaches of section 49

It is illegal to publish material which breaches section 49 – that is, material which identifies a juvenile who should have anonymity. The maximum fine is currently £5,000, but see p. 62, Fining power to be without limit. Section 49 says that the proprietor, editor or publisher of a newspaper can be prosecuted. For a TV or radio programme the case will be against 'the body corporate which provides the service' and any person whose 'functions in relation to the programme correspond to those of an editor of a newspaper'. The Attorney General has to consent to such prosecutions.

see p. 97, The 1933 Act and the internet

👁 **Case study**

In 2003 a district judge fined the *Plymouth Evening Herald* £1,500 for publishing a photograph of a 15-year-old boy convicted at a youth court of stabbing a fellow pupil. The district judge said evidence by friends and relatives that they had recognised the boy, even though his face was pixellated, meant that the paper had breached section 49 (*Media Lawyer*, 4 March 2004).

👁 **Case study**

Section 49 anonymity only applies to a report referring to a youth court case.

In 2010 Ian Carter, formerly Group Editor of East Surrey and Sussex Newspapers, was acquitted of breaching section 49. The *Croydon Advertiser* had published an interview in which a juvenile victim of a stabbing told of his experience. It included a photo of the teenager, and was published eight days after another juvenile had appeared in a youth court charged with the stabbing. But District Judge Suzanne Bayne, at South Western Magistrates Court, Battersea, acquitted Mr Carter after accepting the defence argument that the news story was not a report of proceedings in court – the interview published had not mentioned the courts or that a juvenile was being prosecuted. Ms Bayne said there was nothing in the article which identified the stabbing victim 'as a witness in current proceedings' (*Media Lawyer*, 16 July 2010).

When section 49 anonymity ceases to apply

Section 49 gives a youth court the power to lift a juvenile's anonymity to allow the media to identify him or her, 'to any specified extent', in three types of circumstance.

 → glossary

(1) *To avoid injustice* – This power is rarely exercised. A youth court could use it to allow a media report of a preliminary hearing to identify a juvenile defendant whose lawyer says he/she wants publicity to help trace witnesses to prove an **alibi** – 'My client John Doe was at the funfair that night, not the crime scene. Did anyone see him at the funfair?' It might also do so to quash rumours suggesting that the victim was in fact the defendant.

(2) *Unlawfully at large* – A youth court, if asked to do so by or on behalf of the Director of Public Prosecutions, can lift the section 49 anonymity to help to trace a juvenile who is 'unlawfully at large' after being charged with or convicted of a violent or sexual offence, or any offence for which a person aged 21 or over could be jailed for 14 years or more. This would allow the media to name and publish a photograph of a juvenile who has failed to answer bail or escaped from secure accommodation, and who is a potential threat to public safety.

(3) *In the public interest* – A youth court can lift the anonymity of a juvenile it convicts of any offence if satisfied that doing so is 'in the public interest'.

- Before taking this decision it must give the prosecution and defence the opportunity to argue for or against lifting the anonymity.

This power to lift the anonymity is section 49(4A) of the 1933 Act, is inserted there by section 45 of the Crime (Sentences) Act 1997. It can be used when a youth court feels that the media should be able to identify – for the benefit of the community – a juvenile who has persistently offended or committed a notorious crime.

 See also ch. 15, pp. 183–184, Challenges to youth court anonymity, for the grounds the media can cite, from official guidance for courts and prosecutors, to argue in court for the removal of such a juvenile's anonymity.

! Remember

A court can only lift section 49 anonymity 'in the public interest' if the juvenile has been convicted.

👁 **Case study**

The ability of youth courts to lift section 49 'to any specified extent' is illustrated by a decision of Newbury youth court in 2006. It decided it was in the public interest to allow media reports to name a 14-year-old girl convicted of drink-driving. But it refused to permit publication of recent photographs of her or to allow her school to be named. Shortly after the court decided this, the girl, who was first convicted of drink-driving when she was 12, threw a punch at the prosecutor and hurled a two-litre jug of water at the magistrates (*Media Lawyer*, 28 March 2006).

Anonymity expires when the juvenile turns 18

Section 49 anonymity automatically expires when the juvenile concerned reaches the age of 18, whether he/she is a defendant, witness or victim/alleged victim. This was made clear in 2003 when the High Court upheld the decision of South Shields youth court that a defendant who was 17 when proceedings against him began no longer had anonymity when the case resumed after his 18th birthday (*Todd v Director of Public Prosecutions* [2003] All ER (D) 92 (Oct)).

▌ Juveniles in adult courts

A juvenile may appear in the (adult) magistrates court if jointly charged with an adult. The juvenile may be tried there as a co-accused, or the magistrates can remit the juvenile's case to the youth court for trial or sentencing. If the adult's case is sent for trial to the Crown court, the juvenile's case may be sent there too if the magistrates think a joint trial is in the interests of justice – for example, to avoid making witnesses testify in two trials. Also, a juvenile defendant's case can be sent by a youth court to a Crown court for trial or committed there for sentence.

▌ Section 39 reporting restrictions in adult courts

There is no automatic ban on identifying a juvenile who appears as a defendant, witness or victim/alleged victim in a criminal court other than a youth court.

- But the adult courts have discretion to impose anonymity under section 39 of the Children and Young Persons Act 1933.

If a section 39 order is made, its scope normally is that no report of the case shall reveal:

- the name;
- or address;

- or school;
- or any particulars 'calculated' (that is, likely) to lead to the identification of any person aged under 18 'concerned in the proceedings', either as a defendant or witness or a victim/alleged victim;
- or include any picture or television footage of, or including, any such juvenile.

'Calculated' survives from the Act's original wording.

As with the section 49 restriction, a journalist must take care not to breach a section 39 order by including too much detail about any juvenile protected by it. There is a blanket ban on identifying the juvenile's school unless the court decides otherwise.

 Ch. 15 gives guidance on how the media can challenge section 39 orders which are invalid or unnecessary.

- A court, to pay proper heed to the principle of open justice, should not make a section 39 order merely because of the juvenile's age, or as an order arbitrarily covering all juveniles in the case. It should consider for each whether there is good reason for anonymity.
- Sections 39 or 49 of the 1933 Act can only provide anonymity for a living juvenile, not one who is dead – for example, a murder victim.
- A court cannot use section 39 to give anonymity to an adult.

 see also pp. 98–99, Cases of abuse within a family

But anonymity for a juvenile under section 39 may mean that an adult defendant or adult witness in a case cannot be identified either.

For example, if a father is charged with assaulting his child, and if the child's identity is protected by a section 39 order, the family relationship cannot be included in any report which names the father as the defendant, because giving the relationship would identify the child. Even mentioning the child's age could in some cases reveal a familial relationship.

Section 39 orders can also be made in civil courts and by coroners, see chs. 12 and 16.

! Remember

see p. 62, Fining power to be without limit

A section 39 order can apply to a juvenile 'in respect of whom the proceedings are taken'. It can be used to prevent a media report of truancy case from identifying a child whose parent is prosecuted in the (adult) magistrates court for failing to ensure the child attends school. The effect would be that the report could not identify the parent either, or – unless the court made an exception – the school.

Recent breaches of section 39 orders

A person or organisation breaching a section 39 order can currently be fined up to £5,000.

👁 Case study

The Sun, Daily Mirror and the *Wigan Evening Post* apologised to a judge at Chester Crown court in 2008 after each breached, to some extent, a section 39 order made in a murder case. *The Sun* published details of a disability condition of one of the convicted juvenile defendants, and the *Evening Post* published an address for him, although the order covered both matters. The judge had also said in the order that only one particular photograph could be published of two juvenile witnesses (the murder victim's teenage daughters). But the *Mirror* published a different photograph. The judge said that, in view of the apologies, he would not refer the breaches to the Attorney General for possible prosecution. The judge also said: 'The common theme of these things is that it almost always seems to be a sub editor or features editor who is not aware of something which the news department are' (*Media Lawyer*, 12 February 2008).

see the section 39 case in this book's Late News

When does section 39 cease to apply to a juvenile?

Section 39 anonymity automatically expires when the juvenile reaches the age of 18. This can be inferred from the decision on the scope of section 49 in *Todd v Director of Public Prosecutions* and the fact that section 39 refers to identifying 'any child or young person', by definition someone under the age of 18. It is also a recognised legal principle that Article 10 of the European Convention on Human Rights requires any statutory restriction on reporting to be construed as narrowly as possible.

see p. 95, Anonymity expires when the juvenile turns 18

▌ The 1933 Act and the internet

In 2012 in the High Court Mr Justice Tugendhat said there is force in the argument that the wording of section 39 may not give a court jurisdiction to prohibit information – a child's identity – being published on the internet, as the section's wording refers to print newspapers or sound or television broadcasts (*MXB v East Sussex Hospitals NHS Trust* [2012] EWHC 3279 (QB)). The same argument could apply to section 49. Ethically no-one should take advantage of any such loophole.

ch 1, p. 7, Convention rights, explains Article 10

▌ Jigsaw identification

- The term 'jigsaw identification' describes the effect when someone to whom the law has given anonymity is nevertheless identified by the media to the public because of a combination or accumulation of detail published.

It can occur when two or more media organisations cover the same case. Each may publish a report which in itself preserves the anonymity. But jigsaw identification will occur if someone who reads, views or hears the reports of more than one organisation can, by combining the different detail in each, recognise the person who should be anonymous.

Jigsaw identification can also occur if a media organisation publishes a series of sequential reports in which it allows too much detail gradually to accumulate. The term is also used to describe such an accumulation in a *single* report.

The examples given below relate to anonymity for juveniles. But jigsaw identification can also destroy anonymity granted under other law – for example, the anonymity automatically given to alleged victims of sexual offences, explained in ch. 10.

 Sexual offences law is explained in ch. 10. Other law giving anonymity is explained in chs. 11, 13, 16 and 17.

Example 1 A juvenile in a youth court, who has anonymity under section 49 of the Children and Young Persons Act 1933, admits causing criminal damage to a sports car owned by local millionaire John Doe. One local paper reports: 'A 15-year-old boy vandalised a sports car owned by London tycoon John Doe, costing him £5,000 in repairs.' Another local paper reports: 'A 15-year-old boy vandalised his rich neighbour's sports car, causing £5,000 damage.' Neither paper names the boy. The second paper does not name Doe. But anyone reading both will know the boy is Doe's neighbour, which identifies the boy locally.

Example 2 A juvenile, who should have anonymity after a section 39 order was made under the 1933 Act, gives evidence at Crown court in a murder trial. A local radio station describes her as 'a 16-year-old who works as a shop assistant in London'. Another radio station does not mention her job but describes her routine as 'commuting each morning to work in Charing Cross'. A newspaper reports that she lives in Islington. This accumulation of detail could lead to those who know her, and who listen to both stations and read that newspaper, realising that she is the witness.

Cases of abuse within a family

There is a particular danger of jigsaw identification in media coverage of court cases concerning violence or sexual abuse allegedly inflicted on a child by a relative or family 'friend' – for example, when a father, stepfather or a mother's live-in partner is the adult defendant. In such cases, when the abuse is physical but not sexual, it is standard practice for magistrates or the Crown court judge to make a section 39 order. In cases where the charge is of sexual abuse, the child has automatic anonymity under other law, see ch. 10.

When covering such abuse cases in courts, a media organisation has two options:

(a) *the report can name the adult defendant* – but if the defendant is a relative, the report must not include any detail of the defendant's relationship to the child, to protect the child's anonymity. This can severely restrict what evidence is published – for example, about how the defendant had opportunity to abuse the child, or even the child's age. Lord Justice Maurice Kay made this comment in the Court of Appeal in 2005, alluding to a case in which a father was convicted of conspiracy to rape a child and of distributing indecent photographs of her: 'Offences of the kind established in this case are frequently committed by fathers and step-fathers....If the offender is named and the victim is described as "an 11-year old schoolgirl", in circumstances in which the offender has an 11-year old daughter, it is at least arguable that the composite picture presented embraces "particulars calculated (likely) to lead to the identification" of the victim.' (*R v Teesside Crown Court, ex p Gazette Media Company Ltd and others* [2005] All ER (D) 367 (Jul).

(b) *the report does not identify the adult defendant in any way*, and therefore can refer to the familial or household relationship between the defendant and child, can definitely refer to the child's age, and can include greater detail of evidence, while preserving the child's anonymity.

An editor's instinct is usually that it is in the public's best interests for people charged with crime – and particularly those convicted of it – to be named, as a deterrent and so that a community can be wary of that individual. This is achieved by the approach in (a), if it is possible to construct a meaningful report without revealing the family relationship. But another editor may feel that the public interest is best served by the approach in (b) which can make clear that the alleged abuse was – for example – by a relative. Approach (b) allows more evidence to be published and more questions to be raised about why the community, social services or the police remained unaware of the abuse within that household.

Jigsaw identification would occur if two media organisations covering the case adopted different approaches. If one followed policy (a), naming the adult defendant but obscuring his relationship to the child victim, and the other followed approach (b), not identifying the defendant but reporting, for example, that he was the child's father, anyone reading both reports would be able to identify the child, even though neither report named him/her. To avoid jigsaw identification of the child, all the newsrooms involved need to adopt the same approach.

 See ch. 10, p. 111, Ethical considerations, on the ethical ban on identifying children in sex cases.

Anti-social behaviour injunctions and criminal behaviour orders

see Useful Websites at the end of this chapter

Anti-social behaviour orders (ASBOs) are due to be replaced by new injunctions and criminal behaviour orders (CBOs) under proposals in the Anti-Social Behaviour, Crime and Policing Bill, which is expected to become law in 2014.

As an Act its numbered clauses, referred to later, will become its sections. The government's intention is that these injunctions and CBOs will also replace other orders, including drinking banning orders. The Bill details when the media will be able to identify juveniles as being involved in such court proceedings.

Injunctions to prevent nuisance and annoyance

ch. 12 explains the High Court and county courts

The Bill is due to replace 'stand alone' ASBOs with 'injunctions to prevent nuisance and annoyance'. These, like ASBOs, will be civil orders which may be granted against adults by the High Court or a county court, and against juveniles – people under the age of 18 – by a youth court. Various bodies, including police and local authorities, will be able to apply for injunctions banning, for example, juveniles from streets where they have been creating a nuisance or from possessing cans of spray paint in public places. They will be 'stand alone' because they can be imposed on a person even if he or she has no criminal conviction. Breaching the injunction will be a contempt of court – and the maximum punishment for a juvenile aged 14 to 17 will be three months detention.

No automatic anonymity in reports of injunctions hearings

Provisions in clause 17 of the Bill mean that:

- the automatic anonymity for juveniles normally given by section 49 of the Children and Young Persons Act 1933 relating to media reports of youth court hearings see earlier, will *not* apply to hearings in which the court considers or decides on applications for 'injunctions to prevent nuisance and annoyance'.

So, the default position will be that the media can identify juveniles concerned in these proceedings, even if the court decides against imposing an injunction.

- But clause 17 says the youth court will have discretion to grant the juvenile anonymity by making an order under section 39 of the 1933 Act.

Ch. 15 explains how a journalist can argue in courts against reporting restrictions, and pp. 184–185, Anti-social behaviour cases – arguments for identifying juveniles, provide arguments she/he can make that a juvenile made subject to an injunction should be identified in a report of the hearing.

Criminal behaviour orders

ch. 5, pp. 51–52, Taking a vehicle without authority, explains the 'joy-riding' offence

The Bill has provision for 'criminal behaviour orders' (CBOs) which can be imposed on defendants, including juveniles, after they are convicted of an offence. They will replace what became known as 'bolt-on' ASBOs – an order 'bolted on' to a criminal conviction. The Bill says an application for a CBO may only be made by the prosecution. It can be presumed that a CBO may be imposed on a juvenile after – for example – he/she is convicted of shoplifting or taking a car without the owner's consent ('joy-riding'), banning him or her from entering shops or interfering with cars. Breaching a CBO will be a criminal offence. A juvenile convicted of a serious breach could be given a training and detention order.

Anonymity in reports of hearings to decide whether to impose a CBO

Any criminal court will be able to impose a CBO, but for juveniles this is most likely to be the youth court. Clause 22 of the Bill provides that:

- if – and only if – the youth court makes a CBO against the juvenile the automatic anonymity in section 49 of the 1933 Act lapses as regards that juvenile, allowing media reports of the CBO hearing to identify him or her;
- but the youth court has discretion to preserve the anonymity by making an order under section 39 of the 1933 Act.

The section 49 anonymity will continue to apply for any juvenile witnesses in the CBO hearing, and may still apply for the juvenile defendant in respect of the earlier hearing in the youth court which he/she was convicted of an offence. As has been the case with 'bolt-on' ASBOs, the court should – if section 49 anonymity remains in place for the earlier hearing – say enough in the CBO hearing to explain the behaviour which led to the CBO being imposed.

The journalist could remind the court clerk that the Justices' Clerks' Society issued guidance to its members that when a court draws up an ASBO it should include details of the anti-social behaviour which led to the order being made.

A journalist could argue that it would be for the good of the community for the section 49 anonymity to be lifted 'in the public interest' in respect of the criminal conviction – and that for the same reason section 39 anonymity should not be imposed in relation to the CBO.

see Useful Websites at the end of this chapter for this guidance

See p. 94, When section 49 anonymity ceases to apply, on the youth court's power to consider 'the public interest' and ch. 15, pp. 179–182, The Children and Young Persons Act 1933, for specific arguments which can be made against the juvenile having anonymity.

No automatic anonymity for alleged breaches of CBOs

A juvenile alleged to have breached a CBO may be charged with this as a criminal offence, which will normally be dealt with at a youth court. Clause 29 of the Bill says that the usual anonymity under section 49 of the 1933 Act for juveniles appearing in a youth court does not apply to a juvenile accused of breaching a CBO.

- So the media *can* identify a juvenile defendant when reporting a youth court's proceedings for alleged breach of a CBO, whether or not it convicts him or her of this, though any juvenile witness will have automatic anonymity under section 49.
- But the youth court can decide to give the juvenile defendant anonymity. Clause 29 of the Bill will give youth courts the discretionary power to provide anonymity for a juvenile defendant accused of breaching a CBO. Confusingly, it does so by saying that the court could use section 45 of the Youth Justice and

Criminal Evidence Act 1999 to confer the anonymity. Section 45 is in effect an updated version of section 39 of the 1933 Act, but has not yet been brought into force. As explained earlier, clause 22 of the Bill already refers to section 39 of the 1933 Act as an anonymity measure, rather than to section 45 of the 1999 Act, so there seems to be confusing inconsistency in the Bill. It says that if a court does confer section 45 anonymity for such a juvenile it must give its reasons for doing so. Again, a journalist covering the hearing could argue that the juvenile should not have anonymity – see ch. 15, pp. 184–185, Anti-social behaviour cases – arguments for identifying juveniles.

 Check www.mcnaes.com for updates on the Anti-Social Behaviour, Crime and Policing Bill becoming law. A full explanation of the law on juveniles' anonymity in reports of ASBO and drinking banning order cases will remain in www.mcnaes.com ch. 9 until such orders are replaced.

➡ Recap of major points

- Most juveniles charged with a crime are dealt with by youth courts. The public cannot attend these courts, but journalists can.

- Section 49 of the Children and Young Persons Act 1933 bans media reports from identifying anyone aged under 18 involved in youth court cases, whether as defendant, witness or crime victim.

- This anonymity can be lifted, in the case of a convicted juvenile, to allow the media to identify him/her in the public interest – for example after persistent offending.

- There is no automatic anonymity for juveniles involved in adult court proceedings. But an adult court can make an order under section 39 of the 1933 Act to give the juvenile anonymity.

- Courts can impose orders to ban anti-social behaviour. The default position in law is that a juvenile made subject to such an order, or accused of breaching one, can be identified, unless a section 39 order is made.

((•)) Useful Websites

www.direct.gov.uk/en/YoungPeople/CrimeAndJustice/index.htm
  Government guidance on the youth justice system

http://webarchive.nationalarchives.gov.uk/20100418065544/http:/asb.homeoffice.gov.uk/uploadedFiles/Members_site/Documents_and_images/Evidence_and_court/JCS_ASBOGuide_May06_0041.PDF
  Justices' Clerks' Society Good Practice Guide on ASBOs

www.parliament.uk/briefing-papers/RP13-34
  A House of Commons Library Research Paper's explanation of the Anti-social Behaviour, Crime and Policing Bill

Sexual offences

Chapter summary

The law gives victims of sexual offences, including rape, lifetime anonymity in media reports of these crimes and of any prosecutions which follow. In recent years several media organisations have been fined for publishing detail which breached this anonymity and so caused considerable distress to those identified. As this chapter explains, the anonymity may be removed in some circumstances, allowing the media to identify the individual, but a journalist should consider if this would be ethical.

▌ The scope of automatic anonymity for complainants of sexual offences

Section 1 of the Sexual Offences (Amendment) Act 1992 says that after an allegation of a sexual offence is made, it is illegal to include in any publication:

- any matter which is likely to lead members of the public to identify, during his/her lifetime, the person who is the victim/alleged victim of that offence.

It says the ban includes in particular, if likely to identify that person:

- his/her name;
- his/her address;
- the identity of any school or other educational establishment he/she attends;
- the identity of his/her workplace;
- any still or moving picture of him/her.

Section 6 of the 1992 Act defines publication as any speech, writing, relevant programme or other communication in whatever form addressed to the public at large or to any section of the public, and a 'picture' as 'a likeness however produced'.

The anonymity is automatic, lifelong, and applies from the time an allegation is made, by the alleged victim or anyone else – for example, when a parent complains to police, or to a journalist, that a child has been sexually abused.

It remains in place regardless of whether the allegation is later withdrawn, or whether the police are told, whether an alleged offender is prosecuted and whether anyone is convicted.

The anonymity also applies to anyone who is the target of an attempt or conspiracy to commit a sexual offence, even if the attempt or conspiracy failed.

In rare circumstances a court may lift the anonymity, or it may be waived. But it usually applies.

The wide application of the anonymity

Parliament decided in 1976 that the violation of rape and the potential for victims to suffer embarrassment, and further trauma when testifying in court, justified giving them anonymity. This anonymity has since been extended to victims and alleged victims of other sexual offences. It applies to crime stories as well as court reports. Thus, it applies in respect of a news website report that a rape may have taken place, as in 'Police in Southampton are investigating a rape'. Nothing should be published which suggests the identity of the victim or alleged victim, for example a picture of the house where the attack is said to have taken place.

The anonymity also applies to reports of the trials of those accused of sexual offences (though the defendant can be named), as well as courts martial and civil cases. So, if a woman who alleges she was raped sues the alleged rapist in a civil court, she remains anonymous, irrespective of whether she wins damages.

Similarly, anyone who claims at an employment tribunal that he or she was the victim of a sexual offence must be anonymous in reports of the case.

ch. 17. explains employ- ment tribunals

If a journalist working on a biographical feature is interviewing someone who says that as a child or adult he or she was sexually attacked or sexually molested, the anonymity applies unless the individual gives valid, written consent to be identified – discussed later in this chapter.

👁 Case study

Trinity Mirror Southern Ltd was fined a total of £10,000 in 2011 after it admitted that the *Aldershot News and Mail*, *Farnborough News and Mail*, *Fleet News and Mail* and the *Yateley News and Mail* had published in a report of a court case the names of two women who were victims of sexual assault. It was also ordered to pay each of them £5,000 compensation. Human error was blamed for this breach of the Sexual Offences (Amendment) Act 1992. A Crown Prosecution Service lawyer said: 'The disregard by the newspapers of these women's automatic right to anonymity proved traumatic to those involved and required extensive extra police and victim support'. (Hampshire Constabulary's *Frontline* magazine, issue 163, July 2011).

Care needed with detail

Section 1 prohibits publication of matter 'likely to lead' to identification. A report of a sexual offence which refers to the alleged victim's school or workplace – both of which are specified in the legislation as likely to lead to identification – and gives his/her age could prompt speculation likely to lead to identification. Although saying the victim is a student at a specific university is unlikely to identify him or her, giving further detail, such as that the victim is a 25-year-old music student, is likely to do so. In 1983 the then Solicitor General said that a report of a rape case could be illegal if the detail included was sufficient to identify the victim in the minds of some people even though not in the minds of the community generally.

Jigsaw identification

Jigsaw identification could occur if in reports of a rape trial a town's newspaper described the alleged victim as 'a mother of three' who lived and worked locally, a TV station described her as 'a nurse', and a radio station described her as 'a woman in her thirties' who worked at night. This accumulation of detail could identify her to colleagues and acquaintances. For a definition of jigsaw identification, see ch. 9, pp. 97–98, Jigsaw identification.

Media organisations covering cases involving sexual abuse of a child by an adult in the same family (or household) should agree whether their reports (a) name the adult defendant, but omit any detail of any relationship to the child, or (b) do not identify the adult defendant, and report that the alleged abuse was familial.

Journalists should also pay heed to relevant parts of the Editors' Code of Practice or the Ofcom Broadcasting Code, which are explained later in this chapter.

see also ch. 9, pp. 98–99, Cases of abuse within a family

Case study

The *Luton Herald and Post* was fined £1,000 in 2013 for publishing detail which breached the 1992 Act by identifying a woman victim of a sexual offence. In a report of a trial in which the defendant faced rape and sexual assault charges, the newspaper included the victim's age, said she had come to the UK to study, named her home country, gave the approximate date and location of her arrival, named the placement agency she had used and the institution where she was studying, said how she had met her attacker and referred to her living arrangements and professional aspirations (*Media Lawyer*, 8 October 2013).

Invalid orders purporting to give an adult defendant anonymity

The media may decide, when covering a court case involving alleged sexual abuse within a family, that the only way to preserve anonymity for the alleged victim(s) is not to publish anything identifying the adult defendant. But occasionally

see ch. 15, p. 186, Sexual offence law does not give ano- nymity to defendants

magistrates courts and Crown court judges have sought to make that choice for the media by passing an order, purportedly under the Sexual Offences (Amendment) Act 1992, stating that the adult defendant should not be identified. The reason usually given is that the order is needed to protect the anonymity of the alleged victim(s). But the Act gives no power to courts to impose such an order.

▶ Sexual offences for which alleged victims have anonymity

The 1992 Act, as amended by the Sexual Offences Act 2003, applies the anonymity for victims and alleged victims to almost all offences with a sexual element. The most serious are **indictable-only**, with a maximum sentence of life imprisonment. These include:

→glossary

- *Rape* – penetration of vagina, anus, or mouth without consent, by penis. If the victim is aged under 13, any such conduct is defined as rape, even if the victim says there was no compulsion, because the victim is so young. Males and females can be rape victims but only males can be rapists; females can be guilty of inciting or aiding rape.

- *Assault by penetration* – of vagina or anus, without consent and otherwise than by penis – for example, by finger or object.

- *Causing or inciting a child under 13 or a person who has 'a mental disorder impeding choice' to engage in sexual activity* in which the activity caused or incited involves penetration by penis or otherwise.

- *An attempt, conspiracy, or incitement* to commit any of the above offences.

- *Aiding, abetting, counselling, or procuring* the commission of any of them.

→glossary Some sexual crimes are **either-way** charges. For some, an offender can be sentenced to a jail term of up to 14 years. Either-way charges include:

- *Sexual assault* – intentional sexual touching, without consent.

- *Administering a substance* – for example, spiking someone's drink with a drug – to enable the perpetrator to engage him/her in sexual activity.

- *Trespass with intent to commit a sexual offence.*

- *Sexual intercourse with a girl who has reached the age of 13 but who is under 16* – this offending is not classed as rape if there is no compulsion, but could be very serious and exploitative if the perpetrator is much older.

- *Abuse of a position of trust, through sexual activity with someone aged under 18* – so, for example, a male teacher having consensual sex with a 17-year-old girl is not a crime because she is over 16, the age of sexual consent, unless she was a pupil at the school where he works, in which case the sexual relationship is criminal abuse of his position of trust as a teacher.

- *Sexual activity by a care worker*, for example, in a hospital, if it involved such activity with a person in his/her care who has a mental disorder, and not involving penetration (which would be indictable-only).

- *Engaging in sexual activity in the presence of a child*, or causing a child to watch a sexual act, for the perpetrator's sexual gratification.

- *Arranging or facilitating commission of a sex offence against a child*, anywhere in the world.

- *Meeting or intending to meet a child following sexual grooming*, for example, by an adult contacting a child over the Internet – the child has anonymity even if the meeting did not take place.

- *Sexual activity by an adult with a child family member* (NB: It is incorrect to describe such an offence as incest, because incest is a consensual relationship).

- *Taking an indecent photograph of a child.*

- *Causing or inciting child prostitution.*

- *Trafficking a person into or within the UK for sexual exploitation*, for example, prostitution; or causing or inciting an adult to be a prostitute, or controlling such a prostitute, for gain. Some journalists may not realise that the 2003 Act, by amending the 1992 Act, extended anonymity to cover adults who are or have allegedly been, for example, 'controlled' prostitutes or have allegedly or actually been trafficked to be prostitutes.

- *Exposure* (colloquially called 'flashing') of genitals with the intent to cause alarm or distress.

- *Voyeurism* – observing for sexual gratification someone else or people doing something private (for example, taking a shower, or having sex), knowing they did not consent to being observed because – for example – a hidden camera was used.

Buggery is no longer illegal between consenting adults, but is an offence if perpetrated on someone aged under 16 – a victim who should therefore have anonymity.

A sexual offence which allegedly occurred before 1 May 2004 will be charged according to older definitions, with the anonymity applying. One such older offence is 'indecent assault'.

The anonymity does not apply to two adult relatives who are charged with consensual, illegal sexual activity with each other – which would have been charged as 'incest' under the old law – or to adults accused of sexual activity in a public lavatory. But if only one of them is charged, the other retains anonymity. It also does not apply in cases involving a person accused of sexual activity with an animal.

Liability for breach of the anonymity provision

Section 5 of the 1992 Act says those who can be prosecuted if a publication/broadcast breaches the anonymity are the newspaper or periodical's proprietor, editor and publisher, or any 'body corporate' (for example, a company) providing the programme service and any person whose functions in relation to the programme correspond to those of an editor of a newspaper, or as regards any other form of publication, any person publishing it.

It is a defence for the person accused to show that he/she was not aware, and neither suspected nor had reason to suspect, that the material published would be likely to identify the victim/alleged victim of a sexual offence. Currently the maximum fine is £5,000. But see p. 62: 'Fining power to be without limit'.

 See www.mcnaes.com ch. 10 for other case studies of media organisations being fined for breaching the anonymity of victims of sexual offences.

▶ When does the anonymity cease to apply?

The anonymity does not apply to dead people, so will not apply to someone raped and murdered.

By court order, at the request of a defendant

- A court due to try someone for a sexual offence can, on the application of a defendant or a co-defendant, remove an alleged victim's anonymity if it is satisfied that:
  - it should be lifted to induce people likely to be needed as witnesses to come forward; and that
  - otherwise the conduct of the applicant's defence at the trial is likely to be substantially prejudiced.

 A defendant may argue that he needs witnesses to come forward to support an alibi.

Allowing the media to identify the alleged victim when reporting the alibi defence could jog the memories of members of the public about where and when he/she was seen, and who, if anyone, was with him/her at the time of the alleged offence.

Courts are rarely asked to lift anonymity on this ground, specified in section 3 of the 1992 Act. If the alleged offence is indictable- only – for example, rape – a Crown court has power to waive the anonymity. A magistrates court does not because it cannot try the case.

By court order, to lift 'a substantial and unreasonable' restriction on reporting

- The court trying a sexual offence can lift an alleged victim's anonymity if it is satisfied that:
  - the anonymity would impose a substantial and unreasonable restriction on media reporting of the trial; and that
  - it is in the public interest to remove or relax it.

Again, if the alleged offence is indictable-only, only a Crown court has power to waive the anonymity. Cases in which courts are asked to lift anonymity on the above ground, specified in section 3, are very rare.

👁 Case study

Police were hunting a known criminal, Arthur Hutchinson, after three members of the same family were murdered at their Sheffield home after a wedding party. To help trace Hutchinson, police publicly named him as the suspect, and he was captured. The media had also named the murder victims. Some time after being charged with the murders, Hutchinson was also charged with raping a teenage girl linked to the family, in the same terrible attack. The media had not previously been told of the rape allegation. At Hutchinson's trial on the murder and rape charges, lawyers acting for newspapers argued that it would be impossible for them to report it at all if their coverage could not identify the girl as the alleged rape victim, because if they could not do that their reports could not identify the family involved. It was pointed out that publishing Hutchinson's name or that he was charged with three Sheffield murders would in itself be enough for the Sheffield public to remember who the family was and therefore to identify the girl, and that evidence of the rape and murders was inextricably linked. The judge agreed that the media could identify the girl, and thus the family, because anonymity would otherwise impose a substantial and unreasonable restriction on reporting of the trial, and it was in the public interest for the trial to be fully reported (*R v Arthur Hutchinson* (1985) 129 SJ 700; (1985) 82 Cr App 51). Hutchinson was convicted.

If the victim/alleged victim gives written consent

The media may identify someone as being the victim/alleged victim of a sexual offence if he/she consents. But section 5 of the 1992 Act specifies that:

- the consent must be in writing;
- the person waiving his/her anonymity must be aged 16 or over; and
- the consent will not be valid if it is proved that anyone 'interfered unreasonably with the peace and comfort' of the individual with the intention of obtaining it.

So, the law guards a victim against being pressured into giving consent, and makes clear that anyone under 16 is regarded as too immature to consent. Parents of victims under 16 cannot consent on their behalf.

A court's permission is not needed for this consent to be given. Instances occur fairly regularly of written consent being given, particularly after a perpetrator is jailed. For example, a woman who has been raped may feel that allowing the media to identify her sends a powerful signal to other rape victims that they can find the courage to seek justice, and that there is no stigma in being a victim.

If the case is 'other than' the sexual offence alleged

ch. 5, p. 52, Other noteworthy crimes, gives definitions of these offences

People alleged to have falsely claimed to police that they have been victims of sexual offences may be charged with wasting police time, or perjury, or perverting the course of justice.

- A person appearing in court on such a charge – for example, perjury – in relation to a false allegation of a sexual offence can be identified in reports of those proceedings as someone who was previously said to be the victim of a sexual offence.

This is because section 1(4) of the 1992 Act says that an alleged victim of a sexual offence can be identified in articles which consist 'only of a report of criminal proceedings other than' proceedings for the sexual offence. This would also allow the media covering a burglary case to report that the woman home owner had asserted in court that the burglar raped her, or, in a case involving a woman defendant accused of attacking a man, that the defendant claimed that her alleged victim had in fact raped her. But there would still need to be ethical consideration of whether the report should identify her as regards such statements.

▶ Orders to protect the public from risk of sexual offences

The Sexual Offences Act 2003 gave courts the power to make, in civil law, a Sexual Offences Prevention Order (SOPO) to restrict the behaviour of a sexual offender to protect the public from the risk of 'serious sexual harm'. An order can, for example, ban an offender from loitering near schools or making unsolicited approaches to women. Breaching a SOPO is a crime. In 2013 the government announced that SOPOs would be replaced by Sexual Harm Prevention Orders, for a person convicted or cautioned for a sexual offence, and that it would introduce Sexual Risk Orders to restrict an individual's behaviour if he or she poses a risk of sexual harm, even if he/she has never been convicted.

Check www.mcnaes.com for updates about these new orders, and see www.mcnaes.com ch. 10 for detail of a case in which an offender unsuccessfully sought anonymity in media reports of SOPO proceedings.

▌ Ethical considerations

The Editors' Code of Practice, used by the Independent Press Standards Organisation, and by its predecessor body the Press Complaints Commission, states in clause 11 that the press must not identify victims of sexual assault or publish material likely to contribute to such identification 'unless there is adequate justification and they are legally free to do so'.

The term 'sexual assault' here includes all sexual attacks, eg rape.

ch. 2 introduces the code. Appendix 2, pp. 443–447 shows it in full

- Clause 7 (Children in sex cases) says: 'The press must not, even if legally free to do so, identify children under 16 who are victims or witnesses in cases involving sex offences.'

It adds that in any press report of a case involving a sexual offence against a child:

- the child must not be identified;
- the adult may be identified;
- the word 'incest' must not be used where a child victim might be identified;
- care must be taken that nothing in the report implies the relationship between the accused and the child.

Clause 7 is subject to the code's public interest exceptions, but clause 11 is not, though the term 'adequate justification' arguably embraces the idea of the public interest. The code says there would have to be 'exceptional public interest' to override the normally paramount interests of a child under 16 – but the Editors' Codebook says a girl can be identified as an under-age mother if her parents consent.

 see Useful Websites at the end of this chapter

In the three year period from 2011 to 2013 the Press Complaints Commission issued 11 adjudications censuring media organisations for publishing material which identified or had potential to identify victims of sexual offences – for example, in the *Luton Herald and Post* case discussed earlier. In some of these cases the PCC ruled that material published was likely to identify a child victim. In 2011 the PCC issued guidance – see Useful Websites at the end of this chapter – stressing that 'editors should err on the side of caution' on what detail is published.

 for adjudications see www.mcnaes.com ch. 10

Rule 1.8 of the Ofcom Broadcasting Code says broadcasters should 'be particularly careful not to provide clues' which may lead to the identification of children when by law they should have anonymity 'as a victim, witness, defendant or other perpetrator in the case of sexual offences featured in criminal, civil or family court proceedings'. This rule also warns against jigsaw identification and that inadvertent use of the term 'incest' may identify such a child. See ch. 3 for an introduction to the Ofcom code.

((•))
See
Useful
Websites
at the end
of this
chapter

▐ Relatives of alleged and convicted sex offenders

In guidance on reporting cases involving paedophiles, the PCC drew attention to the rights of relatives and friends of people accused of sex crimes: 'Not only do they also have a right to respect for their private lives under Clause 3, but the Code also makes clear [under Clause 9] that the "press must avoid identifying [them] without their consent" – or unless there is a public interest in doing so.'

➡ Recap of major points

- It is illegal for the media to identify the victims or alleged victims of sexual offences – including rape and sexual assault – in reports of these crimes or of court cases which follow.

- The law gives anonymity to the victims and alleged victims of voyeurs and 'flashing', and to people allegedly or actually trafficked to be prostitutes.

- A court can remove the anonymity in certain circumstances, but this rarely happens.

- There is a danger of 'jigsaw identification', particularly when several media organisations are covering a case of alleged sex abuse within a family.

- A victim/alleged victim who is 16 or over can waive his/her anonymity by giving a media organisation written consent to being identified.

((•)) Useful Websites

www.cps.gov.uk/legal/p_to_r/rape_and_sexual_offences/index.html
   Crown Prosecution Service guidance on prosecution of sexual offences

http://pcc.org.uk/news/index.html?article=NzM0Nw==
   PCC guidance on reporting court cases involving sexual offences

www.pcc.org.uk/advice/editorials-detail.html?article=OTQ=
   PCC guidance to editors on the reporting of paedophile cases

www.editorscode.org.uk/
   The Editors' Codebook provides detailed advice on clauses 7 and 11 of the Editors' Code of Practice

http://stakeholders.ofcom.org.uk/broadcasting/broadcast-codes/broadcast-code/
   The Ofcom Broadcasting Code

Court reporting – other restrictions

Chapter summary

Earlier chapters show that reporting crime and courts is not a job for an untrained amateur. Reporting restrictions can dictate what is published. Breaching them is an offence. This chapter details more restrictions, including permanent bans on using cameras and audio-recording devices in any court. Revealing how individual jurors voted in verdicts is also illegal. Reporting what a court has heard in private can be punished as contempt of court. The chapter also outlines how courts can ban the media from identifying some adult witnesses, and blackmail victims, or order the media to postpone reporting a case. Chapter 15 shows how to challenge a reporting restriction as invalid or unnecessary. Chapter 21 deals with defamation dangers in court reporting.

▶ Ban on photography, filming and sketching in courts and precincts

More than 80 years ago, Parliament banned photography in courts. Case law means the ban includes filming in courts. As explained later, the ban has been relaxed to some extent to allow the proceedings in the Supreme Court and Court of Appeal to be broadcast. But there are no plans to relax it to allow defendants, witnesses or jurors to be filmed or photographed in courts.

A primary reason for the ban is that photography and filming, and any publication of images gained, would put added strain on witnesses, defendants and jurors.

Section 41 of the Criminal Justice Act 1925 makes it illegal to:

- take or try to take any photograph or film; or

- make or try to make – with a view to publication – any portrait or sketch of:

 - any person in any court, its building, or within its precincts,
 - any person 'entering or leaving' a court building or its precincts;

- publish such a photo, film, portrait or sketch.

Section 41 applies to criminal and civil courts and inquests. 'Any person' includes judges, magistrates, coroners, jurors, witnesses, defendants and any other party.

- The Act does not define 'precincts', which causes practical difficulties.

The term includes rooms, foyers or corridors within the courthouse property. It is unclear to what extent it includes areas immediately outside, not part of the property. If unsure, check with the particular court.

Journalists standing on the public pavement frequently photograph and film judges, lawyers, defendants and witnesses entering or leaving court buildings, for example the Royal Courts of Justice in London. Where this practice has become customary, it is rare for a court to object, though it would seem to breach the section 41 ban on showing people 'entering or leaving'. Jurors should not normally be photographed, as this might be regarded as a contempt in common law, as explained later in this chapter.

Breaches of section 41 can be punished with fines up to £1,000.

Artists' sketches of court cases

The media publish artists' sketches of scenes in court, including the face of the defendant, to illustrate newsworthy cases. To comply with section 41, these artists visit the court's public gallery or press bench, memorise the scene and characters, but do the actual sketching elsewhere. A government consultation paper made no objection to sketching in a courthouse press room.

Jury visits to the scene of crime or death

If a judge or coroner decides that a jury should visit an outside location such as a crime or accident scene to help jurors understand evidence, the visit should not be filmed, photographed or sketched without the court's permission. The court may allow this, as long as no juror can be identified through what is published.

Some broadcasting allowed

The Constitutional Reform Act 2005 ensured that the Supreme Court could allow broadcasting of its proceedings which, being concerned with points of law, are argued from documentary evidence and unlikely to involve witnesses in person.

Part of the Crime and Courts Act 2013 enables the Lord Chancellor by order and with the agreement of the Lord Chief Justice, to permit broadcasting from other courts by disapplying section 9 of the Contempt of Court Act, which is explained later in the chapter, and section 41 of the 1925 Act. Such an order was made in October 2013 permitting the Court of Appeal to allow broadcasting of legal argument and judgments in its cases. These courts retain discretion to approve arrangements for broadcasting and to ban it in particular cases. The government said in 2012 that it also intended to allow broadcasts of judges' sentencing remarks in the Crown courts.

ch. 8 explains the work of Crown courts, the Court of Appeal and the Supreme Court

Photography and filming could be contempt of court

- Despite the existence of the 1925 Act, a court may deem photography or filming in court or in its precincts, or even elsewhere, for example on the pavement outside, to be a contempt of court in common law

see also ch. 18 pp. 214–215, Contempt in common law

A photographer's conduct could be regarded as contempt if it amounted to 'molestation' – interference with the administration of justice. Case law suggests that running after a defendant for a short while in order to photograph him/her would not usually be seen as molestation. But stalking a defendant or witnesses further, or jostling them, could be contempt as it might deter them or other witnesses from giving evidence.

👁 Case study

In 2009 Mr Justice Keith warned photographers to stop taking pictures of two young brothers as they arrived at Sheffield Crown court in cars under blankets, saying he would take action if he thought a contempt had taken place. The brothers had admitted inflicting, when aged 10 and 11, horrific violence on two boys in a village near Doncaster (*Press Gazette*, 7 September 2009).

The fine or prison sentence to punish such a contempt is at the judge's discretion. Members of the public have been swiftly punished, particularly for attempts to intimidate a witness.

👁 Case study

In 2004 a man was jailed for nine months for using a mobile phone to take pictures in Birmingham Crown court. The judge believed there was a 'sinister motive' (*Media Lawyer*, 8 October 2004).

▌ Ban on audio recording in court

It is illegal to use any audio-recording device in a court, including a tape-recorder, or a mobile phone's recording facility, without the court's permission.

- One aim of this ban is to prevent witness testimony being broadcast, which for some witnesses would increase the strain of giving evidence.

- It is also to stop secret recordings being made in the public gallery by, for example, a defendant's criminal associates, who could use it to intimidate or humiliate a prosecution witness or help dishonest witnesses collude in false corroboration.

For example, a witness could listen to a recording of another's evidence, and repeat the same information in his/her own evidence but claim to have recalled it independently.

The ban is contained in section 9 of the Contempt of Court Act 1981, which makes it a contempt to:

- use a tape-recorder or any other audio-recording device in court, or take one into a court for use, unless the court gives permission;

- broadcast any audio-recording of court proceedings, or play any of it in the hearing of any section of the public;

- make any unauthorised use of a recording, if recording has been allowed.

ch. 14, p. 154, Procedural rules and open justice, explains what the Rules and Direction are

A court has discretion to allow audio-recording, including by a journalist – for example, for note-taking – and to allow publication of the sound recording. Rule 16.9 of the Criminal Procedure Rules says that anyone who wants permission to record must apply to the court as soon as reasonably practicable, and notify the parties in the case, and anyone else the court specifies, that permission is being sought. An applicant must explain why the court should permit the use of an audio-recorder and why publication of the recording should be permitted, if this is proposed. Criminal Practice Direction 16A.2 says that a relevant factor in the court's decision on whether to permit audio-recording may be 'the existence of any reasonable need' on the part of the applicant for the recording to be made.

The penalty for breaching section 9 of the 1981 Act is a jail term of up to two years and/or an unlimited fine.

▌ Tweeting, emailing and texting 'live' reports from court

Reporters should not make or receive calls on mobile phones during court hearings – doing so could be punished as a contempt because it is disrespectful, and potentially disruptive and damaging to the administration of justice. A judge might fine or jail a reporter whose mobile phone ringtone interrupts a witness's testimony, particularly if the witness is already finding it difficult to testify. The normal rule is that mobile phones must be turned off in court. The rule derives from the **inherent jurisdiction** courts have to govern their own proceedings.   → glossary

But journalists and legal commentators who want to use 'live, text-based communications' to report court cases no longer need to ask the court's permission, the then Lord Chief Justice, Lord Judge, said in guidance in December 2011. It means journalists can use internet-connected laptops or mobile phones in courts to e-mail or text court reports, or post them directly on the internet, including on Twitter. The devices must be silent and unobstrusive. The guidance, which applies to 'court proceedings which are open to the public and to those parts of the proceedings which are not subject to reporting restrictions', indicates that this general permission for the media to use the devices in court is only for 'journalistic purposes.' It also says a court can decide 'at any time' to forbid all use of such devices. It also stresses that photography in court is still forbidden, adding: 'Any equipment which has photographic capability must not have that function activated.' Members of the public must still ask the court's permission to use such devices.

As he handed down his guidance to reporters, Lord Judge said: 'Twitter as much as you like from today' (*Media Lawyer*, 14 December 2011).

The Supreme Court has a general rule allowing the use of live, text-based communications, though not in some types of case.

 See Useful Websites at the end of this chapter for the Lord Chief Justice's guidance and the Supreme Court's rule.

▌Confidentiality of jury deliberations

It is a contempt of court to breach the confidentiality of a jury's deliberations, whether the jury is in a Crown court, an inquest or a civil case. Juries arrive at their verdicts in secret discussions, in rooms guarded against intrusion. The secrecy helps jurors to be frank in discussions, without fear of a public backlash for an unpopular decision or retribution from a vengeful defendant they convict. For the role of juries in criminal trials, civil cases and inquests, see chs. 8, 12 and 16.

- Section 8 of the Contempt of Court Act 1981 says it is contempt of the court to obtain, solicit or disclose any detail of:
  - statements made;
  - opinions expressed;
  - arguments advanced; or
  - votes cast

by members of a jury during its deliberations.

The ban applies even if what is published does not identify any individual juror or even a particular trial. The penalty for a contempt by breaching section 8 is a jail term of up to two years and/or an unlimited fine.

After a trial the media is safe to publish a juror's general impressions of his/her experience of jury service, provided the individual is willing to volunteer these, and is not asked about statements made, opinions expressed, arguments advanced or votes cast in the course of the deliberations, and does not refer to such matters in what is published. A juror could be interviewed, for example, on whether he/she felt in general that evidence was clearly presented. Journalistic investigations of alleged miscarriages of justice such as a controversial murder conviction some-times prompt jurors from the trial to speak up months or years later. Some have contacted journalists to say that, in the light of new evidence which has emerged, they are no longer certain of the accused's guilt. The safest course is to seek legal advice before conducting or publishing such an interview.

👁 Case study

In 2009 the High Court fined *The Times* £15,000 and ordered it to pay £27,426 costs for breaching section 8. The newspaper had published an article about the 10–2 major-ity verdict by a Crown court jury which convicted a childminder of a child's manslaughter. It quoted but did not name the jury foreman, who had approached the newspaper, as expressing doubt about the medical evidence, and quoted him saying that, early in its deliberations, the jury voted 10–2 in an initial indication of its consensus and that the majority of jurors – because of what he called 'common sense' rather than 'logical think-ing' – held to their initial view that the defendant was guilty. *The Times* denied contempt. But the High Court ruled that *The Times* had, by using these quotes, breached section 8 by disclosure of 'votes cast', 'opinions expressed' and 'statements made' during the jury's deliberations, even though jurors' identities were not disclosed, and the foreman's descriptions of the jury's deliberations were brief and possibly inaccurate. (*Attorney General v Michael Alexander Seckerson and Times Newspapers Ltd* [2009] EWHC 1023 (Admin)). The jury foreman was fined £5,000 for his part in the breach (*Media Lawyer*, 20 December 2009).

▌ Contempt risk in identifying or approaching jurors

There is a risk of a media organisation being accused of common law contempt if it identifies a juror against his/her wishes, even after a trial. The disclosure could be held to interfere with the judicial process by putting the juror at risk of harm from anyone unhappy with a verdict. A reporter deemed to have harassed a juror for an interview might be held to be in contempt, because harassment could discourage people from serving as jurors.

 Case study

In 2013 a judge at Oxford Crown court held a hearing to consider an explanation of why Lucy Ford, who works for *The Banbury Guardian*, photographed two jurors outside the courthouse and had asked them to help her identify a defendant. The judge accepted that their being photographed was an accident because they had walked into her picture, and that there was no attempt to intimidate them (*Holdthefrontpage*, 12 February 2013).

See ch. 18 about common law contempt. See also ch. 37, p. 432, Identifying jurors, on the statutory ban on identifying jurors who have served in trials in Northern Ireland.

A juror discharged during a case for late attendance or being drunk may well be named in court, and could be punished by the judge. In the absence of any court order to the contrary, the media can safely identify the juror, if named, and say how he/she was dealt with.

▌ Section 11 orders – blackmail, secrets, personal safety

A court can ban the media from reporting a person's name, or other information, in coverage of a case.

Section 11 of the Contempt of Court Act 1981 says:

- A court can ban the publication of a name or other information in connection with the proceedings as long as it has first allowed that information to be withheld from the public.

Section 11 orders are not used routinely, but a typical use would be to:

Protect the identity of victims/alleged victims of blackmail – The target of blackmail involving a threat to reveal an embarrassing secret will be less likely to report the threat to police, and be a witness, if it is likely that his/her identity will be given in open court, and be reported by the media when the secret emerges in evidence. In blackmail trials, the alleged victim is usually referred to in open court simply by a letter of the alphabet, for example, Ms X. This protects the administration of justice as a continuing process, as identifying any alleged victim of blackmail publicly in court reports makes it less likely that other blackmail victims will contact police.

Protect commercially sensitive information, secret processes – for example, a company sues another for damages over breach of confidence about valuable

ch. 5, p. 51, Crimes against property or involving gain, gives the definition of blackmail

→ glossary

research data. The court may hear evidence about the data **in private** to preserve its confidentiality – if it does not stay confidential, the case would be pointless. A section 11 order could ban reports of the case publishing details of the data.

Protect national security, state secrets – for example, a defendant prosecuted under the Official Secrets Act 1911 is accused of betraying UK military secrets to a foreign power. The court may well go into private session to hear evidence about those secrets. A section 11 order could be used to ban publication of such material, should it leak out. It could also ban the media from identifying intelligence officers who are witnesses, as identification would end their usefulness as undercover agents and might put them at risk.

ch. 33 explains official secrets law

Protect a person from the risk of harm – A court might be persuaded that the name and address of a witness, or the address of a defendant – for example, a sex offender – should not be published, to prevent an attack on that person by criminals or vigilantes. But the media can oppose such orders on the grounds that they are unnecessary – see ch. 15, pp. 175–176, Anonymity and risk of attack?

Two-stage process

A section 11 order is the second step in a two-stage process. The court first has to rule that a name or other information should not be given in proceedings held in public. Only then it can impose a section 11 order. If the name or information then slips out by mistake in a public session – for example in what a witness or lawyer says – or if the media have discovered it by other means, it is illegal to publish it in any context which connects it to the case. A section 11 order remains in force indefinitely, unless a court revokes it.

When a section 11 order is in force, journalists need to guard against 'jigsaw identification' – see ch. 9, pp. 97–98, Jigsaw identification.

Breaching a section 11 order is an offence of contempt of court punishable by a jail term of up to two years and/or an unlimited fine.

But section 11 only bans the reporting of the name or matter 'in connection with the proceedings'.

◗ Ban on reporting a court's private hearing

Courts sit in private, with the public and media excluded, for some cases, including when considering whether mentally ill people should be confined in hospitals, and hearings involving state secrets. The media is automatically banned from publishing what is said in some categories of cases heard by a court in private – that is, **in chambers** or **in camera**.

→ glossary
→ glossary

Section 12 of the Administration of Justice Act 1960 makes it a contempt of court to publish, without the court's permission, a report of proceedings it has heard in private and which:

- relate to the exercise of the inherent jurisdiction of the High Court with respect to children;
- fall under the Children Act 1989 or the Adoption and Children Act 2002 or otherwise relate wholly or mainly to the maintenance or upbringing of a child;
- fall under the Mental Capacity Act 2005, or under any provision of the Mental Health Act 1983 authorising an application or reference to be made to the First-Tier Tribunal, the Mental Health Review Tribunal for Wales or to a county court;
- involve national security;
- involve a secret process, discovery or invention;
- are those, of any kind, where the court expressly bans publication of all or specified information relating to the private hearing.

ch. 13 explains children cases in family courts, and ch. 17 explains tribunals

A reporter may be told what has happened in a private hearing by one of the parties. But in these particular types of cases section 12 automatically prohibits the publication of anything heard by a court in private, to protect the welfare, including the privacy, of children, and the mentally ill or incapacitated; and state or commercial secrets.

A breach of section 12, if proved as contempt, is punishable by a jail term of up to two years, and/or an unlimited fine.

- Any document 'prepared for use' in a court's private hearing is deemed to be part of those proceedings. If a case falls into the section 12 categories, the court will regard publication by the media of information or quotations from such a document, such as a psychiatric report or a report on a couple's fitness as parents, as a contempt.

Some detail can be published about a private hearing

Some material about a private hearing in these types of case can be published. Section 12 makes clear that publishing the text, or a summary, of any order made in such a hearing is not contempt unless the court has specifically prohibited its publication.

In *Re B (A Child)* [2004] EWHC 411 (Fam), Mr Justice Munby stated that section 12 did not itself ban publishing a reference to 'the nature of the dispute' being heard in the private hearing. He added that what could be published without breaching section 12 included:

- the names, addresses, or photographs of parties and witnesses involved in the private proceedings;

- the date, time or place of hearings in the case;
- and 'anything which has been seen or heard by a person conducting himself lawfully in the public corridor or other public precincts outside the court.'

ch. 18 explains contempt law and ch. 21 explains privilege

But he added that a court could ban publication of even these details, or that automatic restrictions under other law could apply.

If the court hearing in private does not fall into the section 12 categories, a media organisation may safely be able to publish an account of it, for example, if guided by a person who was in it. But a media report of a case heard in private is not protected by any statutory privilege in relation to libel law, and will not be protected by section 4 of the Contempt of Court Act 1981 if it creates a substantial risk of serious prejudice to an 'active' case.

Ban on publishing material from court documents

ch. 14, pp. 161–164, Access to documents in civil cases, explains inspection rights.

Even if a case is heard in public, a journalist should exercise care before quoting from a document used in it if the material has not been read out in court.

As explained in ch. 12, civil cases are conducted mainly by reference to documents.

In a civil case, it is safe to quote from any document the journalist obtains with the court's permission, or from any case document he/she is able to inspect by right. For example, if the civil case is heard in public, it will be safe to quote from any **skeleton argument** provided to a journalist by lawyers involved unless the court forbids this.

→ glossary

Any reporting restriction, for example protecting the identity of a child or alleged victim of a sexual offence, must be observed in what is reported from such documents.

In criminal cases, the media has recently gained a qualified right to see case material – see ch. 14, pp. 158–161, Access to material in criminal cases.

Journalists should beware of the risk of contempt incurred by publishing material from a document which they have obtained from one side or the other in criminal or civil proceedings, without the court's permission, and which one party was compelled or had a duty to produce as part of the **'disclosure'** process and which has not been read out in open court. 'Disclosure' is the pre-trial exchange of evidence and information. Contempt law applies because of the danger that parties who feared that material they provided to the other side might be published, even though it was not used in court, would refuse to cooperate fully with the disclosure process.

→ glossary

Again, publishing material not aired in open court is not protected by statutory privilege in relation to libel law, or by the Contempt of Court Act 1981 if the strict liability rule is breached.

▌ Lifetime anonymity for adult witnesses

A criminal court can ban the media from disclosing an adult witness's identity if there is concern that he/she is scared or distressed about testifying, by using discretionary powers in section 46 of the Youth Justice and Criminal Evidence Act 1999 (the 1999 Act).

- Section 46 says a court can order that an adult witness should have lifetime anonymity in reports of the case if the court is satisfied:
  - that the quality of his/her evidence, or of his/her level of cooperation in preparations for the case, is likely to be diminished by fear or distress in connection with being identified by members of the public as a witness in that case, and that
  - granting anonymity is likely to improve the quality of the witness's evidence or the level of his/her cooperation.

A main purpose of this law is to provide better protection for witnesses who fear that the fact that they have given evidence, or are due to testify, will provoke hostility from criminal elements in their communities.

Section 46 says a party in the proceedings in a criminal court – including the defence, though it is usually the prosecution – can ask the court to make the anonymity order, called a 'reporting direction', to cover a witness aged 18 or over. The court may hear this request in camera.

The scope of a section 46 order

A section 46 order makes it illegal to include in any publication during the witness's lifetime any matter likely to lead members of the public to identify him/her as a witness in the proceedings.

It says information likely to identify such a witness includes in particular:

- the witness's name and address;
- the identity of any educational establishment he/she attends;
- the identity of any place where he/she works; and
- any still or moving picture of him/her.

Any detail which risks revealing the witness's identity should be left out. The witness may be the alleged victim of the offence(s) being tried. If so, the effect on reports will be major and similar to that of the lifetime anonymity automatically given to victims/alleged victims of sexual offences, who do not need section 46 anonymity. When a section 46 order is made, journalists should ensure they avoid jigsaw identification.

A section 46 order *cannot* be used to give a defendant anonymity.

 Ch. 9, pp. 98–99 explains, Jigsaw identification. Ch. 10 explains anonymity for victims of sexual offences.

Factors a court must consider

When deciding whether to grant section 46 anonymity, the court must take into account the witness's view about anonymity; the nature and circumstances of the alleged offence(s) being tried; the witness's age, social and cultural background and ethnic origins; his/her domestic and employment circumstances, religious beliefs, or political opinions; and any behaviour towards the witness on the part of the defendant, or the defendant's family or associates, or anyone else likely to be a defendant or witness in the proceedings.

The court must also consider:

- whether it would be in the interests of justice to make the anonymity order; as well as
- the public interest in avoiding imposing a substantial and unreasonable restriction on reporting the proceedings.

Breaches of section 46 orders

see ch. 10
on sexual
offences

Publishing material which breaches the section 46 anonymity brings the same liability as breaching a sexual offence victim's anonymity, with the same maximum fine.

Anyone prosecuted for breach of section 46 has a defence if he/she can prove that:

see ch.
15, pp.
185–186,
Section 46
anonymity
for adult
witnesses,
on chal-
lenging
section 46
orders

- he/she was not aware, and neither suspected nor had reason to suspect, that the publication included the matter or report in question; or that
- the witness concerned gave written consent for the matter to be published.

This 'written consent' defence will fail if it is proved that the consent was obtained by interfering with the witness's 'peace or comfort'.

The court which bestowed the section 46 anonymity, or a higher court, can make 'an excepting direction' to remove the anonymity entirely or relax it to some extent, if satisfied that doing so is necessary in the interests of justice, or that the restriction imposes a substantial and unreasonable restriction on reporting the proceedings, and that it is in the public interest to remove or relax the restriction.

▌ Other anonymity orders

www.
mcnaes.
com ch.
4 on ano-
nymity
for police
inform-
ants

The High Court has power to ban publication of the identities of people concerned in its proceedings, and uses it to give anonymity to children involved in high-profile cases or news stories. The court also usually gives anonymity to mentally incapacitated adults when protecting their interests in civil cases. A media organisation which publishes information identifying such people, in breach of such an order, could be punished for contempt of court. The High Court's powers derive from its inherent jurisdiction and from Article 8 of the European Convention on Human Rights, concerning privacy.

For further detail of use of such orders in family law, see ch. 13, pp. 145–146, Anti-publicity injunctions in family cases. For their use in privacy cases, see ch. 26.

The Civil Procedure Rules govern the conduct of civil cases in county courts and the High Court. Rule 39.2(4) states: 'The court may order that the identity of any party or witness must not be disclosed if it considers non-disclosure necessary in order to protect the interests of that party or witness'.

 For information on anonymity for persons subject, as suspected terrorists, to a 'terrorism prevention and investigation measures', see the chapter on www.mcnaes.com 'Terrorism and the effect of counter-terrorism law'.

▶ Indefinite anonymity for convicted defendants

In exceptional instances, the High Court has banned the media from publishing the new identities and whereabouts of people who became notorious after committing, or being associated with, horrific crimes. The aim was to help rehabilitate them after their release from prison, and protect them from public hostility and possible vengeance attacks.

Mary Bell – The first such case concerned Mary Bell. In 1968, when she was 11, she was convicted of the manslaughter of two young boys, and sentenced to detention for life. When released on licence in 1980, the Home Office gave her a new identity to help her rehabilitation.

Venables and Thompson – In 2001 Dame Elizabeth Butler-Sloss granted indefinite anonymity to Jon Venables and Robert Thompson. In 1993 when they were 11, they were convicted of the murder of two-year-old James Bulger in Merseyside.

Maxine Carr – Similar anonymity was given to Maxine Carr, former girlfriend of school caretaker Ian Huntley. In 2003 Huntley was convicted of murdering two schoolgirls in Soham, while Carr was convicted of conspiring to pervert the course of justice by giving him a false alibi. She was acquitted of knowing, when she gave it, that he had murdered the girls.

→ glossary

Kenneth Callaghan – In 2009 Mr Justice Stephen in the High Court in Belfast banned the media from publishing any photograph which would identify Kenneth Henry Callaghan, then 39, and any information identifying his address, place of work, or any location at which he stays or which he frequents. He had become eligible for parole after serving 21 years for raping and murdering a woman. The judge also banned publication of any photo which identified any serving prisoner being assessed for release at a unit run by the Northern Ireland Office unless the NIO was first given 48 hours' notice of the intention to publish.

 See www. mcnaes. com for more detail of these cases

▌ Ban on publishing 'indecent' matter

Section 1 of the Judicial Proceedings (Regulation of Reports) Act 1926 prohibits publication in any court report of any 'indecent matter or indecent medical, surgical or physiological details.... the publication of which is calculated to injure public morals.' It is unlikely that mainstream media organisations would be prosecuted today under this law. For more detail, see www.mcnaes.com ch. 11.

▌ Section 4(2) of the Contempt of Court Act 1981

A court has power, under section 4(2) of the Contempt of Court Act 1981, to order the postponement of publication of reports of a court case, or any part of a case, where doing so appears necessary to avoid a substantial risk of prejudice to the administration of justice in that case, or any other case which is pending or imminent.

This restriction is best understood in the context of contempt law, so is explained in ch. 18, see pp. 228–230, Section 4(2) orders. See also ch. 15, pp. 176–179, Section 4(2) orders, for grounds on which a section 4(2) order may be challenged.

▌ Postponed reporting of 'special measures' and section 36 orders

Courts can make special arrangements to help a 'vulnerable' or 'intimidated' witness give evidence. The law temporarily bans the media from reporting that a court made such an arrangement, and why, because in some cases a jury might be influenced in its verdict if it knew why such a measure had been taken – for example, knowing a witness was allegedly intimidated by people suspected of being the defendant's associates might prejudice jurors against the defendant.

Special measures

Section 19 of the Youth Justice and Criminal Evidence Act 1999 allows courts to make a 'special measures direction' in a case involving a 'vulnerable' or 'intimidated' witness. Such measures can include:

See also ch. 14, p. 153, One journalist can stay, on this exclusion power

- letting a witness give evidence behind a screen so he/she cannot see or be seen by the defendant;

- allowing a witness to give evidence by live video link or by a video recording;

- excluding the public and all but one reporter while a witness testifies;

- having lawyers and the judge remove wigs and gowns to make the court less strange to a child witness.

The definition of 'vulnerable' can include any witness (other than the defendant) any witness aged under 18, or one with mental disorder or physical disability. The definition of an 'intimidated' witness can include an alleged victim of a sex offence, a witness in which the alleged crime is said to involve a gun or knife, and a witness the quality of whose evidence is, in the court's view, likely to be diminished because of fear or distress connected with testifying.

A special measures direction is not automatic, so a witness aged under 18 or the alleged victim of a sexual offence will not necessarily be thought to need a special measure.

Restrictions on reporting special measures and section 36 orders

Section 47 of the 1999 Act contains automatic reporting restrictions which ban the media from publishing during a trial the fact that a section 19 (special measures) order has been made, varied or discharged; or anything from discussion or argument in court about such an order. There is also an automatic ban on the media reporting during a trial that the judge has made an order under section 36 of the 1999 Act to prohibit a defendant representing himself or herself from personally cross-examining a witness. Judges use this power in sexual offence cases to protect the alleged victims. Often the cross-examination will be done by a specially briefed lawyer, although such a defendant conducts the rest of the case him/herself. It is also illegal for the media to report during the trial any discussion in court on whether a section 36 order should be made or varied, or that it has been discharged.

These restrictions apply to proceedings in magistrates courts as well as to jury trials. Their purpose is to stop jurors (who would not be in court when an order was made or discussed) being prejudiced against the defendant or a witness by learning, before they reach all verdicts in the case, why the court considered making or made the order.

It will be safe to report, during a trial, anything the jury sees anyway – for example, that a witness is giving evidence by video, and anything the judge says to the jury to explain the effect of a section 19 or section 36 order – for example, why a lawyer steps in to act for a defendant who is otherwise representing himself.

But it would, for example, be illegal to publish the fact, beyond any explanation the judge gives to the jury, that most reporters were ordered to leave the courtroom. These reporting restrictions cease to have effect when the relevant case, against all defendants involved, is determined by acquittal, conviction, or otherwise, or is abandoned, or if the court lifts the restrictions during the trial itself.

Liability for breaching the section 47 reporting restrictions is the same as for breaching an order under section 46.

It is a defence for a person charged with breaching section 47 to prove he/she was not aware and neither suspected nor had reason to suspect that such matter was included in what was published. An adult witness subject to a special measures direction under section 19 of the Act may also have been granted lifetime anonymity, in respect of media reports of the trial, under section 46 – see p. 123, Lifetime anonymity for adult witnesses.

! Remember

Decisions on special measures and cross-examination issues are likely to be taken in pre-trial hearings, or when a jury is kept out of the courtroom, so other statute, or contempt law, will probably also be in effect to restrict contemporaneous reporting of what is decided about such measures and issues – see chs. 6, 7, 8 and 18.

▶ Postponing reports of 'derogatory' mitigation

Section 58 of the Criminal Procedure and Investigations Act 1996 allows a court to postpone a media report of a derogatory allegation which is made in a 'speech in mitigation' but has not been given in evidence, if it feels that someone's reputation may have been unfairly besmirched. This restriction is rarely used.

 Ch. 6, p. 60, Sentencing by magistrates, explains when a speech of mitigation is made. More details of this postponement power can be read in www.mcnaes.com ch. 11.

▶ Extradition hearings

Media coverage of hearings in the UK on whether a person should be extradited to another country are not affected by any automatic reporting restriction. These hearings usually take place in Westminster Magistrates Court.

➡ Recap of major points

- It is illegal to take photographs of, film, or sketch people in a court or its precincts.
- It is also illegal to make an audio-recording of a court hearing without permission.
- Journalists have a general permission to tweet, email or text from the courtroom when reporting, but other use of mobile phones there is punishable as a contempt of court.
- It is illegal to seek to discover, or to publish, what a jury discussed in deliberating on a verdict, or how an individual juror voted in the verdict.
- Publication of material identifying a juror may be held to be a contempt of court.
- In certain categories of case it is contempt of court to publish material heard by a court in private.

- An order under section 11 of the Contempt of Court Act 1981 prohibits publication of a name or information which has been withheld from the public proceedings of the court – for example, the name of a blackmail victim.

- Section 46 of the Youth Justice and Criminal Evidence Act 1999 allows a court to give an adult witness in a criminal case lifelong anonymity in media reports.

- In exceptional cases, the High Court has given convicted offenders indefinite anonymity, so the media cannot reveal their whereabouts after they are released.

((•)) Useful Websites

www.judiciary.gov.uk/Resources/JCO/Documents/Guidance/crown_court_reporting_restrictions_021009.pdf
> Guidance on reporting restrictions, issued by the Judicial College (formerly the Judicial Studies Board)

www.justice.gov.uk/guidance/courts-and-tribunals/courts/procedure-rules/criminal/rules-menu.htm

www.justice.gov.uk/courts/procedure-rules/criminal/rulesmenu
> Criminal Procedure Rules 2013 and Criminal Practice Directions

www.judiciary.gov.uk/publications-and-reports/guidance/2011/courtreporting
> Lord Chief Justice's guidance on use of live-text communications

www.supremecourt.gov.uk/docs/pr_1102.pdf
> Supreme Court ruling on use of live-text communications

12

Civil courts

Chapter summary

Civil law cases are a rich source of news. Civil courts deal with private disputes and wrongs. Some cases involve companies or individuals suing for damages. Some are brought against the state and public bodies, for example when a hospital trust is sued for medical negligence by a patient. Most civil litigation is dealt with in county courts. The High Court deals with complex or high-value claims. Few civil cases involve juries. Bankruptcies and company liquidations are civil law matters. Magistrates have some civil law functions.

▌ Types of civil litigation

Most civil litigation is concerned with:

- breaches of contract, including recovery of debt;
- torts – that is, civil wrongs for which monetary damages can be awarded. Torts include negligence, trespass and defamation;
- breach of statutory duty;
- proceedings by financial institutions against mortgagors;
- possession proceedings by landlords against tenants, usually for failure to pay rent;
- 'Chancery' matters, discussed later;
- insolvency, including bankruptcy and the winding up of companies;

- family law cases, including divorce; disputes between estranged parents over residence arrangements for and contact with their children;
- applications by local authorities to take into care children considered at significant risk of violence or neglect which are family law cases too.

ch. 13 explains family law

County courts

County courts deal with most civil cases. There are about 170 county courts in England and Wales – their areas are no longer the same as counties. Reforms in the Crime and Courts Act 2013 mean that from April 2014 they are due to be integrated administratively to be a single national county court.

The High Court

The High Court deals with the most complex or serious civil cases, and those of highest value. The administrative centre of the High Court is at the Royal Courts of Justice in London. Outside London it is divided administratively into 'district registries', which have offices and courtrooms, mostly in cities, and share buildings with the larger county court centres.

The High Court comprises three divisions:

- the *Queen's Bench Division* (QBD), within which there are also specialist courts: the Admiralty Court, the Commercial Court, and the Technology and Construction Court;
- the *Chancery Division*, which deals primarily with company work, trusts, estates, insolvency, and intellectual property. County courts also have limited jurisdiction in this area;
- the *Family Division*, see ch. 13.

High Court judges normally sit singly to try cases. The High Court is also an appeal court in civil law. In appeals and for some other functions two or three judges hear the case, and it is then known as the Divisional Court. A QBD court carrying out certain functions is referred to as the Administrative Court. It handles judicial review of the administrative actions of government departments and of other public authorities, and of the decisions of some tribunals.

ch. 17 explains tribunals.

 See ch. 8, p. 86, The High Court which explains its role as a criminal court.

Court of Appeal

The Court of Appeal, Civil Division, is for most cases the court of final appeal in civil law. It hears appeals from the county courts and the High Court. Some are

The hierarchy of the civil and criminal courts is shown in Figure 1 on p. 5.

heard by three judges, but usually by two. When there are three, each may give a judgment but the decision is that of the majority. In a limited number of cases, appeals can be made to the Supreme Court. The Court of Appeal's procedures in civil cases are similar to those in its criminal cases, see ch. 8, p. 84, The Court of Appeal.

▌ Types of judge in civil courts

Three types of judge preside in the county courts and High Court.

- *District judges* – appointed from among practising solicitors and barristers. Their casework includes many of the fast track and small claims cases, discussed later, family disputes and insolvency. They may be referred to in media reports as, for example, District Judge John Smith, but are increasingly being referred to as, in this instance, Judge John Smith. Deputy district judges are part-time appointments.

- *Circuit judges* – In the busier county courts there may be two or more senior judges known as circuit judges; in some regions they travel round a circuit of several towns or cities to hear cases, hence the origin of the title. Circuit judges may also sit in Crown courts in criminal cases. Recorders are barristers and solicitors who sit part-time with the jurisdiction of a circuit judge. Retired circuit judges who sit part-time are known as deputies. Circuit judges hear some fast track and most multi-track trials, discussed later, and may also hear appeals against the decisions of district judges. Appeals from a circuit judge lie direct to the Court of Appeal.

- *High Court judges* – these are more experienced, and so more senior, than circuit judges.

▌ Legal terms for parties in civil cases

ch. 13 explains divorce law

→ glossary

In many types of civil actions, the party, whether a person or organisation, who initiates the action – for example, claims damages for a tort – is called the claimant. He/she was formerly called the 'plaintiff'. The party against whom the action is taken is the defendant. In some actions, for example bankruptcy and divorce cases, the person initiating the claim is the petitioner and the other party the respondent. In civil courts it is also possible for a party to rely on or produce **hearsay** evidence.

▌ Media coverage of civil cases

ch. 21 explains privilege

The media have privilege against defamation actions for reports of what is said in open court. In civil cases, there is also privilege for media reports based on case documents made available by the court, discussed later in this chapter.

Settlements

A case in which one party sues another may well be settled before a full trial, usually by one side paying the other a sum of money. The settlement means there will be no court judgment on the facts.

- A media report of a settlement should not suggest that the side paying the money has admitted liability – that is, blame – for the wrong allegedly suffered by the other, unless liability *is* admitted. Wrongly suggesting that a settlement indicates an admission of liability could be defamatory.

A private health clinic might sue for libel if a report wrongly suggests it has admitted liability for medical complications after cosmetic surgery, even though it *has* paid out to settle the case.

Reporting restrictions and contempt law

Judges in civil cases have, if they decide to impose a reporting restriction, some of the same powers used by criminal courts, outlined in earlier chapters. A judge in a civil court can, under section 39 of the Children and Young Persons Act 1933, ban the media from identifying a juvenile concerned in the case as a claimant, witness or victim. Judges in civil cases – particularly in family law cases, as explained in ch. 13 – can also use their **inherent jurisdiction** to order that certain people, especially children, are protected by anonymity in reports.

chs. 9, 10 and 11 explain restrictions

→ glossary

The Contempt of Court Act 1981 applies to media reports of civil cases, in that once a case is active nothing must be published which creates a substantial risk of serious prejudice to it. But as juries are rarely used in civil cases, the Act is generally much less restrictive of pre-trial coverage than it is for criminal cases.

ch. 18 explains contempt law

The bans on taking photographs, sketching, filming or audio-recording in court apply to civil courts, as do other statutory and common law protections of the confidentiality of jury deliberations, and of jurors and witnesses generally.

'Payments into court'

The defendant in certain types of civil action, for example, a contract dispute or in a defamation case, may make a payment into court before the start of the trial. This is a formal offer of payment made in the hope that the claimant, who will be told of the sum offered – will accept it as a settlement. Journalists who discover that such an offer has been made should not report it unless and until it is referred to in open court at the end of the trial, if the case goes to trial. Disclosing that an offer has been made at any earlier stage will probably be regarded as contempt of court as it could prejudice the court's decision at trial. The judge in the case, or the jury, if there is one, is not told of the payment before reaching a judgment or verdict. If at the end of the trial the court finds for the claimant, but awards less than the amount in the defendant's pre-trial offer, the claimant will have to pay that part of his/her own costs which was incurred after the date the payment into court was made.

▌ Starting civil proceedings

Most civil actions in the High Court and county courts are begun by the court issuing a claim form – it used to be called a writ. The claim form, which is prepared
by the claimant, sets out the nature of the claim against the defendant, and the
→ glossary remedy or remedies sought. The remedy wanted might be an **injunction** – an order
compelling the other party to do something, or stop doing something – or an order
for the defendant to pay a debt, or to pay damages. The claim form is served on
the defendant.

The vast majority of money claims – for example, for debts – do not proceed
to trial as the defendant usually does not file any defence. The claimant simply
writes to the court asking for judgment to be entered 'in default'. If damages are
claimed there might be a hearing to decide the sum. Once a judgment is entered
in the court's records the claimant can enforce it, seeking the money from the
defendant. The court's enforcement procedures could include bailiffs taking the
defendant's goods to sell to pay the money owed.

▌ Case documents

Journalists have rights to see case documents in civil proceedings because otherwise it may be impossible to report a case meaningfully, in particular trials, in
that evidence is presented in the case documents and may not be aired orally in
court. These rights are explained in ch. 14. pp. 161–164, Access to documents in
civil cases.

▌ Trials in civil cases

A defendant who wants to dispute a civil claim must file a defence within 28 days
of service of the claim form. A civil trial is confined to issues which the parties set
→ glossary out in their **statements of case** (previously known as pleadings), which comprise
the 'particulars of claim', the defence to the claim, any counter-claims or reply to
the defence and 'further information documents'. As a general rule, the public,
including journalists, have the right to see these documents.

Each case is allocated to an appropriate 'track' based upon various factors
including the value of the claim and its complexity.

The three tracks are:

- small claims track;
- fast track;
- multi-track.

While the money value of the claim is not necessarily the most important factor,
the general approach is that a claim which exceeds £10,000 (£1,000 for personal

injury) but not £25,000 will be allocated to the fast track. Claims below these levels – but not possession claims – are allocated to the small claims track.

Cases allocated to the fast track are intended to be heard within 30 weeks and to be concluded in a hearing lasting no more than one day.

The multi-track covers a wide range of claims. Many are only a little more complicated than those on the fast track. Others will require more preparations, and the judge will normally arrange a case-management conference (which sometimes he/she conducts by telephone). Efforts are made to encourage a negotiated (or mediated) settlement.

Most civil cases are resolved without reaching trial.

Small claims hearings

Cases on the small claims track are decided at a county court by a district judge and are intended to be heard within three months. The procedure is designed to allow litigants to present their own case, without the need for a lawyer. Proceedings are informal. The judge must give reasons for the final decision. These cases are now heard in public, though this will often be in the district judge's 'chambers' (that is, a private room) with access allowed.

Full trials

In fast track and multi-track claims there is, if necessary, a formal trial. This is by a judge with no jury, unless the case is in the few categories where there may be a jury, see later in the chapter.

Most parties involved in trials at county courts and the High Court instruct solicitors to prepare their cases. Solicitors either brief counsel (that is, instruct a barrister to provide further advice and to argue the case in court) or represent the client themselves in a county court trial. Solicitor-advocates can appear for their clients in the higher courts without needing to brief a barrister. Claimants and defendants may represent themselves in court and can be assisted by some other lay person (often called a 'McKenzie friend').

see ch. 1, pp. 8–9, The legal profession

Full trial procedure

Unless there is a jury, civil trials are now largely based on documents, read beforehand by the judge, with each party disclosing its documents to the other side before the trial. The documents are those listed earlier, plus witness statements, and each party also supplies a 'skeleton argument' setting out its case. In the trial, witnesses may do no more than confirm that their written statement is true, although usually the judge allows some supplementary questions.

The claimant's witnesses testify first, and are cross-examined by the defendant or his/her advocate. If the defendant calls witnesses there will be the same process of (a short) examination and cross-examination. Expert evidence may be admitted only with the court's permission. Unless expert evidence is likely to be strongly contested the court appoints a single expert who is jointly instructed by the parties.

After all the evidence, the parties or their advocates make their submissions on the evidence and law. Finally, the judge gives his/her judgment and explains his/her reasons for it.

see p. 39, Standard of proof in criminal law

- In civil law, the standard of proof – the test used by a judge (or jury, see later) to decide which of any competing pieces of evidence will be accepted as the truth – is on 'the balance of probabilities'.

This is a lower standard of proof than that needed for criminal convictions.

In more difficult cases a judge may 'reserve' – delay – giving judgment, to have more time to weigh evidence and check the law. The judge may read the judgment out in court at a later date or have it printed and 'hand it down' at a subsequent hearing. Court reporters are usually provided with copies of printed judgments. After the judgment (or, in jury trials, the verdict, discussed later) there is usually an argument about costs, an issue on which the judge must make an appropriate order, as it is not simply a question of the loser paying the winner's costs, though the loser can expect to pay a major part of these.

> ch. 14, p. 163, Judgments and orders, explains what rights journalists have to see judgments.

Trials with juries

In a civil law, there is a right to apply for trial by a jury if the claim involves an:

- allegation of fraud; or
- false imprisonment; or
- malicious prosecution.

As ch. 19 explains, the Defamation Act 2013 removed the presumption of jury trial in defamation cases, but left the court with the discretion to call a jury.

The reasons why juries can be used in these categories of case have been described in a House of Lords judgment as 'historical rather than logical'. They include the notion that defamation cases and those involving fraud claims particularly concern allegations against someone's honour; that in a defamation case, a jury may understand nuances in current meanings of words which a judge – who may be remote from everyday 'street language' – may not; and that false imprisonment or malicious prosecution cases usually involve allegations against an arm of the state such as the police, and so a jury is needed to give the public confidence that the case has been independently decided as a judge alone might be seen as another arm of the state.

A judge has discretion to allow jury trial in other types of civil case, but such instances are exceptional.

If there is a jury trial, the judge will sum up the case after each side has made final submissions. In some cases the judge may ask the jury for a general verdict, but in more complicated cases the judge will set out a series of questions for jurors to answer in the verdict. Juries decide the level of damages if the verdict is for the claimant. Juries in civil cases are selected at random from the electoral role, as are juries in criminal trials. A county court jury consists of eight people and a High Court jury of 12.

▶ Civil functions of magistrates

Magistrates have various civil powers. The role of magistrates courts in family law cases – for example care proceedings – is outlined in ch. 13. Magistrates also hear appeals from decisions of local authority committees on licensing public houses, hotels, off-licences and betting shops.

▶ Bankruptcy

The civil courts deal with bankruptcy cases. Some yield news stories of wild extravagance at the expense of creditors or the Inland Revenue. In law the term bankruptcy only applies to people. Companies go into liquidation, see below.

 www.mcnaes.com ch. 12 explains bankruptcy procedures, what being bankrupt means, the libel danger in wrongly stating someone is bankrupt and how bankruptcies are announced. It also explains that court documents in a bankruptcy case can be inspected by a journalist.

▶ Company liquidation

Care should be taken, when reporting that a limited company has gone into liquidation, to make the circumstances clear. There are different types of liquidation. Misuse of terms could create a libel problem.

 www.mcnaes.com ch. 12 explains liquidation terms.

➡ Recap of major points

- County courts handle most civil litigation. The High Court deals with the more serious or high-value claims.

- Civil case hearings are mainly conducted by reference to documents. A journalist has rights to see the key documents of cases heard in public.

- Civil courts can impose reporting restrictions. Contempt law applies to media coverage reports of their cases, but is less restrictive if no jury is involved.

- Magistrates handle some types of civil case.

- The county courts deal with bankruptcy cases.

- Journalists need to take care before suggesting a person is bankrupt or a company is insolvent, because this could be defamatory if untrue.

((•)) Useful Websites

www.judiciary.gov.uk/you-and-the-judiciary/going-to-court/county-court/county-court
   Judiciary webpage about the county courts

www.adviceguide.org.uk/england/law_e/law_legal_system_e/law_taking_legal_action_e/small_claims.htm
   Citizens' Advice guide to small claims

www.judiciary.gov.uk/you-and-the-judiciary/going-to-court/high-court
   Judiciary webpage about the High Court

www.insolvency.gov.uk/
   Insolvency Service website – explains bankrupty and compulsory liquidation

www.insolvencydirect.bis.gov.uk/bankruptcy/bankruptcysearch.htm
   Individual Insolvency Register – shows who is currently bankrupt

Family courts

Chapter summary

Family law, a branch of civil law, includes many cases involving disputes between estranged parents after marital breakdown, for example, about contact with a child, and cases brought by local authorities seeking to protect children. A court can remove a child from his/her parents because of suspected abuse or neglect. Reporting restrictions and contempt of court law severely limit what the media can publish about most family cases, to protect those involved, particularly children, who in most instances must not be identified. This chapter examines the main restrictions. But because of the complexity of court rules and the restrictions, a fuller version of this chapter is provided in www.mcnaes.com ch. 13.

▶ Introduction

The term 'family cases' covers a range of matters in civil law. They have been dealt with by magistrates courts, county courts, or the High Court Family Division, with cases transferred between these courts. A new Family Court, due to begin operating in 2014, will amalgamate this system into one, unified court. But it will continue to operate from existing courthouses, with a role for magistrates and with judges continuing to preside in the most complex cases.

see ch. 12 for over-view of civil court system

▶ Types of case in family courts

Two major categories in family court proceedings are 'private' and 'public' law cases.

Private law cases include:

- Matrimonial cases – proceedings for divorce, judicial separation, or nullity, or to end a civil partnership.

- Enforcement of financial arrangements between estranged couples.

- Other disputes between estranged parents about their children, such as where they live, and the absent parent's rights to contact, leading to the courts making residence and contact orders under the Children Act 1989.

- Applications for court orders to enforce the return of a child abducted, for example, by one parent in defiance of the other's rights.

- Paternity disputes.

- Applications in domestic violence cases for 'non-molestation' orders.

- Applications to protect a person from a 'forced marriage'.

'Public law' cases include:

- Applications, mainly by local authorities, for court orders allowing social workers to intervene to protect a child they suspect is being neglected or abused in his/her home. The orders are made under the Children Act 1989. The courts can also make emergency protection orders allowing police or social workers to remove a child if there is immediate concern for his/her safety.

- Adoption cases – a court can sanction adoptions of children who have been removed from their birth parents by a local authority in public law cases. Other adoptions may formalise existing relationships, and therefore are private law cases.

▶ Reporting family law cases

see www.
mcnaes.
com ch
13 for the
rules

Rules – currently the Family Procedure Rules 2010 ((SI 2010/2955) – bar the public from family cases involving children but allow journalists to attend these and most types of family case. But reporting family law cases is fraught with difficulties because of anonymity provisions under the Children Act 1989, the contempt of court provisions in section 12 of the Administration of Justice Act 1960 and other extremely tight restrictions. A result is that much of what reporting there is consists of anonymised articles involving, for example, parents' claims that they have suffered a miscarriage of justice at the hands of social workers, medical experts or the courts.

Disputes between parents over where a child will live are almost invariably shrouded in anonymity almost as soon as they arise, because of the 1989 Act's restrictions.

This complex net of restrictions has led to criticism that family courts operate in 'secret'.

Reforms

In 2013 Sir James Munby became President of the Family Division. He has pledged to make family courts more transparent by changes to 'improve access to and reporting of' their cases, while preserving the privacy of families involved. He said that court rules would change. In January 2014 he issued guidance to judges to increase the number of judgments published by family courts

The government too is planning change, in that the Crime and Courts Act 2013 contains powers, not in force by late 2013, to repeal reporting restrictions in the Magistrates' Courts Act 1980. The repeal will be part of the measures to harmonise law for the new unified Family Court, and – as this chapter explains – will not in itself be any improvement for the media in what can be reported.

see Useful Websites at the end of this chapter for this guidance

! Remember

Ethically journalists should not normally interview children aged under 16 on matters concerning their welfare without the consent of a parent or responsible adult. See ch. 27, pp. 332–334, Protecting children's privacy and welfare.

▌ Anonymity under the Children Act 1989

Section 97 of the Children Act 1989 restricts media coverage of family law cases by making it an offence to publish:

- a name or other material intended or likely to identify a child – someone under the age of 18 – who is involved in any current case in a magistrates court, a county court or the High Court in which any power under the Act has or may be exercised with respect to that or any other child;
- an address, as being that of a child involved in such an ongoing case;
- detail identifying the child's school.

Section 97 anonymity automatically applies to children in unresolved residence and contact disputes between parents, and those who are the subject of intervention by social workers. It applies to any report of what is said in court or a written judgment, as well as to any wider feature about a child who is involved in an ongoing case. Clearly, it also means the child's family cannot be identified. Avoid jigsaw identification.

see ch. 9, pp. 97–99, Jigsaw identification

- Breaching section 97 by publishing material identifying a child covered is punishable by a fine of up to £2,500. It is a defence for an accused person to prove that he/she did not know, and had no reason to suspect, that the published material was intended or likely to identify the child.

Adoptions

Section 97 also bans reports of adoption proceedings – journalists cannot attend them – from identifying the child concerned while he/she is under the age of 18.

When does anonymity under the Children Act 1989 cease?

- Section 97 (4) of the Children Act 1989 says that, if a child's welfare requires it, a court may waive to any specified extent the anonymity otherwise automatically bestowed on a child. The Lord Chancellor may also do so, with the Lord Chief Justice's agreement.

Judges have waived the anonymity to allow the media reports to identify and show pictures of children abducted by a parent or hidden from social workers, in the hope – usually borne out – that the public will help find them.

Anonymity ends when the case concludes

The Court of Appeal has ruled that section 97 anonymity only applies while Children Act proceedings are going on, and ends with the case (*Clayton v Clayton* [2006] EWCA Civ 878). The then President of the Family Division said that if a court felt that anonymity should continue beyond a case's conclusion to protect a child's welfare or privacy it should issue an **injunction** to continue it. The High Court or a county court can order that the anonymity continue until the child is 18.

 → glossary

! Remember

A journalist who wants to identify a child as having been involved in a case under the 1989 Act – for example in a story about a mother's battle with social workers, or a parent's account of the break-up of a marriage – should be sure that the proceedings have ended and that no order has been made to continue a child's anonymity.

Wards of court

Children who have been made wards of court by the High Court, or who are the subject of proceedings to make them wards, are automatically protected by section 97 anonymity while the case is ongoing (*Kelly v British Broadcasting Corporation* [2001] Fam 59).

👁 Case study

In 2001 Bobby Kelly, aged 16, ran away from home and joined the 'Jesus Christians' cult. His family made him a ward of court. A BBC reporter traced and interviewed him. Mr Justice Munby ruled in the High Court that the media did not require the court's permission to interview a ward of court or to publish the interview. But he warned that the media should observe reporting restrictions (*Kelly v British Broadcasting Corporation*). Anonymity might apply, and a published interview should not breach contempt law in respect of matter heard by a court in private (as this chapter explains). The BBC was allowed to identify Bobby. He was homesick but said 'you have to give everything up to work for God.'

see Useful Websites at the end of this chapter for the Bobby Kelly story

▶ Anonymised judgments

In county courts and the High Court the texts of family case judgments, if published, are usually anonymised to prevent a child or adult being identified. It is an offence to report an anonymised judgment in a way which identifies any protected person.

▶ Contempt danger in reporting on private hearings

Section 12 of the Administration of Justice Act 1960 makes it a contempt of court to publish, without a court's permission, a report of a private hearing if the case falls into certain categories, including those which:

- relate to the exercise of the inherent jurisdiction of the High Court with respect to children;
- are under the Children Act 1989 or the Adoption and Children Act 2002 or which otherwise relate wholly or mainly to the maintenance or upbringing of a child;
- are under the Mental Capacity Act 2005, or any provision of the Mental Health Act 1983 authorising an application or reference to be made to the First-Tier Tribunal, the Mental Health Review Tribunal for Wales or to a county court;
- are of any kind where the court expressly bans publication of all or specified information relating to the private hearing.

ch. 17 explains the tribunal system

The section 12 prohibition applies broadly across family cases heard in private. The definition of 'private' includes some cases which journalists may attend. It could also be a contempt to publish information from a document prepared for use in a private hearing (*Re F (A Minor) (Publication of Information)* [1977] Fam 58; [1977] 1 All ER 114). This would include a witness statement in a dispute between parents over contact arrangements regarding children, or a social worker's report for a court about a child, irrespective of whether the information published was anonymised.

see p. 144, The definition of 'private'

It might also be a contempt to publish any of the judgment, unless the judge authorises publication.

- But section 12 does allow publication of any order a court makes in private proceedings, unless the court specifically bans publication of the order.

Also, section 12 does not stop the media making basic reference to a case being heard in private.

> For more detail on section 12 of the 1960 Act, see ch. 11, pp. 120–122, Ban on reporting a court's private hearing.

The definition of 'private'

Section 12 reporting restrictions apply if a family case is heard in private. The position by late 2013 remained that if a county court or High Court excludes the public from a family case, it is classed as private, even if journalists attend. The section 12 restrictions apply unless the judge lifts them. If they are not lifted, a journalist can only report limited detail about the hearing.

If magistrates exclude the public from a family case, journalists in late 2013 still had an automatic right to attend it under section 69 of the Magistrates Courts' Act 1980, under which a hearing is not classed as private unless journalists too are also excluded by specific order of the court. But Part 27.11 of the Family Procedure Rules 2010 classes such hearings at magistrates courts as private, even if journalists attend. The 2010 rules mean that it is not clear if section 12 of the 1960 Act applies to limit reports of family proceedings in magistrates courts, in addition to the restrictions in the 1980 Act's section 71 which are discussed later in this chapter. In his guidance, the President said: 'Until this issue has been definitively resolved, it would be prudent for everyone to proceed on the basis that section 12 continues to apply even where representatives of the media are present.'

 see Useful Websites, at the end of this chapter for this guidance

When sections 69 and 71 of the 1980 Act are repealed as part of reforms to create the new, unified Family Court, the only access right for the media in any family case involving children will be – unless subject to any other change – in the 2010 rules. This will mean that the reporting restrictions in section 12 of the 1960 Act will definitely apply to such cases in which magistrates preside, as they will in all tiers of the Family Court, unless the court lifts them or new rules are introduced. Check www.mcnaes.com for updates.

Disclosure Restrictions

Part 12.73 of the Family Procedure Rules, reflecting section 12 of the 1960 Act, says no information 'relating to' court proceedings concerning children and held in private, whether or not the information is in documents filed with the court, may be communicated to the public, or to anyone other than lawyers, officials or other specified categories of people, without the court's permission. There is a similar ban for adoption cases. These rules therefore implicitly forbid, for example, a parent of a child taken into local authority care, or a lawyer, giving a journalist information about the proceedings (other than the few details permitted by section 12 of the 1960 Act), unless the court authorises it. The ban applies whether or not journalists attend the private hearing.

 See also www.mcnaes.com ch. 13 for courts' powers to authorise journalists to see case documents: 'Can journalists see documents? See too this book's Late News item on case documents.

The ban does not stop a parent telling in general terms how they feel about the court case or of the wider experience of, for example, a child being removed from them – though any anonymity applying under the Children Act 1989 must be preserved in any report.

▶ Other reporting restrictions in family cases

The reporting restrictions of the Children Act 1989 and those in Administration of Justice Act 1960 are referred to earlier. Other restrictions can apply in family cases, depending on the type of case

Section 71 of the Magistrates' Courts Act 1980 restricts what may be published from evidence given in 'family proceedings' in a magistrates court – and the 1989 Act anonymity restrictions could also apply to the same hearings if the case concerns that Act.

Automatic reporting restrictions under section 2 of the Domestic and Appellate Proceedings (Restriction of Publicity) Act 1968 cover some types of family case – for example, about neglect to pay maintenance, or for declarations about parentage, legitimacy or marital status – in any court which hears such a case or an appeal, including the magistrates courts, county courts and High Court.

Divorce cases, referred to later in this chapter, have their own reporting restrictions.

! Remember

A full explanation of reporting restrictions and journalists' rights to attend family cases is provided in mcnaes.com ch. 13. Also, the High Court Family Division has published a detailed guide to reporting family proceedings – see Useful Websites at the end of this chapter.

Anti-publicity injunctions in family cases

The High Court has inherent jurisdiction to order that a person must be anonymous in published reports of its proceedings and judgments. It is a contempt to breach such an injunction. Injunctions can be issued to protect children and men-tally or physically incapacitated adults in family cases, and in other types of case in which the court is ruling on their medical treatment, or whether they should be kept alive.

 See www.mcnaes.com ch. 13 for the procedure to alert the media to applications for family law injunc-tions, and for instances of them restricting media coverage of a criminal trial and an inquest.

News-gathering activity can be banned

ch. 10 explains anonymity for victims of sexual offences

An injunction can forbid news-gathering or other activity which is deemed likely to jeopardise a person's welfare or privacy, or could lead to the subjects feeling harassed. Mr Justice McKinnon made such an order in 2008 banning the media from approaching two women whose father was jailed for life at Sheffield Crown court after repeatedly raping them, as children and adults, fathering children. Nobody involved was named in reports of the father's trial.

But it was feared that news-gathering activities could lead to their being identi-fied in local communities.

Coverage of divorce, nullity, judicial separation and civil partnership cases

Divorce, judicial separation, or nullity cases, or proceedings to end a civil part-nership, have usually been dealt with by county courts, although some have been transferred to the High Court.

Most divorce proceedings are uncontested. Lists of petitioners granted a decree nisi – the first stage of a divorce – are read out in open court. The decree ends the marriage when it is made absolute, usually after six weeks. In a contested case, the husband, wife and possibly other witnesses may give evidence in court.

Reporting restrictions, explained in www.mcnaes.com ch. 13, apply to divorce, judicial separation and nullity cases, and proceedings to end a civil partnership – whether the report is of a hearing in a contested case or of case documents open to inspection. Rules on when such cases can be heard in private are also explained in www.mcnaes.com ch. 13. In matrimonial cases there may be hearings on financial orders (previously known as 'ancillary relief') – that is, the division of property and other financial arrangements between estranged couples.

Inspection of evidence and copy of decree

Part 7.20 of the Family Procedure Rules 2010 permits anyone, in a period of 14 days after the decree nisi is made, to inspect and make copies of evidence filed with the application for the divorce if it is not contested. Part 7.36 allows anyone to obtain from the court a copy of the decree absolute.

see this book's Late News on decrees

▌ The Court of Protection

The Court of Protection is a specialist court established by the Mental Capacity Act 2005 to make decisions for people who lack the mental capability to decide for themselves – for example on financial or welfare matters or medical treatment. It usually sits in private and has its own procedural rules. Its judgments are usually anonymised. For more detail, see www.mcnaes.com ch. 13.

➡ Recap of major points

- Family courts are difficult to report, because reporting restrictions apply in many cases.
- A child involved in ongoing proceedings under the Children Act 1989 should not be identified in media reports of such cases, unless the court authorises it.
- The High Court has had for decades wide-ranging powers to protect the welfare of children and others, including anonymity orders, and the new, unified Family Court will retain these powers.

((•)) Useful Websites

www.judiciary.gov.uk/Resources/JCO/Documents/Guidance/family-courts-media-july2011.pdf
    An official guide for journalists, judges and practitioners explaining the law on reporting family courts, endorsed by the President of the Family Division, the Society of Editors and the Judicial College

http://news.bbc.co.uk/1/hi/uk/852109.stm

and http://news.bbc.co.uk/1/hi/uk/853876.stm
    BBC reports on Bobby Kelly, when he was a ward of court

www.judiciary.gov.uk/Resources/JCO/Documents/Guidance/transparency-in-the-family-courts-jan2014.pdf
    The President's 2014 guidance to family courts

14

Open justice and access to court information

Chapter summary

Open justice is vital to a democracy. If justice is done in secret the public can have no confidence in it, because secrecy may hide injustice. Journalists are the public's eyes and ears in courtrooms, so need to know their rights of admission to courts. This chapter explains them, and refers to case law and statute which journalists can cite to oppose attempts to exclude them from courts. But the law does allow courts to sit in private on occasion. This chapter also explains the rights journalists have to see court documents needed to report civil and criminal cases. Other chapters refer to admission rights for particular types of court – youth courts in ch. 9, family courts in ch. 13, coroners courts in ch. 16, and employment tribunals in ch. 17.

▶ Open courts – a fundamental rule in common law

In 1913, the House of Lords in *Scott v Scott* [1913] AC 417 affirmed the common law rule that normally courts must administer justice in public. One law lord, Lord Atkinson, said:

> The hearing of a case in public may be, and often is, no doubt, painful, humiliating, or deterrent both to parties and witnesses, and in many cases, especially those of a criminal nature, the details may be so indecent as to tend to injure public morals, but all this is tolerated and endured, because it is felt that in public trial is to be found, on the whole, the best security for the pure, impartial, and efficient administration of justice, the best means for winning for it public confidence and respect.

www.mcnaes.com ch. 14 gives more detail of *Scott v Scott*.

A major benefit of open justice is that a witness who testifies in public is less likely to lie. A public lie is more likely to be exposed than one told behind closed doors. Other benefits of open justice were categorised by Lord Woolf in the Court of Appeal judgment in *R v Legal Aid Board ex p Kaim Todner* [1998] 3 All ER 541:

> It is necessary because the public nature of proceedings deters inappropriate behaviour on the part of the court. It also maintains the public's confidence in the administration of justice. It enables the public to know that justice is being administered impartially. It can result in evidence becoming available which would not become available if the proceedings were conducted behind closed doors or with one or more of the parties' or witnesses' identity concealed. It makes uninformed and inaccurate comment about the proceedings less likely.

As Lord Woolf noted, any reporting restriction is a departure from the open justice principle, and so must have an overriding justification. Chapter 15 provides specific grounds on which journalists can challenge reporting restrictions or decisions to exclude them from hearings. The foundation of such challenges is that general benefits always flow to society from open justice.

In private, in chambers and in camera

- The term **in chambers** refers to occasions when a hearing, usually a preliminary one in a case, is held in the judge's chambers or another room rather than a formal courtroom. →glossary

- The term **in camera** is used when the public and media are excluded from all or part of the main hearing in a case – such as a criminal trial. The hearing is effectively being held in secret. →glossary

- The term **in private** is used to cover both the above terms. But a hearing may be held in chambers for administrative convenience, rather than because of a decision or rule that it should be private – see later in the chapter. →glossary

The limited scope of common law exceptions to open justice

It is generally acknowledged that excluding the press and public from a court case is only justified in common law in three sets of circumstances:

- when their presence would frustrate the process of justice – *for example, when a woman or child cannot be persuaded to give evidence of intimate sexual matters in the presence of many strangers;*

- when unchecked publicity would defeat the whole object of the proceedings, *for example:*
  - *when a case concerns ownership of a trade secret, and publicity would reveal the secret to commercial rivals, or*
  - *when a case concerns a matter relating to national security which could be damaged by publicity, or*
  - *when the court is considering granting an order to one party that another party must produce evidence which it might destroy, before the order is served on it, if it were to be tipped off by reports of an open court hearing that such an order is being sought;*

ch. 13 explains family law

- when the court is exercising a parental role to protect the interests of vulnerable people, mainly:
  - *children, for example, in family law or care cases, or*
  - *people with mental incapacity or mental illness;*

and unchecked publicity could harm the welfare of those involved.

Statutes and procedural rules allow courts to exclude the public and, in some instances, journalists, in specified circumstances, as this chapter explains later. These statutory powers cover, to an extent, the same kinds of occasion for which common law justifies exclusion. Common law can be used if no statutory power covers the occasion, but does not give courts a general licence to sit in private.

Lord Diplock, emphasising that common law rarely justified departing from the open justice principle, said in a 1979 House of Lords judgment that the rule should only be set aside when:

www. mcnaes. com ch. 14 provides more detail of this case

> the nature or circumstances of the particular proceeding are such that the application of the general rule in its entirety would frustrate or render impracticable the administration of justice or would damage some other public interest for whose protection Parliament has made some statutory derogation from the rule' (*Attorney General v Leveller Magazine Ltd* [1979] AC 440 at 449, 450).

▶ Contempt and libel issues in reports of private hearings

If a case being heard in private falls into certain categories – for example, it is about national security or the upbringing of children – it is a contempt for anyone, including a journalist, who discovers what has been said in its private hearing to publish such information, or material from documents prepared for use in the case – see the explanation of the Administration of Justice Act 1960 in ch. 11, pp. 120–122, Ban on reporting a court's private hearing.

Publishing information from a private hearing in any court case:

- is not protected by section 4 of the Contempt of Court Act 1981 if the publication creates a substantial risk of serious prejudice or impediment to an 'active' case – see ch. 18, p. 227, Court reporting – the section 4 defence;

- is not protected by privilege if someone defamed by it sues for libel – see ch. 21, pp. 264–268, Privilege.

▌ The media's role

A journalist's vital role in reporting court cases as trustee for the wider public has been recognised in many judgments. In *R v Felixstowe Justices ex p Leigh* [1987] QB 582; [1987] 1 All ER 551, Lord Justice Watkins said:

> " The role of the journalist and his importance for the public interest in the administration of justice has been commented upon on many occasions. No-one nowadays surely can doubt that his presence in court for the purpose of reporting proceedings conducted therein is indispensable. Without him, how is the public to be informed of how justice is being administered in our courts? "

Other cases which can be cited

Scott v Scott, Attorney General v Leveller Magazine Ltd and other cases referred to in this chapter can be cited by a journalist when challenging exclusion from a court hearing.

for challenge procedure, see ch. 15

A journalist can also direct the court to guidance issued by the Judicial College: 'Reporting Restrictions in the Criminal Courts' – see Useful Websites at the end of the chapter. This states: 'The test is one of necessity. The fact, for example, that hearing evidence in open court will cause embarrassment to witnesses does not meet the test for necessity.' It also reminds courts that imposing a reporting restriction to stop some detail being published might avoid the need for exclusion.

A defendant's embarrassment is insufficient reason to exclude the media

A High Court judge criticised Malvern magistrates' decision to sit in camera to hear mitigation for a woman who admitted driving with excess alcohol. Her solicitor had asked the court to sit in private because she would refer to embarrassing details of her pending divorce which – the court was told – had made her suicidal and drink to excess. He said her emotional state meant she could not speak about this in open court. The High Court agreed that magistrates did have power to sit in camera but Lord Justice Watkins said that in this case their reason for doing so was 'wholly unsustainable and out of accord with [the open justice] principle' (*R v Malvern Justices, ex p Evans* [1988] QB 540; [1988] 1 All ER 371, QBD).

Journalists can sometimes stay when the public is excluded

If the public are lawfully excluded, it does not follow that journalists must necessarily go too.

Rowdy supporters of a defendant may be banned or ejected from a court's public gallery. But journalists are not going to be rowdy, so should be let into the court. In 1989 a Court of Appeal judgment acknowledged that there might be cases during which the press should not be excluded with the other members of the public (*R v Crook (Tim)* (1989) 139 NLJ 1633 CA).

The public and press should not be excluded for longer than necessary

If a court rules that a journalist should be excluded he/she should point out that the Court of Appeal said in 1989 that a judge should be alive to the importance of adjourning into open court as soon as exclusion of the public was not plainly necessary (*Re Crook (Tim)* (1991) 93 Cr App R 17, CA).

Criminal courts cannot sit in private to protect a defendant's business interests

The risk that publicity might severely damage a defendant's business does not justify a criminal court sitting in private (*R v Dover Justices, ex p Dover District Council and Wells* (1991) 156 JP 433).

▌ Articles 6 and 10

Article 6 of the European Convention on Human Rights says everyone is entitled to a fair and public hearing. The rights which Article 6 primarily protects are those of parties in civil litigation and defendants in criminal cases rather than those of the media or wider public. A journalist challenging exclusion from a court should cite Article 10, which protects the right to freedom of expression and to impart information.

 Ch. 1 explains the Convention's effect, and Articles 6 and 10 are set out in Appendix 1, pp. 441–442.

▌ Statute law on open and private hearings

Magistrates' cases – Section 121 of the Magistrates' Courts Act 1980 says magistrates must sit in open court when trying a case or considering jailing someone, or hearing a civil law complaint, unless another statute permits them to sit in private.

Indecent evidence – Section 37 of the Children and Young Persons Act 1933 gives any court the power to exclude the public – but not journalists – when a witness aged under 18 is giving evidence in a case involving indecency.

Sexual history – Section 43 of the Youth Justice and Criminal Evidence Act 1999 requires a court hearing an application to introduce evidence or questions about a complainant's sexual history, for example in a rape case, to sit in private. This reflects the sensitivity of someone who may have suffered rape being questioned about her/his sex life. The court must give its decision on whether such evidence will be allowed, and its reasons, in open court.

One journalist can stay – Section 25 of the 1999 Act allows a court to make a 'special measures direction' to exclude the public and some journalists when, for example, a witness is due to testify in a sexual offence case or there are reasonable grounds for believing that someone other than the defendant wants to intimidate the witness. But it says one journalist must be allowed to stay in court.

 Ch. 11, pp. 126–127, Postponed reporting of 'special measures' and section 36 orders, explains special measures directions.

The 1999 Act says that even if, under this section, some journalists and the public are excluded from a courtroom, the proceedings are still legally deemed to be being held in public 'for the purposes of any privilege or exemption from liability available in respect of fair, accurate and contemporaneous reports'. This is a reference to contempt and libel law, explained in chs 18 and 21.

Sentence review for informants – Section 75 of the Serious Organised Crime and Police Act 2005 says a Crown court may exclude the public and press when reviewing a sentence previously imposed on a defendant who pleaded guilty, and who has given or offered assistance – for example, information – about a crime to a prosecuting or investigating agency such as the police. But the public and press can only be excluded if the judge considers this is in the interests of justice and necessary to protect someone's safety, for example because the informant would be at risk of retaliation if the fact that he/she gave such assistance was publicised. In the review, the original sentence could be reduced as a reward for the assistance offered. If the original sentence was lenient because the defendant had already offered such assistance, the review can increase it if he/she knowingly failed to provide it. If a defendant has failed to honour a pledge of assistance, a journalist has strong grounds for arguing that a lenient sentence should be reviewed in open court as the public should be confident that the defendant received an appropriate sentence. The Act allows the court to ban publication of anything about the proceedings 'as it thinks appropriate'.

Official secrets trials – The public and media may be excluded from secret trials, see ch. 33, p. 399.

Closed material procedure – Controversial provisions for 'closed material procedure' were enacted in Part 2 of Justice and Security Act 2013 to allow courts considering civil claims to hear evidence in private, without the claimant having access to it, if the court accepts that disclosing the evidence to the public and claimant would damage national security. The government said this would allow it to contest compensation claims from terror suspects without the security services having to reveal sensitive evidence in open court.

Detail about Part 2 of the Justice and Security Act 2013, and events which led to this legislation being created, can be read on www.mcnaes.com ch. 14.

Procedural rules and open justice

Courts have procedural rules which add detail to statute. The wording of some rules gives courts wide discretion to sit in private. A journalist facing exclusion because of a procedural rule should argue that the court's interpretation of it must fully recognise the common law protection of open justice, and Article 10, and cite *Scott v Scott*, in which Lord Shaw stressed that judges must be vigilant to ensure that the open justice principle is not usurped.

- Lord Shaw said: 'There is no greater danger of usurpation than that which proceeds little by little, under cover of rules of procedure, and at the instance of judges themselves.'

Criminal cases: rules on open and private hearings

Procedure for criminal cases in magistrates courts, Crown courts and the Court of Appeal (Criminal Division) is governed by the Criminal Procedure Rules (SI 2013/1554) and the Criminal Practice Directions.

See Useful Websites at the end of this chapter for these Rules and the Directions.

Rule 16.2 says that a court must have regard to the importance of dealing with criminal cases in public and of allowing them to be reported. Rule 37.2 states specifically that the general rule is that a trial or sentencing in a magistrates court must be in public.

Rule 16.6, for magistrates and Crown courts, says that if the prosecution or defence want to argue that a trial or part of it should be heard in private (that is, in the limited circumstances when a court has power to waive the open justice rule) they must apply in writing to the court not less than five business days before the trial is due to begin – though rule 16(3) allows a court to hear an application sent later than this – and that the court officer must at once display notice of the application prominently in the courtroom's vicinity, and give the media notice of it. The application itself shall be heard in private, unless the court orders otherwise, and if in a Crown court shall be heard after the **arraignment** but before the jury is sworn. The rule adds that if a court orders that a trial will be heard wholly or partly in private it must not begin until the day after the application was granted, giving the media some time to challenge the order.

→glossary

ch. 8 explains Crown courts

Ch. 15 explains how a journalist can in any court oppose or challenge an access restriction.

The Criminal Procedure Rules allow courts to conduct some procedures in private – for example, an application to a Crown court judge for bail after magistrates have refused it. But the presumption in law is that a journalist can be allowed into a bail hearing – see www.mcnaes.com ch. 14.

Civil cases: rules on open and private hearings

The Civil Procedure Rules (CPR) cover civil proceedings in the Queen's Bench and Chancery divisions of the High Court and the county courts.

Part 39(2) of the CPR says that the general rule is that a hearing is to be in public but that a hearing, or part of it, may be in private if:

- publicity would defeat the object of the hearing;

- it involves matters relating to national security;

- it involves confidential information (including information relating to personal financial matters) and publicity would damage that confidentiality;

- it is necessary to protect the interests of any child or protected party;

- it is an application **without notice** – *that is, one party in the case is not yet* →glossary
  aware of the proceedings – and it would be unjust to any respondent for there to be a public hearing;

- it involves uncontentious matters arising in the administration of trusts or of a deceased's estate;

- the court considers a private hearing necessary in the interests of justice.

The Practice Direction which supplements this rule lists types of case which shall, 'in the first instance', be listed as private. These include a claim by a mortgagee for possession of land; landlords' applications for possession of residential property because rent is allegedly owed; and proceedings brought under the Consumer Credit Act 1974 and the Protection from Harassment Act 1997 (the latter would include some domestic violence cases).

! Remember

A journalist can try to persuade the judge that cases in these categories should be heard in public. The Practice Direction states that the judge should have regard to 'any representations' made.

The CPR also provide for other types of hearing to be held in private. A journalist excluded from a civil court should ask which rule applies.

www.mcnaes.com ch. 14 provides summaries of cases when media organisations, by referring to Part 39(2) of the Civil Procedure Rules, have successfully argued for their rights to attend the hearings of civil cases, even when a party asserted this would expose 'confidential' information. See Useful Websites at the end of this chapter for these rules. For general information on civil courts, see ch. 12. Other rules apply to the family courts – see ch. 13.

▌ Hearings in chambers are not always private

ch. 11, pp. 120–122, Ban on reporting a court's private hearing, explains the 1960 Act

A hearing may be in chambers – for example, a judge's office – rather than in public in a courtroom, merely because of routine, administrative convenience. Lord Woolf (later Lord Chief Justice) said in the Court of Appeal in 1998 that members of the public and journalists who asked should be given permission to attend a hearing in chambers if this was practical and the case was not in a category listed in section 12 of the Administration of Justice Act 1960. (*Hodgson v Imperial Tobacco* [1998] 2 All ER 673; [1998] 1 WLR 1056).

▌ What information and help must criminal courts provide?

Many court clerks are helpful in providing basic detail about a case to reporters in court, such as how to spell the defendant's name. But since 2011 the Criminal Procedure Rules have set out when court officers must provide certain information on request.

Rule 5.8

Rule 5.8 gives members of the public, including reporters – whether in the courtroom or phoning – the right to obtain from a criminal court certain details of a case. This applies if the 'court officer' has the details, if the case is ongoing or the verdict in the case was not more than six months ago, and if no reporting restriction prohibits the details being supplied. The 'court officer' must in these circumstances supply the details verbally or by other arrangements prescribed by the Lord Chancellor

The details are: the date of any public hearing in the case, unless any party has yet to be notified of that date; each alleged offence and any plea entered; the court's decision at any public hearing, including any decision about bail, or the sending of the case to another court; whether the case is under appeal; the outcome of any trial and any appeal; and the identity of the prosecutor, the defendant, the 'parties' representatives' – normally lawyers – including their addresses, and the judge, magistrate or magistrates, or justices' legal adviser by whom a decision at a hearing in public was made.

Rule 5.8 says that the request for these details may be made orally and makes clear that no reasons for the request need to be stated. It says the court officer must also supply details of any reporting or access restriction ordered by the court.

It also says the requestor must pay 'any fee prescribed'. But as yet there has been no announcement that journalists will be expected to pay for these basic details.

But rule 5.8 says that a request for such detail about any other case – which would include an older case – must be in writing, unless the court otherwise permits, and must explain why the information is required. It adds that if any other information about a case is requested, or a request is made to see a document containing information about the case, the court can decide this at a hearing, public or private, or without a hearing.

See also p. 158, Journalists' access to case material in court proceedings'

Protocol on court lists and registers

Under a protocol agreed between the Newspaper Society, the Society of Editors and Her Majesty's Courts and Tribunals Service (HMCTS), the Service sends free of charge and by email to local newspapers copies of the daily lists of defendants due to appear in magistrates courts and copies of these courts' 'registers', which briefly record each day's details of convicted defendants and punishments.

see Useful Websites at the end of this chapter for the protocol

A Home Office circular (no. 80/1989) said the lists should contain each defendant's name, age, address, the charge he/she faces and, where known, his/her occupation.

It is likely that qualified privilege protects a fair and accurate media report of court lists and registers should anyone sue for a defamatory error published by the media but which was in the document when supplied by HMCTS. But a journalist at a court hearing should quote the defendant's details and charge(s) as given at the hearing, and not rely on the list or register. A report of the hearing will be protected by privilege, if the relevant defence's requirements are met.

see ch. 21 on privilege and ch. 9 on youth courts

If the register includes details of juvenile defendants, check whether they were dealt with by the youth court, in which case usually they must not be identified.

Crown court lists can be accessed from an internet service, www.courtserve.net/homepage.htm as well as being seen at the courts, but give less information than those of magistrates courts.

The protocol agreed between media organisations and the Courts and Tribunals Service says: 'Crown court staff are encouraged to cooperate with local newspapers when they make enquiries'.

Magistrates' names

As well as Rule 5.8, case law says the names of magistrates – also known as 'justices of the peace' (JPs) – dealing with a case *must* be given by the court to the media and public. The High Court made this clear in 1987 in *R v Felixstowe Justices, ex p Leigh*, cited earlier. In that judgment, Lord Justice Watkins said any attempt to give magistrates anonymity was inimical to the proper administration of justice, adding: 'There is, in my view, no such person known to the law as the anonymous JP'.

A defendant's details should be given in court

The Home Office, in circular no. 78/1967 and in a similar circular in 1969, said defendants' names and addresses should be stated orally in magistrates courts.

The 1967 circular said: 'A person's address is as much part of his description as his name. There is, therefore, a strong public interest in facilitating press reports that correctly describe persons involved.' The High Court ruled in 1988 that a defendant's address should normally be stated in court (*R v Evesham Justices, ex p McDonagh* [1988] QB 553; [1988] 1 All ER 371).

The Judicial College guidance says: 'Announcement in open court of names and addresses enables the precise identification vital to distinguish a defendant from someone in the locality who bears the same name and avoids inadvertent defamation.'

((•))

see Useful
Websites
at the end
of this
chapter
for this
guidance

Facts of an admitted case should be stated

((•))

see Useful
Websites
at the end
of this
chapter
for the
Directions

If a defendant pleads guilty to a charge the prosecution should state in open court the facts of the offence, before any sentence is imposed, so that the public and media know the circumstances. This requirement is imposed by Criminal Practice Direction D Sentencing.

Details of witnesses in criminal cases

A Home Office statement on standards of witness care, issued in 1998, said that unless it was necessary for evidential purposes, defence and prosecution witnesses should not be required to give their addresses in open court.

Fines

A public register shows if fines imposed by criminal courts are unpaid – see later in the chapter.

▌ Journalists' access to case material in court proceedings

Journalists can safely report information from documents as read out in a court's public proceedings or officially provided by the court, if any reporting restriction in place is obeyed. But there are contempt risks in publishing information gleaned from case documents in other circumstances, as explained in ch. 11.

see ch.
21 on
privilege

A media organisation may face a libel action if it publishes defamatory matter from a document not read out in open court, unless the document was officially made available.

Access to material in criminal cases

In 2012 the Court of Appeal ruled that *The Guardian* newspaper should have been given access to documents used in an extradition hearing (*R (on the application of Guardian News and Media Ltd) v City of Westminster Magistrates Court*, [2012] EWCA Civ 420). This ruling was a landmark victory for the media because it established a presumption in law that journalists covering hearings in courts should be able to see case material, to aid that coverage. Provisions in Part 5B of the Criminal Practice Directions which came into force in October 2013 reflect this.

Practice Direction Part 5B

Part 5B says that the opening notes, written submissions and **skeleton arguments** used by counsel in the criminal courts should normally be provided to journalists who want them. Skeleton arguments are documents in which each side sets out the basis of their case. Part 5B says that other documents and information can also, be provided to the public or journalists, at the discretion of the courts. → glossary

A request for access to documents should first be addressed to the party who presented them to the court. If the party – for example, the prosecution – refuses, the request can be made to the court, the Direction says.

It adds that in the case of requests for information by reporters or lawyers acting for media organisations 'there is a greater presumption in favour of providing the requested material, in recognition of the press' role as "public watchdog" in a democratic society', adding: 'The general principle in those circumstances is that the court should supply documents and information unless there is a good reason not to in order to protect the rights or legitimate interests of others and the request will not place an undue burden on the court.'

It goes on:

> Opening notes and skeleton arguments or written submissions, once they have been placed before the court, should usually be provided to the media.
>
> It may be convenient for copies to be provided electronically by counsel, provided that the documents are kept suitably secure.
>
> If there is no opening note, permission for the media to obtain a transcript of the prosecution opening should usually be given – [although a transcript will have to be paid for.]

The Practice Direction stresses that the media are expected to be aware of the limitations on the use to which such material can be put – for example, that legal argument held in the absence of the jury should not be reported before the conclusion of the trial. It states: 'It is not for the judge to exercise an editorial judgment about "the adequacy of the material already available to the paper for its journalistic purpose" but the responsibility for complying with the Contempt of Court Act 1981 and any and all restrictions on the use of the material rests with the recipient.'

 see ch.18, p. 229, Proceedings in court in the absence of the jury

It also says some information should be given when requested by a member of the public or a journalist, who could simply ask court staff for it and need give no reason for wanting it. This class of information is detailed in rule 5.8 the Criminal Procedure Rules, explained earlier.

 ch. 18 explains the 1981 Act

Applications to the court for other information or material – which includes documents, photographs, DVD recordings and closed-circuit television footage – must be made in writing, and must be notified to the other parties.

Skeleton arguments and written submissions are likely to fall into the category of documents which are treated by a court as having been read aloud in their entirety, even though they were neither read not summarised aloud, and 'should generally be made available on request', the Practice Direction says.

Documents which *have* been read aloud in their entirety – such as opening notes, statements, including experts' reports and admissions – should usually be provided on request unless doing so would disrupt the court proceedings or place an undue burden on the court, advocates or others it adds.

In the case of documents which are read aloud in part, or summarised aloud, the Direction says:

> Open justice requires only access to the part of the document that has been read aloud.
>
> If a member of the public requests a copy of such a document, the court should consider whether it is proportionate to order one of the parties to produce a suitably redacted version. If not, access to the document is unlikely to be granted; however open justice will generally have been satisfied by the document having been read out in court.
>
> If the request comes from an accredited member of the press…there may be circumstances in which the court orders that a copy of the whole document be shown to the reporter, or provided, subject to the condition that those matters that had not been read out to the court may not be used or reported. A breach of such an order would be treated as a contempt of court.

! Remember

for the Authority, see Useful Websites at the end of this chapter

The term 'accredited' here refers to journalists able to produce a press card recognised by the UK Press Card Authority.

The Direction says courts considering applications for material will take account of factors including:

- whether a request is for the purpose of contemporaneous reporting; a request after the conclusion of the proceedings will require careful scrutiny;
- the nature of the information or documents sought and the purpose for which they are required;
- the stage of the proceedings at the time of the application;
- the value of the documents in advancing the open justice principle, including enabling the media to discharge its public watchdog role by reporting the proceedings effectively;

- any risk of harm which access may cause to the legitimate interests of others;
- any reasons given by the parties for refusing to provide the material requested as well as any other representations received from the parties.

The Practice Direction indicates that journalists should only apply to the court for material covered by existing protocols after first trying to obtain that information under those protocols from the relevant organisation(s), which would be from:

- Her Majesty's Courts and Tribunals Service, as regards information in lists and registers from magistrates courts, see earlier;
- the Crown Prosecution Service or the police, as regards material covered by the protocol called 'Publicity and the Criminal Justice System'.

The 'Publicity and the Criminal Justice System' protocol

The Crown Prosecution Service in 2005 issued a protocol 'Publicity and the Criminal Justice System' which says that material on which the prosecution relied in a trial, and which *should* normally be released to the media included:

- maps and photographs, including custody photos of defendants, and diagrams produced in court;
- videos showing crime scenes;
- videos of property seized – for example, weapons, drugs, stolen goods;
- sections of transcripts of interviews which were read to the court;
- videos or photographs showing reconstructions of the crime;
- CCTV footage of the defendant, subject to copyright issues.

The protocol also says that material which *might* be released following consideration by the CPS, in consultation with the police, victims, witnesses, and others directly affected by the case, such as family members, includes:

- CCTV footage showing the defendant and victim, or the victim alone, which the jury and public had seen in court;
- video and audio tapes of police interviews with defendants, victims and witnesses;
- victim and witness statements.

((•))

see Useful
Websites
at the end
of this
chapter
for the
protocol

The protocol also enables the media to ask the CPS head of strategic communications to become involved in the event of a dispute over disclosure.

Access to documents in civil cases

The Civil Procedure Rules cover county courts, the High Court and the Court of Appeal Civil Division. These allow non-parties, such as journalists, access to

((•))

see Useful
Websites
at the end
of this
chapter
for these
Rules

documents filed with the court in civil claims lodged after 2 October 2006, when rule changes took effect.

This access is important, as civil cases are now largely conducted by reference to documents rather than by the systematic taking of oral evidence. A civil trial may be impossible to report meaningfully if a reporter has not read key documents.

Pending and ongoing civil trials

Parts 5.4 and 5.4C of the CPR says any person who pays the prescribed fee may see a civil court's register of claims – that is, its list of cases – and, as a general rule, can obtain a copy of any 'statement of case' if the relevant claim has been listed for a hearing and all defendants have filed acknowledgements of service or defences.

'Statement of case', which is defined in Part 2.3, means the claim form, particulars of claim (if not in the claim form), defence, and also any counter-claim or reply to the defence. For further detail, see Part 16 of the CPR.

'Further information documents' supplied in response to a request under Part 18 of the rules are also part of a statement of case.

((•))

see Useful
Websites
at the end
of this
chapter
for the
Journal
report

👁 Case study

The *Journal* newspaper was able to publish the story of a footballer's dispute with his former landlords because reporter Emma King asked Newcastle county court if she could see the claim form. Former Sunderland player El Hadji Diouf had been taken to court by the landlords. They said he owed them £12,000 but agreed a settlement with him before the case was due to start, which included a confidentiality clause. Emma asked the court if she could see the claim form as it was a public document. She argued it was in the public interest to publish the allegations in it. Diouf's barrister initially opposed her request, citing the confidentiality agreement. But he was advised by Judge Christopher Walton that a report of the case would be in the public interest because the footballer was a well-known figure (*Holdthefrontpage* website, 13 May 2011).

The Court of Appeal has ruled that if a party to a civil court case objects to a document being made available for publication, a court will require 'specific reasons' why the party will be damaged by its publication, and that 'simple assertions of confidentiality', even if supported by both parties in the case, should not prevail (*Lilly Icos Ltd v Pfizer Ltd* [2002] EWCA Civ 2).

A non-party may obtain a copy of any other document filed with the court if it gives permission. But a party or any person identified in a statement of case may apply to the court for restrictions on access to such documents.

Witness statements

A statement of case does not include witness statements. But Part 32.13 of the CPR says: 'A witness statement which stands as evidence-in-chief is open to inspection during the course of the trial unless the court otherwise directs.' This enables public access during the course of the trial to written evidence relied on in court but not read out. But the court may rule that a witness statement should not be made available because of the interests of justice, the public interest, or the nature of medical evidence or confidential information, or because of the need to protect the interests of any child or protected party.

Interlocutory hearings and judicial reviews

The CPR rules on access to documents apply to interlocutory hearings and judicial reviews.

 www.mcnaes.com ch. 14 has case studies of how the media has used CPR rules to gain access to case documents in civil cases – for example, cases brought against News Group Newspapers Ltd for alleged phone-hacking – and how judges have interpreted the rules. A case study warns too on how to avoid libel pitfalls when basing news reports on case documents.

! Remember

Qualified privilege *will* protect media reports of documents made available to the media as copies, or for public inspection, by a court, if the defence's requirements are met and any reporting restriction is obeyed. See ch. 21 on privilege. Family courts have their own procedural rules, which normally mean that no document can be disclosed other than to a limited range of people – see ch. 13.

Skeleton arguments

Each side in a civil case draws up a skeleton argument, a document summarising its arguments in law. It is now established principle that a civil court can allow a journalist to see these and 'written openings' used by counsel (*GIO Personal Investment Services Ltd v Liverpool and London Steamship Protection and Indemnity Association Ltd (FAI General Insurance Co Ltd intervening*) [1999] 1 WLR 984; and the *Guardian v Westminster City Magistrates* case cited earlier).

Judgments and orders

CPR Practice Direction 39A states that when a hearing takes place in open court members of the public can obtain a transcript of any judgment given or a copy of any order made, subject to payment of the appropriate fee. When a judgment is given or an order is made in a private hearing, a non-party wanting a copy will need permission from the judge involved.

👁 Case study

Mr Justice Jacob said in the Chancery Division in January 1998 that, with very rare exceptions, and even when a hearing was in private, no judgment could be regarded as a secret document. (*Forbes v Smith* [1998] 1 All ER 973).

See www.mcnaes.com ch. 12 for information about bankruptcy records and ch. 13 in this book for divorce records.

see www. mcnaes. com ch. 14 for an outline of this case

Access to statements of case and witness statements after a civil case concludes

The High Court ruled in 2004 that anyone, including a journalist, can obtain access to witness statements relating to a case which has concluded – including a case settled without a judgment (*Chan U Seek v Alvis Vehicles Ltd and Guardian Newspapers* [2004] EWHC 3092 (Ch)).

However, a party to a case can object to such access. If a judge holds a hearing to decide the access issue, costs could be awarded against a journalist or media organisation whose application fails.

▶ Public register of monetary judgments, orders and fines

((•))
see Useful Websites at the end of this chapter

A public register shows the names and addresses of people and businesses with county court and High Court monetary judgments against them, if these sums were not paid within a required timescale. The register also shows if these are recorded as having being paid later or as still unpaid. This information stays on the register for six years. It is run by the Registry Trust and can be searched online. Not all High Court judgments are shown.

The register has been extended to include records of:

see ch. 17 on tribunals

- fines which were not paid quickly, or which remain unpaid, after being imposed in criminal cases by magistrates courts or Crown courts;
- Child Support Agency liability orders (see www.mcnaes.com ch. 13, Types of cases in family courts);
- Tribunals' 'enforced' awards – sums owed after a tribunal has ordered them to be paid, eg after a successful claim at an employment tribunal.

A fair and accurate report of matter on the register is protected from a libel action by qualified privilege if the requirements of the defence are met – see ch. 21, pp. 270–271, Stories from documents open to public inspection. Take care to understand what the register shows.

➡ Recap of major points

- A journalist arguing against being excluded from a court represents the wider public's interest in open justice.
- Common law, statute, and courts' procedural rules enshrine the open justice principle, but do allow courts to sit in private in some circumstances.

- Criminal courts should give reporters basic details of cases, including magistrates' names. Defendants' details should normally be given in open court.

- Reporters covering criminal trials should be allowed to see case material unless a legal reason prevents this.

- A protocol enables the media access to some types of prosecution material, for example, photos and video footage, to help it report a trial.

- The Civil Procedure Rules enable journalists to get copies of and inspect documents in civil cases.

((•)) Useful Websites

www.judiciary.gov.uk/Resources/JCO/Documents/Guidance/crown_court_reporting_restrictions_021009.pdf
> Guidance on reporting restrictions, published by the Judicial College, the Newspaper Society, the Society of Editors and Times Newspapers Ltd

www.justice.gov.uk/courts/procedure-rules/criminal/rulesmenu
> Criminal Procedure Rules 2013 and Criminal Practice Directions

www.justice.gov.uk/courts/procedure-rules/civil/rules
> Civil Procedure Rules and Practice Directions

www.newspapersoc.org.uk/pera-publications#registers
> Protocol agreed by Her Majesty's Courts and Tribunals Service on magistrates courts lists and registers, and cooperation by Crown courts

www.presscard.uk.com/
> UK Press Card Authority

www.cps.gov.uk/publications/agencies/mediaprotocol.html
> 'Publicity and the Criminal Justice System' – protocol for release of prosecution material to the media, agreed by the Crown Prosecution Service and the Association of Chief Police Officers

http://www.thejournal.co.uk/news/north-east-news/el-hadji-diouf-agrees-out-of-court-4431319
> *Journal* story on the Newcastle county court case involving footballer El Hadji Diouf

www.trustonline.org.uk/about-us/
> Registry Trust public register

15

Challenging the courts

Chapter summary

Courts often restrict media coverage of cases, and journalists must be prepared to challenge invalid or overly broad restrictions – they may be the only people in court arguing for the open justice principle (see ch. 14). This chapter explains the case law journalists can cite when opposing reporting restrictions, and how to make challenges.

▌ Why a challenge may be needed

A criminal or civil court may try to restrict reporting of case when it has no power to do so, or to impose a restriction which is valid but wider than necessary.

The benefits of open justice are best protected by unrestricted reporting. A journalist challenging a proposed or existing reporting restriction, or possible exclusion from a court, should remind the court of those general benefits – explained in ch.14 – as well as raise specific points about the particular case.

It is an established principle that any court should only impose the minimum reporting restriction needed to achieve its objective. The Master of the Rolls, Lord Neuberger, said in the Court of Appeal in 2011 that courts *'should ensure that the restrictions on access and reporting are the minimum necessary to enable justice to be done in that case'* (emphasis added) (*Elena Ambrosiadou v Martin Coward* [2011] EWCA (Civ) 409).

▌ A reporting restriction must be obeyed

Reporting restrictions, even if they are invalid or too broad, must be obeyed unless the court amends or lifts them (*Lakah Group and Ramy v Al Jazeera Satellite Channel* [2002] EWHC 2500; [2002] All ER (D) 383 (Nov) (QB)).

▌ The media's right to be heard

A court should hear representations from a media organisation or a journalist opposing or querying a reporting restriction or a decision to sit in private.

This principle is recognised in rule 16.2(3) of the Criminal Procedure Rules 2013 (SI 2013/1554) which cover magistrates and Crown courts, it says a court should not impose a restriction unless each party and any other person directly affected – which would include the media – was present or had had an opportunity to make representations. This is re-stated in Criminal Practice Direction 16B in which the Lord Chief Justice details how the rules should be applied.

((•))

see Useful
Websites
at the end
of this
chapter
for the
Rules and
Direction

Notice of applications for restrictions and of opposition to them

Rule 16.4(3) requires that parties applying for a reporting restriction, or for a court hearing to be held partly or entirely in private, should, if the court directs, give the media advance notice. Rule 16.5(3) imposes obligations on media organisations to apply 'as soon as reasonably practicable' if they wish to oppose a reporting or access restriction and to give notice to the parties (for example, the defence and prosecution in a criminal case) that such representations are to be made and why the restriction is opposed or should be amended. However, rule 16.3 gives the courts discretion to hear applications for restrictions, or media representations against them, made without notice and made verbally rather than in writing. The Direction says that the order itself should state that any interested party – which would include a journalist – who was not there or represented when it was made has permission to apply to make representations within a limited period, such as 24 hours.

! Remember

Journalists opposing applications for reporting or access restrictions, or their continuation, should tell the court if they were disadvantaged because no notice was given of it. The court may allow them more time to prepare argument.

The Direction says open justice is 'an essential principle' in criminal courts, and that a court needs to be satisfied that the purpose of the proposed order to restrict reporting or access cannot be achieved by a lesser measure, such as special measures or clearing the public gallery – usually while allowing media representatives to stay in court. It adds that the terms of any order must be proportionate so as to comply with Article 10 of the European Convention on Human Rights, which covers freedom of expression and to impart and receive information.

see ch.
1, p. 7
Convention
rights, on
Article 10

The order must be in writing, worded in precise terms and specify the legal power under which it is made, as well as its precise scope and purpose and, if appropriate, the time at which it will cease to have effect, the Direction says. The order must also state 'in every case, whether or not the making or terms of the order may be reported or whether this itself is prohibited'.

The media should be told of a restriction made

Rule 16.8 of the Criminal Procedure Rules 2013 says that if a reporting or access restriction is made, the court officer should record the reason for this, and that a notice of the restriction should be displayed somewhere prominent in the court-room's vicinity and communicated to reporters.

The Practice Direction says a copy of the order should be provided to any local or national media, and court staff should be prepared to answer any inquiry about a specific case, but that it will remain the responsibility of those reporting the case to ensure the order is not breached and to make inquiry in case of doubt.

Judicial College guidance for criminal courts

((•))

see Useful
Websites
at the end
of this
chapter
for this
guidance

Guidance entitled 'Reporting Restrictions in the Criminal Courts', published by the Judicial College, has been drawn up by media organisations and the judiciary, It can be cited usefully in challenges to actual or proposed reporting restrictions or threatened exclusions, and is endorsed by the Lord Chief Justice in Practice Direction 16B.

The guidance says (its page numbers given) that courts should:

- check, before making an order, that no automatic reporting restriction already applies – if one does, an order is unnecessary (p. 14);
- invite media representations when first considering making orders to restrict reporting or exclude the media (pp. 4, 5 and 14);
- hear media representations as soon as possible, because contemporaneous court reporting is important and news is perishable (pp. 6 and 14);
- recognise that the media have expertise in reporting restrictions and are well placed to represent the wider public interest in open justice (p. 14);
- have procedures to notify the media that an order has been made, and give them copies of the written notice as soon as possible (p. 5).

The need for an order must be 'convincingly established', the guidance says (pp. 6 and 15).

▶ Common Law

A court has no common law power to restrict reporting – see *Independent Publishing Company Limited v Attorney General of Trinidad and Tobago and Another* ((PC) [2005] 1 AC 190). Courts have common law powers in some circumstances to order that a name or matter should not be aired in public in its proceedings, but have no common law power to order that something said in open court cannot be reported, or to make orders limiting what the media may report other than by way of court reporting. A reporting restriction must be authorised by statute.

▶ Methods of challenge

Journalists challenging proposed or actual reporting restrictions or exclusion of the media from a court should raise the issue as soon as possible.

An approach to the court by a reporter or editor

In court, the reporter should approach the clerk as the first step – for example, if a hearing is under way, by asking an usher to pass the clerk a note.
Journalists should refer to the Judicial College guidance (discussed earlier).

If an order has already been made, the clerk can be asked to:

- supply it in written form, if this has not already been provided;
- specify in writing why it was made, if the order does not make this clear;
- state in writing the statute and section under which it was made, if the order does not state this.

Such a request might prompt the court to reconsider the order, especially if a reporter – or an editor, by fax, letter or email – quotes case law against it.

Journalists opposing a restriction or exclusion should remind the court of their and the public's Convention rights under Article 10.

ch. 1, p. 7, Convention rights, explains Article 10

- Raising a query or challenge in person in court, or by an editor writing to the court, has the advantages that doing so may resolve the matter quickly, and is the cheapest method as there is no need to involve a lawyer.

A reporter whose argument is being opposed by both the defence and prosecution should remind the court of the warning by Court of Appeal judge Sir Christopher Staughton that '….when both sides agreed that information should be kept from the public, that was when the court had to be most vigilant' (*Ex p P* [1998] CA Transcript 431, quoted with approval in the Supreme Court in the second paragraph of *Guardian News and Media Ltd's Application* [2010] UKSC 1).

Costs

Courts do not normally make costs orders against journalists or a media employer when these informal challenges are made, even if they fail. But it is important to make the challenge as early as possible.

Challenges taken to a higher court

If a challenge by a reporter or an editor fails, the court's decision can be challenged in a higher court.

Judicial review by the High Court of restrictions imposed by magistrates

A journalist or media organisation can apply to the Queen's Bench Divisional Court, part of the High Court, for **judicial review** of a decision by a magistrates court.

→ glossary

- But this normally involves hiring lawyers, and there is a court fee, and, if the challenge fails, the journalist or media organisation may have to meet some or all of the costs of any party which opposed the application. An applicant may have to bear its own costs even when successful.

Crown court restrictions can be challenged at the Court of Appeal

Decisions by Crown court judges to impose reporting restrictions or exclude the media can be challenged under section 159 of the Criminal Justice Act 1988, which gives the media a route of appeal to the Court of Appeal.

- The disadvantages are that the appeal may not be considered quickly, so a story may have lost any news value, and the appeal will normally involve hiring lawyers, paying a court fee, and, even if it succeeds, costs.

 Ch. 8, p. 84, The Court of Appeal, explains that court's role. There are case studies of the Press Association's successful use of the section 159 appeal route on p. 181, Is the juvenile concerned in the proceedings? and p. 187, Sexual offence law does *not* give anonymity to defendants.

((•))

for the
Rules, see
Useful
Websites
at the end
of this
chapter

Rule 69 of the Criminal Procedure Rules 2013 sets out the procedure to appeal to the Court of Appeal against a reporting or access restriction in a criminal case.

▶ Convention rights of anonymity

Lawyers acting for defendants or arguing on the behalf of witnesses may urge courts to use powers based on Article 2 (the right to life), Article 3 (the right to freedom from degrading treatment including torture) and/or Article 8 (privacy rights) in the European Convention on Human Rights to provide anonymity or otherwise restrict reporting. The statute empowering this is the Human Rights

Act 1998. As explained in ch. 11, the High Court has used such powers to ban the media from reporting new identities given to a few, notorious defendants after release from prison. But it is exceptionally rare for criminal courts to use any power to ban the media from identifying a defendant facing trial, and rare too for them to ban publication of a defendant's address or to use Convention powers to protect a witness's identity, bearing in mind that there are other, statutory powers to protect witnesses from publicity if this is felt necessary.

see ch. 1, p. 7, The Human Rights Act 1988

 See also p. 173, Someone else may be wrongly perceived as the defendant.

The Supreme Court said, in (*Application by Guardian News and Media Ltd and others in Ahmed and others v HM Treasury* [2010] UKSC 1) that, in 'an extreme case', a court has power to ban the media from identifying a witness or 'a party' to a case, such as a defendant, if doing so is necessary to protect that person or his/her family from risks to their lives and safety which could arise, for example, because of what the person had said about 'some powerful criminal organisation'. It said the sources of a court's power to make an anonymity order to protect such a person from 'a threat of violence arising out of its proceedings' were the person's rights under Articles 2 and 3. But it removed the anonymity lower courts had given four men who were appealing against asset-freezing orders made under anti-terrorism law. The Court said that the men's right to respect for privacy and family life under Article 8 did not over-ride the media's rights under Article 10 as there was a 'powerful, public interest' in identifying them.

see also, p. 175 Anonymity and risk of attack?

! Remember

A court considering how the Convention applies must carry out the 'balancing test' if, for example, the media asserts its Article 10 rights against someone's rights under Article 8 – see ch. 1, pp. 7–8, Weighing competing rights.

 The High Court has used the Convention in the context of family law to ban media reports from identifying a defendant in a criminal case – see www.mcnaes.com ch. 13

▶ Challenging restrictions under contempt law

Courts have discretionary powers to restrict reports of proceedings. These include those in sections 11 and 4(2) of the Contempt of Court Act 1981.

Section 11

Courts have common law powers to order that a name or other information should be withheld from the public during proceedings. A court which uses this power can then make an order under section 11 of the Contempt of Court Act 1981 indefinitely banning publication of the name or information – such as a defendant's address – in connection with reports of the proceedings. The media generally accept that blackmail victims should have this anonymity, but have opposed defendants being given it, and may object if it is used for witnesses for invalid or insufficient reasons.

 See ch. 11, pp. 119–120, Section 11 orders – blackmail, secrets, personal safety, and ch. 14, pp. 157–158. A defendant's details should be given in court, for case law that a defendant's address should normally be stated in court.

'In connection with the proceedings'

A section 11 order only bans publication of a name or matter 'in connection with the proceedings' – that is, a particular court case. It does not stop the media referring to someone by name in other contexts.

 See the case study in www.mcnaes.com ch. 10 about a man who won section 11 protection to stop a newspaper publishing his address in a report of a court hearing to impose a sexual offences prevention order (SOPO) on him – but the newspaper was able to report from other sources his previous offences and the view that he remained a danger to women. See more detail on such orders later in this chapter.

Has the name or matter been withheld from the public?

A section 11 order cannot be made if the name or matter has already been mentioned in public proceedings in the case. In *R v Arundel Justices, ex p Westminster Press* [1985] 2 All ER 390; [1985] 1 WLR 708) magistrates made a section 11 order banning publication of the name and address of a man charged with burglary offences. The High Court held in a judicial review that the magistrates had no power to make the order as the defendant's details had already been given in public – when the clerk routinely checked the information with the defendant in the first hearing.

A court which has made a deliberate decision to withhold a name or matter from its public proceedings can use a section 11 order to forbid its publication after it is mentioned by mistake (*Re Times Newspapers Ltd* [2007] EWCA Crim 1925; *Re Trinity Mirror plc and others* (2008), [2008] QB 770 [2008] EWCA Crim 50)).

Is anonymity necessary for justice to be done?

see www. mcnaes. com ch. 14 for this case

Section 11 orders may only be made when they are necessary in the interests of the administration of justice. In *Attorney General v Leveller Magazine Ltd* [1979] AC 440 at 449-450. Lord Diplock said that departure from the open justice rule was only justified:

> where the nature or circumstances of the particular proceeding are such that the application of the general rule in its entirety would frustrate or render impracticable the administration of justice or would damage some other public interest for whose protection Parliament has made some statutory derogation from the rule.

The High Court in Northern Ireland said in 1997: 'The use of the words "some other public interest" indicates that Lord Diplock had in mind the protection of the public interest in the administration of justice rather than the private welfare of those caught up in that administration'. The observation came as it refused to grant anonymity to a man charged with indecent assault. His lawyer had argued that, in the light of incidents involving others facing similar allegations, he was likely to be attacked if it became known in his community that he faced this charge (*R v Newtownabbey Magistrates' Court, ex p Belfast Telegraph Newspapers Ltd* [1997] NI 309).

see also, p. 175 Anonymity and risk of attack?

for this guidance see Useful Websites at the end of this chapter.

Someone else may be wrongly perceived as the defendant

The Judicial College guidance warns courts that banning publication of a defendant's address creates the risk that the public might think, wrongly, that someone entirely unconnected with the case, but with the same or a similar name, is the defendant.

Section 11 is not to protect the 'comfort and feelings' of defendants

A section 11 order should not be made for the 'comfort and feelings' of a defendant – *R v Evesham Justices, ex p McDonagh* [1988] QB 553; [1988] 1 All ER 371. Evesham magistrates agreed that a defendant's address should not be given in court because he feared harassment by his ex-wife, and made a section 11 order banning its publication. But in a judicial review quashing the order Lord Justice Watkins said that 'it is well established practice that, save for a justifiable reason' a defendant's address has to be given publicly in court. He said:

> There are undoubtedly many people who find themselves defending criminal charges who for all manner of reasons would like to keep unrevealed their identity, their home address in particular. Indeed, I go so far as to say that in the vast majority of cases, in magistrates' courts anyway, defendants would like their identity to be unrevealed and would be capable of advancing seemingly plausible reasons why that should be so. But section 11 was not enacted for the comfort and feelings of defendants.

It was only in rare circumstances, conforming to those set out in *Attorney General v Leveller* (discussed earlier), that a court would protect a defendant from publicity, he added.

Section 11 is not to protect a defendant's business interests

A section 11 order cannot not be used to protect a defendant's business interests, the High Court held in *R v Dover Justices, ex p Dover District Council and Wells* (1991) 156 JP 433).

Section 11 anonymity is not to protect a defendant's children

A section 11 order cannot be used in a criminal case to shield the children of a defendant from the effects of publicity about a case. The Court of Appeal ruled in 2008 that Croydon Crown court was wrong to use an order to stop the media naming a man who had admitted 20 charges of downloading child pornography from the internet. The judge who made the order justified it by saying the defendant's daughters, aged six and eight, who were neither victims nor witnesses in the case, would suffer significant harm if their father was identified. The Court of Appeal said the judge was wrong to conclude that the children's privacy rights under Article 8 of the European Convention outweighed those of the media and the public under Article 10. Sir Igor Judge said: '…there is nothing in this case to distinguish the plight of the defendant's children from that of a massive group of children of persons convicted of offences relating to child pornography'. Allowing the defendant anonymity would be 'to the overwhelming disadvantage of public confidence in the criminal justice system' *(In Re Trinity Mirror and others,* cited earlier).

Section 11 and civil orders imposed on sexual offenders

Police can apply in civil law for orders restricting the behaviour of convicted sexual offenders if it suggests they may reoffend – for example, banning them from loitering near schools. Home Office guidance says it is normal practice for some police forces to ask magistrates, at the outset of the application hearing, to make a section 11 order to stop the offender being identified in reports, and suggests that any disorder arising from public knowledge of his involvement in the hearing would make him more likely to abscond. But it adds: 'It is, of course, for the court to decide whether such a prohibition is necessary.' The media can argue that such a hearing needs unrestricted reporting because the public should be able to recognise such offenders.

see also
www.
mcnaes.
com ch.
10

 For more on such orders, see ch. 10, pp. 110–111, Orders to protect the public from risk of sexual offences.

Anonymity should not be used to spare witnesses in criminal cases from embarrassment

A section 11 order made by a Crown court judge giving anonymity to a witness on the grounds that the stress of publicity might cause her to relapse into heroin addiction was criticised in the High Court. Lord Justice Brown said: 'There must be many occasions when witnesses in criminal cases are faced with embarrassment as a result of facts which are elicited in the course of proceedings and of allegations made which are often without any real substance. It is, however, part of the essential nature of British criminal justice that cases shall be tried in public and reported and this consideration must outweigh the individual interests of particular persons' *(R v Central Criminal Court, ex p Crook* (1984) *The Times,* 8 November).

Section 11 anonymity in civil cases

In *R v Legal Aid Board, ex p Kaim Todner,* cited earlier, Lord Woolf said that in general, parties and witnesses in civil cases had to accept the embarrassment, damage to their reputation, and possible consequential loss which could be inherent in being involved in litigation, and that their protection was that normally a public judgment would refute unfounded allegations.

In a few civil cases courts have ruled that the potential psychological harm to a claimant of his/her medical condition being made public justified an anonymity order. See *H v Ministry of Defence* [1991] 2 QB 103; [1991] 2 All ER.

Anonymity and risk of attack?

Lawyers sometimes urge courts to give a defendant or witnesses anonymity, or to ban publication of their addresses, on the grounds that they are at risk of violence from criminals or vigilantes.

Case law says:

- a court asked to give a defendant or witness anonymity, or ban publication of their address, on safety grounds must be satisfied that the risk to their safety is 'real and immediate'; and

- the risk must have an objective, verifiable basis – be backed by evidence to the court, and not be assessed merely on the person's subjective fears.

If allegations against a defendant, and his identity, are already public knowledge, there is no justification for restricting media reports.

In the House of Lords in 2007 Lord Carswell referred to the established criterion that there should be 'a real and immediate risk' to life to justify anonymity. A real risk was one which was objectively verified, and an immediate risk was one which was present and continuing, he said, adding: 'It is in my opinion clear that the criterion is and should be one that is not readily satisfied: in other words, the threshold is high' (*Re Officer L* [2007] UKHL 36).

The test is the same, whether the person said to be at risk is a defendant or witness, whether the anonymity being sought is for the proceedings – that the person should not be identified in court – argued from common law or Convention rights, or whether the anonymity sought would be in media reports, argued from Convention rights and/or by reference to section 11 of the Contempt of Court Act.

see pp. 170–171, Convention rights of anonymity

Police and prison officer defendants – risk of attack

Lawyers defending police or prison officers often argue that their clients should have anonymity or that the media should not publish their home addresses because the crime of which they are accused or the general nature of their job or duties puts them at risk of attack or harassment from vengeful criminals.

👁 Case study

Two senior police officers were charged in 2010 with misconduct in a public office after alleged improper interference in prosecutions for speeding. Aldershot magistrates, after hearing an objection from a reporter, refused the officers' request for a section 11 order banning publication of their home addresses. They sought judicial review, arguing that publication would put them at risk because of their past involvement in investigating serious crime. The High Court, refusing to make an order, noted that the Press Association, which with a regional media group had argued against a ban, had shown that anyone could use internet records of electoral registers, at a cost of £4.95, to discover the officers' addresses within five minutes. Any risk to the officers' safety, if it existed, would be from someone who targeted them, who would be not be deterred merely because the media had not published the addresses, it said, adding that the type of charges the officers faced were unlikely to provoke a vigilante attack (*R (on the application of Harper and Johncox) v Aldershot Magistrates' Court and others* [2010] EWHC 1319 (Admin).

see also the Duggan inquest case study, ch. 16, p. 196

Police officers as witnesses: risk of attack

Police firearms officers involved in fatal shootings while on duty have been given anonymity at inquests – *R (on the application of Officer A and another) v HM Coroner for Inner South London* [2004] All ER (D) 288 (Jun).

Section 4(2) orders

Courts have power to postpone publication of media reports of all or part of a case under section 4(2) of the Contempt of Court Act 1981, to 'avoid a substantial risk of prejudice' to later stages of the same case or to other cases pending or imminent. See also ch. 18, pp. 228–229, Section 4(2) orders.

Postponement orders frequently mean that when the restriction no longer applies the case receives substantially less coverage than it would otherwise have done, especially if the order means that coverage of a sequence of trials has, because of the practicalities of media production, to be compressed into one day's publication on the day the last trial ends. Many details will never be published and the benefits of open justice will have been eroded.

see ch. 14 on the benefits of open justice

In 2006 the head of the Metropolitan police's counter-terrorism branch, Peter Clarke, said section 4(2) orders – imposed because of argument that reports of one terrorism trial could prejudice others then pending – were causing long delays in publication of reports of these trials. He said it had led to myths that the terrorism threat had been exaggerated (*Media Lawyer*, 15 December 2006).

Journalists challenging a section 4(2) order should refer the court to pp. 20 and 21 of the Judicial College guidance – see Useful Websites at the end of this chapter.

When a court is considering an application for a section 4(2) order, the prosecution should assist the court in an objective and unpartisan spirit in respect of the proper principles to be applied (*Ex p. News Group Newspapers Ltd, The Times*, May 21, 1999, CA).

The risk of prejudice must be substantial

A section 4(2) order should only be made if the risk of prejudice to current or pending proceedings is substantial.

In 1993 in the Court of Appeal the Lord Chief Justice, Lord Taylor, said that in determining whether publication of information would cause a substantial risk of prejudice to a future trial, a court should credit that trial's jury with the will and ability to abide by the judge's direction to decide the case only on the evidence before it. The court should also bear in mind that the staying power and detail of publicity, even in cases of notoriety, were limited and that the nature of a trial was to focus the jury's minds on the evidence put before them rather than on matters outside the courtroom (*R v Beck, ex p Telegraph plc* [1993] 2 All ER 971). See also Sir Igor Judge's comments on juries, cited later in this chapter.

In 1994 Mr Justice Lindsay refused to make a section 4(2) order postponing reporting of civil cases involving pension funds, although criminal proceedings were pending. He said a risk of prejudice which could not be described as substantial had to be tolerated as the price of an open press and that even if the risk was properly to be described as substantial, a postponement order did not automatically follow (*MGN Pension Trustees Ltd v Bank of America* [1995] 2 All ER 355, Ch D).

Principles for decisions on section 4(2) orders

In *R v Sherwood, ex p Telegraph Group* [2001] EWCA Crim 1075; [2001] 1 WLR 1983, The Court of Appeal set out three principles on section 4(2) orders:

(1) Unless the perceived risk of prejudice was demonstrated, no order should be made;

(2) The court had to ask whether an order was necessary under the European Convention on Human Rights. Sometimes wider considerations of public policy would come into play to justify refusing to make a section 4(2) order even though there was no other way of eliminating the prejudice anticipated;

(3) Applications for postponement orders should be approached as follows:
   (i) Would reporting give rise to a substantial risk of prejudice? If not, that would be the end of the matter;
   (ii) if such a risk was perceived to exist, would an order eliminate it? If not, obviously there could be no necessity to impose such a postponement. But even if the judge was satisfied that an order would achieve the objective, he/she would have to consider whether the risk could satisfactorily be overcome by less restrictive means;
   (iii) the judge might still have to ask whether the degree of risk of prejudice contemplated should be regarded as tolerable in the sense of being the lesser of two evils, when compared to the harm which a 4(2) order could cause to the benefits of open justice.

Risk of prejudice in sequential cases

Lord Justice Farquharson said in *R v Beck, ex p Daily Telegraph* (cited earlier) that the fact that an accused expected to face a second indictment after a trial of the first did not in itself justify making a section 4(2) order. It depended on all the circumstances, including the nature of the charges, the timing of the second trial, and where the second trial would be heard. If substantial prejudice to the accused could be avoided by extending the period between trials, or transferring the case to another court, then that course should be followed.

Risk of prejudice if one defendant is sentenced before others tried

ch. 18. p. 225, The 'fade factor' and limited publication, explains the term

In 2006 the Court of Appeal overturned a section 4(2) order postponing reporting of the sentencing of terrorist Dhiran Barot. The judge had made the order on the grounds that reports would prejudice the forthcoming trial of other defendants. Lawyers for the media argued that five months would elapse before that jury trial and so the 'fade factor' would mean that contemporaneous reporting of Barot's sentencing would not create a risk of serious prejudice.

Sir Igor Judge said in the Court of Appeal that although there was a primacy in the right to a fair trial it did not follow that a section 4(2) order should have been made. The right to a fair trial had to be balanced with the hallowed principle that the media had the freedom to act as the eyes and ears of the public. Juries had 'passionate and profound belief in, and a commitment to, the right of a Defendant to be given a fair trial', he said, emphasising the capacity of juries to concentrate on the trial evidence (*R v B* [2006] EWCA Crim 2692).

> For more detail of Sir Igor's remarks in this case, see ch. 18, pp. 224–225, Juries are told to put pre-trial publicity out of their minds.

The possibility of retrial does not mean a hearing is 'pending or imminent'

see ch. 18, pp. 217–218, Proceedings become active again when an appeal is lodged

The mere fact that a defendant has lodged an appeal against a conviction does not mean that a re-trial is 'pending or imminent', and so cannot justify use of section 4(2) to postpone the reporting of another case he or she is involved in (*Beggs v The Scottish Ministers* [2006] ScotCS CSIH_17 (16 March 2006)).

Section 4(2) cannot be used to protect reputation or safety

Magistrates and Crown court judges have occasionally made section 4(2) orders for a purpose other than avoiding a substantial risk of prejudice to a current or future hearing. Such orders are invalid. For example, a section 4(2) order cannot be used to ban publication of a name or material to encourage a witness to give evidence, or to protect anybody's reputation or general welfare or safety. The Court of Appeal made this clear in *Re Trinity Mirror plc and others* and in *Re Times Newspapers Ltd*, cited earlier in this chapter.

Section 4(2) orders cannot restrict reports of events outside the courtroom

Section 4(2) refers only to postponing reports of a court's proceedings – but some courts have tried to use it temporarily to ban reporting of an external event, or of a statement not made in the proceedings. The Court of Appeal accepted, in *R v B* cited earlier, that such use is beyond the section's scope, and unnecessary because a media organisation can face proceedings under the Contempt of Court Act's strict liability rule for publishing anything which creates a substantial risk of serious prejudice or impediment to an active case.

ch. 18 explains the strict liability rule

The Children and Young Persons Act 1933

The Children and Young Persons Act 1933 contains in its sections 39 and 49 provisions dealing with anonymity for juveniles – people under the age of 18, referred to in the Act as 'children and young persons'. The anonymity given under either provision may be challenged.

ch. 9 explains the scope of these section 39 and 49 restrictions

Challenging section 39 orders

Section 39 gives a court discretion to order that reports of a court case should not identify any specified juvenile 'concerned in the proceedings'. In a criminal case this definition includes a juvenile who is a defendant or witness. It also includes a juvenile who is the victim or alleged victim of the crime – the Act says it includes a juvenile 'in respect of whom the proceedings are taken'. In a civil case it covers a juvenile who is claimant, respondent or witness.

Courts often make section 39 orders without properly considering whether they are necessary, and make invalid orders. As explained earlier, the Criminal Procedure Rules require courts to hear media challenges to any reporting restrictions. Section 39 orders are probably challenged the most.

Crown court judges tend to protect a juvenile defendant's identity with a section 39 order made pre-trial. They may consider lifting it if the juvenile is convicted and should give the media opportunity to argue for this. A court is less likely to lift the order after an acquittal.

((•))

see Useful Websites at the end of this chapter for this CPS guidance

Crown Prosecution Service guidance on lifting section 39 anonymity

Guidance issued by the Crown Prosecution Service in 2011 to prosecutors gave the following circumstances as examples of cases of a strong public interest in favour of lifting the section 39 restrictions in the case of a convicted juvenile:

- significant public disorder where the public would rightly need to be satisfied that offenders were brought to justice, and there was a need to deter others;
- serious offences which undermined the public's confidence in the safety of their communities;
- hate crimes which could have a corrosive impact on the confidence of communities.

CPS guidelines accept that in some cases allowing the media to identify a convicted (and therefore punished) juvenile can help deter others from committing crime.

www. mcnaes. com chapter 38 'incitement of hate' outlines hate crimes

Principles to guide a court about section 39 orders for juvenile defendants

Lord Justice Simon Brown in *R v Crown Court at Winchester, ex p B* [2000] 1 Cr App R 11 identified seven principles a court deciding whether to make a section 39 order should consider:

(1) In deciding whether to impose or lift reporting restrictions, the court will consider whether there are good reasons for naming the defendant;

(2) It will give considerable weight to the offender's age and the potential damage to the child or young person of public identification as a criminal before he/she has the benefit or burden of adulthood;

(3) It must have regard to the welfare of the child or young person;

(4) The prospect of being named in court with the accompanying disgrace is a powerful deterrent and naming a defendant in the context of his punishment serves as a deterrent to others. These deterrents are proper objectives for the court;

(5) There is a strong public interest in open justice and in the public knowing as much as possible about what has happened in court, including the identity of those who have committed crime;

(6) The weight to be attributed to different factors may shift at different stages of the proceedings, and, in particular, after the defendant has been found, or pleads, guilty and is sentenced. It may then be appropriate to place greater weight on the interest of the public in knowing the identity of those who have committed crimes, particularly serious and detestable crimes;

(7) The fact that an appeal has been made may be a material consideration.

Is the juvenile concerned in the proceedings?

Section 39 orders cannot validly be used if the juvenile is not 'concerned in the proceedings', so criminal courts should not use this power to give a child anonymity when his or her parent is the defendant, unless the child is a witness or the victim or alleged victim of the offence, or is the juvenile 'in respect of whom the proceedings are taken' – for example, in a truancy case in which a parent is prosecuted for failing to ensure a child attends school.

In 2000 Mr Justice Elias said in the High Court:

> Sadly, in any case where someone is caught up in the criminal process other members of the family who are wholly innocent of wrongdoing will be innocent casualties in the drama. They may suffer in all sorts of ways from the publicity given to another family member. But I do not consider that in the normal case that is a relevant factor or a good reason for granting a direction under section 39 (*Chief Constable of Surrey v JHG and DHG* [2002] EWHC 1129 (Admin); [2002] All ER (D) 308 (May)).

Journalists should heed clause 9 of the Editors' Code of Practice. This says that relatives of people convicted or accused of crime should not generally be identified without their consent, unless they are genuinely relevant to the story. And the Ofcom Broadcasting Code's section 8 warns that children do not lose their right to privacy because of the notoriety of their parents.

chs. 2 and 3 introduce these codes

But sometimes a defendant's children *are* relevant in a court case. Moreover, the media – even if they do not wish to publish the name of a child – may have to challenge the section 39 order if its blanket anonymity for a child has the effect of preventing reports from identifying the adult defendant.

👁 Case study

The Court of Appeal in 2013 said that Recorder J.J Wright had been wrong to impose at Swindon Crown court a section 39 order which banned the media from identifying the 15-year-old boy whose father – a former Army officer – was on trial for defrauding taxpayers of more than £180,000 to send his three sons to an independent boarding school. The trial was already well under way – the prosecution having already identified in open court all three sons, including the 15-year-old, and media reports having mentioned them – when the *Recorder* made the order. The boy was not a witness. The father was convicted on most charges (*R v Robert Jolleys, ex p Press Association* [2013] EWCA Crim 1135).

The High Court made a similar ruling in 2008 – that section 39 cannot be used to spare the embarrassment of a defendant's children if they are 'not concerned in the proceedings' (*Crawford v Director of Public Prosecutions The Times*, 20 February 2008).

The identity of the juvenile is already in the public domain

In *R v Cardiff Crown Court, ex p M (a minor)* (1998) 162 JP 527, DC, the High Court ruled that if a section 39 order was not made when the case was first listed, publicity identifying the juvenile might make it inappropriate to make an order at a later stage.

Section 39 orders cannot specifically give adults anonymity

The Court of Appeal ruled in 1991 that section 39 orders could not be used to ban the publication of the identity of an adult defendant (*R v Southwark Crown Court, ex p Godwin* [1992] QB 190; [1991] 3 All ER 818).

Lord Justice Glidewell said:

> In our view, section 39 as a matter of law does not empower a court to order in terms that the names of [adult] defendants should not be published.... If the inevitable effect of making an order is that it is apparent that some details, including names of [adult] defendants, may not be published because publication

would breach the order, that is the practical application of the order; it is not a part of the terms of the order itself. 🔊🔊

see ch. 9, pp. 98–99, Cases of abuse within a family

In 2005 the Court of Appeal ruled there was no power under section 39 to prohibit identification of adults charged with sexual offences against children. But it warned of the danger of publishing material which might identify the children if the adult's name was published (*R v Teesside Crown Court, ex p Gazette Media Co Ltd* [2005] EWCA Crim 1983).

Which proceedings are covered by a section 39 order?

In 1993 Lord Justice Lloyd in the Court of Appeal said the word 'proceedings' in section 39 must mean proceedings in the court making the order and not any proceedings anywhere (*R v Lee* [1993] 2 All ER 170; [1993] 1 WLR 103, CA). So, a section 39 order made in a magistrates court does not apply to reports of the case when it reaches Crown court – but the Crown court can make a new order.

An order must be clear about whom it protects

The child or children covered by a section 39 order should be clearly identified (*R v Central Criminal Court, ex p Godwin and Crook*, cited earlier).

There must be a good reason for a section 39 order

A court should not make a section 39 order automatically, merely because of a juvenile's age, or unthinkingly as a 'blanket' order covering all juveniles in the case.

- In *R v Lee*, cited earlier, Lord Justice Lloyd pointed out that the 1933 Act made a distinction between section 49 anonymity, automatic in the juvenile (now youth) court, and section 39 anonymity, which is not automatic, in the Crown court – 'a distinction which Parliament clearly intended to preserve.'

A section 39 order cannot validly be made in respect of a dead juvenile

see Useful Websites at the end of this chapter for the Judicial College guidance

Courts sometimes make section 39 orders attempting to ban the identification of dead children. Several High Court judges have said the courts do not have this power. The Judicial College guidance says that for section 39 to apply the juvenile 'must be alive' and cites in support *Re S (a child) (Identification: Restrictions on Publication)* [2005] 1 AC 593.

Victim is too young to need section 39 anonymity

The Judicial College guidelines say: 'Age alone is not sufficient to justify imposing an order as very young children cannot be harmed by publicity of which they will be unaware...'.

Courts have accepted that a baby or a toddler who is the victim/alleged victim of a crime does not need section 39 anonymity, because by the time they are old enough to be harmed by the case's publicity it is likely to have been forgotten.

👁 **Case study**

In 2013 the High Court upheld a refusal by Lowestoft magistrates court to grant section 39 anonymity for a three-year-old girl in a case in which her mother Tess Gandy, aged 35, was convicted of being drunk in a public place while in charge of the girl, having been cautioned previously for a similar offence. Section 39 anonymity would have prevented the media identifying Gandy, a local councillor. Her identity in the case was protected by a temporary injunction until the High Court made its decision. It ruled that the child was too young to be directly affected by publicity about her mother's conviction, and that open justice and the Article 10 rights of the media and public should prevail (*R (on the application of A) v Lowestoft Magistrates' Court, with the Crown Prosecution Service and Archant Community Media Ltd as interested parties* [2013] EWHC 659 (Admin)).

A section 39 order cannot be in force if the juvenile has turned 18

A section 39 order can only be made to give anonymity to a person aged under 18. Case law on section 49 of the Act, and the wording of section 39 itself, make clear that section 39 anonymity expires when a juvenile turns 18.

 See ch. 9, p. 97, When does section 39 cease to apply to a juvenile? for this case law.

An order cannot be made simply because a defendant was under the age of 18 when the offence was committed.

▌ Challenges to youth court anonymity

Section 49 of the Children and Young Persons Act 1933 gives all juveniles 'concerned' in youth court proceedings, and appeals from youth courts, automatic anonymity in media reports.

A youth court which convicts a juvenile can, by using section 49(4A) of the 1933 Act, inserted by section 45 of the Crime (Sentences) Act 1997, make an order that the anonymity should be lifted if it is satisfied that it is 'in the public interest' to do so.

In 1998 the Home Office and Lord Chancellor's Department issued a joint circular 'Opening up youth court proceedings' which said that lifting the anonymity would be particularly appropriate in respect of a juvenile defendant:

- whose offending was persistent or serious; or
- whose offending had had an impact on a number of people; or
- in circumstances when alerting people to his/her behaviour would help prevent further offending.

 See ch. 9, p. 94, When section 49 anonymity ceases to apply

 see Useful Websites at the end of this chapter about circular

It said occasions when it would not be in the best interests of justice to lift section 49 anonymity included:

- when publicity might put the offender or his/her family at risk of harassment or harm;
- when the offender was particularly young or vulnerable;
- when the offender was contrite and ready to accept responsibility for his/her actions;
- when public identification of the offender would reveal the identity of a vulnerable victim and lead to unwelcome publicity for that victim.

👁 Case study

In 2001 the High Court upheld a youth court's decision to lift the section 49 anonymity in the case of a 15-year-old offender who had admitted taking a car without the owner's consent. He had previous, similar convictions for 'joy-riding', and the media had been told he had been arrested 130 times (*McKerry v Teesdale and Wear Valley Justices* (2000) 164 JP 355; [2000] Crim LR 594).

The guidance issued in 2011 by the Crown Prosecution Service on circumstances when there is a strong public interest in favour of lifting section 39 anonymity also applies to the lifting of section 49 anonymity for a convicted juvenile

> ((•)) See p. 179, Crown Prosecution Service guidance on lifting section 39 anonymity, and Useful Websites at the end of this chapter.

Anti-social behaviour cases - arguments for identifying juveniles

check www. mcnaes. com for news of updated guidance

Courts have the power to make civil orders to curb anti-social behaviour – see ch. 9, pp. 99–102, Anti-social behaviour injunctions and criminal behaviour orders. Courts have powers to make a section 39 order to provide anonymity for juveniles made subject to such measures, or those accused of breaching them. A journalist who wants a court to permit a report to identify a juvenile in such a case can cite Home Office guidance, 'Publicising anti-social behaviour orders', issued to local authorities in 2005: See Useful Websites at the end of this chapter.

This says that orders against anti-social behaviour protect local communities, and that: 'Publicity should be expected in most cases.'

The guidance said the benefits of publicity included:

- public reassurance that action was being taken to protect the community's human rights;
- enforcement – local people have the information to identify individuals who breached such orders;

- deterrence - if a person subject to such an order knew people might identify him/her for breaching it, a breach would be less likely, while others who saw publicity about such orders might be deterred from anti-social behaviour.

A Home Office factsheet 'Replacing the ASBO' said in 2013 that allowing the media to identify the juvenile in reports of hearings to decide on whether to impose a criminal behaviour order CBO and reports of CBO breach cases 'may be necessary, in some circumstances, to help in enforcing the order and to protect victims and communities'.

Case law on ASBOs will be relevant to the new injunctions and CBOs.

((•))

for factsheet, see Useful Websites at the end of this chapter

- Mr Justice Wilson said in the High Court in 2001 that in most cases magistrates should not ban identification by the media of a child subject to an ASBO, because the effectiveness of such orders would often depend on the local community knowing that the ASBO applied to that child (*Medway Council v BBC* [2002] 1 FLR 104).

▌ Section 46 anonymity for adult witnesses

Section 46 of the Youth Justice and Criminal Evidence Act 1999 gives courts the power to stop the media identifying an adult witness during his/her lifetime. The court must be satisfied that the quality of the witness's evidence, or level of cooperation in connection with preparations for the case, is likely to be diminished by reason of his/her fear or distress in connection with being identified as a witness by members of the public. It must also be satisfied that anonymity is likely to improve the quality of his/her evidence or the level of his/her cooperation. Ch. 11, pp. 123–124, Lifetime anonymity for adult witnesses, provides general detail about this power.

A journalist wishing to challenge the imposition or continuation of a section 46 order should follow the rule 16 procedure in the Criminal Procedure Rules, explained earlier in this chapter, and can make the following arguments.

Is there 'fear' or 'distress', and would the quality of evidence really be diminished?

Home Office explanatory notes to the 1999 Act state: 'Neither "fear" nor "distress" is seen as covering a disinclination to give evidence on account of simple embarrassment.'

👁 Case studies

In 2010 at the Old Bailey Judge Jeremy Roberts refused to make a section 46 order requested by the prosecution. It wanted anonymity for a 58-year-old woman, a prosecution witness in a case in which two men faced charges relating to possessing unlicensed herbal medicines. The judge, after hearing the Press Association's arguments that such an order would not be justified, said he did not believe that the quality of her evidence was likely to be diminished if he did not make the order, adding: 'She is a responsible, obviously intelligent lady. She has held a very responsible position in the past' (*Media Lawyer*, 10 February 2010).

At Blackpool magistrates court in 2009 a journalist successfully opposed a prosecution application that section 46 anonymity was needed for a barrister to improve the quality of his evidence. He was a prosecution witness in an assault case in which – the prosecution said – the defendant was expected to make derogatory allegations (*Media Lawyer*, 7 April 2009).

Does the section 46 order serve much purpose?

If a prosecution witness's identity is known to the defendant – almost always the case – the defendant will tell associates who he/she is. In such cases, the only purpose of section 46 anonymity would be to shield the witness's identity from the rest of the population. A journalist can ask the court why a witness's identity has to be shielded if the defendant already knows it and can tell others.

👁 Case study

In 2007 a judge at Kingston Crown court made a section 46 order banning identification of witnesses due to testify as the victims of an attempted robbery. But she lifted it after the Newsquest newspaper group and local reporters pointed out that the defendants knew the witnesses, whose identities were already in the public domain as they had previously been named in open court, and that if the order remained in force the media would no longer be able to identify the victims or say where the offence occurred (*Holdthefrontpage* website and *Media Lawyer*, 19 and 20 September 2007).

▌ Sexual offence law does *not* give anonymity to defendants

As ch. 10 explains, the Sexual Offences (Amendment) Act 1992 automatically bans media reports from identifying the victims or alleged victims of sexual offences. Occasionally magistrates and judges assert that the Act allows them to ban the media from identifying a defendant, insisting that anonymity for a defendant is necessary as an extra precaution to prevent media reports including detail likely to identify a victim/alleged victim. But there is no such power in the Act.

Case study

In 2012 the Court of Appeal ruled that a judge at Cambridge Crown court was wrong to ban the media from identifying a convicted rapist, purportedly under section 1 of the 1992 Act. The judge had ruled such a ban was necessary to stop the media, by naming the rapist, inadvertently identifying the victim as a side-effect. The Court of Appeal agreed with the Press Association's Legal Editor Mike Dodd (who is co-author of *McNae's*) that the Act contains no power to grant anonymity to a defendant. The Court agreed that the responsibility for ensuring the lifelong anonymity automatically granted by the Act to sexual offence victims rested with editors, and those reporting such a trial, not with the trial court (*R (Press Association) v Cambridge Crown Court* [2012] EWCA Crim 2434).

▌ Postponement of reports of derogatory mitigation

Section 58 of the Criminal Procedure and Investigations Act 1996 allows courts to ban, for 12 months, publication of an assertion which is derogatory of a person's character and which is made during a speech in mitigation. The banning order cannot be made if the assertion was aired in the trial or at any other stage of the proceedings prior to the mitigation speech.

> See mcnaes.com ch. 11 for more details of this restriction and for grounds of challenge if it is made invalidly.

➡ Recap of major points

- Challenges to reporting restrictions can be made by a reporter addressing the court, or by an editor writing to it. If this fails, the challenge can be taken to a higher court.

- An order under section 11 of the Contempt of Court Act 1981 should only be made if the relevant name or matter has already been deliberately withheld by the court from its public proceedings.

- A court order bestowing anonymity on safety grounds is only justified if the risk which publicity would create for that person is 'real and immediate', verified by evidence.

- An order under section 4(2) of the Contempt of Court Act to postpone media reporting of a case should only be made to avoid a substantial risk of prejudice to a pending or imminent hearing.

- A section 39 order cannot be made in respect of an adult or a dead juvenile. It can be argued that a baby or toddler is too young to need it.

- Journalists arguing for a youth court, magistrates court or Crown court to permit reports of a case to identify a juvenile defendant can cite Home Office and CPS guidance on this.

- An anonymity order under section 46 of the Youth Justice and Criminal Evidence Act 1999 should only be made if the witness is eligible and if the order is needed to achieve one of the section's purposes.

((•)) Useful Websites

www.justice.gov.uk/courts/procedure-rules/criminal/rulesmenu
    Criminal Procedure Rules 2013

www.judiciary.gov.uk/Resources/JCO/Documents/Guidance/crown_court_reporting_restrictions_021009.pdf
    Judicial College guidance: 'Reporting Restrictions in the Criminal Courts'

http://dugganinquest.independent.gov.uk/docs/Anonymity_ruling__27_6_13(1).pdf
    Coroner's anonymity order for the inquest into Mark Duggan's death

www.newspapersoc.org.uk/18/aug/11/cps-guidance-to-prosecutors-on-lifting-reporting-restrictions-on-youths-convicted-of-crime
    Crown Prosecution Service 2011 guidance to court on lifting anonymity for juvenile offenders

www.cps.gov.uk/legal/p_to_r/reporting_restrictions/index.html
    Crown Prosecution Service's current guidance to prosecutors about anonymity for juveniles

www.justice.gov.uk/downloads/youth-justice/courts-and-orders/YouthCourt2001.pdf
    A report citing on its p. 15 the Home Office circular 'Opening up youth court proceedings'

http://webarchive.nationalarchives.gov.uk/20100405140447/http:/asb.homeoffice.gov.uk/uploadedFiles/Members_site/Documents_and_images/Enforcement_tools_and_powers/ASBOs_PublicisingGuidance_0031.pdf
    Home Office guidance: 'Publicising anti-social behaviour orders'

www.gov.uk/government/uploads/system/uploads/attachment_data/file/251312/01_Factsheet_Replacing_the_ASBO_-_updated_for_Lords.pdf
    Home Office Factsheet 'Replacing the ASBO'

Coroners courts

Chapter summary

Coroners investigate certain types of death to establish the cause. The inquests they hold are court hearings, often newsworthy. This chapter outlines coroners' duties and explains why some inquests have juries. The Contempt of Court Act affects what can be reported, and coroners can impose reporting restrictions to give witnesses and children anonymity. Media coverage of inquests must be sensitive to the grief of the bereaved. In another role, coroners courts decide whether a found object should be classed as historical 'treasure'.

▶ Changes to the coroner system

A coroner – the office dates from the twelfth century – is appointed to serve a district. Coroners must have practised as a barrister or solicitor for five years (in 2013 the government agreed that suitably qualified legal executives could also become coroners). There remain some who are not lawyers but practised as doctors. The Coroners and Justice Act 2009 says new coroners must be legally qualified. Coroners investigate the causes and circumstances of certain types of death, in some cases having hearings in their courts to do so. The other role of the coroner system is to decide whether found objects from bygone centuries should be classed as 'treasure'. Both types of hearing are called inquests.

The 2009 Act has reformed the system. Coroners' districts became known as areas, and some were merged to form larger ones. The former offices of coroner, deputy coroner and assistant deputy coroner became, respectively, senior coroner, area coroner and assistant coroner.

Chief Coroner

The 2009 Act created the national post of Chief Coroner, whose duties include providing leadership for coroners, setting national standards for their work, approving coroner appointments (which are made by local authorities), directing coroners to begin investigations into a particular case, if necessary, and reporting annually to the Lord Chancellor on how the coroners system is performing.

Rules

((•)) see Useful Websites at the end of this chapter

Section 45 of the 2009 Act enables the Lord Chancellor to make rules to govern coroners' procedures. The Coroners (Inquests) Rules 2013 (SI 2013/1616) which took effect in England and Wales in July 2013 are among rules which replaced the Coroners Rules 1984.

Investigations into deaths

Under the 2009 Act a coroner must investigate certain categories of death: those for which he/she has reason to suspect that the cause is unknown; if the death is 'violent or unnatural'; or if the person died while in custody or while otherwise held in state detention. 'Violent or unnatural' deaths include those caused by crime, accidents, suicide, neglect or lack of care, excessive alcohol, drug abuse or any other form of poisoning. Police and doctors have a duty to report such deaths to the local coroner, and anyone concerned about the circumstances of a death can report it. Those in 'state detention' include people held in police stations, prisons, immigration detention centres and mental hospitals.

The reforms in the 2009 Act are due to lead in October 2014 to the appointment in each area of a 'medical examiner' – an experienced doctor whose duties will include scrutinising how doctors certify all other local deaths, a safeguard to help ensure that the coroner is told of any death which could fall into these categories. A coroner has the right at common law to take possession of a body to make his/her inquiries.

Deaths leading to inquests

Not all investigations require an inquest. There would be no need if, for example, a post mortem examination showed that someone died of natural causes. But holding an inquest means a coroner can require witnesses to testify. Inquests help keep communities and institutions vigilant about fatal dangers, and reassure the public that suspicious deaths are investigated. Inquest determinations on how people died are included in national statistics such as those for road accidents.

! Remember

An inquest is a fact-finding hearing to establish the reason for a death. It does not rule on who, if anyone, might be criminally responsible – that is the role of the criminal courts in, for example, murder cases. The civil courts decide if any party must pay damages to a deceased person's family.

A coroner's jurisdiction to hold an inquest arises from the fact that the body is in his/her district. A coroner must hold an inquest if a body has been brought into his/her district from abroad and he/she has reason to suspect the death was violent or unnatural, which is why, for example, the deaths of United Kingdom service personnel overseas give rise to inquests in the UK.

Purpose of inquests into deaths

The purpose of a coroner's investigation into a death, and therefore of an inquest, if one is held, is to determine:

- who the deceased was; and
- how, when and where he/she came by his/her death; and
- to make findings on the particulars about the death which have to be registered according to statute.

Establishing a deceased's identity is usually straightforward, but may require lengthy investigation if, for example, a decomposed body is found. The particulars, which have to be communicated to the Registrar of Births, Marriages and Deaths, include the deceased's name, the date and place of death and his/her gender, age, address and occupation.

In most inquests the decisions are made by a coroner alone. But juries figure in some inquests to decide on facts, with a coroner presiding to rule on law and procedure.

Inquests which have juries

The practice of having juries in some types of inquests helps safeguard civil liberties and public health – for example, by providing scrutiny other than by officialdom of police, prisons and workplace safety.

Under the 2009 Act, an inquest must be held with a jury if the senior coroner has reason to suspect that the death falls into one of the following categories:

- the deceased was in custody or otherwise in state detention, and the death was either violent or unnatural, or the cause is unknown;
- the death resulted from an act or omission of a police officer or member of a police force of the armed services in the execution of his/her duty;
- the death was caused by those types of accident, poisoning or disease which by law must be notified to a government department or inspector, such as workplace fatalities.

An inquest into any other type of death can also be held with a jury if the senior coroner thinks there is 'sufficient reason'. An inquest jury comprises at least seven and not more than 11 people. Jurors are selected randomly from electoral rolls.

Information about inquests

Rule 9 of the Coroners (Inquests) Rules 2013 says a coroner must notify the dead person's next of kin and any 'interested person who have made themselves known' to the coroner of the date, time and place of the inquest hearing within one week of setting the date, and must make such details publicly available before it commences. Guidance from the Chief Coroner makes clear that this is to ensure that the media can attend if they wish.

👁 Case study

Lincolnshire county coroner Stuart Fisher showed in 2006 how helpful coroners can be. After being called by a Press Association reporter about an inquest he had held the previous day into a baby's death. Mr Fisher fetched the file on the hearing from the boot of his car, and proceeded to read his conclusions as well as evidence from witnesses (*Media Lawyer*, 13 April 2006).

Admission to inquests

A coroner investigating a death by means of an inquest may hold three types of hearing – 'a pre-inquest review hearing' (rule 6), the opening of the inquest and the full hearing.

The 'opening' is usually an initial, brief hearing for the coroner formally to ascertain the identity of the deceased. The inquest can then be adjourned – there having already been a post mortem examination and possibly burial or cremation – and is usually resumed after a period of weeks or months to hear evidence gathered about the circumstances of the death.

Rule 11 says that generally any pre-inquest hearing and the inquest hearings must be held in public but that:

- a coroner may direct that the public be excluded from a pre-inquest review hearing if he/she considers it would be in the interests of justice to do so.

- a coroner who does not have immediate access to a courtroom or other appropriate place in which to open the inquest may open it privately and then announce that it has been opened at the next hearing held in public.

- a coroner in the case of any of these types of hearing can direct that the public (a term which here would include journalists) should be excluded from all or part of it because he/she considers it would be in the interests of national security to do so.

There is nothing in the rules to stop a coroner allowing journalists to attend a pre-inquest review if the only reason the public has been excluded is to avoid noisy disruption to the process of justice.

▌ The airing of evidence

Unlike the criminal courts, where the process is accusatorial, adversarial and subject to strict rules on how evidence is given, an inquest is inquisitorial. The coroner can 'lead' witnesses through their evidence.

see ch. 6, p. 60, Hostile witnesses and leading questions

Rule 23 allows a coroner to take written rather than oral evidence from any witness if satisfied that this evidence is unlikely to be disputed, or that it is not possible for the witness to attend at all or within a reasonable time, or that there is a 'good and sufficient reason' why he/she should not attend or to believe he/she will not attend. So, the coroner may decide, for example, that a busy hospital doctor has no need to attend an inquest to testify in person.

But the rule says the coroner must, in any circumstance in which he/she accepts written evidence, announce the nature of the evidence and the witness's full name at the inquest hearing, and that any 'interested person' is entitled to see a copy of any written evidence.

The rule adds that: 'A coroner may direct that all or parts only of any written evidence submitted under this rule may be read aloud at the inquest hearing.'

Coroners generally do read aloud written evidence. But if it is not read out a journalist would have a strong argument, because of the Article 10 rights, the open justice principle and the decision of the Court of Appeal in *R (Guardian News and Media) v City of Westminster Magistrates' Court* [2011] 1 WLR 3253; [2011] EWCA Civ 1188, to be allowed to see it.

 See ch. 14, pp. 158–159, Access to material in criminal cases, about this case and ch. 1, p. 7, Convention rights, on Article 10 rights.

Coroners do not usually read out suicide notes, to spare the bereaved further anguish.

Access to documents

The 2009 Act was intended to increase transparency in inquest procedure. Reflecting this, the 2013 rules require coroners to keep a recording of every inquest hearing, including 'pre-inquest reviews', and the rules formalise when a coroner must disclose documents. Rule 13 says that a coroner must provide, to anyone who is an 'interested person' in the case – for example, the dead person's next of kin – any document in the case or a copy of it, or must make the document available for inspection by that person as soon as is reasonably practical, including the post-mortem report and where available the recording of the inquest hearing.

ch. 14 covers these criminal court rules

'Document' here means any medium in which information is recorded. There is no case law yet on whether a journalist is an 'interested person' under rule 13. But the recent creation of rules for criminal courts giving journalists qualified access to case documents, and the Court of Appeal decision in the *Guardian News and Media* case mean there are strong arguments that journalists should have similar access to inquest documents.

Rules 14 and 15 permit a coroner to redact a document before disclosure, or to refuse to disclose it in some circumstances – for example, when it relates to commenced criminal proceedings. A coroner may also restrict how a disclosed document can be used – and a next of kin or journalist who ignores that restriction could be punished for contempt of court. For example, a coroner is highly likely to order that no part of a disclosed recording of an inquest should be posted on social media or broadcast as doing so could, for example, humiliate a witness who broke down when testifying and deter witnesses from giving evidence in future inquests. If a coroner discloses a document before or during an inquest no fee can be charged for it. Rules set out what fee can be charged if a request for disclosure is made after an inquest.

Determinations and conclusions – formerly 'verdicts'

An inquest produces a decision on what caused a death, determined by the coroner, or the jury if there is one. These decisions, announced at the inquest, have traditionally been referred to as verdicts. It has become the journalistic convention to report that a coroner's jury *returns* a verdict and that a coroner sitting without a jury *records* a verdict. The 2009 Act uses the term 'determination' to denote a decision as to the identity of the deceased, and how, when and where he/she died. But it seems likely that 'verdict' will continue to be used colloquially.

Determinations and 'findings' – 'findings' are particulars which statute requires to be registered. Determinations can, as was the case with verdicts, be expressed in 'short form conclusions' comprising of single words or short phrases including 'natural causes', 'accident', 'road traffic collision', 'misadventure', 'drug related', 'industrial disease', 'unlawful killing', or 'suicide'. An 'open' determination is recorded or returned when an inquest decides there is insufficient evidence for any other conclusion.

Narrative conclusions

Recent years have seen increasing use of **narrative verdicts** – statements summing up the coroner's or jury's conclusions on how the deceased came to die, providing some factual detail. Under the 2013 rules this practice will continue because they permit a coroner or a jury to deliver 'a brief narrative conclusion' as well as or rather than a 'short-form' one. This also fulfills a requirement that a coroner should allow a jury to express a brief conclusion about disputed facts at the centre of the case, so that inquest procedure complies with Article 2 of the European Convention on Human Rights, the right to life, on the principle that a jury must be able to express conclusions in a way which can help avoid similar loss of life. Coroners also usually make concluding remarks to focus public attention on lessons to be learnt from a death, and have a legal duty to produce reports for the Chief Coroner if an inquest has revealed circumstances which could continue to place lives at risk.

See, ch. 1, p. 6, The European Convention on Human Rights. Article 2 is set out in Appendix 1, p. 441.

Related criminal proceedings

When a person is suspected of crime in connection with a death, an inquest is usually opened, then adjourned until after any criminal proceedings have ended. The inquest may then be resumed if there is sufficient cause. For example, if someone accused of a murder is acquitted, an inquest may subsequently return a determination of unlawful killing while not attributing blame. If a public inquiry is instigated under the Inquiries Act 2005 to consider why a person or people died – for example, in a rail crash – the Lord Chancellor can direct that any inquest should be adjourned. It will not be reopened unless there is an exceptional reason.

ch. 17 outlines the law on public inquiries

Review of inquest decisions

There is no direct route of appeal against an inquest decision, but an aggrieved person with sufficient legal interest in the case – for example, a deceased's next of kin – can apply to the High Court for judicial review. This could result in that court making an order to quash an inquest determination and to order that a fresh inquest be held in the interests of justice.

→ glossary

Defamation and contempt issues in media coverage

An inquest is a type of court proceeding, so fair, accurate and contemporaneous reports of an inquest held in public are protected from libel actions by absolute privilege. Non-contemporaneous reports are protected by qualified privilege if the requirements of that defence are met.

privilege is explained in ch. 21

An inquest is covered by the Contempt of Court Act 1981 (the 1981 Act). As explained in ch. 18, it is illegal to publish material which creates 'a substantial risk of serious prejudice or impediment' to an active case. The Court of Appeal has ruled that an inquest becomes 'active' when it is opened (*Peacock v London Weekend Television* (1986) 150 JP 71). It seems unlikely that a coroner, being an experienced professional, could be prejudiced in his/her considerations by media coverage. But the media should take care, in an inquest case in which a jury is or could be involved, not to publish material which creates a substantial risk of serious prejudice to its deliberations. The media should also avoid publishing material which could breach the Act by affecting a witness's testimony.

An inquest may precede a hearing in a criminal court into the same events – for example, an inquest might be opened then adjourned because someone is charged with murder. The media can safely report that inquest hearing contemporaneously, if it is held in public, because the report – provided it is fair, accurate and published in good faith – will be protected by section 4 of the 1981 Act unless the coroner has made an order under section 4(2) postponing reporting of the hearing.

Reporting restrictions

Coroners can make orders restricting media reports of inquests, for example by using section 39 of the Children and Young Persons Act 1933 to give a juvenile witness anonymity, the law of which is explained in ch. 9.

 Coroners also have **inherent jurisdiction** in common law and under Article 2 of the European Convention on Human Rights to order that a witness should have anonymity in inquest proceedings – for example, to prevent a real and immediate risk to their life (*R (on the application of Officer A) v HM Coroner for Inner South London and others* [2004] EWHC Admin 1592). Article 8 rights – for example, for the protection of family life – may also be cited in favour of anonymity.

> See also ch. 15, pp. 175–176, Anonymity and risk of attack? on anonymity for police officers.

👁 Case study

ch. 11, pp. 119–120, Section 11 orders, explains these orders

Prior to the 2013 inquest into the death of Mark Duggan, who was fatally shot by a police officer after a mini-cab was stopped in London in 2011, Judge Cutler ordered that 24 officers, including the one who fired the fatal shot and colleagues in that firearms unit, could give evidence anonymously and made orders under section 11 of the Contempt of Court Act banning media reports of the inquest from identifying them; See Useful Websites at the end of this chapter. Duggan's death sparked rioting in London and other cities. Under law which enables judges to preside over complex inquests Judge Cutler was appointed to be an assistant coroner to preside at the Duggan inquest, which had a jury. In January 2014 the jury returned a verdict that Mr Duggan was lawfully killed – although it also found that he did not have a gun when police shot him.

Publication of material heard in any part of an inquest held in private could be deemed a contempt of court and will not be protected by privilege in libel law.

Common law and statutory protections of witnesses and jurors, including section 8 of the 1981 Act, apply to inquest proceedings, as does the ban on photography, filming and audio recording in courts. Ch. 11 explains these laws.

Media challenges to reporting restrictions or lack of access

Any media challenge to a reporting restriction imposed by a coroner, or to a decision to exclude the media from an inquest, must – if the coroner will not reconsider – be made to the High Court as an application for judicial review.

◗ Ethical considerations when covering deaths

chs. 2 and 3 introduce the codes, and see Useful Websites at the end of this chapter

The Editors' Code of Practice and the Ofcom Broadcasting Code set out ethical standards, explained in ch. 27, to minimise media intrusion into bereaved people's grief and shock. These are particularly pertinent to coverage of inquests. The Editors' Code and the Ofcom code also say that excessive detail about suicide methods should not be published.

The Samaritans have published media guidance on reporting suicides.

◗ Treasure inquests

Historically, coroners courts have decided whether historical objects found on or buried in the ground should be classed as 'treasure'. The Crown or a franchisee has legal rights to take possession of valuable objects ruled to have been treasure deliberately hidden by a past generation – for example, buried for safety during warfare. The Treasure Act 1996 amended this ancient law to encourage those who use metal-detectors to declare discoveries so that museums can decide if they want the objects found. The Act has various definitions of treasure, including:

- a found object which is not a single coin and which contains at least 10 per cent of gold or silver, and which is at least 300 years old, and any other object found with it;
- a find of ten or more coins found together whatever their metallic content, which are at least 300 years old.

District coroners have been responsible for holding inquests to decide if an object is treasure. The Coroners and Justice Act 2009 was due to relieve them of this duty by creating a national post of Coroner for Treasure, the idea being that an individual with particular expertise could preside at all treasure inquests. But by late 2013 the government had not provided funding for the post. Anyone with reasonable grounds for believing an object they have found might be classed as treasure is required to notify a coroner within 14 days of the discovery or the realisation. Failure to do so is punishable by a fine, or a jail term of up to three months.

The coroner, once notified, or if he/she has reason to suspect any other found object is treasure, must hold an investigation, which could involve an inquest, with a jury if there is 'sufficient reason'.

If the find is ruled to be treasure, the British Museum or National Museum of Wales is given the opportunity to acquire the find. There is a system for the finder to be paid a reward, based on the treasure's market value, from public funds, and it is also possible for some to be awarded to the owner of the land on which the treasure was found.

The reward may be reduced, or not even offered, if the finder was trespassing or illegally disturbing an archaeological site. If the object is not classed as treasure or no museum wants it, the finder can keep or sell it, subject to any rights of the land's owner or occupier.

➡ **Recap of major points**

- The purpose of an inquest is to find out who a deceased person was and how he/she died.

- A coroner can exclude the public and journalists from an inquest on grounds of national security.

- Coroners can impose reporting restrictions.

- Inquests are court hearings, and so are covered by the law of contempt of court, which can affect media coverage.

- A treasure inquest decides if a found, historical object should be classed as 'treasure', in which case a museum is given the opportunity to acquire it.

((•)) **Useful Websites**

www.legislation.gov.uk/uksi/2013/1616/article/34/made
    The Coroners (Inquests) Rules 2013

www.gov.uk/after-a-death/
    Government guidance on inquests into deaths

www.judiciary.gov.uk/Resources/JCO/Documents/coroners/guidance/chief-coroners-guide-to-act-sept2013.pdf
    Chief Coroner's Guidance to the Coroners and Justice Act 2009 – see paragraphs 110–116

www.judiciary.gov.uk/about-the-judiciary/office-chief-coroner/the-chief-coroner
    Information about the Chief Coroner

www.coronersociety.org.uk/
    The Coroners Society of England and Wales

www.courtsni.gov.uk/en-GB/Services/Coroners/Pages/default.aspx
    Coroners Service for Northern Ireland

www.inquest.org.uk/
    Inquest – a charity providing free advice to the bereaved on contentious deaths

www.samaritans.org/media-centre/media-guidelines-reporting-suicide
    The Samaritans' media guidelines on reporting suicides

www.gov.uk/treasure
    Government guidance on treasure

http://dugganinquest.independent.gov.uk/docs/Anonymity_ruling__27_6_13(1).pdf
    Anonymity ruling by coroner for the inquest into Mark Duggan's death

Tribunals and public inquiries

Chapter summary

Tribunals are specialist judicial bodies which decide disputes in particular areas of law. The UK has a wide range of tribunals with a huge annual caseload which can yield news and human interest stories. Tribunals adjudicate issues such as asylum and immigration cases; the rents tenants can be charged; whether a patient in a secure mental health hospital is safe to return to the outside world; benefit entitlements; and employment disputes. Some tribunals are termed a 'commission' or 'panel'. Some regulate professions and decide, for example, whether doctors or lawyers should be banned from practising because of misconduct. The term 'public inquiry' denotes other kinds of legal, investigatory processes.

▐ Tribunals in the administrative justice system

Most tribunals are official bodies which make decisions determining someone's legal rights. There are more than 70 types of tribunal. The majority rule on disputes between an individual, or a private organisation, and a state agency, for example, about tax obligations; benefit entitlements, or immigration status. The annual workload of tribunals in this 'administrative justice' system can exceed a million cases, compared to about 65,000 civil and 200,000 criminal justice cases a year.

Tribunals listed here are among those which may be of particular interest to journalists:

The Immigration and Asylum Chamber hears appeals against decisions made by the Home Secretary and his/her officials in asylum, immigration and nationality matters.

The Special Immigration Appeals Commission (SIAC) hears appeals against Home Office decisions to deport, or exclude, someone from the UK on national security or public interest grounds, and appeals against decisions to deprive someone of UK citizenship.

The Health, Education and Social Care Chamber of the First-tier Tribunal hears, for example, appeals from doctors and dentists who have not been included on lists which allow them to provide work in NHS primary care, and appeals from people who have been banned from working for organisations concerned with children and vulnerable adults.

This chamber includes the First-tier Tribunal (mental health) for England (formerly the mental health review tribunals) which hears appeals from patients detained under the Mental Health Act 1983 for release from secure mental hospitals. Wales has a separate mental health review tribunal.

The Property Chamber (Residential Property) of the First-tier Tribunal hears for example, appeals against rent levels fixed by a rent officer for regulated tenancies.

The First-tier Tribunal is a generic tribunal created to merge the administration of most tribunals dealing with appeals against decisions made by state officials. A decision of the First-tier Tribunal may, in some instances, be appealed to, or be reviewed by, the next tier of the administrative justice system, known as the Upper Tribunal.

 www.mcnaes.com ch. 17 gives an outline of the procedural rules of these tribunals, on who can attend them, and of powers they have to prohibit the disclosure or publication of specified documents or information relating to their proceedings.

▌ Examples of disciplinary tribunals

The disciplinary tribunals listed below, being those of regulated professions, are not part of the 'administrative justice' system.

The Medical Practitioners Tribunal Service of the General Medical Council hears complaints against doctors in its Fitness to Practice Panels. These normally sit in public, but can sit in private – for example, when considering confidential information concerning a doctor's health.

The Solicitors Disciplinary Tribunal must, in general, sit in public to hear allegations of professional misconduct against solicitors. But it can in some circumstances exclude the public from all or any part of a hearing.

 For detail on these disciplinary tribunals, and those for barristers and nurses, see www.mcnaes.com ch. 17.

▌ Defamation and contempt issues in reporting tribunals

A tribunal is classed as a court if it exercises 'the judicial power of the State', a definition in section 14 of the Defamation Act 1996 and section 19 of the Contempt of Court Act 1981.

Tribunals which are courts

The Upper Tribunal, the Special Immigration Appeals Commission and the Employment Appeal Tribunal were each created by statute to be a 'superior court of record', and so are courts under the 1996 and 1981 Acts. There is case law that employment tribunals and First-tier tribunals in the administrative justice system run by Her Majesty's Courts and Tribunals Service, including mental health review tribunals, also meet this definition. If a tribunal is classed as a court, this determines how defamation and contempt laws apply to journalists covering its cases.

Privilege in coverage of tribunals

If a tribunal is classed as a court, then under the Defamation Act 1996 a fair and accurate media report of its hearings held in public, if published contemporaneously, is protected by absolute privilege, and a non-contemporaneous report is protected by qualified privilege under Part 1 of the Act's Schedule 1, with no requirement to publish 'explanation or contradiction'. These defamation defences are explained in ch. 21.

In 2009 the High Court ruled that a media account of the proceedings of the Solicitors Disciplinary Tribunal enjoyed absolute privilege (*Imran Karim v Newsquest* [2009] EWHC 3205 (QB), which means that the High Court classed it as a court. But such case law does not exist or is not conclusive for some tribunals.

However, the disciplinary tribunals of some other professions, and other types of tribunal, derive their powers from an Act of Parliament. In the case of any tribunal constituted by or under, or exercising functions under, statutory provision, a media report of its public proceedings will be protected by qualified privilege bestowed by paragraph 11 of Part 2 of Schedule 1 to the Defamation Act 1996, if all the requirements of that defence are met. Again, these include that the report fairly and accurately reflects the proceedings. Also, a requirement is that, at the request of anyone defamed by the published report, a reasonable letter or statement of explanation or contradiction must be published.

see ch. 21, pp. 268–269, The requirements of qualified privilege

! Remember

This type of qualified privilege also protects fair and accurate reports of the findings (but not of the proceedings) of the disciplinary committees of certain private associations – for example, in the field of sport, business and learning. See ch. 21, p. 272, Disciplinary actions by private associations.

Proceedings are not always formal

The proceedings of many tribunals are not as formal as those in an ordinary court of law. An appellant might not be represented by a lawyer. Journalists should remember that qualified privilege does not extend to any published matter which is not 'of public interest' and the publication of which is not 'for the public benefit' – so a flare-up at a hearing of irrelevant, personal abuse may well be such matter.

Contempt issues in coverage of tribunals which are courts

If a tribunal is classed as a court the Contempt of Court Act 1981 applies, which means that the media should not publish material which could create 'a substantial risk of serious prejudice or impediment' to any of the tribunal's 'active' cases. The 1981 Act is explained generally in ch. 18. Under the Act's Schedule 1, a tribunal case is 'active' 'when arrangements for the hearing are made or, if no such arrangements are previously made, from the time the hearing begins. It remains 'active' until 'the proceedings are disposed of or discontinued or withdrawn'.

In many instances, it would be unlikely that media stories about an 'active' tribunal case – for example, published before its full hearing – could create a substantial risk of serious prejudice or impediment, in that judges and/or professionals such as doctors or lawyers preside in tribunals, and are unlikely to be influenced by media reports. But there is a possibility that such media reports could affect witnesses in their testimony.

Other restrictions

Media contact with a witness prior to such a hearing could be punished as contempt in common law if it was ruled to amount to interference with him/her, and unauthorised use of cameras or audio-recorders in a hearing could also be punishable as illegal under the 1981 Act or the Criminal Justice Act 1925. If a tribunal classed as a court holds a hearing in private, it may be ruled to be a contempt if a media organisation reports what was said in that hearing, if the case concerns mental health, national security, the welfare or upbringing of children, or secret processes and in any other case where the tribunal has expressly prohibited publication of information.

Chapter 11 explains these restrictions.

 See www.mcnaes.com ch. 17 'Tribunals which are courts' for further detail of relevant law.

▌ Employment tribunals

Employment tribunals adjudicate on complaints against employers – for example, of unfair dismissal or of 'constructive dismissal' in which a person claims that he/she had to quit the job because of improper conduct by another/others in the workplace. These tribunals also adjudicate on complaints of discrimination by employers on grounds of gender, race or age.

Employment tribunals, formerly known as industrial tribunals, are based in regional centres. For some types of case an employment tribunal has three members: a lawyer who is chair, and now officially termed an 'employment judge'; and two lay members – someone with experience as an employer and someone with a background as an employee, for example, a trade unionist. But unfair dismissal claims are now among those which can be decided by an employment judge sitting alone.

Procedure

Employment tribunal hearings in England, Wales and Scotland are governed by rules set out in the Employment Tribunals (Constitution and Rules of Procedure) Regulations 2013 (SI 2013/1237).

Northern Ireland has its own system of employment tribunals.

Hearings in employment tribunal cases tend to be informal. A case may have more than one 'preliminary hearing' for rulings by an employment judge on whether the case can proceed, or on case management. If it proceeds there is a further hearing, referred to in the rules as the 'final' hearing. This may last several days. In it the tribunal first decides on *liability* – whether the complaint against the employer is justified. This decision may be announced in summary on the same day it is made but may not be revealed until sent out later in a written judgment. If the employer is held liable, subsequently – often after an adjournment of some weeks – there is another 'final hearing' in which the tribunal decides the *'remedy'*, for example requiring the employer to pay compensation to someone sacked unfairly. If the tribunal finds employment law has been breached it can also impose a financial penalty on the employer.

Rule 46 of the 2013 regulations permits all or part of a tribunal hearing to be conducted 'by use of electronic communication', including by telephone, provided that members of the public attending the hearing are able to hear what the Tribunal hears and see any witness as seen by the Tribunal.

Appeals on points of law from employment tribunal decisions can be made to the Employment Appeal Tribunal (EAT) based in London.

((•))

see Useful Websites at the end of this chapter for these rules

Information about pending cases and judgments

Employment tribunal staff are instructed to provide journalists with the details of the parties in a case, and the nature of the claim, once it is listed for a hearing. Lists of hearings due to take place can also be obtained a week in advance, for a fee, through the *CourtServe* website. Journalists wanting a copy of a judgment can, if a regional tribunal office refuses to supply it, get it from the public register of judgments which keeps them for at least six years.

EAT judgments can be read online at its website.

((•))

for these sites, see Useful Websites, at the end of this chapter

Admission to employment tribunal cases

Rule 56 of the 2013 regulations states that a preliminary hearing shall be conducted in public if it involves a ruling on a 'preliminary issue' or is considering if all or part of a claim or response should be struck out – for example, because it has no reasonable prospect of success. A preliminary hearing can be held in private if dealing with case management or exploring if there can be a settlement. Rule 59 says final hearings shall be in public. But rules 56 and 59 are subject to other rules which empower a tribunal to sit in private.

see ch. 1, pp. 6–7, The European Convention on Human Rights, and ch. 26 on privacy

Rule 50 says that a tribunal can sit in private if it considers this necessary 'in the interests of justice' or in circumstances set out in section 10A of the Employment Tribunals Act 1996 or to protect a person's rights under the European Convention on Human Rights – for example, the right to privacy.

Section 10A of the 1996 Act says that an employment tribunal can decide to sit in private:

- when a witness's evidence is likely to contain:
  - information which he/she cannot disclose without breaking statutory law or without breaking an obligation of confidence; or
  - information which would cause substantial injury to his/her or the employer's interests, other than interests in collective negotiations over pay and conditions.

→ glossary

The rule 50 provision that an employment tribunal can exclude the public (and therefore journalists too) from a hearing in order to protect a person's Convention rights is a new statutory power, reflecting **case law** developments. It is likely to lead to more instances of people or companies arguing that cases should be heard in private. Journalists wishing to argue against an order to exclude them should remember that, according to rule 50, a tribunal deciding whether to sit in private 'shall give full weight to the principle of open justice' and to the right to freedom of expression (in the Convention's Article 10).

see also ch. 14 on Open Justice

The rule adds that any person with a legitimate interest (which would include a journalist wanting to cover the case) who has not had a reasonable opportunity to make representations against such an order 'may apply to the tribunal in writing for the order to be revoked or discharged, either on the basis of written representations or, if requested, at a hearing.'

Case study

The High Court has ruled that an employment tribunal is not empowered to sit in private merely because there is to be evidence of a sensitive or salacious nature when sexual misconduct is alleged (*R v Southampton Industrial Tribunal, ex p INS News Group Ltd and Express Newspapers plc* [1995] IRLR 247).

A Minister of the Crown, under the 1996 Act's section 10 and rule 94 of the 2013 regulations can direct an employment tribunal to hear a case in private in the interests of national security – if the tribunal has not already decided to do so.

Witness statements

In an employment tribunal, as in a civil court, usually a witness's written statement is his/her **evidence-in-chief**. The witness may give oral evidence too, but a journalist will probably need to see the written statement to understand the case. Rule 44 of the 2013 regulations says that any witness statement which stands as evidence in chief shall be available for inspection during the hearing by members of the public (and therefore journalists) attending it unless the tribunal decides that all or any part of the statement is not to be admitted as evidence. But the tribunal has the power under rules 50 (for example, on privacy grounds) or 94 (national security grounds) to revoke this inspection right.

 → glossary

see ch. 12, p. 135, Full trial proce-dure, for civil court procedure

Reporting and disclosure restrictions

Rule 50 empowers employment tribunals, on their own initiative or at the request of a party, to make an order 'with a view to preventing or restricting the public disclosure of any aspect of those proceedings' if the tribunal considers this necessary 'in the interests of justice' or in order to protect the Convention rights – including the privacy – of any person, or in the circumstances described in section 10A of the 1996 Act (which are set out earlier).

Such an order can ban indefinitely the disclosure of parts of the evidence, and/or the identities of 'specified parties, witnesses or other persons referred to in the proceedings' or in any documents 'forming part of the public record' of the case, including its listing and judgment.

Such an order can, then, permanently prevent a media report of the case from identifying who the complainant and/or respondent (for example, the employer) is. The order could make it illegal to publish any identifying detail – not just a person's name – and if so care must be taken by journalists to avoid 'jigsaw identification'.

see ch. 9, pp. 97–98, jigsaw identifica-tion

This new power in rule 50 to protect people's Convention rights co-exists with older powers to restrict reporting, explained in the next section, which are set out in the 1996 Act's section 11 relating to cases in which sexual misconduct is alleged, and in section 12 relating to cases in which discrimination on grounds of disability is alleged. These older powers allow employment tribunals to ban temporarily any media report of these types of case from identifying people involved in them. It seems likely that anyone arguing in such cases to be granted anonymity will now seek it under rule 50 in respect of Convention rights, under which it may be indefinite, not temporary. But the media can argue that principles laid down in judgments about these older types of reporting restriction should apply too when tribunals decide if rule 50 restrictions are justified.

Anonymity in sexual misconduct and disability cases

Section 11 of the Act and Rule 50 of the 2013 regulations give employment tribunals discretionary power to make temporary anonymity orders, known as 'restricted reporting orders', in cases involving allegations of sexual misconduct – for example, that a woman was forced to leave her job because her boss sexually harassed her. Sexual misconduct is defined as a sexual offence or sexual harassment or other adverse conduct (of whatever nature) related to sex, or to the sexual orientation of the person at whom the conduct is directed.

In a restricted reporting order, an employment tribunal can prohibit the inclusion in reports of any matter likely to lead members of the public to identify:

- the person making the allegation of sexual misconduct; and/or
- anyone 'affected' by it, for example the person(s) accused of such misconduct or any witness due to give evidence in such proceedings.

The tribunal can decide in each such case who should have such anonymity, if anyone. It may, for example, decide not to grant anonymity for the accuser but order it in respect of the person accused, to safeguard his/her reputation until judgment on whether the accusation is proved. Such an order cannot specifically bestow such anonymity on an employer that is a company or institution, so its corporate name can be published if this does not identify a person named in the order (*Leicester University v A* [1999] IRLR 352). But in a case where the employing organisation is small, for example a small firm, it may be that to preserve anonymity for the person the firm itself cannot be identified in media reports while the order remains in force, because reference to the person's gender or age or job description would in itself be enough to identify him/her to people who know he/she works there.

◉ Case study

In 1997 the Court of Appeal said it was important that tribunals should recognise that their power to make these orders in cases of sexual misconduct was not to be exercised automatically, and that the public interest in the media's ability to communicate information should be considered (*Kearney v Smith New Court Securities* [1997] EWCA Civ 1211).

Section 12 of the 1996 Act and rule 50 of the 2013 regulations allow employment tribunals to make restricted reporting orders when considering claims that an employer unlawfully discriminated on disability grounds, if evidence 'of a personal nature' is likely to be heard and is likely to cause significant embarrassment if published.

Rule 50 says a restricted reporting order made under section 11 or 12 of the Act shall specify the person whose identity is protected, and may specify particular matters of which publication is prohibited as likely to lead to that person's identification, and that the order should also specify the duration of the restriction. The rule adds that a notice that such an order has been made should be displayed on the notice board of the Tribunal with any list of cases taking place, and on the door of the room in which the case affected by the order is being heard.

! Remember

The automatic reporting restrictions in the Sexual Offences (Amendment) Act 1992 mean that anyone in employment tribunal proceedings who states that they are, or who is alleged to be, a victim of a sexual offence – for example, rape or sexual assault – must not be identified in media reports of the case in his/her lifetime, unless they have given valid, written consent for this. This is law is explained in ch. 10. It applies irrespective of whether a restricted reporting order under the Employment Tribunals Act 1996 has been imposed or expired.

The 1996 Act says that once the employment tribunal has made a restricted reporting order under sections 11 or 12:

- it can revoke (that is, cancel) the order at any stage – for example, while the case is ongoing, or when it makes a verbal announcement of its decision on *liability* – to permit media reports to immediately identify the person formerly covered by the order;
- but, anyway, if not revoked the order only has effect 'until the promulgation of the decision of the tribunal', according to the Act. Under regulations published in 2004, this meant the date when the ruling on *liability* was sent to the parties, or in cases where there needed to be a ruling on *remedy*, the date that ruling was sent to them – see the earlier explanation of these terms. The 2013 regulations replaced those of 2004, and, as explained earlier, require the tribunal to state the duration of a section 11 or 12 order when making it. Under the Act it can only last until 'promulgation'.

Penalty for breach of anonymity

Publishing matter which breaches a restricted reporting order made under the Act's section 11 or 12 is a summary offence punishable by a fine of up to £5,000. Any proprietor, editor or publisher held responsible will be liable to pay it. It is a defence for the person or company prosecuted to show that he/she/it was not aware, and neither suspected nor had reason to suspect that the published matter breached the order.

National security reporting restrictions

Rule 94 of the 2013 regulations, reflecting section 10 of the 1996 Act, says that a Minister of the Crown can order an employment tribunal to conceal the identity of a witness in a case concerning national security issues, and order it to keep secret all or part of the reasons for its decision in such a case, or the tribunal on its own initiative can take either of these courses of action. When the tribunal has taken such steps, it is an offence to publish anything likely to lead to the identification of the witness or to publish any part of a decision the tribunal intended to keep secret. The maximum fine is £5,000.

Challenging reporting restrictions

A journalist covering an employment tribunal case may wish to challenge the imposition or continuation of a disclosure restriction made under rule 50, or use of the 1996 Act's section 11 or 12, or the restriction's scope or duration. Rule 50(4) gives anyone 'with a legitimate interest' the right to make a challenge by written or verbal representations, just as it does in the case of an order that a hearing should be in private, see earlier. Again, rule 50 (4) requires the tribunal considering imposing a restriction, or deciding on a challenge to it, to give full weight to the open justice principle and Article 10 rights.

👁 Case study

In 2013 the Associated Newspapers group successfully argued at an employment tribunal that anonymity orders should cease to apply. The tribunal had rejected a man's claims of constructive dismissal, unfair dismissal and sexual harassment. The complainant had been a managing director. His allegations included that he was obliged by his boss, the group's chief executive, to take part in sex parties against his will. The tribunal, having ruled the claims were 'totally without merit', then ruled that the complainant did not deserve to retain anonymity because any damage to his reputation was because of 'his own actions'. It also ruled that the chief executive should not retain anonymity either, having found that there were 'sexual encounters' from 2001 to 2009 which involved both men having sex with women other than their wives and partners. The tribunal said that the chief executive was responsible for a company ethos which allowed the managing director to rule over employees 'by fear', and that removal of the chief executive's anonymity in reports of the case would let employees know why this was (*Media Lawyer*, 20 August 2013).

An employment tribunal can take account of previous publicity when refusing to make a restricted reporting order. In 2000 a tribunal refused to make such an order which would have granted temporary anonymity to a businessman accused of sexual harassment. Both parties wanted the order made. But the *Daily Record* successfully argued that both parties had previously willingly given information about the case to the media (*Scottish Daily Record and Sunday Mail Ltd v Margaret McAvoy and others*, EAT/1271/01).

Where a restricted reporting order is imposed under the Act's section 11 or 12, but a settlement is reached without the case proceeding to judgment, the restriction remains in place indefinitely (*Fiona Davidson v Dallas McMillan* [2009] CSIH 70). However, it can be lifted if there is a change in circumstances for example, a person who wanted anonymity originally now wishes the media to be able to identify him/her (*Tradition Securities & Futures SA and another v Times Newspapers Limited and others*, UKEATPA/1415/08/JOJ; UKEATPA/1417/08/JOJ).

Contempt and defamation law affecting coverage of employment tribunals

Employment tribunals and the Employment Appeals Tribunal are classed as courts. Therefore, as explained earlier in this chapter about all such tribunals, media reports of their hearings can enjoy privilege against libel actions, and the Contempt of Court Act 1981 and other contempt law apply to their proceedings. This includes the ban in section 9 of the 1981 Act on unauthorised use in their hearings of audio-recording devices (*Neckles v Yorkshire Rider Ltd* [2002] All ER (D) 111 (Jan)).

▐ Public inquiries

Public inquiries can be broadly categorised either as local inquiries, set up routinely in certain circumstances, or those which are set up ad hoc to consider a matter of national concern.

Local public inquiries

Some Acts of Parliament provide that an inquiry hearing must be held before certain decisions are made affecting the rights of individuals or of public authorities. An inquiry might be held, for example, before planning schemes are approved. In some cases, an 'inspector' appointed by a Minister to chair the inquiry decides the matter at issue. In others, he/she must report to the Minister, who subsequently announces a decision and the reasons for it. Some statutes under which inquiries are held stipulate that they must be held in public. In others, this is discretionary. Local authorities and health trusts also have general statutory powers under which they can fund an ad hoc inquiry into a matter of local (or national) concern, though it will be at their discretion whether it is held in public.

Public inquiries into matters of national concern

Public inquiries initiated ad hoc by government Ministers have in recent years included:

- The inquiry chaired by Sir Brian Leveson into the culture, practices and ethics of the press, which was established under the Inquiries Act 2005 (the 2005 Act) www.levesoninquiry.org.uk/

    ch. 2 gives context about the Leveson inquiry

- The Hutton inquiry set up in 2003 into the death of Dr David Kelly, who committed suicide after investigation by his employer, the Ministry of Defence, into his contact with BBC journalists about the government's stated justification for the Iraq war. This inquiry was held on a non-statutory basis by a chair appointed by the Secretary of State for Constitutional Affairs. See www.the-hutton-inquiry.org.uk/.

If an inquiry is held on a non-statutory basis, it has no legal powers to compel witnesses to give evidence, but is seen as a flexible option when full cooperation is anticipated.

If the inquiry is established under the 2005 Act, under section 19 a Minister or an inquiry's chair can decide on various grounds – for example, national security or to protect the 'efficiency' of the inquiry – that it should hear evidence in private.

 www.mcnaes.com ch. 17 sets out the reporting restrictions which can be imposed under the Act, including by the chair of such an inquiry. It also outlines the powers of the chair to compel production of evidence – including from a journalist – and explains how section 18 of the Act gives journalists some rights to obtain or view a record of an inquiry's evidence and documents, but says that audio recording and televising of the proceedings need the chair's permission.

Coverage of public inquiries: defamation law

ch. 21, pp. 268–269, The requirements of qualified privilege

Reports of public inquiries held under the Inquiries Act 2005 have, under its section 37, the same privilege 'as would be the case if those proceedings were proceedings before a court'. This means that, as regards proceedings held in public, absolute privilege applies under section 14 of the Defamation Act 1996 to contemporaneous reports and qualified privilege applies under Part 1 of Schedule 1 to the 1996 Act to non-contemporaneous reports, if the respective requirements of these defences are met, including that the reports fairly and accurately reflect the proceedings.

The Schedule is set out in this book's Appendix 3. Part 1 of the Schedule also applies qualified privilege, subject to the same requirements, to media reports of the proceedings in public 'of a person appointed to hold a public inquiry by a government or legislature anywhere in the world'. Media reports of public inquiries of the type defined in paragraph 11 in Part 2 of the Schedule enjoy qualified privilege subject to the additional requirement to publish 'explanation or contradiction' if this is requested. The 1996 Act does not make clear in Part 2 of the Schedule how what it describes as a person appointed by 'a Minister of the Crown' to run an inquiry differs from what Part 1 of the Schedule describes as a person appointed to do this 'by a government', see earlier. But it is an established legal principle that when an event/circumstance is described both generally and specifically in a statute, the part which is most specific applies.

Privilege will not apply to media reports of any matter aired in a private session of an inquiry. As is the case with administrative tribunals, proceedings of public inquiries are not as formal as those in an ordinary court of law, so some extra care must be exercised in what is reported if qualified privilege under the 1996 Act is relied on – see p. 202, Proceedings are not always formal.

The findings of a public inquiry are usually published by a government department, by Parliament or by the relevant local authority. Under the 1996 Act:

- a fair and accurate media report of such findings, when they have been officially published by a government or legislature anywhere in the world, is protected by qualified privilege under Part 1 of the Act's Schedule 1 (paragraph 7).

- a fair and accurate media report of findings officially published by a local authority anywhere in the world is protected by qualified privilege under Part 2 of the Schedule (paragraph 9).

➡ Recap of major points

- Most types of tribunals adjudicate in disputes in specialist areas of law. Some are regulatory tribunals for professions, for example doctors, lawyers.

- Employment tribunals can make temporary anonymity orders in cases involving sexual misconduct.

- Media reports of the public proceedings of tribunals are protected by qualified privilege and, as regards those classed as courts, by absolute privilege when reports are contemporaneous.

- For any tribunal classed as a court, contempt law applies.

- Media reports of the public proceedings of public inquiries are, as regards defamation actions, protected by either qualified privilege or absolute privilege.

((•)) Useful Websites

http://www.justice.gov.uk/tribunals/rules
    Procedural rules for the First-tier Tribunal and the Upper Tribunal

http://www.justice.gov.uk/tribunals/employment

https://www.gov.uk/employment-tribunals
    Government guidance on employment tribunals

http://www.legislation.gov.uk/uksi/2013/1237/regulation/1/made
    Procedural rules for employment tribunals

http://www.justice.gov.uk/tribunals/employment-appeals
    Government guidance on Employment Appeals Tribunal

https://www.gov.uk/employment-tribunals

www.direct.gov.uk/en/Employment/index.htm
    Government guidance on employment rights

http://www.justice.gov.uk/tribunals/employment/hearings
    Details of register of employment tribunal judgments

www.employmenttribunalsni.co.uk/
    Northern Ireland industrial tribunal service

www.legislation.gov.uk/ukpga/2005/12/notes/contents/
    The government's explanatory notes to the Inquiries Act 2005

http://www.courtserve.net/
    CourtServe website

18

Contempt of court

Chapter summary

The law of contempt protects the integrity of the administration of justice, and the fundamental principle that a defendant is presumed innocent until proven guilty. Contempt law most affects journalists when they publish material which might affect a trial, by making a jury more likely to find a defendant guilty – or innocent – or by influencing a witness's evidence. Publications may also 'impede' the course of justice by creating a risk that witnesses will refuse to come forward to help the prosecution or defence. Media organisations which have committed contempt by publishing prejudicial material have been fined heavily. The law of contempt applies as much to material on the internet as to print and broadcast coverage.

▶ What does contempt of court law protect?

The law of contempt of court protects the judicial process. Anyone who is disruptive or threatening in a courtroom can be punished immediately for contempt, by being sent by the magistrates or judge to the court's cells, and in some cases subsequently to jail, as contempt is a criminal offence.

The greatest risk of the media committing contempt is by publishing material which could prejudice a fair trial by:

- giving the impression that a defendant or suspect is the sort of person who is likely to have committed the crime, or vilifying a suspect to the extent that witnesses might refuse to come forward to help his/her defence or the prosecution case;

- seeking to discover or publishing information from the jury's confidential discussions about a verdict – this would breach the Contempt of Court Act 1981– see ch. 11, pp. 117–118, Confidentiality of jury deliberations;

- publishing material which breaches the **common law** of contempt, eg by 'vilifying' a person for being a witness at a trial – see later in this chapter;

- contaminating a witness's evidence by interviewing him or her in detail, or offering payment for his/her story before a trial – see later in this chapter;

- publishing material in breach of a court order made in common law or under the Contempt of Court Act 1981, for example, by naming a blackmail victim in reports of a trial – see ch. 11 pp. 119–120, Section 11 orders – blackmail, secrets, personal safety.

! Remember

The Court of Appeal has ruled that the punishment for publishing material in breach of an order made under a statute other than the 1981 Act – for example, under the Children and Young Persons Act 1933, explained in ch. 9 – should be that specified by that statute, rather than as a contempt (*R v Tyne Tees Television* [1997] EWCA Crim 2395; *The Times*, 20 October 1997).

▌ Types of contempt

There are two types of contempt – common law contempt and strict liability contempt. Common law contempt consists of publishing material which creates a substantial risk of serious prejudice to proceedings which are pending or imminent with the intention of creating that risk, or of behaviour or conduct which interferes with the administration of justice.

Strict liability contempt, which is governed by the Contempt of Court Act 1981, consists simply of publishing material which creates a substantial risk of serious prejudice or impediment to 'active' proceedings – the court decides whether the publication has created the risk, and the motives of the writer and publisher are irrelevant.

 See p. 219, What type of material can cause a substantial risk of *serious prejudice or impediment*.

The media's approach to contempt has caused concern. In March 2011, the Attorney General, Dominic Grieve QC, expressed alarm about the media's approach to crime reporting, saying there was 'frenzied interest' in high-profile arrests which stopped abruptly only when a suspect was charged or released, and warned that the law might have to be changed to give arrested people anonymity until they were charged.

▶ Contempt in common law

Common law contempt makes it an offence to publish material which creates a substantial risk of serious prejudice to legal proceedings which are imminent or pending, if it can be proved that there was intent to create such a risk.

- The term 'intent' could mean either deliberate intention to create such a risk, or recklessness in publishing material which the person responsible for the publication should have foreseen would create such a risk.

The Contempt of Court Act 1981 largely superseded the common law by creating the strict liability rule in respect of a case which is 'active' under the Act. Common law contempt still applies to material published before proceedings become active (and arguably may apply to material published at later stages in the proceedings). Prosecutions of the media for common law contempt are extremely rare as the prosecution has to prove that the journalist or editor intended to create a serious risk of prejudice.

👁 Case study

In 2010 the Police Service of Northern Ireland sought a High Court injunction to stop the BBC broadcasting a documentary about the 1972 bombings in the village of Claudy in which nine people died and 30 were injured. Police argued that even though no proceedings were active, the programme – which the BBC refused to allow an officer to see before it was broadcast – was a contempt, would interfere with the administration of justice or could breach confidentiality. Mr Justice Seamus Treacy rejected the 'unprecedented' application, saying it was based on pure speculation, was not supported by any legal authority, and, if allowed, would significantly extend the boundaries of the law (*Media Lawyer*, 3 November 2010).

Witness interviews and 'molestation'

Publishing detailed accounts of a witness's evidence while a case is active could breach the strict liability rule. But even if the intention was not to publish any interview with a witness until after the trial, a reporter who interviews a witness about a case before he/she has testified might be held guilty of common law contempt for having contaminated the witness's memory, for example by telling him/her what other witnesses said, or by saying anything which could influence what the witness remembered or otherwise affected his/her testimony.

It could also be a contempt by 'molestation' for a journalist to pester a witness so much for a pre-trial interview, or in photographing him/her, that he/she was deterred from testifying. A media organisation's offer to 'buy up' a witness who has yet to give evidence to tell his/her story after the trial could amount to common law contempt if it was held to have influenced how the witness testified.

Ch. 2, p. 19, Payments to witnesses, gives detail of clause 15 of the Editors' Code of Practice. There is similar provision in the Ofcom Broadcasting Code, see ch. 3, p. 23, Ofcom – its role and sanctions.

Vilifying a witness

Media organisations which publish, after the end of a trial, criticism of a witness which was so abusive that a judge could rule that it was likely to deter others from being witnesses in future could be punished for common law contempt for 'vilifying' the witness.

 Ch. 11 explains that publishing information from some types of court document, photography or filming in a courtroom, or harassment of a defendant or witness by photographers or film crews could be ruled to be a contempt in common law.

▶ Contempt of Court Act 1981 – strict liability

A primary purpose of the Contempt of Court Act 1981 was to replace some aspects of the common law of contempt, and give greater certainty about what constitutes a contempt. Section 1 of the Act made contempt by publication a strict liability offence in the case of 'active' criminal or civil proceedings.

- The strict liability rule says it is a contempt to publish material which creates a substantial risk of serious prejudice or impediment to 'active' legal proceedings.

Strict liability means that the prosecution, when seeking to prove that a contempt was committed, does not have to prove that the editor or media organisation responsible intended to create the risk. The court simply judges the actual or potential prejudicial effect of what was published. Prosecutions for contempt are usually of the relevant publishing company.

- The Act defines publication as any writing, speech, broadcast or other communication addressed to any section of the public – and includes material on websites.

Breaching the strict liability rule is punishable by an unlimited fine and/or a maximum of two years' in jail.

Who can prosecute for contempt of court?

Proceedings for contempt under the strict liability rule can be initiated only by a Crown court or higher court, or by the Attorney General or with the Attorney General's consent.

 ch. 1 p. 9, High offices in law, explains the Attorney General's role

Magistrates cannot punish contempt of court by publication. A contempt in respect of proceedings in a magistrates court (although none appears to have been recorded) would have to be dealt with by the High Court.

In 1997 the Court of Appeal ruled that only in exceptional circumstances should trial judges deal with such an alleged contempt themselves (*R v Tyne Tees Television*, *The Times*, 20 October 1997). Crown court judges usually refer such matters to the Attorney General, who decides if the case should be referred to the High Court.

When are criminal proceedings active?

The strict liability rule applies only if proceedings are 'active'.

The Act says a criminal case becomes active when:

ch. 4 explains these early stages of a criminal case.

- a person is arrested, or
- an arrest warrant is issued, or
- a summons is issued, or
- a person is charged orally.

These steps all mean that there is a definite prospect of an individual facing trial. A criminal case, if not already active because one of the above four events has occurred, also becomes active when the accused is served with a document specifying the charge(s).

A potential problem for the media is that the police may not make clear, after a crime is committed, if a person is under arrest or simply 'helping police with their inquiries'. Journalists must press for clarification.

When do criminal proceedings cease to be active?

Criminal proceedings cease to be active when any of these events occur:

- the arrested person is released without being charged (except when released on police bail);
- no arrest is made within 12 months of the issue of an arrest warrant;
- the case is discontinued;
- the defendant is acquitted or sentenced; or
- the defendant is found unfit to be tried, or unfit to plead, or the court orders the charge to lie on file.

 Ch. 4, pp. 41–42, The Crown Prosecution Service explains police bail and arrest warrants.

A defendant can be ruled to be unfit to be tried or unfit to plead if he/she suffers acute physical ill-health or mental illness. An order that a charge should 'lie on file' means the defendant has not been acquitted or convicted, but that the court agrees that the charge is no longer worth proceeding with. If after a lengthy trial a defendant is convicted of four charges but the jury cannot agree on the fifth, the judge may order that charge to 'lie on file' because the expense of a retrial for that charge would be excessive, or a conviction would not lead to a longer prison sentence.

Period between verdict and sentence at Crown court

A Crown court case remains active, even though all the verdicts have been reached, until the defendant is sentenced. It is technically possible for a media organisation to breach the strict liability rule during this period, although the jury's involvement has ended. But Crown court judges are regarded as too experienced to be influenced by media coverage, so it is thought unlikely that there will be any substantial risk of serious prejudice, whatever is published after all verdicts but before an adjourned sentencing. Media organisations are generally safe in publishing background features about such a case, including material which did not feature in the trial, as soon as the last verdict is given, although judges have been known to order the postponement of publication of such material until after sentencing. The judiciary told the Law Commission in April 2013 that it believes that a case should cease to be active when the final verdict is delivered.

Proceedings become active again when an appeal is lodged

The 1981 Act states that:

- when an appeal is lodged, the case becomes active again, so strict liability contempt resumes;
- the case ceases to be active when the hearing of any appeal is completed – unless in that appeal a new trial is ordered or the case is remitted to a lower court.

Lawyers often announce at the end of a criminal or civil case that their clients will appeal, but it usually takes some weeks for an appeal to be prepared and lodged, so there is a time when the case is not active between, in a criminal case, the sentence and the lodging of an appeal.

- Even if an appeal is lodged against a Crown court conviction, the media still have considerable freedom relating to what can be published about such a case, although it has become active again, as the appeal will be heard by the judges of the Court of Appeal.

see ch. 8, p. 84, Court of Appeal

It can safely be assumed that nothing the media publishes will create a substantial risk of serious prejudice to the way these judges approach the case. But if they order a retrial – that is, another jury trial – the media must be wary of publishing anything which creates a risk of serious prejudice to the retrial, as witnesses and potential jurors will be considered susceptible to publicity about the case before and during the retrial.

Where to check if an appeal has been lodged

Appeals to the Court of Appeal from Crown courts may be lodged at the Crown court office. Appeals on a point of law to the Queen's Bench Divisional Court (the High Court) from a Crown court appeal hearing must be lodged at the Royal Courts of Justice in London. Appeals from magistrates court summary trials may be lodged at a local Crown court office.

see ch. 15, p. 178, The possibility of retrial, for the similar ruling in the *Beggs* case

---

👁 Case study

The High Court in Belfast in 2002 refused to issue an injunction to stop Ulster Television broadcasting a programme featuring new material which had not been put before the jury in a trial in which two men were convicted of murder. The men's lawyers said they intended to appeal and the material could prejudice the jury at any retrial. But Mr Justice Kerr said the possibility of a retrial was a matter of speculation.

Police appeals for media assistance

Sometimes when police have obtained a warrant for someone's arrest, they seek media help in tracing him/her. The warrant makes the case active under the 1981 Act. Police may supply the suspect's photograph and/or description for publication, even though identification may be an issue in the case. If the person is armed or likely to be violent, police may say so, to warn the public.

- Technically, a media organisation publishing such a photograph, description or warning about the person's character could be accused of creating a substantial risk of serious prejudice to such an active case.
- But the then Attorney General said in the House of Commons during the debate on the Contempt of Court Bill in 1981:

" The press has nothing whatever to fear from publishing in reasoned terms anything which may assist in the apprehension of a wanted man and I hope that it will continue to perform this public service. "

- There is no known case of a media organisation being held in contempt for publishing such a police appeal. But there is no defence in the 1981 Act for assisting the police in this way.

The Attorney General's comments would not apply to information supplied by police which was published or repeated after the person's arrest.

Section 3 defence of not knowing proceedings were active

Section 3 of the Act provides a defence for an alleged breach of the strict liability rule. The defence applies if:

- the person responsible for the publication, having taken all reasonable care, did not know and had no reason to suspect when the material was published that relevant proceedings were active.

The person accused of contempt must prove that all reasonable care was taken. So, to be sure that the section 3 defence can be used, a journalist reporting a crime story must check regularly with police, especially before a deadline, about whether someone has been arrested or charged, as either event would make the case active, and the story would need to be re-edited to remove any detail likely to breach the strict liability rule. For some news stories it might be necessary for journalists to check with magistrates courts whether arrest warrants or summonses have been issued.

If the police or court spokesperson says the case is not active, the journalist should keep a note of what was said, by whom and when, to prove that he/she took reasonable care to establish if the case was active.

 See p. 231, Contempt of civil proceedings, for detail of when a civil case is active. See ch. 16, p. 195, Defamation and contempt issues, for when an inquest is active, and ch. 17, p. 201, Contempt issues in coverage of tribunals, for detail of when cases before certain types of tribunal are active.

What type of material can cause a substantial risk of serious prejudice or impediment?

The 1981 Act does not define what creates a substantial risk of serious prejudice or impediment to an active case. But cases in which editors and media organisations have been convicted of contempt show that material which could be held to be in contempt of court in active cases includes:

- references to a suspect or defendant's previous convictions;
- information suggesting he/she is dishonest or of bad character in other ways;
- any evidence seeming to link him/her directly to the crime of which he/she is suspected or accused;
- any other suggestion that he/she is guilty.

If the person is tried, the magistrates or jury will probably not be told of his/her previous convictions, while character evidence may be admissible only in certain circumstances.

It could also be strict liability contempt in an active case to publish:

ch. 6 explains when 'bad character' evidence is admissible

- a witness's detailed account of a relevant event after a case becomes active – the risk this presents is explained later in this chapter.
- a photograph or footage or physical description of a suspect when visual identification of the alleged perpetrator is or is likely to be an evidential issue because:
  - a police identity parade is to be held; and/or
  - a witness is expected to testify at the trial on such identification.

! Remember

Contempt law is enforced more strictly in Scotland. This means particular care must be taken in cross-border publication, including on the internet. See the mcnaes.com chapter on Scotland.

References to a defendant's previous convictions

Coverage in *The Times* of a knife attack in which one woman died and another was injured which detailed the attacker's previous conviction for the manslaughter of her own mother did not amount to a breach of the strict liability rule, the High Court ruled in a decision published in February 2013. But it was 'deeply regrettable' that the newspaper had detailed Nicola Edgington's previous conviction, said Sir John Thomas, the then President of the Queen's Bench Division, sitting with Mr Justice Eady. The court stressed that those who reported crime should recognise that they published articles making assumptions about the extent of the issues likely to be disputed in forthcoming criminal trials at their peril. Sir John added: 'If there is created a substantial risk of serious prejudice, the danger is that those most immediately concerned in the case, not only any accused person but also the victims and their families, may unnecessarily be deprived of access to justice. That should be a danger no editor wants to create.' The court said it had 'narrowly reached the conclusion' that Attorney General Dominic Grieve QC had failed to prove that *The Times* breached the strict liability rule with its coverage of the incident in Bexleyheath in which Nicola Edgington attacked and injured Kerry Clark before stabbing and killing grandmother Sally Hodkin nearby. Edgington was convicted on 7 February 2013, of having murdered Mrs Hodkin and attempting to murder Ms Clark on Monday 10 October 2011 (*Attorney General v Times Newspapers Ltd* [2012] EWHC 3195 (Admin)).

Information suggesting a suspect or defendant is dishonest or of bad character

The *Daily Mirror* and *The Sun* were fined £50,000 and £18,000 respectively in July 2011 over their coverage the previous December of the arrest of former teacher Chris Jefferies, the landlord of murdered landscape architect Joanna Yeates. The court heard that one *Daily Mirror* front page carried the headline 'Jo Suspect is Peeping Tom' beneath a photograph of Mr Jefferies, and another front-page headline read 'Was Killer Waiting In Jo's Flat?', with sub-headings below reading 'Police seize bedding for tests' and 'Landlord held until Tuesday'. *The Sun's* front-page headline read 'Obsessed By Death' next to a photograph of Mr Jefferies and below the words 'Jo Suspect 'Scared Kids'. Attorney General Dominic Grieve QC said material in the articles gave an 'overall impression' that Mr Jefferies had a 'propensity' to commit the kind of offences for which he had been arrested. The Lord Chief Justice, Lord Judge said section 2(2) of the Contempt of Court Act 1981 provided that the strict liability contempt rule applied only to a publication which created a substantial risk that the course of justice in the proceedings in question 'will be seriously impeded or prejudiced' and went on: 'Dealing with it briefly, impeding the course of justice and prejudicing the course of justice are not synonymous concepts. If they were, they would not have been identified as distinct features of the strict liability rule.' The issue of impeding the course of justice outside the trial process was 'less well trodden'. Vilification of a suspect under arrest readily was a potential impediment to the course of justice, he said, adding:

> At the simplest level publication of such material may deter or discourage witnesses from coming forward and providing information helpful to the suspect, which may, (depending on the circumstances) help immediately to clear him of suspicion or enable his defence to be fully developed at trial.

He said that it was not an answer to argue that on the evidence actually available, the combination of the directions of the judge and the integrity of the jury would ensure a fair trial – the evidence at trial may be incomplete 'because its existence may never be known, or indeed may only come to light after conviction' (*Attorney-General v MGN Ltd and another* [2011] All ER (D) 06 (Aug)). Mr. Jefferies was released without charge after his arrest. Another man was convicted of murdering Ms Yeates.

 Mr Jefferies won damages from newspapers for libel, see ch 4, p. 43, The risk of libel in media identification of crime suspects

👁 Case study

In 2011 the *Daily Mail* and *The Sun* were found guilty of strict liability contempt, after both mistakenly published on their websites a photograph which showed a man, who was on trial for murder, posing with an automatic pistol. The case was the first time website operators in the UK had been found guilty of contempt. The photograph was taken from a social networking web page. Lord Justice Moses, sitting with Mr Justice Owen in the Queen's Bench Divisional Court said: 'The criminal courts have been troubled by the dangers to the integrity and fairness of a criminal trial, where juries can obtain such easy access to the internet and to other forms of instant communication. This case demonstrates the need to recognise that instant news requires instant and effective protection for the integrity of a criminal trial.' The newspapers were found to have created a 'a substantial risk' of prejudicing the trial of Ryan Ward, who was eventually convicted of murdering father-of-two Craig Wass by hitting him on the head with a brick when he intervened in a row to protect Ryan's girlfriend. The offending photograph of Ward appeared on the two newspapers' websites alongside their reports of the first day of the trial. They were removed immediately the newspapers were alerted to the risk – the *Daily Mail* had used the picture uncut, but *The Sun* had cropped it, although part of the barrel of the gun could still be seen. No juror saw the pictures. The Divisional Court said that although the jury was warned against researching material on the internet, a juror would not have understood the trial judge's instructions to have prohibited reading online news reports of the case (*Attorney General v Associated Newspapers Ltd and another* [2011] All ER (D) 45 (Mar)). The court fined each paper £15,000 and ordered them to pay the Attorney General's costs of £28,117 (*Media Lawyer*, 19 July 2011).

Publishing a witness's detailed account

Publishing a witness's detailed account of a relevant event after a case becomes active may be deemed a contempt because of the risk that:

- the witness may, because such a detailed account has been published, feel obliged to stick to it and therefore less able honestly to retract or vary some detail after further reflection; or

- the witness's evidence may not figure in the trial at all, because it is ruled inadmissible or has been retracted – but if it has already been published other witnesses or jurors in the case may have read or heard it and been influenced by it.

Visual identification

Publishing a photo or footage or description could influence or confuse a witness who gives identification evidence so that the court may not be sure if the witness's evidence – for example, from an 'identity parade' – is based on what was seen during the crime or on recollection of a subsequently published photograph or footage or description.

Police investigating crimes often ask the media to publish a sketch or computer generated image of an alleged offender's face, as described by a witness, or issue a physical description, in an attempt to get the public to give information about the individual's identity.

The strict liability rule means that the image and description must usually not be published again after the case becomes active.

👁 Case study

In 1994 *The Sun* was fined £80,000 and its editor Kelvin MacKenzie £20,000 after it published a photograph of a man charged with murder. The picture was published before an identity parade in which he was picked out by witnesses (*The Independent*, 6 July 1994).

! Remember

The examples of prejudicial material in this chapter relate mainly to the contempt risk of saying or suggesting that a suspect or defendant is guilty – but the strict liability rule can be breached by publishing material suggesting or asserting a suspect's innocence.

 The High Court and Crown courts can grant injunctions to prevent the media publishing material deemed capable of creating a substantial risk of serious prejudice to a criminal case or to restrain reporters' attempts to interview witnesses before a trial – see www.mcnaes.com ch. 18.

What can be published after a criminal case becomes active?

Contempt law does not mean that the media cannot publish anything about a crime after a case becomes active.

Non-prejudicial, basic information about the crime can be published. For example, the media can report that there was an alleged robbery, where it took place and that later someone was arrested. Do not report that 'the robber was later arrested' as this says the arrested person is guilty of the offence. Note the Attorney General's concern about 'frenzied interest' in high-profile cases.

In most cases, it will not be contempt to name the arrested person, because he/she will be named at the trial. But it may be unsafe in libel law to name an arrested person before he/she is charged, and other law gives pre-charge anonymity to teachers accused by pupils, as ch. 4 explains.

In contempt law it is safe to identify the alleged victim(s) of crime before any prosecution begins. But a reporting restriction may apply to media reports of the court case, as chs. 9 and 11 explain. The victim/alleged victims of a sexual offence has automatic anonymity from the time the offence is alleged – see ch. 10.

Common ground

It is not prejudicial to publish material which will be common ground between the defence and prosecution at the trial, such as non-prejudicial background material about a defendant and any alleged victim. Also, in a murder case, there will rarely be dispute about where the body was found. In contested cases, the nature and extent of a victim's injuries will probably be common ground because much of the forensic or medical evidence will be beyond dispute – the trial issue will be how the injuries were caused or who caused them.

How the courts interpret the strict liability rule

In *A-G v MGN Ltd* [1997] 1 All ER 456 Lord Justice Schiemann set out the principles a court should follow when deciding whether published material created a substantial risk of serious prejudice in cases with a potential for jury trial. The court, he said, should consider what risk occurred at the time the material was published. The mere fact that by reason of earlier publications there was already some risk of prejudice did not in itself prevent a court finding that the later publication had created a further risk. The court should consider:

- the likelihood of the publication coming to a potential juror's attention;
- its likely impact on an ordinary reader;
- and, crucially, the residual impact on a notional juror at the time of the trial.

Juries are told to put pre-trial publicity out of their minds

At the start of Crown court trials judges tell juries to decide their verdicts only on the evidence presented to them, and to put pre-trial publicity about the case, or media coverage of the trial, out of their minds. They are also warned not to research the internet for material.

Judges have made clear that juries must be trusted. In 1996 the then Lord Chief Justice, Lord Taylor, dismissed an appeal by Rosemary West, who was convicted of a series of murders, which was based in part on claims that she had not had a fair trial because of adverse publicity. He said:

> But, however lurid the reporting, there can scarcely ever have been a case more calculated to shock the public who were entitled to know the facts. The question raised on behalf of the defence is whether a fair trial could be held after such intensive publicity adverse to the accused. In our view it could. To hold otherwise would mean that if allegations of murder are sufficiently horrendous so as inevitably to shock the nation, the accused cannot be tried. That would be absurd.

More recently, senior judges have firmly re-stated the view that jurors given directions by a judge are capable of looking at the evidence fairly. In *Re B* [2007] EMLR 5; *The Times*, 6 November 2006, Sir Igor Judge, as he then was, presiding at the Court of Appeal, stressed the robustness and independence of juries in a case in which the court lifted an order postponing reporting of a hearing at which Dhiren Barot, self-confessed terrorist, was to be sentenced.

He said, at paragraphs 31 and 32 of the judgment, that 'juries up and down the country have a passionate and profound belief in, and a commitment to' the defendant's right to a fair trial and went on:

> They know that it is integral to their responsibility. It is, when all is said and done, their birthright; it is shared by each one of them with the defendant. They guard it faithfully. The integrity of the jury is an essential feature of our trial process. Juries follow the directions which the judge will give them to focus exclusively on the evidence and to ignore anything they may have heard or read out of court.

The judge at the trial would give the jury appropriate directions, he said, adding:

> We cannot too strongly emphasise that the jury will follow them, not only because they will loyally abide by the directions of law which they will be given by the

judge, but also because the directions themselves will appeal directly to their own instinctive and fundamental belief in the need for the trial process to be fair.**""**

There were, he added, at least two safeguards against the risk of prejudice – the media's responsibility to avoid inappropriate comment which might interfere with the administration of justice, and the trial process, including the integrity of the jury.

The 'fade factor' and limited publication

The 'fade factor' recognises that the public will probably have forgotten detail in reports published in the early stages of a criminal case, eg soon after the crime, or about the time that someone is arrested or charged, by the time a jury is selected. Others factors a court takes into account include the area where the material was published, and the likely extent to which it was read – or, if broadcast, seen or heard – in that area.

see p. 220, References to a defendant's previous convictions

But some material may be so striking, even when published some time before a trial, as to create a substantial risk of serious prejudice or impediment to the trial. This has been said to include, especially, disclosure of a defendant's criminal record.

Case study

The lapse of time was a factor in assessing the substantial risk of serious prejudice in a contempt case in 1997. The *Daily Mail* and *Manchester Evening News*, which carried stories describing how a home help was caught on video film stealing from an 82-year-old widow, were found not guilty of contempt of court in the Queen's Bench Divisional Court. Mr Justice Owen said his initial view was that the stories were a plain contempt of court as they carried the clearest statements that she was guilty at a time when proceedings against her were active. The key issue was whether the stories created a substantial risk that the criminal proceedings against her would be seriously prejudiced. But the stories were several months old by the time of the trial, and he had concluded that the contempt allegation was not made good. But Lord Justice Simon Brown warned the media against thinking that when someone was apparently caught red-handed there was no possibility of a not guilty plea at trial (*A-G v Unger* [1998] 1 Cr App R 308).

! Remember

The 'fade factor' alone might not be enough to avoid liability for contempt if the court holds that published material has created an impediment to the course of justice – see the Jefferies case on pp. 220–221, Information suggesting a suspect or defendant is dishonest or of bad character.

Publishing material shortly before or during a trial

The 'fade factor' offers no protection if the material concerned is published shortly before a trial begins or after it has started. In 2008 ITV Central was fined

£25,000 for contempt for broadcasting an item on the morning on which the trial of five men was due to start which reported that one defendant was in jail serving a sentence for murder.

👁 Case study

In 2002 the *Sunday Mirror* was fined £75,000 for publishing an article which led to the collapse of the first trial of two Leeds United footballers on assault charges. The two-page spread was published while the jury was deliberating and had been sent home for the weekend. It contained an interview in which the victim's father said his son was the victim of a racial attack – the jury had been told that there was no evidence of a racial motive – and a story commenting on a major witness's credibility. In the contempt proceedings, counsel for the Attorney General estimated the cost of the aborted trial at £1,113,000 and the cost of the subsequent retrial £1,125,000 (*Attorney General v Mirror Group Newspapers Ltd* [2002] EWHC 907 (Admin)).

Archive material on news websites

The protection of 'the fade factor' does not apply to material which, since it was originally published, remains accessible to the public in a media organisation's online archive. Although judges instruct juries not to do research on defendants, jurors (and witnesses) might nevertheless search the internet for such material. Jurors might find stories in news archives referring to a defendant's previous convictions, or accounts of the crime they are trying which were published before the case became active. They might also find accounts published by foreign media which ignore UK contempt law.

UK media organisations say it would be impossible to keep checking whether anything in their online archives refers to people who have since become involved in any of the thousands of cases which are active at any time. But,

- if a media organisation's attention is drawn to archived material which, in the view of the defence or prosecution creates a substantial risk of serious prejudice or impediment to a particular active case, the safest course to avoid a contempt problem is to remove it or block public access to it until the case is no longer active.

see also Late News section of this book about online archives

Lord Falconer, the former Lord Chancellor, suggested in 2008 that the Attorney General should be able to identify 20 or so high-profile cases where there was a distinct contempt risk and write to warn the media to remove prejudicial material from their websites.

In 2012 a juror was jailed for six months for contempt because she used the internet to research the defendant, despite the judge forbidding this. The trial at Luton Crown court had to be halted, and the defendant re-tried.

▶ Media could face huge costs if 'serious misconduct' affects a case

Under the Courts Act 2003 the Lord Chancellor made regulations in 2004 allowing a magistrates court, a Crown court, or the Court of Appeal to order a third party (which could be a media organisation) to pay costs which were incurred in a court case as a consequence of that party's 'serious misconduct' (Costs in Criminal Cases (General) (Amendment) Regulations 2004 (SI 2004/2408)). The 'serious misconduct' could be held to have occurred through publication of material, or through a reporter's action even if there was no strict liability contempt. The measure was largely inspired by the costly abandonment of the trial in the Leeds footballers case following a *Sunday Mirror* article, referred to earlier. If 'serious misconduct' not amounting to a contempt was held to have occurred in future, the media organisation involved could become liable for huge costs.

Regulation 3F(4) says the court must allow the third party against whom such a costs order is sought to make representations, and may hear evidence. An appeal against such an order made by magistrates may be made to the Crown court, an appeal against a Crown court order may be heard in the Court of Appeal. There is no appeal against such an order made in the Court of Appeal.

▶ Court reporting – the section 4 defence

In some circumstances, a media report of a court hearing might create a substantial risk of prejudice to a later stage of the same case or to another case due to be tried.

Before the Contempt of Court Act 1981, even a fair and accurate report of proceedings in open court could be held to create such risk of prejudice, and so be contempt. But section 4 of the 1981 Act gives the media a defence, saying a person cannot be found guilty of breaching the strict liability rule in respect of a report of a court hearing which is held in public which is:

- a fair and accurate report of that hearing;
- published contemporaneously;
- and in good faith.

The Act does not define 'good faith', but the overall effect of section 4 is that courts are expected to make a specific order restricting the media if they do not want all, or part of, any hearing in public to be reported contemporaneously.

The section 4 defence does not protect reports of a court hearing held in private – see also ch. 11, p. 120, Ban on reporting a court's private hearing.

see ch. 21, p. 266, Reports must be contemporaneous, for the definition

Inaccurate reporting of a current jury trial

The section 4 defence does not protect an unfair or inaccurate court report. The High Court fined the BBC £5,000 in 1992 for an inaccurate report of a continuing trial before a jury, saying it contained errors which created a substantial risk of serious prejudice since it was foreseeable that publication would delay and obstruct the course of justice (*A-G v BBC* [1992] COD 264).

▶ Section 4(2) orders

In some circumstances, it might be argued that fair, accurate and contemporaneous reporting of a trial could prejudice a later stage of that case, or another, linked, case.

ch. 4, p. 39, Standard of proof in criminal law, explains this principle

If several defendant are to be dealt with in a series of trials, publishing reports of the first in the series could arguably influence people who read or see them and who are then selected as jurors for the next or subsequent trials, which could concern different allegations against the same defendant(s).

The jury in the second trial, because of the principle of the presumption of innocence for defendants, may well be told nothing about the earlier trial.

But a juror in the second trial who remembers media reports of the first might be more likely to find a defendant guilty, especially if he/she was convicted in the first trial.

To avoid this danger, section 4(2) of the 1981 Act gives a court power to postpone publication of reports of a hearing or trial. In the earlier example, a judge could order that no report of the first trial should be published until the second has finished.

Section 4(2) says a court may order the postponement of the reporting of a case, or part of a case:

- where this appears to be necessary for avoiding a substantial risk of prejudice to the administration of justice in those proceedings;
- or in any other proceedings, pending or imminent; and that
- the period of postponement may be as long as the court thinks necessary for this purpose.

Note that a court may make a section 4(2) order if there is a substantial risk of any prejudice, not necessarily 'serious' prejudice. Publishing material which breaches a section 4(2) order is punishable as contempt, with an unlimited fine and/or up to two years in jail.

Normally all charges against a defendant can be reported prior to any trial, even under the automatic reporting restrictions of other statutes as described in chs. 6, 7 and 8. But in cases involving a defendant who faces more than one trial, a Crown

→ glossary

court judge may at a stage prior to trial – for example, at the **arraignment** – make a section 4(2) order postponing publication of the charge(s) the defendant is due to face in any subsequent trial until after the end of the first trial, to stop potential jurors in the first trial knowing that the same defendant is to face another trial.

 Ch. 15, pp. 176–179, Section 4(2) orders, explains the grounds on which the media may challenge the imposition of an order.

What if a section 4(2) order is not made?

Pleas made in a hearing before the trial – sometimes, a defendant facing a number of charges will, when arraigned, plead guilty to some but deny the others, so the jury will try him/her on the charge(s) he/she has denied. If a media organisation carries a report before the end of that trial which mentions that the defendant has admitted, or faces, other charge(s), and if the jury has not been told of other charges and/or any such guilty plea (that is, a previous conviction), the judge might feel obliged, to ensure fairness to the defendant, to stop the trial and order a retrial before a fresh jury elsewhere. Had the judge made a section 4(2) order before the trial began, postponing reporting of the other charge(s) or guilty plea(s), the media's position would have been clear, and they would have obeyed the order. But if the judge did not make such an order, the legal position would be less clear on whether reporting the other charge(s)/guilty plea(s) during the trial was a contempt.

Some legal experts say the section 4 defence should protect the media in such circumstances, arguing that the defence should apply unless the court makes it clear that information aired in open court should not be contemporaneously reported by making a section 4(2) postponement order. But the section 4 defence is subject to 'good faith' in publishing, so it would fail if it could be proved that the person responsible for publication deliberately intended to create prejudice to the subsequent trial. Proof of such intent could lead to the offence being regarded not as a breach of the 1981 Act but as a graver contempt at common law.

Proceedings in court in the absence of the jury

During trials judges often have to rule on the admissibility of evidence or other matters after hearing argument from defence and prosecution lawyers, while the jury is kept out of the courtroom. The process of making such a ruling is still classed as a public proceeding. But the judge may tell the lawyers not to mention the matters discussed to the jury if the matters are prejudicial. Publishing reports of those discussions and rulings before the verdicts are given could lead to the trial being aborted. Judges may not make section 4(2) postponement orders covering such discussions or rulings in the jury's absence in the expectation that the media will realise that it should not be published prematurely.

The law is not clear

The application of the law of contempt in both the circumstances outlined earlier – that is, publication before a trial of any guilty plea(s)/other charge(s), or contemporaneous reporting of discussions in a jury's absence during a trial – is unclear if no section 4(2) order has been made.

But specialists suggest that journalists would have a defence by arguing that a court could have made an order under section 4(2) and that it should have done so if it wanted material kept from potential jurors, or if it failed to do so it had made that decision on good and sufficient grounds.

Journalists should not, even if no section 4(2) order is made, contemporaneously report things discussed or rulings made when the jury is not in court during a Crown court trial. Even if the publication cannot be held to be contempt, there is a risk – explained earlier in this chapter – that a media organisation might be accused of 'serious misconduct' under section 93 of the Courts Act 2003 and be held liable for the costs of an aborted or delayed trial. The material can be published after all verdicts are reached, unless the judge orders otherwise. But judges have been known to make clear on occasion that they have no objection to contemporaneous reporting of what happened in the jury's absence because they did not think it would be prejudicial. Arguably, a cautious approach should be taken to publication of any other charge(s) faced, or guilty plea(s) entered, by a defendant who is shortly to be tried on other matters, unless it is clear that the jury will be told about them.

▌ Section 5 defence of discussion of public affairs

Section 5 of the Contempt of Court Act says:

❝ a publication made as, or as part of, a discussion in good faith of public affairs will not be treated as contempt of court under the strict liability rule if the risk of impediment or prejudice to particular legal proceedings is merely incidental to the discussion. ❞

The defence was introduced because of complaints that freedom of expression in the UK was unnecessarily restricted by a ruling in a case in 1973.

◉ Case study

The Sunday Times wanted to publish an article raising important issues of public interest about the way the drug Thalidomide was tested and marketed – at a time when civil actions were pending against the manufacturers, Distillers Company (Biochemicals) Ltd, on behalf of children born with deformities because their mothers took the drug during pregnancy. The House of Lords ruled that the proposed article would be contempt in respect of those pending cases. The government-appointed Phillimore Committee said of the decision: 'At any given moment many thousands of legal proceedings are in progress, a number of which may well raise or reflect such issues (matters of general public interest). If, for example, a general public debate about fire precautions in hotels is in progress, the debate clearly ought not to be brought to a halt simply because a particular hotel is prosecuted for breach of the fire regulations.'

The European Court of Human Rights held in 1979 that the Lords' ruling violated the right to freedom of expression under Article 10 of the European Convention on Human Rights.

The government's response was to introduce the section 5 defence. The time of liability for contempt in civil proceedings, explained later in this chapter, was also changed.

◉ Case study

Two newspapers were prosecuted in 1981 for contempt arising from comments published during the trial of Dr Leonard Arthur, a paediatrician accused of murdering a new-born baby with Down's syndrome. It was alleged that the doctor, complying with the parents' wishes, let the infant starve. Dr Arthur was acquitted of murder. The *Sunday Express* admitted that a contempt was committed in a comment article by the editor, John Junor, which said the baby had been drugged instead of being fed and had died 'unloved and unwanted'. The editor was fined £1,000 and Express Newspapers £10,000.

But the *Daily Mail* denied contempt, arguing that its article was protected by section 5. The House of Lords held on appeal that while the article did create a substantial risk of serious prejudice to Dr Arthur's trial, it was written in good faith and, because it was written in support of a 'pro-life' candidate at a by-election, was a discussion of public affairs. Lord Diplock said the article made no express mention of Dr Arthur's case and the risk of prejudice would be properly described as merely incidental (*The Times*, 16 and 19 December 1981; *Attorney General v English* [1983] 1 AC 116).

Safest course

To be sure of section 5 protection a media organisation should not, when publishing a general feature or discussion about a social issue, refer in it to any active case in which the issue figures, and in particular should not suggest that the defendant in such a case is or is not guilty.

▶ Contempt of civil proceedings under the 1981 Act

Under the strict liability rule:

- civil proceedings are deemed to be active from the time a date for the trial or a hearing is fixed.

- A civil case ceases to be active when it is disposed of, abandoned, discontinued or withdrawn.

There is generally less possibility of media coverage creating a substantial risk of serious prejudice to active civil cases than to active criminal cases, as most civil cases are tried by a judge alone, and judges are regarded as highly unlikely to be affected by media coverage.

ch. 12 explains civil courts, and which cases could involve juries

But there remains the possibility that witnesses in a civil case could be affected by media coverage if it delves so deeply into the circumstances of the case that witnesses' evidence given in advance of or at the trial could be coloured or their memories be contaminated by detail they read or see in reports.

When a jury is involved, particular care must be taken not to breach the strict liability rule, and material aired in court in the jury's absence should not be published while the jury is involved in the case.

Case study

Mr Justice Poole, in the High Court sitting in Birmingham in 1999, reminded reporters that civil proceedings remained active until a case ended. A jury had decided in favour of a man claiming damages from West Midlands Police for malicious prosecution. Before the jury decided on the amount of damages, the *Birmingham Post* suggested he would get £30,000. The judge said the proceedings were therefore tainted. The claimant abandoned his case rather than go through a retrial (*Media Lawyer*, Issue 25, January/February 2000).

---

 glossary

Sometimes when a journalist seeks a comment about a civil case, a lawyer involved will insist that little can be published because it is **sub judice** – a term indicating merely that the legal action has begun. But this is not the same as the case being active: a civil case becomes active at what may be a later stage, when a date is fixed for the trial or hearing – and even then, media coverage is not prohibited, provided the strict liability rule is obeyed.

 See ch. 12, p. 133, 'Payments into court', for an explanation of the contempt danger of reporting that such a payment has been made in a civil case.

▌ Other contempts under the 1981 Act

Section 8 of the Act says it is contempt to seek to discover or to publish how an individual juror voted in a verdict, or what was discussed by a jury to reach a verdict.

Section 9 of the Act says it is a contempt to use or take into court for use any audio recorder (except with the court's permission), and to broadcast any such recordings.

Section 11 of the Act gives courts powers, when they allow a name or other information to be withheld from the public, to prohibit publication of that name or material in connection with the proceedings. Breach of a section 11 order would be a contempt.

ch. 11 explains these sections

▌ Contempt in reports of court hearings held in private

see ch. 11, p. 120, Ban on reporting a court's private hearing, on the 1960 Act

Section 12 of the Administration of Justice Act 1960 makes it a contempt for the media to publish an account of what was said or done at a court hearing held in private if the case falls within certain categories. The ban also covers quoting from court documents.

➡ Recap of major points

- For the media, the greatest danger of committing contempt of court lies in publishing material which, under the Contempt of Court Act 1981, could be ruled to have created a substantial risk of serious prejudice or impediment to an 'active' case.

- Certain types of information are more likely than others to be regarded as creating such risk – for example, details of the previous convictions of a defendant awaiting trial.

- Journalists should know when under the Act a criminal or a civil case becomes active, and when it ceases to be active – because the 'active period' determines what can be published.

- Juries are rarely used in civil cases, so the media have greater leeway about what can be published about active civil cases than they have in relation to active criminal cases.

- In prosecuting under the Act for strict liability contempt the Attorney General does not have to prove intent to cause prejudice.

- Under section 4(2) a court can order the media to postpone a report of a court case, or part of it, to avoid a substantial risk of prejudice.

- Section 5 provides a defence for a published discussion in good faith of public affairs where the risk of prejudice is merely incidental to the discussion.

- When during a trial there are legal discussions or rulings which occur in the jury's absence, the media should not report such material until all the verdicts are reached.

- Under the Courts Act 2003, any party, including a media organisation, held to have committed 'serious misconduct' affecting a court case could be liable for huge costs.

((•)) Useful Websites

www.judiciary.gov.uk/Resources/JCO/Documents/Guidance/crown_court_reporting_restrictions_021009.pdf

The Judicial College (formerly the Judicial Studies Board) guidance: 'Reporting Restrictions in the Criminal Courts'

Part 3

Defamation and related law

19

Defamation – definitions and dangers

Chapter summary

This chapter explains what defamation is and why it is of such concern to journalists and publishers. It covers the risks of being sued for libel and losing, and so having to pay huge costs and damages. The chapter explains the definitions of what is defamatory. The following chapters explain who can sue for defamation, what the claimant must do to bring an action, the defences, and reforms in the Defamation Act 2013, which came into effect at the start of 2014. Defamation is one of the greatest legal dangers for anyone who earns a living with words and images – so handling a complaint or drafting an apology about something which has been published is not a job for an inexperienced journalist.

▌ Seeking legal advice

Defamation law is complex, so this book can provide nothing more than a rough guide. While media organisations can sometimes safely go further than many journalists suppose, they also need to stop and reflect before taking what might be a dangerous course of action.

The golden rule for the journalist is that if publication seems likely to bring a threat of a defamation action, they should take professional advice.

But the media's role in exposing wrongdoing is extremely important. As Lord Justice Lawton (then Mr Justice Lawton) said in a case in 1965:

" It is one of the professional tasks of newspapers to unmask the fraudulent and the scandalous. It is in the public interest to do it. It is a job which newspapers have done time and time again in their long history. "

▌ What is defamation?

The law protects an individual's personal and professional reputation from unjustified attack. In civil law a statement making such an attack may be found to be a tort – a civil wrong for which a court may award monetary damages.

Defamatory statements are those published or spoken which affect the reputation of a person, company or organisation. A defamatory statement in written or in any other permanent form is a libel, for which damages can be awarded. But a statement may be protected by a defence.

A defamatory statement which is spoken is the tort of slander, which may also incur damages unless a defence applies. But defamatory statements which are spoken in a broadcast on radio or television, by cable, or spoken in the public performance of a play are classed as libel, by the Broadcasting Act 1990 and Theatres Act 1968 respectively. Libel and slander have different requirements about what a claimant must prove, as chs. 20 and 24 explain.

In the past, juries tried most defamation cases. But the Defamation Act 2013 abolished the presumption of jury trial, so cases will be heard by a judge alone unless the court orders otherwise. This means it will be easier to decide the key issue of the meaning of words complained of – a task which used to fall to the jury but will now be done by the judge.

Definitions of a defamatory statement

A statement about a person is defamatory if it tends to do any one of the following:

- expose the person to hatred, ridicule, or contempt;
- cause the person to be shunned or avoided;
- lower the person in the estimation of right-thinking members of society generally; or
- disparage the person in his/her business, trade, office or profession.

see also
p. 244,
Freedom
of expres-
sion, on
'serious
harm'

The words 'tends to' are important. The claimant does not have to show that the words actually did expose him/her to hatred, etc. But the Defamation Act 2013 introduces a requirement that a claimant must show that the statement complained of caused or is likely to cause his/her reputation 'serious harm'. A company which wishes to sue must show that the statement has caused or is likely to cause it serious financial loss.

Lawyers sometimes find it difficult to decide whether a statement is defamatory, and judges sometimes disagree.

Note the phrase 'right-thinking members of society generally' in the third definition. It is not enough for a claimant in a libel action to show that the words of which he/she complains have lowered him/her in the estimation of a limited class in the community who may not conform to that standard.

! Remember

It is almost always defamatory to say of a person that he/she is a liar, or a cheat or is insolvent or in financial difficulties – whether the statement is a libel will depend on whether the publisher has a defence, for example, it can be proved true.

Meaning of words

The test in law of what words mean is what a 'reasonable person' would think they mean – that is, are they defamatory? It is not necessarily the meaning intended by author or publisher. Sir Anthony Clarke, Master of the Rolls, detailed the principles of deciding meaning in *Jeynes v News Magazines Ltd* ([2008] EWCA Civ 130), saying (at paragraph 14):

> They may be summarised in this way: (1) The governing principle is reasonableness. (2) The hypothetical reasonable reader is not naïve but he is not unduly suspicious. He can read between the lines. He can read in an implication more readily than a lawyer and may indulge in a certain amount of loose thinking but he must be treated as being a man who is not avid for scandal and someone who does not, and should not, select one bad meaning where other non-defamatory meanings are available. (3) Over-elaborate analysis is best avoided. (4) The intention of the publisher is irrelevant. (5) The article must be read as a whole, and any 'bane and antidote' taken together. (6) The hypothetical reader is taken to be representative of those who would read the publication in question. (7) In delimiting the range of permissible defamatory meanings, the court should rule out any meaning which, 'can only emerge as the produce of some strained, or forced, or utterly unreasonable interpretation...' (8) It follows that 'it is not enough to say that by some person or another the words might be understood in a defamatory sense'.

see p. 240, Bane and antidote

The words must be read in full and in their context, because a statement which is innocuous when standing alone can acquire defamatory meaning when juxtaposed with other material. Juxtaposition is a constant danger for journalists, particularly for sub-editors and those dealing with production. Those editing footage must take care how pictures interact with each other, and with any commentary – what meanings are being created?

see also ch. 20, p. 256, Juxtaposition

Inferences

Many statements may carry more than one meaning.

- An inference is a statement with a secondary meaning which can be understood by someone without special knowledge who 'reads between the lines in the light of his general knowledge and experience of worldly affairs'.

For example, an inference is created if someone says: 'I saw the editor leave the pub, and he was swaying and his speech was slurred'. The inference is that the editor was drunk, though the term 'drunk' is not used. But for some statements there may be dispute about whether a defamatory inference was created.

Innuendoes

- An innuendo is a statement which may seem to be innocuous to some people but which will be seen as defamatory by people with special knowledge.

For example, saying 'I saw our editor go into that house on the corner of Sleep Street' would not in itself be defamatory, unless the communication is to someone who knows that the house is a brothel.

The term innuendo comes from a Latin word meaning 'to nod to'.

The libel claimant who argues that he/she has been defamed by an innuendo must show not only that the special facts or circumstances giving rise to the innuendo exist, but also that they are known to the people to whom the statement was published.

👁 Case study

In 1986 Lord Gowrie, a former Cabinet Minister, received 'substantial' damages over a newspaper article which created the innuendo that he took drugs. He had recently resigned as Minister for the Arts and the *Daily Star* newspaper then asked: 'What expensive habits can he not support on an income of £33,000? I'm sure Gowrie himself would snort at suggestions that he was born with a silver spoon round his neck.' His **counsel** said the reference to expensive habits, the suggestion that he could not support those habits on his ministerial salary, the use of the word 'snort' and the reference to a 'silver spoon around his neck' all bore the plain implication to all those familiar with the relevant terminology that Lord Gowrie took illegal drugs, particularly cocaine, and resigned because his salary was not enough to finance the habit.

→ glossary

A journalist would clearly be mistaken to believe that using inference or innuendo is any safer in libel law than making a direct allegation.

Bane and antidote

Just as a defamatory meaning may be conveyed by a particular context, so a defamatory meaning may be removed by the context. A judge said in 1835 that, if in one part of a publication something disreputable to the claimant was stated that was removed by the conclusion, 'the bane and the antidote must be taken together'.

The House of Lords applied this rule in 1995 (*Charleston v News Group Newspapers Ltd* [1995] 2 AC 65), when it dismissed a case in which Ann Charleston and Ian Smith, two actors from the television serial Neighbours, sued the *News of the World* over headlines and photographs in which their faces were superimposed on models in pornographic poses.

The main headline read: 'Strewth! What's Harold up to with our Madge?' The text said:

> What would the Neighbours say…strait-laced Harold Bishop starring in a bondage session with screen wife Madge. The famous faces from the television soap are the unwitting stars of a sordid computer game that is available to their child fans. The game superimposes stars' heads on near-naked bodies of real porn models. The stars knew nothing about it.

The actors' counsel conceded that anyone who read the whole of the text would realise the photographs were mock-ups, but said many readers were unlikely to go beyond the photographs and headlines.

Lord Bridge said it was often a debatable question, which the jury must resolve, whether the antidote was effective to neutralise the bane. The answer depended not only on the nature of the libel a headline conveyed and the language of the text which was relied on to neutralise it, but also on the manner in which all the material was set out and balanced. In this case, no reader who read beyond the first paragraph could possibly have drawn a defamatory inference.

Lord Nicholls warned that words in the text would not always 'cure' a defamatory headline. 'It all depends on the context, one element in which is the layout of the article. Those who print defamatory headlines are playing with fire.' The ordinary reader might not notice words tucked away low down in an article.

Changing standards

Imputations which were defamatory a hundred years ago may not be defamatory today, and vice versa. In the reign of Charles II it was held to be actionable to say falsely of a man that he was a papist and went to mass. In the next reign similar statements were held not to be defamatory.

During the First World War a UK court decided that it was a libel to write falsely of a man that he was a German.

Is it defamatory to call someone homosexual? It used to be, but now no 'right-thinking member of society' would think less of someone because they are gay. So to state wrongly that someone is gay would not in some circumstances be defamatory. But it could be defamatory if it implies the person lied about his/her sexual orientation.

👁 Case study

Singer-songwriter Robbie Williams won 'substantial' damages from publisher Northern and Shell in 2005 after the magazines *Star* and *Hot Star* ran stories alleging that he had omitted from a forthcoming authorised biography details of an alleged sexual encounter with a man in the lavatories of a club in Manchester, and that by disclosing details of his female conquests but not mentioning this episode he was concealing his true sexuality. The allegations, however, were completely false – the publisher apologised, and paid damages and the singer's costs. (*Robert Peter Williams v Northern and Shell Plc*, statement in High Court, 6 December 2005).

◗ Why media organisations may be reluctant to fight defamation actions

Defamation law tries to strike a balance between the individual's right to a reputation and the right to freedom of speech, and so provides defences for the person who makes a defamatory statement about another for an acceptable reason – see subsequent chapters. But media organisations can be reluctant to fight defamation actions, for a variety of reasons.

Uncertainty of how a judge will interpret meanings

- The first is the uncertainty about how a judge will decide the meaning of what was published. For example, a statement which seems innocuous to one person may, equally clearly, be defamatory to another.

Difficulty of proving the truth

Even if a journalist and his/her editor are convinced of a story's truth, they may be unable to prove it in court.

ch. 21
explains
the 'justi-
fication',
or truth
defence

- People needed as witnesses to an event may not want to get involved in a libel case; witnesses' memories may prove unreliable; they may forget detail by the time the trial begins; by the time the case gets to trial they may have moved address and cannot be traced.

Huge damages could be awarded if trial lost

- Media organisations considering contesting a libel action also find it difficult to assess the damages which might be awarded should they lose, especially if they are to be decided by a jury.

Some juries have awarded huge sums.

◉ Case study

In 2000 the magazine *LM* (formerly *Living Marxism*) shut down after a jury awarded a total of £375,000 damages to two television reporters and ITN over a story accusing them of having sensationalised the image of an emaciated Muslim pictured through barbed wire at a Serb-run detention camp in Bosnia (*The Guardian*, 21 March 2000).

The Court of Appeal has the power to substitute its own figure for a jury award it considers to be excessive or inadequate.

In 2002 libel judge Mr Justice Eady said that the ceiling for the most serious defamatory allegations was currently 'reckoned to be of the order of £200,000'.

That was the figure he awarded in that year, when trying a case without a jury, to each of two nursery nurses wrongly accused of sexual abuse (*Christopher Lillie and Dawn Reed v Newcastle City Council, Richard Barker, Judith Jones, Jacqui Saradjian and Roy Wardell* [2002] EWHC 1600 (QB)).

But in October 2005 a jury awarded £250,000 to Rupert Lowe, chairman of Southampton Football Club, over an article which said he had behaved 'shabbily' in suspending the club's manager after child abuse allegations. It was the highest award for more than four years. Since then there have been fewer jury trials and more awards of damages by judges, with damages at much lower levels, though a judge noted in 2012 that the upper limit would now, taking into account factors including inflation, be around £275,000 (*Cairns v Modi* [2012] EWCA Civ 1382).

Huge costs

- Damages might be high, but they are usually much lower than legal costs in the case, which are generally paid by the loser.

In one case Mirror Group Newspapers paid £15,000 in settlement of a defamation action but was then presented with a costs bill of £382,000 – which was reduced on appeal.

In 1994 the BBC had to pay an estimated £1.5 million costs in a case heard by a judge, who awarded £60,000 damages. The libel was contained in a *Panorama* programme, 'The Halcion nightmare', which reported that, long before the sleeping drug Halcion was banned in the UK, there was evidence that it might have had serious adverse side effects.

In June 2010 martial arts expert Matthew Fiddes, a former bodyguard to entertainer Michael Jackson, dropped his defamation case against Channel 4 over a documentary about members of the Jackson family at the doors of the court. By that time, Channel 4's costs exceeded £1.5 million. Mr Fiddes was operating on a no-win, no-fee **Conditional Fee Agreement** (CFA).

→glossary

In addition, provisions in sections 34 to 42 of the Crime and Courts Act 2013 allow a court to impose 'exemplary damages' on a publisher which has not signed up to a press regulator recognised by the recognition body established by the Royal Charter agreed by the Queen in October 2013 as part of the Leveson proposals for a new system of press regulation. The court may also refuse to award costs to a non-regulated publisher which wins its case.

It may be better to settle

It is not surprising that, faced with these kinds of figures and risks over costs and damages, even if the case is won at a trial, ardent campaigning editors may decide either not to carry a story or, having carried it, avoid a trial by apologising and paying damages.

As the vast majority of libel cases settle out of court, with the amounts involved rarely being disclosed, the ongoing cost of libel actions to media organisations is often underestimated. The settlement usually involves paying some or all of the other side's costs.

'No win, no fee' legal representation

see Useful
Websites
at the end
of this
chapter
on 'no
win. no
fee'

see ch. 26
on privacy

The introduction of the Conditional Fee Arrangements, known as 'no win, no fee', for libel cases in 1998 had a serious chilling effect on the media, significantly restricting what the public was able to read and hear, most obviously when articles, books, or programmes were changed because of legal considerations.

Legal aid was never available for launching libel actions, so historically the libel courts were beyond the reach of people on modest incomes. But CFAs meant litigants without the means to sue could do so, represented by lawyers who received nothing if they lost a case but could claim up to a 100 per cent increase on fees if they won. In January 2010 the European Court of human Rights held that a 100 per cent success fee claimed by Naomi Campbell's lawyers from Mirror Group Newspapers was a breach of the publisher's right to freedom of expression.

In 2011 the coalition government announced that it would implement reforms recommended by Lord Justice Jackson in his report on costs and stop success fees and premiums for insurance taken out by claimants to cover a winning defendant's costs from being reclaimed from a defendant who loses a case. That reform has been put on hold while the government draws up a new scheme to protect would-be litigants of modest means from having to pay the costs if they sue a publisher and lose.

The media has argued that the CFA system means it can be held to ransom by an impecunious claimant on a CFA. If the claimant loses, the media defendant is unlikely to recover its costs, while if the claimant wins, the media defendant has to pay not only damages but also the lawyers' 'success fees', and the insurance premiums. In addition, there is no incentive for a claimant on a CFA to exercise any control over what his solicitor spends, as the defendant will pay. The pressure to settle such cases rather than go to court is considerable.

▶ Freedom of expression

ch. 1
explains the
Convention
generally

Most journalists believe that defamation law, in attempting to 'strike a balance' between protecting reputation and allowing freedom of speech, has been tilted historically in favour of claimants.

But developments in recent years, particularly the Defamation Act 2013, seem likely to tilt the balance in favour of freedom of expression. They are:

(1) The Human Rights Act, which took effect on 2 October 2000, requiring courts to pay regard to Article 10 of the European Convention on Human Rights, concerned with freedom of expression. The European Court of Human Rights has said that Article 10 does not involve a 'choice between

two conflicting principles' but 'a freedom of expression that is subject to a number of exceptions which must be narrowly construed'.

(2) The decision of the House of Lords in *Reynolds v Times Newspapers* [2001] 2 AC 127, which greatly extended the ambit of the defence of privilege. This has now taken statutory form in section 4 of the Defamation Act 2013, which introduces a defence of 'publication on a matter of public interest'.

ch. 22 explains this defence

(3) The increased willingness of the courts to strike out cases in which a claimant could not show that a substantial tort had been committed – now given statutory expression in the requirement in section 1 of the Defamation Act 2013 that a claimant must show that a statement has caused or is likely to cause serious harm to his/her reputation.

Other reforms aiding freedom of expression include the introduction of qualified privilege for peer-reviewed publications in scientific and academic journals, the widening of qualified privilege in relation to courts and press conferences and the liberalising of the honest opinion defence, formerly known as 'fair comment'.

ch. 21 explains defences

▌ Errors and apologies

Sometimes publication of the words which cause the libel problem are the result of an innocent error. The arrival of a solicitor's letter from a potential claimant which could start the journey to the High Court is the moment to take legal advice. Libel law is not a matter for an inexperienced person, because of the dangers of aggravating a problem by mishandling it. A reporter who receives a complaint about something which has been published should refer the issue to the relevant executive or editor.

Publishing an apology or an inadequate correction can itself, in certain circumstances, create a further libel problem.

Taking the correct legal steps, including, if necessary, publishing a prompt apology or correction, can remove the heat from a libel threat, and save thousands of pounds even if the claim is settled.

ch. 21, pp. 273–274, Care needed in apologies and corrections

! Remember

The most common cause of libel actions against media organisations is a journalist's failure to apply professional standards of accuracy and fairness. The best protection against becoming involved in an expensive action is to make every effort to get the story right.

➡ Recap of major points

- A defamatory statement made in permanent form is generally libel and if in transient form it is generally slander – if it cannot be defended.

- In a defamation action, the test of what the words actually mean is the test of what a reasonable person would take them to mean.

- Words may carry an innuendo, a 'hidden' meaning clear to people with special knowledge or create an inference, obvious to everybody.

- The financial implications of losing a defamation action in terms of damages and costs are so punitive that journalists must always consider whether what they are writing or plan to broadcast will be defensible if a defamation action results.

((•)) Useful Websites

www.lawsociety.org.uk/for-the-public/faqs/conditional-fee-agreements/
   Law Society explanation of 'no win, no fee' arrangements

http://inforrm.wordpress.com/
   Inforrm blog site, which publishes analysis of defamation and other law

www.legislation.gov.uk/ukpga/2013/26/contents/enacted
   Defamation Act 2013

www.legislation.gov.uk/ukpga/2013/26/notes/contents
   Explanatory Notes to the 2013 Act

The claimant and what must be proved

Chapter summary

This chapter details who can sue for libel, and explains that the law places a low burden of proof on people who do. A claimant has to prove that the material was published to a third party – a formality in a case against the media – that it is capable of bearing the defamatory meaning complained of, that he/she has been identified in it, and that his/her reputation has suffered or is likely to suffer serious harm. But the claimant does not have the burden of proving the material is false. A claimant can sue anyone who 'publishes' the libel, including reporters and the publication's distributors. The practical effects of some of the reforms in the Defamation Act 2013 are not yet clear.

▌ Who might sue?

All citizens as individuals have the right to sue for libel – that is, to be a claimant. The availability of 'no win, no fee' arrangements, described in ch. 19, has opened the libel courts to greater numbers of people. This does reinforce the need for accuracy and to approach stories thus:

- Is what I am writing potentially defamatory?
- If so, do I have a defence?

But, as ch. 19 explains, all would-be claimants now have to pass the 'serious harm' test introduced in the Defamation Act 2013 – failure to get over this hurdle will stop a claim in its tracks.

see also
p. 249,
Disparaging
goods

Corporations, including companies

A corporation can sue for a publication injurious to its trading reputation. But section 1(2) of the Defamation Act 2013 now requires that any body that 'trades for profit' must show that the serious harm it claims to have suffered 'has caused or is likely to cause the body serious financial loss'. Previously the threat of being sued by a company was significant. But companies are now thought likely to find it difficult to prove that they have suffered or are likely to suffer serious financial loss. The mere fact that a company's share price has fallen is insufficient (*Collins Stewart Ltd & another v The Financial Times* [2004] EWHC 2337)). Individual directors and managers can sue if 'identified', see later.

Local and central government

The House of Lords ruled in *Derbyshire County Council v Times Newspapers* [1993] AC 534 that institutions of local or central government could not sue for defamation in respect of their 'governmental and administrative functions' as this would place an undesirable fetter on freedom of speech. But they can sue as institutions for

→ glossary

libels affecting their property, and for malicious falsehood if they can show **malice**.

A council's individual members or officers are able to sue if what is published can be seen as referring to them personally. Lord Keith said in the *Derbyshire County Council* case:

ch. 24
explains
malicious
falsehood

> A publication attacking the activities of the authority will necessarily be an attack on the body of councillors which represents the controlling party, or on the executives who carry on the day-to-day management of its affairs. If the individual reputation of any of these is wrongly impaired by the publication any of these can himself bring proceedings for defamation.

An individual can pursue a defamation claim if what is published 'identifies' him/her, which can occur even if he/she is not named. The legal test for identification is explained later.

As a general rule, an association, such as a club, cannot sue unless it is an incorporated body, but words disparaging an association will almost invariably reflect upon the reputations of one or more of the officials who, as individuals, can sue if 'identified'.

Trade unions

The House of Lords seems to have accepted in the *Derbyshire County Council* case cited earlier that trade unions can sue, even though they are not corporate bodies. A union's officers can sue.

Members of Parliament

The Defamation Act 1996 allows Parliamentarians to waive their Parliamentary privilege in defamation actions and thus sue.

Disparaging goods

Can a publication defame a person or a firm by disparaging goods? It is an increasingly important question as product testing becomes commonplace in newspapers, magazines and other media.

The answer is yes. But it is not enough that the statement should simply affect the person adversely in his/her business – it must also impute to him/her discreditable conduct in that business, or tend to show that he/she is ill-suited or ill-qualified to do it. (See *Griffiths v Benn* [1911] 927 TLR 26, CA, applied in *James Morford and others v Nic Rigby and the East Anglian Daily Times Co Ltd*, Court of Appeal, 17 February 1998.)

For example, it will be defamatory to write falsely of a businessman that he has been condemned by his trade association, or of a bricklayer that he/she does not know how to lay bricks properly, if they can show that their reputations suffered or were likely to suffer serious harm as a result of the publication.

Not all words criticising a person's goods are defamatory – for example, a motoring correspondent could criticise a car's performance without reflecting upon the character of the manufacturer or dealer. But the statement might prompt an action for malicious falsehood: see ch. 24.

The imputations that give most problems in this context are dishonesty, carelessness and incompetence.

In 1994 a jury awarded £1.485 million damages to the manufacturer of a yacht, Walker Wingsail Systems plc, over an article in *Yachting World* which contrasted the manufacturer's striking claims for the yacht's performance with its drastically poorer performance when tested by the journalist.

▶ What the claimant must prove

A claimant suing for libel has to prove that:

- the publication has caused or is likely to cause his reputation to suffer serious harm;

- it may be reasonably understood to refer to him/her – that is, 'identification', and

- it has been published to a third person.

This can be remembered as 'defamation, identification, publication'.

Defamation

Legal definitions of defamatory statements are given in ch. 19, p. 238. Broadly speaking, any allegation or smear which causes or is likely to cause serious harm to a person's reputation among honest citizens will be defamatory.

A claimant does *not* have to prove that the statement is false. If a statement is defamatory, the court assumes it is false. If the statement is true and the journalist can prove it is true then there is a defence, as the next chapter explains.

The claimant does not have to prove intention: it is no use the journalist saying 'I didn't mean to damage this person's reputation'. However, as explained in ch. 21, intent is relevant in the 'offer of amends' defence. As ch. 22 explains, the public interest defence in section 4 of the Defamation Act 2013 provides protection in some circumstances for publication of untrue statements.

Identification

The claimant must prove that the published material identifies him/her.

Some journalists believe they can play safe by not naming an individual – but omitting the name may prove no defence.

- The test in defamation law of whether the published statement identified the claimant is whether it would reasonably lead people acquainted with him/her to believe that he/she was the person referred to.

A judge said in 1826: 'It is not necessary that all the world should understand the libel; it is sufficient if those who know the claimant can make out that he is the person meant' (*Bourke v Warren* (1826) 2 C&P 307). That is still the law.

During the late 1980s and 1990s the Police Federation, representing junior police officers, brought many actions against newspapers on behalf of their members. During the 33 months to March 1996 it launched 95 libel actions, winning them all and recovering £1,567,000 in damages. Many of the officers were not named in what was published, but it was claimed that acquaintances and/or colleagues would realise who they were. The *Burton Mail* paid £17,500 compensation plus legal costs to a woman constable who featured anonymously in a story following a complaint about an arrest. It was argued that the story's details identified her.

Derogatory comments about an institution can reflect upon the person who heads it – newspapers have had to pay damages to head teachers, who were not named in the paper, for reports criticising schools.

Wrong photos or wrong caption

People are identified by what they look like, so using the wrong photo could identify someone in a defamatory context, even if they are not named.

Use of file or 'stock' photographs or film to illustrate news stories or features is fraught with libel risks. A photo of a social function, with people holding drinks, is perfectly acceptable – but if it is later used as a stock shot to illustrate the perils of drinking, those pictured may sue, particularly any who are teetotal.

Confusion about who is shown in a photograph can be very costly. In 2005 the *Sunday Mirror* paid out £100,000 plus costs to a man falsely identified in a photo as the rapist Iorworth Hoare (*Press Gazette*, 3 June 2005).

Importance of ages, addresses and occupations

It can be dangerous to make a half-hearted effort at identification, particularly in reports of court cases.

👁 Case study

In *Newstead v London Express Newspapers Ltd* [1940] 1 KB 377, the *Daily Express* had reported that 'Harold Newstead, a 30-year-old Camberwell man', had been jailed for nine months for bigamy. Another Harold Newstead, who worked in Camberwell, sued the newspaper, claiming that the account was understood to refer to him – and won. He argued that if the words were true of another person, which they were, it was the paper's duty to give a precise and detailed description of that person, but the paper had 'recklessly struck out' the convicted person's occupation and address.

! Remember

A defendant's age, address and occupation, if mentioned in court, or provided by the court, should be given with his/her name in reports of the case, unless the court directs otherwise. Ch. 14 explains that courts should give reporters such details.

Blurring identity increases risk

The problem with not fully identifying the subject of a story is not only that the person may argue in a libel case that he/she was the person referred to, but also that another may claim that the words were taken to refer to him/her. A newspaper quoted from a report by the district auditor to a local council, criticising the council's deputy housing manager. The paper did not name him. But a new deputy manager had taken over. He sued, claiming he was thought to be the offending official.

Defamation of a group

If a defamatory statement refers to someone as being a member of a group, and includes no other identifying detail of that person, all members of the group, if it is sufficiently small, may be able to sue for defamation, even though the publisher intended to refer to only one of them.

For example, saying: 'One of the detectives at Blanktown police station is corrupt', without naming the allegedly corrupt individual, will allow all the detectives there to sue because the statement 'identifies' them to their acquaintances and colleagues. Even if the publisher has evidence that one is corrupt, the rest will win damages. But if the group referred to is large, no one in it will be able reasonably to claim to have been identified merely by a reference to the group. Case law does not set a clear figure for when a group is too large for those in it to claim that reference to the group identified them as individuals. In one case, reference to a group of 35 police dog-handlers based in an area of London was ruled to be sufficient to identify them as individuals.

👁 Case study

A case in 1986 concerned a reference published by a newspaper to an allegation that detectives at Banbury CID had raped a woman. The newspaper did not name those allegedly involved. It was successfully sued by members of the group, which comprised only 12 detectives (*Riches and others v News Group Newspapers Ltd* [1985] 2 All ER 845).

Referring to a group may also identify those with particular responsibility for it. Saying: 'The supermarket in Blanktown Road is run badly' refers to a small group of managers, each of whom could sue.

Juxtaposition

Placing a photograph incorrectly, or using the wrong picture, can cause expensive problems if it wrongly suggests by juxtaposition that someone shown is a person 'identified' in the accompanying story.

In 2002 motivational therapist and part-time nightclub doorman Shabazz Nelson won 'substantial' damages from *The Sun* after it used his picture with an article in which Oasis star Liam Gallagher alleged he and his girlfriend were assaulted by door attendants – referred to as 'monkeys' – at the Met Bar in London. The piece was illustrated by a picture of Mr Nelson, who was working there that night as a doorman. Mr Nelson had not assaulted Mr Gallagher or his girlfriend and had 'conducted himself in a perfectly proper and responsible manner', and was 'understandably concerned' that *Sun* readers who saw the article 'would have understood that he was the subject of Mr Gallagher's claims', Mr Justice Eady was told at the High Court.

Lack of care in the editing and 'voice-over' of footage can also cause trouble, if the commentary is 'juxtaposed' with an unconnected image.

👁 Case study

In 1983 a Metropolitan Police detective constable was paid £20,000 damages by Granada TV after being shown walking out of West End Central police station during a *World in Action* programme on Operation Countryman, an anti-corruption investigation into the force. As he was shown emerging from the station the voice-over said: 'Since 1969 repeated investigations show that some CID officers take bribes.' The officer was not identified by name, and there was no suggestion that he was guilty of such behaviour – he was merely a figure in a background shot. But his recognisable, unexpected guest appearance was enough to earn him healthy damages, because it wrongly 'identified' him as corrupt.

Publication

The claimant must prove that the statement was published. There is no defamation if the words complained of, however offensive or untrue, are addressed, in speech or writing, only to the person to whom they refer. To substantiate defamation, they must have been communicated to at least one other person. In the case of the news media, there is no difficulty in proving this: publication is widespread.

If very few readers see online material

There is an exception to this rule about publication for claimants suing over items on the internet published by foreign parties.

👁 Case study

In 2005 the Court of Appeal rejected a Saudi Arabian businessman's claim for defamation by ruling that it would be an abuse of process for any claimant to bring an action over material on the internet unless 'substantial publication' in England could be shown. In that case, the complained-of material was downloaded by only five people in England – three, including the claimant's lawyers, were in his 'camp', and the other two were unknown. There was no 'real or substantial' **tort** (*Dow Jones and Co Inc v Yousef Abdul Latif Jameel* [2005] EWCA Civ 75).

→ glossary

The court will not assume that internet publication is necessarily substantial publication (*Amoudi v Brisard* [2006] 3 All ER 294). A court in Canada ruled that hyperlinks to articles containing defamatory material did not amount in that particular case to substantial publication of defamatory statements by the publisher of the article containing the hyperlinks (*Crookes v Wikimedia Foundation Inc.* (2008) BCSC 1424).

Who are the 'publishers'?

A person who has been defamed may sue the reporter, the sub-editor, the editor, the publisher, the printer, the distributor and the broadcaster. All have participated in publishing the defamatory statement and are regarded as 'publishers' at common law. However, some may be able to use the defence in section 1 of the Defamation Act 1996 or section 10 of the Defamation Act 2013 – see ch. 21, p. 275, 'Live' broadcasts and readers' online comments.

Repeating statements of others

- Every repetition of a libel is a fresh publication and creates a fresh cause of action. This is called the repetition rule. It is no defence to say that you, the publisher, are not liable because you are only repeating the words of others.

The person who originated the statement may be liable, but anyone who repeats the allegation – for example, by publishing material from a defamatory press release – may also be sued. One of the most common causes of libel actions is repeating statements made by interviewees without being able to prove the truth of the words. Also, a publisher who 'lifts' (copies and publishes) material published elsewhere is also liable.

In 1993 and 1994 papers paid damages to defendants in the *Birmingham Six* case, who were jailed for terrorism but later cleared on appeal. Former West Midlands police officers were accused of fabricating evidence in the case, but prosecution of the officers was abandoned. The *Sunday Telegraph* subsequently reported one of the three officers as referring to the Birmingham Six and saying: 'In our eyes, their guilt is beyond doubt.' *The Sun* newspaper published an article based upon the *Sunday Telegraph*'s interviews. It later carried an apology and reportedly paid £1 million in damages to the six.

see www. mcnaes. com ch. 20 for details of this case

Journalists on local newspapers also need to be alert when handling the bygone days column. A doctor received damages for statements published afresh in 1981 in the 'Looking Back' column of the Evening Star, Ipswich. The statements, repeated from an article published 25 years previously, went unchallenged when first published. But see, The 'single publication rule' and online archives, later in this chapter.

Online archives and repetition

The repetition rule is particularly relevant to websites containing archive material. It dates from the 1849 case of the Duke of Brunswick, who sued a newspaper for defamation after sending his butler to buy a back copy.

Nowadays the Duke would call up the archive version on the internet.

As ch. 21, explains, it is normally a defence to a defamation action that it was not launched until more than a year after the publication – that is, the normal time limit is that a claimant must start the action within those 12 months.

- But under the repetition rule, each time an article or footage or sound-recording in an internet archive is accessed by someone it is viewed as amounting to a new publication, potentially giving rise to a new action.

So, the law currently is that the limitation period – the 12 months – begins afresh each time online material is accessed, no matter when the material was first published. This makes it especially important to remove from an archive material which has been held to be libellous.

In 2006 a businessman, Jim Carr, won two libel damages payouts from the *Sunday Telegraph* over one story. In April that year he won £12,000 and an apology over an article published in November 2005. The newspaper later paid him a further £5,000 in damages over the same defamatory story, which, by an oversight, it had left available on its website.

The 'single publication rule' and online archives

The 'repetition rule' is ended by the 'single publication rule' created by the defence in section 8 of the 2013 Act. The effect will be that from the time this part of the

Act came into force the limitation period for bringing a defamation action – 12 months – runs from date of the first publication 'to the public' of the complained-of statement. So if the allegation appears in a story in the print edition of a newspaper late on the evening of January 1, and is then uploaded on to the newspaper's website at mid-morning on January 2, the limitation period runs from January 1, as this was the first publication. Or, if the article is only online, the first publication is the first time any member of the public accessed it.

Section 8 therefore changes the position under the old law that each time a reader, viewer or listener accesses an article in such an archive, this constitutes a fresh publication which can give rise to a libel action even though the original (the first) publication occurred more than a year ago.

check www. mcnaes. com for updates on the 2013 Act

However, the change is not immediate because the limitation period means the new rule will not apply to website material until a year after section 8 comes into force.

It should be noted that in exceptional circumstances courts can extend the 12-month limitation period. Also, the Act says that the 'single publication rule' will not apply if the manner of the subsequent publication (that is, by the same publisher) is 'materially different' from the manner of the first. The Act says that when a court is deciding if there is such material difference, factors it can consider include 'the level of prominence that a statement is given' and 'the extent of the subsequent publication'. The Act's Explanatory Notes, referring to what may be 'materially different', say:

> A possible example of this could be where a story has first appeared relatively obscurely in a section of a website where several clicks need to be gone through to access it, but has subsequently been promoted to a position where it can be directly accessed from the home page of the site, thereby increasing considerably the number of hits it receives.

Publication by a *different* publisher of the same allegation will trigger a new limitation period in relation to that specific publication, so creating an opportunity for anyone who claims to have been defamed by the allegation to sue that different publisher for defamation.

➡ Recap of major points

- A claimant suing for libel must prove three things:

  (1) it is defamatory and has caused or is likely to cause his reputation serious damage, (2) it may be reasonably understood to refer to him, (3) it has been published to a third person.

- The test of 'identification' is whether the words would reasonably lead people who know the claimant to believe he/she was the person referred to.

- Publication is assumed in the case of traditional media. But this is not always the case with online publication.

- Every repetition is a fresh publication. The journalist is liable for repeating a defamatory statement made by an interviewee or source. A single publication rule is introduced in the Defamation Act 2013.

Defences

Chapter summary

The law provides defences for media organisations sued for defamation – without them many of the stories published and broadcast each day would be suppressed for fear of a libel action. This chapter explains the main defences, and gives practical advice on what a journalist must do when preparing a story to ensure it meets their requirements.

▌ The main defences

Journalists need to know about how defamation defences work, as the steps they take in researching and writing a story will often determine whether a defence is available to avoid a costly defamation action. Some defences are now in the Defamation Act 2013.

The main defences are:

- **truth** – section 2 of the 2013 Act, replacing the common law defence of justification; →glossary
- **honest opinion**, in section 3 of the 2013 Act, replacing the common law defence of honest comment (which was also known as fair comment); →glossary
- absolute privilege; — *fair & accurate report, contemporaneous of a trial*
- qualified privilege; *fair, accurate, contemporaneous, public interest*
- accord and satisfaction;
- offer of amends.

The fact that new statutory defences in the 2013 Act repeal the common law defences of justification and honest comment means that courts must follow the words of the statute when making rulings. Cases decided before the statute came into force may be a guide to the correct approach, but only after the court has first considered the statutory requirements.

▶ Truth – its requirement

The defence requires that the published material complained of can be proved in court to be substantially true. If this requirement is met, it gives complete protection against a libel action (the only limited exception arises under the Rehabilitation of Offenders Act 1974 – see ch. 23).

The defence applies to statements of fact. If the words complained of are an expression of opinion they may be defended as honest opinion.

Media organisations sued for defamation often rely on both truth and honest opinion as defences, applying each as appropriate to different elements of what was published.

- The standard of proof needed for a truth defence is that used in civil cases generally – the material must be proved true 'on the balance of probabilities'.

This is a lower requirement than 'beyond reasonable doubt', the standard of proof in criminal cases. But it means that a media organisation relying on a truth defence must have enough evidence to persuade a judge at trial that its version of the event(s) is correct.

The imputation of the libel must be proved

Section 2(3) of the 2013 Act says that, in a defamation case involving publication of two or more imputations involving the claimant, 'the defence under this section does not fail if, having regard to the imputations which are shown to be substantially true, the imputations which are not shown to be substantially true do not seriously harm the claimant's reputation'.

This means that a defendant does not have to prove the truth of every statement in what was published. But the most damaging imputation must be proved, and the damage to reputation it causes must outweigh any damage caused by unproved allegations. So if a newspaper runs a story saying that a politician is cruel to his children and swears at his neighbours, the former allegation is the most damaging. But if in such a case a media organisation was unable to prove the minor allegations, it might find it harder to persuade a jury that the major allegation is true.

Examples

The *Daily Telegraph* won when it was sued by tennis player Robert Dee after reporting that he was 'ranked as the worst professional tennis player in the world after 54 defeats in a row...' The newspaper pleaded justification (now truth) and fair comment (now honest opinion). Mrs Justice Sharp held that the facts in the story were sufficient to justify any defamatory meaning the words were capable of bearing (*Robert Dee v Telegraph Media Group Ltd* [2010] EWHC 924 (QB); [2010] EMLR 20).

In July 2012 the scientific journal *Nature*, its publisher, Macmillan, and senior journalist Quirin Schiermeier, pleaded justification, as well as honest comment and public interest journalism, when they were sued by Egyptian scientist Professor Mohamed El Naschie over an article which said he published large numbers of his own articles in a specialist journal, *Chaos, Solitons and Fractals* (CSF), of which he was editor-in-chief. He claimed the article meant that he abused his position to self-publish large numbers of his own articles in his journal, that his articles were of poor quality, had received little or none of the peer review to be expected of pieces in academic publications, that he had lied or been cavalier about his academic qualifications, and had been forced to retire because of his faults as editor-in-chief.

Mrs Justice Sharp, who conducted the trial in November and December 2011, dismissed Professor El Naschie's claim in a detailed 91-page decision in July 2012, concluding that the article was substantially true, contained comments which were defensible as honest comment, and was the product of responsible journalism.

Cases in which the media plead justification or truth can be extremely complex.

👁 Case study

In 1997 *The Guardian* newspaper and Granada TV risked paying huge libel damages and costs when they defended a case brought by former Conservative Cabinet Minister Jonathan Aitken over reports in the newspaper and the *World in Action* programme that he was involved in arms dealings with Saudi businessmen and that he allowed an Arab business associate to pay his bill at the Ritz hotel in Paris, in breach of ministerial guidelines. Aitken resigned from the Cabinet in order, he said, to pursue *The Guardian* and 'cut out the cancer of bent and twisted journalism in our country with the simple sword of truth and the trusty shield of British fair play'. *The Guardian* discovered at a late stage in the trial vital evidence of credit card payments found in the records of another hotel. Aitken, who had seemed to be winning, abandoned the case, facing a £2 million costs bill. He was later jailed for perjury (*The Guardian*, 8 June 1999).

Levels of meaning and reporting on police investigations

When considering reports linking a claimant with criminal or wrongful conduct, the courts recognise three levels of meaning:

- the person is guilty of the criminal offence or misconduct (a level 1 meaning – if the court decides this meaning applies, then a publisher using the truth offence will have to prove that the offence or misconduct occurred); or

- he/she is reasonably suspected of the offence or misconduct (level 2); or

- there are grounds for an investigation – for example, by police (level 3).

These are known as *Chase* level 1, 2 and 3 meanings, having been detailed by Lord Justice Brooke in *Chase v News Group Newspapers* [2002] EWCA Civ 1772; [2003] EMLR 2180.

Proving reasonable suspicion or that there were grounds for an investigation

It may be defamatory to say someone is reasonably suspected of an offence, or that there are grounds for investigating his/her conduct, because it implies there was conduct on the person's part which warrants the suspicion. So a successful plea of truth must prove conduct by the individual which gives rise to the suspicion or the grounds. It is no use saying other people told you about their suspicions (*Shah v Standard Chartered Bank* [1999] QB 241).

👁 Case study

In *Chase v News Group Newspapers Ltd* (cited earlier) *The Sun* newspaper paid £100,000 damages to children's nurse Elaine Chase for a story headlined 'Nurse is probed over 18 deaths'. Police were investigating the deaths of a number of terminally ill children she had treated but concluded – after the newspaper's story appeared – that there were no grounds to suspect her of an offence. *The Sun* tried to show there were reasonable grounds for suspicion, but the Court of Appeal said it was relying almost entirely on the fact that a number of allegations against her had been made to the hospital trust and police. The only respect in which the newspaper focused upon the nurse's conduct concerned an allegation made after publication, which the court said could not be taken into consideration.

Avoid implying habitual conduct

The statement that someone 'is a thief' may be true – but if the basis for the statement is just one minor conviction, for example for stealing a packet of bacon from a shop, a defence of truth would almost certainly fail, as the individual would argue that the words meant he was a persistent thief, whereas he was essentially an honest man who had had a single lapse.

Inferences and innuendoes must be proved

see also
ch. 19 on
meanings
of words

The truth defence will involve proving not only the truth of each defamatory statement but also any reasonable interpretation of the words and any innuendoes lying behind them.

Persisting with a truth defence can be financially risky

Persisting in a defence of truth has financial risks. If it fails the court will take a critical view of a defendant's persistence in sticking to a story which it has decided was not true, and may award greater damages.

 See also ch. 19, p. 242, Why media organisations may be reluctant to fight defamation actions.

The investigative journalist – practical advice on procedure

www.mcnaes.com ch. 21 gives tips for journalists beginning to do investigations, to help them be able to prove the truth. For example:

- The journalist should persuade each witness to make a signed statement and date it, before the story is published. In some circumstance it may be best to persuade them to sign an **affidavit**.   →glossary

A media organisation's case is often weakened because a journalist has failed to keep notes or recordings and research in good order to prove what someone said.

▎Honest opinion

The defence of honest opinion protects published opinion, not any statement put forward as factual. The defence is similar to the defence formerly known as fair comment, then as honest comment. But section 3 of the Defamation Act 2013 when creating the honest opinion defence abolished that common law defence. Media organisations using the honest opinion defence will also be prepared to run another defence, such as truth, absolute privilege, or qualified privilege in tandem.

The requirements of honest opinion

The main requirements of the honest opinion defence are:

- the published comment must be the honestly held opinion of the person making it (though it may have been published by another party);
- it must be recognisable to the reader/viewer/listener as opinion rather than as a factual allegation;
- it must be based on a provably true fact or privileged material;
- it must explicitly or implicitly indicate, at least in general terms, the fact or information on which it is based.

All these requirements must be met if the defence is to succeed.

Only comment, not facts

A judge gave an example of an opinion protected by the fair comment defence, saying that if one accurately reported what some public man had done then said 'Such conduct is disgraceful', that was merely an expression of one's opinion, a comment on the person's conduct. But if one asserted that the man was guilty of disgraceful conduct without saying what that conduct was, one was making an allegation of fact for which the only defences were justification (now truth) or privilege.

The requirements of section 3 of the 2013 Act reflect the decision of the Supreme Court in *Spiller and another v Joseph and others* [2010] UKSC 53 that it was incorrect to require that the comment must identify the matters on which it was based with sufficient particularity to enable the reader to judge for himself whether it was well founded. Instead, it said, the requirement was that the comment 'must explicitly or implicitly indicate, at least in general terms, the facts on which it was based'. The new statutory defence provides that an honest person must be able to hold the opinion on the basis of 'any fact' which existed when the statement complained of was published.

for other details of this case, see www. mcnaes. com ch. 22

→ glossary

Case study

Sub-editors must take special care if they introduce comment into headlines. In 2003 *The Daily Telegraph* published articles making allegations about left-wing MP George Galloway after a reporter found documents said to refer to him in a ruined government building in Baghdad soon after the invasion of Iraq. One story was headlined 'Telegraph reveals damning new evidence on Labour MP'. When sued, the paper did not claim the allegations were true but said the headline was an expression of opinion. But the judge said 'damning' had a plain meaning – 'that is to say, that the evidence goes beyond a **prima facie** case and points to guilt'. The MP won the libel case (*George Galloway MP v Telegraph Group Ltd* [2004] EWHC 2786 (QB).

The exception to the rule that comment must be based on a true fact is when the comment is based on privileged material, such as a report of judicial proceedings or proceedings in Parliament. A media organisation can safely make scathing comments about a defendant convicted of a crime, if based on privileged reports of the trial's evidence. The honest opinion defence will succeed in relation to what was published at the time of the conviction even if the defendant is later acquitted on appeal. The honest opinion defence should also protect publication of criticism of judges, magistrates and coroners, based on privileged reports of their actions in court.

Opinion must be 'honestly held', not 'fair'

The law does not require the 'truth' of the comment to be proved – by its nature it cannot be. Comment may be responsible or irresponsible, informed or misinformed – but cannot be true or false. Defendants pleading honest opinion do not need to persuade the court to share their views – but they do need to satisfy it that the opinion on an established fact represents a view that an honest person could hold. Mr Justice Diplock in his summing up to the jury in *Silkin v Beaverbrook Newspapers* [1958] 1 WLR 743 (QB), said: 'The basis of our public life is that the crank and the enthusiast can say what he honestly believes just as much as a reasonable man or woman. It would be a sad day for freedom of speech in this country if a jury were to apply the test of whether it agrees with a comment, instead of applying the true test of whether this opinion, however exaggerated, obstinate, or prejudiced, was honestly held.'

Dishonesty can defeat the honest opinion defence

The defence will fail if a claimant can show that the person expressing the opinion did not in fact hold that opinion. It will also fail if, for example, the editor of a newspaper which published the comment, for example in a column, did so when he or she knew, or should have known, that the author did not hold the opinion being expressed.

Imputing improper motives

Because the Defamation Act 2013 repeals the common law defence of honest comment, earlier cases cannot be taken to be a definitive guide to how the courts will interpret its replacement, the honest opinion defence. But these cases might provide some indication.

The suggestion that someone has acted from improper motives has in the past been hard to defend as honest comment. But judges in the Court of Appeal took a more helpful view when entrepreneur Richard Branson sued his biographer Tom Bower for libel (*Branson v Bower* [2001] EWCA Civ 791; [2001] EMLR 800). Bower wrote of Branson's attempt to run the national lottery: 'Sceptics will inevitably whisper that Branson's motive is self-glorification.' Bower said this was fair comment (which at that time was the name of the honest comment defence) but Branson said it was a factual allegation (that he had a questionable intention in bidding for the national lottery) and was untrue.

Lord Justice Latham, giving the Court of Appeal's judgment, said comment was 'something which is or can reasonably be inferred to be a deduction, inference, conclusion, criticism, remark, observation', and that the judge in the lower court was fully entitled to conclude that Bower was expressing a series of opinions about Branson's motives.

Reviews

The honest opinion defence protects the expressions of opinion contained in reviews of, among other things, performances, books, holidays and restaurants.

Humour, satire and irony

In 2008 Sir Elton John sued *The Guardian* for libel over a spoof article written by Marina Hyde under the headline 'A peek at the diary of...Sir Elton John' – a regular feature in the paper's Weekend section satirising the activities of celebrities and others. Sir Elton claimed the article meant his commitment to the Elton John Aids Foundation was insincere and that once the costs of his White Tie and Tiara fund-raising ball were met only a small proportion of the funds raised would go to good causes. *The Guardian's* defence was that the words were clearly comment and could not have the meaning claimed by the claimant.

Mr Justice Tugendhat struck out Sir Elton's claim, accepting *The Guardian's* argument that the words were a form of teasing, and that had it actually unearthed a story about a charity ball's costs leaving nothing for good causes it would have treated it as a serious story and written it without any attempt at humour (*Sir Elton John v Guardian News and Media Ltd* [2008] EWHC 3066 (QB)).

❚ Privilege

The public interest sometimes demands that there should be complete freedom of speech without any risk of proceedings for defamation, even if the statements are defamatory and even if they turn out to be untrue. These occasions are referred to as privileged. Privilege exists under common law and statute.

❚ Absolute privilege

The defence of absolute privilege, where it is applicable, is a complete answer and bar to any action for defamation. It does not matter if the words are true or false, or if they were spoken or written maliciously.

But while someone may be speaking on an occasion which is protected by absolute privilege it does not follow a journalist's report of the comments will also be protected by absolute privilege. Members of Parliament may say whatever they wish in the House of Commons without fear of being sued for defamation. The reports of Parliamentary proceedings published on Parliament's behalf in *Hansard*, its official record, are protected by absolute privilege; as are reports published by order of Parliament, such as White Papers. But media reports of the contents of Parliamentary publications enjoys only qualified privilege, a defence which, as this chapter explains, depends on there being a proper motive in publication.

The requirements of absolute privilege

ch. 17 explains tribunals

The only time journalists enjoy absolute privilege is when they are reporting court cases or the proceedings of certain types of tribunals.

In this context the requirements of absolute privilege are that what was published was:

- a fair and accurate report of judicial proceedings held in public within the UK, published contemporaneously.

The Defamation Act 2013 extended this protection to reports of proceedings in any court established under the law of a country or territory outside the UK, any international court or tribunal established by the Security Council of the United Nations or by an international agreement. A 'court' includes 'any tribunal or body exercising the judicial power of the State'.

Privilege for court reports is vital for the media because what is said in court is often highly defamatory, and reporting it would be impossible without this protection.

The law thus recognises that the media help sustain open justice, a principle examined in ch 14. Privilege does not apply if the court (or tribunal) hearing is held in private.

Reports must be fair

For absolute privilege to apply, a report of a court case must be 'fair and accurate'. This does not mean that the proceedings must be reported verbatim; a report will still be 'fair and accurate' if:

- it presents a summary of the cases put by both sides;
- it contains no substantial inaccuracies;
- it avoids giving disproportionate weight to one side or the other.

In a case in 2006 (*Bennett v Newsquest*, see *Media Lawyer* newsletter, No. 64), Mr Justice Eady pointed out that a newspaper report of a criminal case, which was the subject of a defamation action, contained inaccuracies, then said:

" The report must be fair overall and not give a misleading impression. Inaccuracies in themselves will not defeat privilege. Omissions will deprive a report of privilege if they create a false impression of what took place or if they result in the suppression of the case or part of the case of one side, while giving the other. "

A media organisation loses the protection of absolute privilege if its report is held to be unfair or inaccurate in any important respect.

- To be fair, a report of a trial must make clear that the defendant denies the charge(s) and, while it proceeds, that no verdict has been reached – for example, the report can conclude by stating: The case continues.

How much of a court case must be reported to be fair?

In 1993 the *Daily Sport* paid substantial damages to a police officer acquitted of indecent assault. It reported the opening of the case by the prosecution and the alleged victim's main evidence, but did not include her cross-examination by the defence, which began on the same day and undermined her allegation. Later the paper briefly reported the officer's acquittal. He still decided to sue. The settlement in the case means that the issue of how much of a day's proceedings in court must be covered for a report to be fair remains something of a grey area.

Trials may last for days, weeks or months, and the defendant may later show that statements made by the prosecution were wrong. Reports of proceedings may be published each day but the safest practice is that if the publication has reported allegations that are later rebutted it should also carry the rebuttals.

Reports must be accurate with quotes attributed

All allegations in court reports must be attributed because a report that presents an allegation as if it were a proved fact is inaccurate. Do not write 'Brown had a gun in his hand' but 'Smith said Brown had a gun in his hand'.

A media organisation is left with no protection at all if it wrongly identifies as the defendant someone who is only a witness or unconnected with the case. A report which gets the charge or charges a defendant faces wrong could prove expensive in libel damages.

 Ch. 20 p. 250, Identification, explains the need for a report to fully identify a defendant.

see also www. mcnaes. com ch 21: 'Case study on accuracy'

Journalists must also avoid wrongly reporting that the defendant has been convicted when he or she has in fact been acquitted. One paper paid damages when it reported a man's acquittal on drug charges – but did so in terms which gave the impression that he was in fact guilty.

The courts do allow some leeway to publications compressing material in reports, (*Elizabeth and Peter Crossley v Newsquest (Midlands South Ltd)* [2008] EWHC 3054 (QB)).

Reports must be contemporaneous

To have the protection of absolute privilege, court reports should be published contemporaneously with the proceedings.

- Contemporaneous means 'as soon as practicable' – for example, in the first issue of a newspaper following the day's hearing. For a broadcaster, it can be construed that the report should be aired on the same day of the hearing or early on the next day.

For a weekly paper, contemporaneous publication may mean publishing the following week.

Sometimes reports of court proceedings have to be postponed because a court order compels this. Section 14(2) of the Defamation Act 1996 says that in these circumstances a story is treated as if it were published contemporaneously if it is published 'as soon as practicable after publication is permitted'.

Even if the report is not contemporaneous, it will still attract qualified privilege under statute and under common law, explained later in this chapter.

Reports of earlier sections of a hearing published to put later reports in context should still be treated as having absolute privilege (The *Crossley* case, cited earlier).

Privilege is only for reports of proceedings

Suppose a 'court report' in the media contains background matter or comment that did not originate from the court? In the *Bennett* case referred to earlier, the judge said this would not destroy the privilege of the report: 'Extraneous comments can be included or other factual material but it must be severable, in the sense that a reasonable reader could readily appreciate that the material did not purport to be a report of what was said in court.'

chs. 11 and 18 explain postponement orders

But the added material itself is not covered by privilege.

Outbursts from the public gallery

Privilege may not protect defamatory matter shouted out in court – for example, from the public gallery by someone who is not part of the proceedings.

But if the shouted comment is by someone who has given evidence as a witness in that case, privilege would protect its inclusion in a court report, provided all the defence's requirements were met.

If the shouted comment is not defamatory, it can in defamation law be reported safely, no matter who made it.

▌ Qualified privilege

Qualified privilege is available as a defence for the publication of certain types of information. This law, in effect, categorises this information as of importance to society. The defence allows these 'statements' – including media reports of certain documents and events – to be freely published in the public interest, with no requirement for the publisher to be able to prove them as true, though there are some requirements.

Qualified privilege by statute

Schedule 1 of the Defamation Act 1996 – now amended and expanded by the Defamation Act 2013 – lists 'statements' to which the statutory form of qualified privilege applies, if the defence's requirements are met. For example, the defence applies to media reports of press conferences, of Parliamentary debates held in public, of public meetings, and of public meetings of councils, their committees and sub-committees. It also applies to media reports of statements issued for the public by government departments, councils, the police and other governmental agencies. It also protects non-contemporaneous reports of court cases, including references to people's past convictions.

The Schedule is set out in Appendix 3 of this book, pp. 448–452.

see also
ch. 23
on past
convictions

The requirements of qualified privilege

The defence's requirements differ from those of absolute privilege. For absolute privilege, the publisher's motive is irrelevant. But a qualified privilege defence will fail if the claimant can show malice by the publisher or author.

Fair and accurate, without malice, and in the public interest

The basic requirements of the qualified privilege defence relating to those 'statements' listed by Schedule 1 are that:

- the published report must be fair and accurate, and published without malice.

There is also a general requirement for qualified privilege that:

- the matter published must be a matter of public interest, the publication of which is for the public benefit.

This can be summed up as 'published in the public interest'.

Malice in this context means ill-will or spite towards the claimant or any indirect or improper motive in the defendant's mind. Lord Nicholls explained in *Tse Wai Chun Paul v Albert Cheng* [2001] EMLR 777, Court of Final Appeal, Hong Kong that the purpose of the qualified privilege defence was to allow someone with a duty to perform, or an interest to protect, to provide information without the risk of being sued – and if a person's dominant motive was not to perform this duty or protect this interest, he/she could not use the defence.

So a journalist or editor could be denied the protection of qualified privilege if, in a defamation action, the court accepted that the motive for publication was not from a duty to inform the public but was spite – for example, the publisher aired a defamatory allegation merely to settle a private score.

 See www.mcnaes.com ch 14 for a case study of how in 2012 the *Mail on Sunday* lost a defamation action when a judge ruled that its report of a court case was not protected by qualified privilege because it was not sufficiently fair or accurate, and therefore publication was not in the public interest.

Is there a requirement to publish explanation or contradiction?

Schedule 1 to the 1996 Act sets out in Part 1 a list of statements having qualified privilege 'without explanation or contradiction' and in Part 2 a list of statements thus privileged but 'subject to explanation or contradiction'.

This difference is important.

- A publisher relying on qualified privilege under Part 2 to protect a report must, to retain the protection, publish a 'reasonable letter or statement by way of explanation or contradiction' if required to do so by anyone defamed in the report.

This would apply, for example, if someone wanted the publisher to air a letter or statement from them to respond to a report of a council meeting which defamed them. Failure to publish such a letter or statement would destroy the defence of qualified privilege for what was published earlier. The Act says such a statement must be published 'in a suitable manner', which means 'in the same manner as the publication complained of or in a manner that is adequate and reasonable in the circumstances'.

! Remember

Get legal advice if any statement that the complainant wants published gives rise – because he/she make counter-allegations – to any risk of libelling another person. Publication of a statement of 'explanation or contradiction' is not protected by privilege under the 1996 Act, so the statement must be 'reasonable' in this respect, though common law privilege may apply.

see also pp. 272–273, Privilege at common law, on replies to attack

A statement listed in Part 1 of Schedule 1 – for example, a report of what is said in public in a legislature such as the UK Parliament or in a public register open to inspection, discussed later in this chapter – is not subject to the requirement to publish such a letter/statement by anyone defamed by the report (though an editor may decide it is newsworthy or ethical to do this).

Part I is the means by which the 1996 and 2013 Acts greatly widened the categories of statements protected, by including reports of proceedings held in public in foreign legislatures, foreign courts and of all public inquiries appointed by governments.

Statute only protects a report of the occasion or material specified

The protection of statutory qualified privilege applies only to reports of the actual proceedings, events or material listed in Schedule 1 of the 1996 Act, as amended by the 2013 Act.

- For example, this qualified privilege in the Schedule's Part 2 protects a report of speeches by councillors in a council meeting held in public, but will not protect a report of defamatory allegations a councillor makes after the meeting when asked to expand on statements made during it.

What the councillor says in the meeting – such as that a builder is corrupt – can, if the meeting was held in public, be safely reported. But if the comment is made afterwards, the publisher who airs it would have no privilege and so would need to rely on the truth defence – that is, would have to prove the builder was corrupt, which might be impossible.

Reports of public meetings, press conferences, scientific and academic conferences

Reports of a public meeting on a matter of public interest held anywhere in the world are now protected by qualified privilege, by virtue of the 2013 Act amending Part 2 of Schedule 1 of the 1996 Act, as are reports of press conferences held anywhere in the world for the discussion of a matter of public interest, and reports of scientific or academic conferences held anywhere in the world, or copies of, extracts from or summaries of material published by such conferences.

What is a public meeting?

Paragraph 12 of the Schedule, following amendment by the 2013 Act, defines a 'public meeting' as:

- a lawful meeting held anywhere in the world for the furtherance or discussion of a matter of public interest, whether admission to the meeting is general or restricted.

This definition is fairly wide, covering public meetings about a particular community or those held about national issues. The term 'restricted' means the definition can apply, for example, to a meeting called by residents of one village who exclude from it people from the neighbouring village. Again, the privilege is subject to the 'explanation and contradiction' requirement.

The nature of press conferences

The 2013 Act extended qualified privilege to coverage of press conferences held anywhere in the world on matters of public interest. This codified in statute a decision by the House of Lords in 2000 that a press conference, held after the issuing of a general invitation to the press, is a form of public meeting.

👁 Case study

Law firm McCartan Turkington Breen sued *The Times* over its report of a press conference, called by people campaigning for the release of a soldier convicted of murder, during which defamatory comments were made about the firm. It had represented the soldier. A jury awarded £145,000 damages to the firm, but on appeal Lord Bingham, the senior Law Lord, said: 'A meeting is public if those who organise it or arrange it open it to the public or, by issuing a general invitation to the press, manifest an intention or desire that the proceedings of the meeting should be communicated to a wider public.' Journalists could be regarded as 'the eyes and ears of the public'.

In *McCartan*, The House of Lords also ruled that a written press release, handed out at the meeting but not read aloud, and reported by the media, was in effect part of the press conference proceedings. This means that fair, accurate reports of documents handed out at a press conference also have qualified privilege, in the context of coverage of the press conference.

Stories from documents open to public inspection

Paragraph 5 in Part 1 of the Schedule gives privilege for a fair and accurate copy of or extract from a document which the law requires to be open to public inspection. This means, for example, that the media have qualified privilege for material quoted fairly and accurately, etc, from publicly-available records such as those at Companies House, the Land Registry or other public registries, even if the records themselves turn out to be inaccurate. The paragraph also gives qualified privilege to media reports of court documents officially made available to them – see ch. 14. But it does not apply to reports of documents released under the Freedom of Information Act, though the public interest defence may apply to such reports. This defence is explained in ch.22.

ch. 30 explains the FOI Act

Reports of statements issued for the public by government agencies

Paragraph 9 in Part 2 of the Schedule gives qualified privilege, subject to explanation or contradiction, to 'a fair and accurate copy of or extract from' a notice or other matter issued for the public by governments anywhere in the world, and authorities anywhere in the world which have governmental functions. This includes government departments, councils and police authorities, so it would cover, for example, fair and accurate reports of official police statements, and statements made on behalf of local authorities, for example, press releases about consumer protection or environmental health matters.

- These statements could be defamatory – for example, a police press release might name a man and say police want to trace him to question him about a murder. But the qualified privilege allows the media to report this without fear of being sued by the man, provided, if asked, that it publishes his 'reasonable letter or statement of explanation or contradiction'.

There will be many occasions when a reporter will wish to report the misdeeds of a person but may be inhibited by the fear of a defamation action. The answer is often to obtain confirmation of the information in the form of an official statement by a police or local authority spokesman.

! Remember

Statutory qualified privilege does not protect reports of information unofficially 'leaked' from such authorities, or of what was said by people who are not official spokesmen or women.

Not all authorities are covered

Paragraph 9 of the Schedule does not cover reports of all statements by people in authority – it does not cover, for example, reports of statements by the spokespeople of British Telecom, a gas board, a water board, the rail companies, London Regional Transport, British Airport Authority or other bodies created by statute which are involved in providing day-to-day services to the public. But it seems likely that a fair and accurate account of the official statements of such a body would be held to be covered by privilege at common law, referred to later in this chapter.

Verbal comments by press officers

Suppose a reporter telephones a press officer at one of the bodies of the type specified under paragraph 9 of the Schedule. Is the report of the spokesperson's verbal comments protected by qualified privilege under the Act? The general position seems to be, yes, unless the spokesperson was given no chance to make considered comments.

👁 Case study

In *Blackshaw v Lord* [1984] QB 1, Lord Justice Stephenson, referring to the protection paragraph 9 gives the media, said: 'It may be right to include...the kind of answers to telephoned interrogatories which Mr Lord [a *Daily Telegraph* reporter], quite properly in the discharge of his duty to his newspaper, administered to Mr Smith [a government press officer]. To exclude them in every case might unduly restrict the freedom of the press...But information which is put out on the initiative of a government department falls more easily within the paragraph than information pulled out of the mouth of an unwilling officer of the department.'

Disciplinary actions by private associations

Paragraph 14 in Part 2 of the Schedule bestows qualified privilege on media reports of the findings or decisions of a wide variety of bodies – for example, in the field of sport, business or learning – anywhere in the world which have a constitution empowering them to make disciplinary decisions about members. So, for example, the media can safely report a decision by the Jockey Club to discipline a jockey, the Football Association to discipline a player, or a scientific association to censure an academic, if the association is of the type listed in paragraph 14. The protection does not apply to a report of the proceedings of such bodies, and is subject to the 'explanation and contradiction' requirement.

Reports about companies

The 1996 and 2013 Acts also greatly extended qualified privilege with respect to reporting company affairs. Earlier, qualified privilege only covered reports relating to proceedings at public companies' general meetings. The Acts extended Part 2 privilege to documents circulated among shareholders of a listed company with the authority of the board or the auditors or by any shareholder 'in pursuance of a right conferred by any statutory provision', and to fair and accurate copies of, extracts from or summaries of any document circulated to members of the company about the appointment, resignation, retirement or dismissal of directors of the company or its auditors.

▎ Privilege at common law

There are some circumstances in which the media can benefit from privilege in common law. This will apply, within certain bounds, to publication of a person's response to an attack on his/her character or conduct. Also, privilege in common law applies to reports of court cases and Parliamentary proceedings, if held in public, in addition to statutory privilege. For more detail, see www.mcnaes.com ch. 21.

▶ 'Accord and satisfaction', apologies and corrections

A media organisation can use the defence of 'accord and satisfaction' to halt a defamation case on the ground that the issue has already been disposed of – for example, by publication of a correction and apology which the claimant accepted at the time as settlement of his/her complaint. But negotiating an apology or correction is not a job for an inexperienced journalist.

'Without prejudice'

A solicitor acting for a client demanding a correction and apology will always avoid suggesting that this action by the media organisation will be enough in itself to settle the dispute and will make it clear that the request is made 'without prejudice' to any other action that might be thought necessary.

What does this mean? The basic principle is that parties attempting to settle their differences before going to law should be encouraged to speak frankly. So anything said or written in the course of negotiations to settle and described as 'without prejudice' (that is, off the record) cannot subsequently be used against a party in court if negotiations fail. The rule applies whether or not the phrase 'without prejudice' is expressly used, but it can be good practice for the media organisation to use it too.

Journalists speaking with someone complaining about a story need to distinguish between:

- discussions over an offer to publish a follow-up story or a correction; and
- discussions over settling a claim.

In the former case, which often involves the journalist and the subject themselves, the discussion need not necessarily be 'without prejudice'; the journalist may well want to refer to this discussion in court, to show fairness or lack of malice, or to mitigate damages.

In the latter case, often involving solicitors and mention of money, the discussion should be 'without prejudice'. As a general rule journalists should notify their insurers about potential claims immediately, and, if there are solicitors 'on the other side', the publisher should also involve its own lawyer.

Care needed in apologies and corrections

It is no defence for a media organisation to publish a correction and apology not agreed by the claimant.

Publishing such apology can make matters worse for the publisher, because:

- a court may find that it constitutes an admission that the material which prompted the complaint was defamatory;
- a badly drafted apology or correction might also repeat the original defamatory statement, further angering the person who complained about it, or even unwittingly libel someone else.

see www.
mcnaes.
com
ch. 21:
'Practical
advice on
waivers'

For example: 'In our article yesterday we said Mr Red hit Mr Green. But we wish to point out that Mr Red says Mr Green struck him first'. If this is published Mr Green may sue over the wording of the apology.

On the other hand, if the jury finds for the claimant, the fact that the media organisation took prompt and adequate steps to correct the error, and to express regret, will reduce the damages.

Complainants might also be prepared to sign waivers – a statements saying they waive their right to legal redress in exchange for the publication of a correction and apology – which will provide a complete defence of 'accord and satisfaction'.

A practical danger for an editor who asks a complainant to sign a waiver is that the reader may not previously have realised that he or she has a claim for damages and, thus alerted, may consult a lawyer. The waiver is therefore most useful when the complainant has already threatened to consult a lawyer.

Inexperienced reporters sometimes try to avoid the consequences of errors without referring them to the editor, by trying to shrug them off, or by incorporating a scarcely recognisable 'correction' (without apology) in a follow-up story – a highly dangerous course of action, which may further aggravate the damage and prompt the potential claimant to take more formal steps to secure satisfaction. Reporters should always tell the editor about a problem immediately so it can be dealt with properly.

▌ Offer of amends

The media can defame a person unintentionally. The classic example was the case of Artemus Jones, in which a journalist introduced a fictitious character into a descriptive account of a factual event in order to provide atmosphere – referring to what he thought of as his fictional character as being at the Dieppe motor festival 'with a woman who is not his wife'.

Unfortunately the name he chose was that of a real person, a barrister – and former journalist – from North Wales. Stung by the comments of his friends the real Artemus Jones sued and recovered substantial damages.

Another example is when a story about one individual is understood to refer to another as in the case of Harold Newstead, explained in ch. 20, p. 251, Importance of ages, addresses and occupations.

The Defamation Act 1996 provides for a defence known as 'offer to make amends'.

To use it, a defendant who is alleged to have published a defamatory statement must make a written offer to make a suitable correction and apology, to publish the correction in a reasonable manner and to pay the claimant suitable damages and legal costs.

If the offer of amends is rejected, and is not withdrawn, it will be a complete defence unless the claimant can show that the defendant 'knew or had reason to believe' that the published statement was false and was also defamatory of the claimant.

Editors planning to make an offer of amends must not delay. If the resulting compensation is to be assessed by a judge he/she will start by deciding what would be 'suitable damages' if the editor had made no offer of amends and will then award a 'discount' of perhaps 50 per cent as a 'reward' for making the offer. The *News of the World* received only a 40 per cent discount after it was slow to respond to a complaint and published an apology six months after the original story.

Once an offer is made it is binding.

▌ Leave and licence

The 'leave and licence' defence is that the claimant suing for libel had previously agreed that the material could be published. If it is clear the material is defamatory, a publisher intending to rely on this defence needs to be sure he/she can prove there was such pre-publication agreement. The person who is going to be defamed by the material should be asked to sign a statement agreeing to its publication or be recorded agreeing. Otherwise it might be difficult to prove that consent was given if it was merely verbal.

Sometimes, even without an explicit agreement, the context will be that leave and licence was given – for example, by a pop star who chooses in an arranged interview to speak on-the-record about false allegations made against him, seeking to dispel them.

But in other circumstances – for example, a media investigation into wrongdoing – the leave and licence defence will not be secured merely by the journalist giving the target the opportunity to comment.

▌ 'Live' broadcasts and readers' online comments

Newsagents and booksellers have a defence of innocent dissemination as they are merely the conduit for the passage of the words complained of and are not responsible for them. But the defence was not available to others, such as distributors and broadcasters.

The Defamation Act 1996, in section 1, and section 10 of the Defamation Act 2013 extended the defence, which now applies to anyone who was not the author, editor or publisher (as defined by the Act) of the statement complained of, who took reasonable care in relation to its publication, and who did not know and had no reason to believe that whatever part he/she had in the publication caused or contributed to the publication of a defamatory statement.

A court deciding whether a person took reasonable care, or had reason to believe that what he/she did caused or contributed to the publication of a defamatory statement, must have regard to:

- the extent of his/her responsibility for the content of the statement or the decision to publish it;
- the nature or circumstances of the publication; and
- the previous conduct or character of the author, editor or publisher.

Section 10 of the 2013 Act says a court does not have jurisdiction to hear and determine an action for defamation brought against a person who was not the author, editor or publisher of the statement complained of unless it is satisfied that it is not reasonably practicable for an action to be brought against the author, editor or publisher.

Live broadcasts protected by section 1

The list of categories of people who are not authors, editors or publishers for the purposes of the defence includes broadcasters of live programmes who have no effective control over the maker of the statement complained of.

In 1999 the research firm MORI and its head, Bob Worcester, sued the BBC over defamatory remarks made by controversial politician Sir James Goldsmith during a live radio interview. The BBC said it had a defence under section 1 – but could it be said it had taken 'reasonable care'? It was argued it should have known Sir James was likely to say something defamatory and it should at least have used a 'delay button'. The case was settled before the jury reached a verdict.

Broadcasters in 'live' situations need to react quickly to halt or cut off defamatory utterances to be sure of benefitting from section 1.

Internet service providers and website operators

The section 1 defence is also available for ISPs (internet service providers) which provide as 'host' a service to enable people and companies to publish their own content on their websites. ISPs play a merely passive role in the process of transmission of any defamatory matter, and are therefore not publishers under section 1. But an ISP could be successfully sued for libel if it failed quickly to take down defamatory material on a site it hosts after receiving a complaint about it. In *Godfrey v Demon Internet Ltd* [2001] QB 201 the ISP was successfully sued for material on a newsgroup it hosted which it left online for about 10 days after receiving a complaint. The claim was for damages for those 10 days.

Section 5 defence

Section 5 of the 2013 Act provides a new defence for website operators, which will be detailed in regulations which, as this book was being completed, were still subject to consultation. But the defence is intended to protect a website operator from a defamation action over postings by users if they follow steps intended to allow the would-be claimant to take action directly against the individual/s who posted the defamatory material.

 See www.mcnaes.com ch 21 for a detailed explanation of this defence when the regulations are settled.

There is also an additional protection for those who 'host', 'cache' or are 'mere conduits' for internet publication - the Electronic Commerce (EC Directive) Regulations 2002/2013. In outline, they are protected from liability to pay damages or any other financial remedy unless and until they have notice of the defamatory publication. This is why many ISPs operate 'notice and take down' procedures.

It is not yet known how these defences will operate in connection with each other.

The moderation of readers' comments posted on websites

Newspapers, magazines, TV channels and radio stations cannot use the section 1 defence in the 1996 Act in respect of content which staff place on their websites, as they are clearly publishers.

As regards comment posted there by readers, the section 1 defence, and that in section 5 of the 2013 Act, as long as the correct procedural steps are followed, will offer some protection. Also, the media organisation might have a defence under Regulation 19 of the Electronic Commerce (EC Directive) Regulations 2002 in relation to comments posted directly on to the sites by readers.

Section 1 or Regulation 19 are unlikely to apply if the media organisation's staff moderate – check – material before it goes online, or subsequently check a comment which is clearly defamatory, or attracts complaint, but let it remain online. But the section 5 defence in the 2013 Act may offer some protection, as it specifies that the defence 'is not defeated by reason only of the fact that the operator of the website moderates the statements posted on it by others'.

- The safest course is to remove a reader's comment from the website quickly if there is a complaint that it is defamatory. The material can be re-posted later if after consideration it is deemed safe.

👁 Case study

In 2009 Mr Justice Eady ruled that the *Croydon Guardian* was not liable as the publisher for comments posted on its website by others. A man had tried to sue for defamation about readers' comments posted about a report of a disciplinary tribunal case in which he was struck off as a solicitor. Mr Justice Eady said the newspaper was protected by the Regulation 19 defence because it had not had actual knowledge of the alleged 'unlawful activity or information' until the man complained, and it had then removed the material including the comments, as soon as it became aware of the nature of his complaint (*Karim v Newsquest Media Group Ltd* [2009] EWHC 3205 (QB)).

▌ Other defences

Defences which might be available are:

The claimant has died A defamation action is a personal action. A dead person cannot be libelled. Similarly, an action begun by a claimant cannot be continued by his heirs and executors if he/she dies.

That proceedings were not started within the limitation period – that is, the person suing did not begin the action within 12 months of the material being published. This should be a complete defence, unless there is a new publication of offending material. The period, formerly three years, was reduced to one year by the Defamation Act 1996 – although the courts may extend it if it is thought to be in the interests of justice to do so. Reporters should date their notebooks, recordings and research material and store them carefully in case this proof is needed if someone sues towards the end of the limitation period, or there is a possibility of using this material again after that. Journalists must remember that every repetition is a new publication.

 See ch. 20, p. 253, Repeating statements of others, for the case of the 'bygone days' column and pp. 254–255, The 'single publication rule' and online archives, on this new defence in the Defamation Act 2013.

➡ Recap of major points

- The main defences against an action for libel are: truth, honest opinion and absolute and qualified privilege.

- It is a complete defence (with one exception arising under the Rehabilitation of Offenders Act 1974) to prove that the words complained of are substantially true.

- A defendant can plead that an article expressing comment was an honestly held opinion on a matter of public interest.

- Absolute privilege applies to court reports, but reports must be fair, accurate, and contemporaneous.

- Qualified privilege is available on many occasions under statute (for example, for a report of a public meeting). The defence is qualified because it is lost if the motive in publishing is malicious.

- Other defences include 'accord and satisfaction' and 'offer of amends'.

((•)) **Useful Websites**

Test whether your story has a defence – see mcnaes.com ch. 21

22

The public interest defence

Chapter summary

This defence, introduced in the Defamation Act 2013, grew from the common law *Reynolds* defence, which was developed to allow journalists to fulfil their duty to report stories in the public interest, even if they included defamatory material they could not prove to be true, if the publication was the product of responsible journalism. Attempts to use the defence led to the courts closely examining whether a story was truly in the public interest, and the way in which it was researched and written. This chapter reviews the old defence, details the requirements of the new statutory defence, and highlights the real difficulties journalists are likely to face in using it. Journalists should never consider using this defence without taking legal advice.

▶ The birth of the defence

The 'public interest' defence created by the Defamation Act 2013 is intended to help liberalise libel law by protecting the publication of defamatory material concerning a matter of public interest, even if at the time the publisher cannot prove the material to be true. Editors hope it will increase the occasions when responsible, investigative journalism can safely be published.

→ glossary The defence's origins are in the '*Reynolds* defence'. This evolved in **common law**, taking its name from the 1998 case in which former Irish premier Albert Reynolds sued Times Newspapers, publisher of the *Sunday Times*, over an article he claimed meant he deliberately and dishonestly misled the Irish parliament by suppressing information about the appointment of Ireland's Attorney General as President of its High Court. Times Newspapers argued in its defence that, in keeping with Article 10 of the European Convention on Human Rights, the

public interest in media coverage of political issues and in scrutinising the conduct of elected politicians should be protected by a common law form of qualified
privilege.

Times Newspapers lost in the High Court. But in the Court of Appeal, the Lord
Chief Justice, Lord Bingham, said: 'As it is the task of the news media to inform
the public and engage in public discussion of matters of public interest, so is that
to be recognised as its duty.' In 1999 the case reached the House of Lords. Times
Newspapers lost, but the court confirmed the principle that in some circumstances
the media have a duty to publish material in the public interest, even if it could not
be proved to be true, and that therefore qualified privilege in common law should,
in those circumstances, protect that publication – and so the *Reynolds* defence was
born (*Reynolds v Times Newspapers* [2001] 2 AC 127).

Lord Nicholls, in the leading speech, set out a non-exhaustive list of factors a
court should consider when examining whether a publication was the product of
responsible journalism, and therefore whether it could be protected by the new
defence.

ch. 1
explains the
Convention's
effect and see
also ch. 21,
pp. 267–272,
Qualified
privilege

Lord Nicholls' list *(with summarised explanation added in italics)*

(1) The seriousness of the allegation. The more serious the charge, the more
the public is misinformed and the individual harmed, if the allegation is
not true – *therefore, the more serious the allegation, the greater should be
the reporter's efforts to ensure that what is published is correct if the story
is to be protected by the new defence.*

(2) The nature of the information, and the extent to which the subject matter
is a matter of public concern – *the less the matter is of public concern, the
weaker the defence. In some cases, if a judge decides the matter is not of
public concern, the defence will fail. Judges often say that what interests
the public and what is in the public interest are two different things.*

(3) The source of the information. *Some informants have no direct knowledge of the events. Some have their own axes to grind, or are being paid
for their stories. It is important to note that courts are wary of unidentified
informants, although a newspaper or broadcaster will not necessarily be
penalised for refusing to identify a source.*

(4) The steps taken to verify the information – *it is always important to
check, whenever possible, to ensure that what you have been told it true
or correct. Making no or insufficient checks before publication will be
regarded as irresponsible journalism and the defence will not apply.*

(5) The status of the information. The allegation may have already been the
subject of an investigation which commands respect – *for example, if a
reputable agency – such as the police – has already decided the relevant
allegations are not true, than the media must have sufficient reason to air
them, if the defence is to apply.*

(6) The urgency of the matter. News is often a perishable commodity – *that is, the courts, when deciding if the defence applies, must take into consideration that journalists need to work and publish quickly.*

(7) Whether comment was sought before publication from the claimant – *that is, ie the person who claims he/she was defamed.* He/she may have information others do not possess or have not disclosed. An approach to the claimant will not always be necessary. *But generally, the person who is the subject of an allegation should be approached. It is also important to make it clear in a story that if the person about whom allegations have been made cannot be contacted, efforts have been made to reach him or her. Only rarely will an approach to the subject not be necessary.*

(8) Whether the article contained the gist of the claimant's side of the story – *that is, the journalism must be fair to benefit from the defence. Leaving out the claimant's side is a recipe for disaster.*

(9) The tone of the article. A newspaper can raise queries or call for an investigation. It need not adopt allegations as statements of fact – *for example, the defence may not apply to material which brashly and unfairly suggests that unproven allegations are true. It is important to mind your phrasing. Make sure that what you write is what you mean – and that your meaning is clear to anyone who reads your copy, including the Man on the Clapham Omnibus. Sloppy writing will almost undoubtedly prove expensive.*

(10) The circumstances of the publication, including the timing – *that is, was it really so urgent that the story had to be published when it was? Could it have waited an hour or two or a day or so?*

The *Jameel* case

The *Reynolds* defence developed further in *Jameel v Wall Street Journal Europe* [2006] UKHL 44 in which Lord Bingham, then the senior judge in the House of Lords, said the material published had to be of public interest and the product of responsible journalism, adding: 'The publisher is protected if he has taken such steps as a responsible journalist would take to try and ensure that what is published is accurate and fit for publication.' He recalled that in *Reynolds* Lord Nicholls had 'listed certain matters which might be taken into account in deciding whether the test of responsible journalism was satisfied' – which he said were 'pointers', not 'hurdles' – and adding that the rationale of the test was that 'there is no duty to publish, and the public has no interest to read, material which the publisher has not taken reasonable steps to verify'.

In the *Jameel* case the *Wall Street Journal* reported that, at the request of US authorities, Saudi Arabia's central bank was monitoring a number of accounts to stop them from being used, 'wittingly or unwittingly', to funnel funds to terrorist groups, and that millionaire Saudi Arabian businessman Mohammed Jameel and his companies were among those being tracked.

Mr Jameel sued for defamation, and a jury found that the article was defamatory of him and his companies, and awarded them damages.

The Court of Appeal rejected the newspaper's appeal against the trial judge's denial of the *Reynolds* privilege, because the newspaper had refused to give Mr Jameel's spokesman 24 hours to produce a response.

But the newspaper won the case on appeal to the House of Lords (which has now been replaced by the Supreme Court). There Lord Bingham said that denying the *Reynolds* privilege just because the newspaper failed to delay publication of the claimants' names and did not wait long enough for them to comment was a very narrow ground – Mr Jameel could only have issued a denial, and Saudi Arabia's central bank would not have admitted to monitoring accounts.

▌ The Act's public interest defence

The new defence in the Defamation Act 2013 of publication on a matter of public interest is detailed in section 4. It abolishes and replaces the *Reynolds* defence, because Parliament's intention was to clarify this area of law. The Explanatory Notes published when the Act was passed state that the new defence is intended to reflect the principles established in the *Reynolds* case and subsequent case law. But the previous cases are not binding authority for the statutory defence, although they might be a 'helpful' guide to interpreting how it should be applied.

Section 4(1) says the defence is available if the defendant can show that the statement complained of was, or formed part of, a statement on a matter of public interest, and that he/she reasonably believed that publishing it was in the public interest.

This provision, say the Explanatory Notes, is intended to reflect the common law *Reynolds* defence as it was detailed in *Flood v Times Newspapers* [2012] 2 AC 273.

The Act reflects the two elements of the common law test. Section 4(1)(a) requires that the words complained of were about a matter of public interest. If the publication passes this test, it then has to meet the requirements of section 4(1)(b), which has subjective and objective elements.

First comes the subjective element, which is the defendant's belief that publication was in the public interest, then comes the objective element, which is the question of whether it was reasonable, in all the circumstances, for the defendant to hold that belief.

The *Flood* case

In the *Flood* case, the *Sunday Times* ran a story saying that Detective Sergeant Gary Flood of the Metropolitan Police extradition unit was being investigated following an allegation of corruption. Det Sgt Flood – who was later completely exonerated by an inquiry – sued for defamation. Mr Justice Tugendhat at first instance ruled that the newspaper report was protected by the *Reynolds* defence. But the Court of Appeal overturned that, taking an extremely narrow view of the defence and holding that it was not available because the journalists responsible for the article had failed to act responsibly by failing adequately to verify the allegations in it.

The Supreme Court reversed that decision, saying that the newspaper was entitled to use the *Reynolds* defence. Lord Brown said:

> In deciding whether Reynolds privilege attaches (whether the Reynolds public interest defence lies) the judge, on true analysis, is deciding but a single question: could whoever published the defamation, given whatever they knew (and did not know) and whatever they had done (and had not done) to guard so far as possible against the publication of untrue defamatory material, properly have considered the publication in question to be in the public interest?

This, said Lord Brown, involved a host of different considerations, starting with the non-exhaustive list of 10 factors identified by Lord Nicholls in the original *Reynolds* case but also including other considerations.

The court must consider all the circumstances

Section 4(2) of the 2013 Act says that in determining whether the public interest defence is made out, the court must have regard to all the circumstances of the case.

Courts will doubtless be looking to see if the journalism was conducted in a responsible manner – and might be expected to have in mind, at least, the non-exhaustive list of 10 factors detailed by Lord Nicholls in the original *Reynolds* case. The Act itself places no requirement on a publisher to demonstrate that what was published was the result of 'responsible journalism', and the abolition of the common law defence means that the *Reynolds* case is no longer a binding authority. But the old cases showing the approach judges have taken to responsible journalism might give some indication of factors which might be taken into account in deciding whether the defendant's belief – that publishing it was in the public interest – *is* reasonable.

Audit trails to justify the public interest element and belief

ch 2, p. 12, outlines the context of the report

Sir Brian Leveson suggested in his 2012 report into the press that any new regulator should require investigative journalists and their editors to produce an 'audit trail' of the development of a story, the investigation itself, and the issues considered and factors discussed when deciding whether to publish, and whether the story was in the public interest.

Whether the courts will require this as part of the public interest defence should become clearer when cases on the new defence have been decided. Some editors are already familiar with such 'audit trail' practices, because, for example, the BBC Editorial Guidelines require that use of undercover tactics must be approved by senior managers as being in the public interest, and because in 2012 the Editors' Code of

Practice was changed to require press editors, in the event of a relevant complaint about reporters' methods, to demonstrate how and with whom they decided that 'public interest' exceptions applied. Chapters 2 and 3 explain these codes.

Section 4(4) of the 2013 Act states that when deciding whether it was reasonable for a defendant to believe that publication was in the public interest, the court 'must make such allowance for editorial judgement as it considers appropriate'.

Defining the public interest

The Ofcom Code and the Editors' Code of Practice have some definitions of what journalism can be considered to be 'in the public interest' – for example, to expose crime or that someone is misleading or endangering the public. The wording of those definitions was influenced by legal judgments in breach of confidence cases about the circumstances when the public interest justifies confidential or private material being published against someone's wishes. But the 2013 Act does not define the public interest. The Explanatory Notes say simply that 'this is a concept which is well-established in the English common law'.

see ch. 25, pp. 310–311, Publication in the public interest, about such cases

The publication must be, or form part of, a statement on a matter of public interest, meaning that the court can either deal solely with the words complained of, or take a holistic view of them in the wider context of the document or article in which they appear when deciding if overall this is a matter of public interest.

It was held that the *Reynolds* defence was available to anyone who publishes material in the public interest, including in a book. The same seems to apply to the new statutory defence.

In *Charman v Orion Publishing Group Ltd and others* [2007] EWCA Civ 972, [2008] 1 All ER 750 the Court of Appeal allowed the use of the defence to defeat a libel claim by a former police officer over Graeme McLagan's book, *Bent Coppers – The Inside Story of Scotland Yard's Battle Against Police Corruption*.

It seems from rulings so far that judges will consider material to be in the public interest if it is of 'real public concern' – but the test is not as strict as saying the public need to know. The concept is also flexible – the degree of public interest required will vary according to the publication and market, as in the *GKR Karate* case in 2000, in which a judge found in favour of the *Leeds Weekly News*, a free newspaper which was sued over a front page article warning readers about the activities of doorstep salesmen selling karate club membership.

The judge said the fundamental question was one of public interest, and the people of Leeds clearly had an interest in receiving this information (*GKR Karate Ltd v Yorkshire Post Newspapers Ltd* [2001] 1 WLR 2571).

The responsible journalism test

The courts examined the issue of 'responsible journalism' in a number of cases, which might throw light on the approach they will take in future.

The *Reynolds* case – Although the House of Lords in *Reynolds* established the *Reynolds* defence, it also decided, by a majority, that the *Sunday Times* could not take advantage of it as it had conspicuously failed to 'give the gist of the subject's response' (point 8 – see p. 282, Lord Nicholl's list). Asked at the trial why his account contained no reference to Mr Reynolds' explanation, the reporter said: 'There was not a word of Mr Reynolds' defence because I had decided that his defence…there was no defence'. Mr Reynolds had addressed the Irish parliament on the issue, but the paper did not report his statement.

On the steps taken to verify the story (Lord Nicholls' point 4), the reporter, asked why he took no notes during his inquiries, said: 'I was not in note-taking mode'.

The *Loutchansky* case – *The Times* in 1999 published articles alleging that international businessman Grigori Loutchansky controlled a major Russian criminal organisation involved in money-laundering and smuggling nuclear weapons.

The High Court judge rejected its claim to a *Reynolds* defence. The case went to the Court of Appeal, which agreed that the articles dealt with matters of public concern (Lord Nicholls' point 2), but made the following points:

- implicating Mr Loutchansky in misconduct of the utmost gravity was manifestly likely to be highly damaging to his reputation, so a proportionate degree of responsibility was required of the journalist and the editor (Lord Nicholls' point 1). But *The Times* had failed to show this – the allegations were vague, the sources unreliable, insufficient steps were taken to verify the information, and no comment was obtained from Mr Loutchansky before publication.

- The High Court judge was entitled to find that 'such steps as were taken' by the reporter in his unsuccessful attempts to contact either Mr Loutchansky or his company, Nordex, or its lawyers were far less diligent than required by the standards of responsible journalism (Lord Nicholls' point 7).

- On the question whether the coverage contained the gist of Mr Loutchansky's side of the story (Lord Nicholls' point 8), it only contained the bare statement that he had 'repeatedly denied any wrongdoing or links to criminal activity', which was insufficient, given the seriousness of the unproven allegations published.

Both the *Reynolds* and *Loutchansky* cases demonstrate the importance of journalists having a good shorthand note to support what they write. Asked in court in the *Loutchansky* case to produce the note he made of a vital conversation he said he had had with his most important source, the reporter replied that he thought he must have made the note on a scrap of paper which he had subsequently thrown away (Lord Nicholls' point 4).

The Court of Appeal rejected the newspaper's appeal (*Loutchansky v Times Newspapers Ltd* [2001] EWCA Civ 1805).

The source of the information and the steps taken to verify it – Lord Nicholls' third and fourth points – require more than a journalist making a number of calls which do not actually yield useful information or verification. In *Lord Ashcroft v*

Stephen Foley, Independent News and Media and Roger Alton [2011] EWCA 292
(QB) Mr Justice Eady agreed with the claimant's argument that if sources provided no relevant information, or none that was relied upon, the fact that they had been contacted was irrelevant. He added: 'Journalists, in other words, cannot collect "brownie points" for having rung round a number of people who had no relevant information to give.'

Seeking comment from the claimant

A key point in many cases involving the *Reynolds* defence was whether the publisher sought comment from the claimant (Lord Nicholls' seventh point).

Any damaging story should be put to the subject before publication. As Lord Nicholls said: 'He [the subject] may have information others do not possess or have not disclosed.' The courts regard observance of the practice as one indication of responsible journalism. But point 7 also states: 'An approach to the claimant will not always be necessary' – the view the court took in the *Jameel* case because of its special circumstances.

Journalists should always try to put defamatory or damaging allegations to the subject if they intend to report them in the public interest.

▶ Websites

The new defence is available to anyone who publishes material – so will cover bloggers, Twitter-users and everyone else with access to the world-wide web.

But in the *Flood* case – discussed earlier – the court held that the *Sunday Times* was protected by the Reynolds defence in relation to the copy of the story in its internet archive only until the date on which it was told that Det Sgt Flood had been exonerated. Mr Justice Tugendhat held that its failure to make clear that Mr Flood was innocent, for example by adding an indication to this effect to the online story, could not be said to be responsible journalism.

All journalists should keep the internet in mind when dealing with investigative stories – and ensure that archive material is updated to reflect changes in circumstances.

▶ A delicate balance

This new defence in the 2013 Act is extremely important to the media, journalists and editors but also to those who might seek to sue. It seeks to strike a balance between the right to reputation and a free press – but when it succeeds it means that a would-be claimant is deprived of any remedy for what might be a defamatory publication which severely damages his/her reputation. So the journalist's activities and professionalism will be closely scrutinised – in effect, the journalist's conduct will be on trial rather than that of the defendant.

▶ Neutral reportage

The 'public interest' defence created in the 2013 Act includes protection of neutral reportage – that is, when a dispute or issue is being reported even-handedly in instances in which the fact that allegations are being made by one person against another, or that something is a matter of controversy, is itself a matter of public interest, even though the publisher cannot prove which people in a dispute or opposed in the controversy are telling the truth.

Section 4(3) says that if the complained-of statement (the reportage) was 'an accurate and impartial report of a dispute to which the claimant is a party', a court must, when determining whether it was reasonable for the publisher to believe that publishing the statement was in the public interest, disregard any omission by the publisher 'to take steps to verify the truth of the imputation conveyed by it'.

Again, when considering if the defence applies, judges can be guided, but not bound, by case law, outlined below, on a variant of the *Reynolds* defence which became known as the neutral reportage defence.

The *Al-Fagih* case

In *Al-Fagih v HH Saudi Research & Marketing (UK) Ltd* [2001] EWCA Civ 1634 the Court of Appeal ruled that a newspaper could rely on the Reynolds defence where it reported, in an entirely objective manner, an allegation about someone made by an opponent during a political dispute. The defence was not lost merely because the newspaper had not verified the allegation. The newspaper had argued that where two politicians made serious allegations against each other, it was a matter of public importance to report the dispute, provided that this was done fairly and accurately and the parties were given the opportunity to explain or contradict.

The *BNP* case (*Roberts v Searchlight*)

This showed that a 'neutral reportage' defence could be used even when, by contrast with *Al-Fagih*, the journal and its staff are clearly not neutral. The test was whether the journalist has reported the matter neutrally. The anti-fascist magazine *Searchlight* reported a dispute between British National Party factions, repeating defamatory allegations made in the BNP's own bulletin. The magazine, its editor and a journalist successfully argued that they had a defence of qualified privilege in common law as they were merely reporting the allegations, not adopting or endorsing them (*Christopher Roberts and Barry Roberts v Gerry Gable, Steve Silver and Searchlight Magazine Ltd* [2006] EWHC 1025 (QB)).

➡ Recap of major points

- The *Reynolds* defence protected publication of material if it could be shown to be a matter of public interest, responsibly reported.

- The new statutory 'public interest' defence, which has its origins in the *Reynolds* defence, has two principle elements – the publication must be a statement on a matter of public interest, and the defendant's belief that it was reasonable.

- Judges will be guided to an extent by case law on the *Reynolds* defence, and the new defence can protect 'neutral reportage' – accurate and impartial reports – of a dispute in which the claimant is involved.

((•)) Useful Websites

www.legislation.gov.uk/ukpga/2013/26/contents/enacted
The Defamation Act 2013

www.legislation.gov.uk/ukpga/2013/26/notes/contents
The Explanatory Notes to the Act

www.bailii.org/uk/cases/UKSC/2012/11.html
The Supreme Court decision in *Flood v Times Newspapers Ltd*

www.bailii.org/uk/cases/UKHL/2006/44.html
The House of Lords decision in the *Jameel* case

www.bailii.org/uk/cases/UKHL/2006/44.html
The House of Lords decision in the *Reynolds* case

www.bbc.co.uk/journalism/law/reynolds-defence/
BBC College of Journalism's guidance on the *Reynolds* defence

23

The Rehabilitation of Offenders Act 1974

Chapter summary

The Rehabilitation of Offenders Act allows people to live down previous criminal convictions after a specified period, which varies with the length of the sentence they receive. It limits the defences journalists have against libel claims over a published reference to a 'spent' conviction about which a claimant can prove malice. The Act presents no problem for journalists if revelation of someone's criminal record is in the public interest.

▶ Rehabilitation periods

 The Act created the concept of **spent convictions**. Convictions become 'spent' after a 'rehabilitation period', which varies according to the sentence imposed. Some convictions, such as murder, which carry an automatic life sentence, are never spent.

The aim was to allow people convicted of less serious offences to live down previous convictions and get a fresh start. There is no legal obligation to declare a 'spent' conviction when applying for most jobs, whatever the application form says, although there is for some posts, such as working with children.

The Act also seeks to stop the media referring to someone's spent conviction for no good reason.

Rehabilitation depends on the length of an offender's sentence. Serious crimes for which convictions never become spent are those for which an offender is given a jail sentence of more than 30 months, whether the sentence is immediate or suspended, or a term of more than 30 months of youth custody, detention in a young offender institution or corrective training. Terms of preventive detention or an extended sentence for public protection, given for violent or sexual offences, never become spent.

 Various types of sentence are explained in ch. 6, pp. 60–63, Sentencing by magistrates, and ch. 8, p. 83, Sentencing at Crown court.

The rehabilitation periods determining when less serious convictions become spent vary from 10 years, for a prison sentence greater than six months, to six months, for an absolute discharge. But a further conviction during the rehabilitation period can extend it. Cautions become spent immediately. Rehabilitation periods for many convictions are halved for those under 18, and in some cases are even shorter for those aged 12 to 14. Suspended sentences are treated as if they were put into effect.

Section 18 of the Policing and Crime Act 2009 amends section 5 of the Rehabilitation of Offenders Act to insert subsection (4C), setting the rehabilitation period for orders made on conviction of offences of loitering or soliciting for purposes of prostitution under section 1(2A) of the Street Offences Act 1959 at six months from the date of the conviction.

 See Useful Websites at the end of this chapter and www.mcnaes.com ch. 23 for a detailed breakdown, issued by Nacro the crime reduction charity, of rehabilitation periods arising from particular sentences.

▌ The Act's effect on the media

The Act limits the defences available for a media organisation sued for libel for publishing reference to a person's spent conviction.

see ch. 21 for explanation of all these defences

(1) A defence of justification – that the report of the previous conviction was true – will fail if the claimant can prove that the conviction was spent and the publication was malicious. This breaches the principle that truth is a complete defence to a defamation action because the Act aims to deter the media from referring to a spent conviction without good reason.

(2) The defences of absolute or qualified privilege are not available for reporting a spent conviction which is mentioned in court proceedings but is then ruled inadmissible by the court.

Example: A man sues a newspaper for defamation after it publishes an accurate reference to his previous criminal conviction. The defences available are:

- *Justification*– because there was a conviction. Defamation law accepts that the conviction is proof that the person committed that crime. So a media organisation, once it proves the conviction – for example, from a court record – is not required to re-prove that the person suing committed the offence.

- *Qualified privilege* – protects non-contemporaneous reports of court cases if the defence's requirements are met. Mention of a conviction is, in effect, a report of the court case in which the conviction occurred when the defendant pleaded guilty or when magistrates or a jury announced the guilty verdict. The defence also protects quotations from the case, such as the judge calling the convicted defendant 'a scoundrel'.

see ch. 19,
p. 239, on
inferences

- *Honest opinion* – protects opinion expressed about the person based on the fact of the conviction, if the defence's requirements are met. If a council election candidate has a criminal conviction, an editorial comment column could safely publish the author's honestly held opinion that the conviction made the person unfit for public office. Similar comments from others could also be safely published, if they are their honestly held opinions. Even if no such comment is made explicitly, a media organisation publishing the conviction in this context creates an inference that it means the person could be regarded as unfit for public office. The honest opinion defence should protect the media organisation over that inference.

Even if the conviction referred to is 'spent', the above defences apply, unless the publication was malicious – for example, there was no public interest in referring to it.

But a claimant would win if it was proved at a defamation trial that there was malice. There would be malice if a journalist or editor published a reference to a spent conviction merely to further some interest of his/her own or in spite. In such a case the Act means the justification defence cannot be used, although the conviction is a fact. Proof of malice also destroys the qualified privilege defence. The honest opinion defence would also be undermined, as the published comment must be based on a matter of public interest – and a provably malicious reference to the conviction would be much harder to justify as being for the public good. A comment must also be based on a privileged statement or a fact defensible by justification.

! Remember

In most news stories the media can refer to and comment on spent convictions – disclosing a council candidate's previous conviction or the criminal record of a dodgy businessperson – with no fear of libel consequences because the disclosures are in the public interest and no malice is involved.

▌ Spent convictions revealed in court proceedings

A person giving evidence in any civil proceedings should not, generally, be asked questions about spent convictions.

The Act does not apply to later criminal proceedings. Rehabilitated people who appear before criminal courts again, after their convictions have become spent, can still be asked about them.

Absolute or qualified privilege applies to media reports of a spent conviction mentioned in a court case unless the court ruled that the conviction was inadmissible.

Judges have been directed that spent convictions should never be referred to in criminal courts unless this is unavoidable, and that no one should refer in open court to a spent conviction without the judge's authority.

▌ Criminal penalties

There is no criminal penalty for journalists who mention a spent conviction. But it may well be an offence for a public servant to disclose details of spent convictions other than in the course of official duties.

ch. 28 explains data protection

It is a criminal offence to get information of spent convictions from official records by fraud, dishonesty or bribery.

➡ Recap of major points

- Convictions become spent at the end of the rehabilitation period.

- A conviction which led to a jail term of more than two-and-a-half years is never spent.

- The rehabilitation period varies between 10 years (in respect of a jail sentence exceeding six months) and six months (after an absolute discharge), though some offences are spent immediately.

- The Act restricts the libel defences available to journalists who refer with malice to spent convictions.

((•)) Useful Websites

www.nacro.org.uk/what-we-do/resettlement-advice-service/advice/legislation/rehabilitation-of-offenders-act-1974,1646,NAP.html#2
   Nacro, Rehabilitation of Offenders Act 1974, rehabilitation periods chart

www.justice.gov.uk/downloads/offenders/rehabilitation/rehabilitation-offenders.pdf
   Ministry of Justice guidance to the Act – includes a chart on rehabilitation periods

24

Slander, malicious falsehood and obscenity

Chapter summary

Defamation in its spoken form is slander – and can present journalists with problems. This chapter examines those problems, and looks at malicious falsehood, which occurs with the publication of a statement which is not defamatory but is false and can be shown to have caused financial loss. It also briefly examines obscenity.

▌ Slander

 The most obvious difference between the **torts** of libel and slander is, as ch. 20 explains, that libel is in permanent form (eg written words, a drawing or a photograph), while slander is spoken or in some other transient form.

But:

- defamatory statements broadcast on radio or television, or in a cable programme are treated as libel – Broadcasting Act 1990;
- as are defamatory statements in a public performance of a play – Theatres Act 1968.

ch. 20 explains what a libel claimant must prove

In slander, as with libel, the statement must be published to a third person, and must refer to the claimant.

Another difference between libel and slander is that while damage is presumed in a libel action, a claimant in a slander action must prove the damage suffered, except in the case of:

- an imputation that an individual has committed a crime punishable by death or imprisonment; or
- any statement calculated to disparage an individual in his office, profession, calling, trade or business.

Journalists are less likely to become involved personally in a slander action than a libel action, but must be aware of the dangers.

Suppose X says that Y, a borough council member, used his position to secure building contracts – actionable because it disparages Y in his office of councillor. A reporter checking the story will have to interview people to reach the truth, and must be wary of being sued for slander over the questions asked during interviews in which the original slander might be repeated to a third party. There is also a risk that a message left on an answering machine could spark an action for slander if it is heard or re-played by someone other than the claimant. There is also a risk if broadcasters shout allegations, in public, at people who have refused to be interviewed about them – the broadcast itself could spark a libel action, while the fact that the question was shouted might tempt the subject into trying to sue for slander as well.

▶ Malicious falsehoods

Publication of a false statement may still cause a person financial damage even though it does not cast aspersions on his/her character or fitness to hold a certain office or to follow a particular calling. For example, a false statement that a solicitor had retired from practice would doubtless cause loss as the lawyer's clients would seek other solicitors to do their work. But it is clearly not defamatory to be considered retired.

The wronged person cannot sue for libel or slander if a published statement is not defamatory – but might be able to bring an action for malicious falsehood.

The claimant must prove the statement is untrue – in contrast with libel, where the court assumes that a defamatory statement is false.

The claimant in a malicious falsehood action must also prove that the statement was published maliciously.

As with the defence of qualified privilege in libel, malice means a statement made by someone who knows it is false, or is reckless as to its truth. But a defendant who believes a statement is true but publishes it with the aim of injuring the claimant will also be viewed as motivated by malice (*Spring v Guardian Assurance plc* [1993] 2 All ER 273, CA). Negligence – that is, wrongly believing a statement is true, and so failing to check it, when there was no aim to injure – is not malice.

The claimant in a malicious falsehood case does not have to prove that he/she has suffered actual damage if the words are in permanent form, such as printed words, and calculated – likely – to cause financial damage, or they are spoken or written and likely to cause him/her financial damage in his office, profession, calling, trade or business.

But once a claimant has proved financial damage, he/she can also claim damages for emotional distress, hurt feelings and so on – and they could well be substantial because the defendant will be shown to have acted maliciously.

👁 **Case study**

Former Conservative Party co-treasurer Peter Cruddas was awarded £180,000 in damages in his High Court libel and malicious falsehood action over a *Sunday Times* allegation about charging £250,000 to meet David Cameron. The 59-year-old businessman sued Times Newspapers Ltd and two members of the newspaper's Insight team over three articles which appeared in March 2012, claiming that they meant that, in return for cash donations to the Conservative party, he corruptly offered for sale the opportunity to influence government policy and gain unfair advantage through secret meetings with the Prime Minister and other senior Ministers. He also said the articles meant he made the offer even though he knew the money offered for meetings was to come, in breach of the ban under UK electoral law, from Middle Eastern investors in a Liechtenstein fund and that he was happy that the foreign donors should use deceptive devices to conceal the true source of the donation.

Finding that Mr Cruddas was defamed, and that the newspaper was also guilty of malicious falsehood, Mr Justice Tugendhat, said the journalists responsible for the story had the 'dominant intention to injure Mr Cruddas'.

But Mr Cruddas received no damages on the malicious falsehood claim, the judge saying that while the defendants had acted maliciously, and that the articles were likely to cause him pecuniary damage in respect of his profession and business, there was no point in considering damages now, as they would not increase the total awarded for the libel because he could not recover twice for the same damage. But he would consider the issue at a later date, if necessary. The *Sunday Times* is seeking to appeal.

Limitation period

The limitation period for bringing a malicious falsehood action is one year, the same as for a defamation action – Defamation Act 1996.

Corrections

An editor may realise that the facts of a story are wrong, but they were not defamatory and it was an honest mistake. In such a case, he/she should act quickly to publish an adequate correction to avoid being accused of malice should there be a legal action.

Slander of goods and title

Two types of malicious falsehood are known as slander of goods (false and malicious statements disparaging the claimant's goods), and slander of title (false and malicious denial of the claimant's title to property).

The word slander is misleading in both cases. The damaging statement can be in permanent form or spoken.

▌ Obscenity

It is an offence to publish obscene material – the test is whether the words or material published would tend to deprave and corrupt those likely to read them.

The Obscene Publications Act 1959 introduced a defence that the publication was 'for the public good…in the interests of science, literature, art, or learning, or of other objects of public concern'. The Obscene Publications Act 1964 made it an offence to possess an obscene article for publication for gain.

➡ Recap of major points

- Slander, a civil wrong (like libel), concerns defamatory words which (unlike libel) are spoken or in some other transient form.

- In slander (unlike libel), actual damage may need to be proved.

- Malicious falsehoods are false statements that, though not defamatory, may still be damaging. The claimant must prove that the statement is untrue and was published maliciously.

Part 4

Confidentiality, privacy and copyright

Breach of confidence

Chapter summary

The law of breach of confidence is based upon the principle that a person who has been given information in confidence should not take unfair advantage of it. This chapter explains the kind of information and relationships considered confidential. If a media organisation publishes this type of information, it needs a legal defence to avoid having to pay damages. Governments, businesses and individuals use this law to protect information they regard as officially or commercially secret, or private.

   The main means of preventing a breach of confidence is an injunction banning publication of confidential information. This area of law is also the foundation of the law of privacy, which is the focus of the next chapter.

▶ Development of the law

The law on breach of confidence is at its most straightforward in protecting commercial secrets. An employee has a duty to protect commercially-sensitive information he/she creates or gains in the course of employment – for example, data on market research or development of new products. That duty arises from the employment relationship. If an employee disloyally passes that information to the employer's commercial rival, that is a breach of confidence. In most instances the betrayed employer could, apart from sacking the employee, successfully sue him/her and the rival in the civil courts for damages to compensate for any financial loss suffered, because breach of confidence is a **tort**, a civil wrong. The duty to → glossary preserve confidentiality can automatically pass to anyone else who receives the material and realises its confidential nature. So, a media organisation to which a business's commercial secrets are leaked could also be successfully sued if it publishes these, unless it has a defence.

The law of breach of confidence can also protect material which is personally private. Queen Victoria's husband Prince Albert used the law in 1848 to prevent commercial publication of private family etchings which depicted their children and pets. Copies had been purloined from the printers to which they had been sent by the Royal household to be printed merely as a personal collection (*Prince Albert v Strange* (1848) 1 Mac. & G. 25).

But the wide scope the law now has to protect personal privacy, and the use of breach of confidence law by successive governments to protect official secrets, are comparatively recent developments.

◗ Development of privacy law

Until 2000, UK law recognised no general right to privacy. But people who believed their privacy was about to be infringed could try to use the law of breach of confidence to prevent intrusions. Their main difficulty lay in the different nature of the two kinds of right. An obligation of confidence, by definition, arises, first, from the circumstances in which the information is given – a relationship which gives rise to one party owing a duty of confidence to another.

pp. 305,
Breach of
confidence
and official
secrets,
explains
Spycatcher

In contrast, a right of privacy relating to information would arise from the nature of the information itself, based on the principle that certain kinds of information were private and for that reason alone should not be disclosed. Many cases involving invasions of privacy did not result from breaches of confidence.

The law evolved as judges began to abandon their strict view on the circumstances in which an obligation of confidence could occur. In the *Spycatcher* case in the House of Lords in 1988 Lord Goff of Chieveley said (*A-G v Times Newspapers* (1992) 1 AC 191):

> " A duty of confidence arises when confidential information comes to the knowledge of a person (the confidant) in circumstances where he has notice, or is ruled to have agreed, that the information is confidential, with the effect that it would be just in all the circumstances that he should be precluded from disclosing the information to others. "

Lord Goff said he had expressed the duty in wide terms to include the situation where 'an obviously confidential document was wafted by an electric fan out of a window into a crowded street, or when an obviously confidential document such as a diary was dropped in a public place and then picked up by a passer-by.'

In this scenario the passer-by has no relationship with the person whose information he/she has picked up – but, because it is obviously confidential, in law the passer-by should not, for example, give or sell it to a media organisation for publication, unless there is a legal defence.

In 2000 the Human Rights Act 1998 came into force, and incorporated into UK law the European Convention on Human Rights, which guarantees the right to respect for privacy and family life, as ch. 1 explains. In cases involving alleged breach of personal privacy, the courts started abandoning the legal contrivance of implying a confidential relationship where none existed, and so a separate type of tort – misuse of private information – developed. This is the focus of the next chapter, but the roots of that law are explained here.

In the *Douglas* case, which is explained later in this chapter, Lord Justice Sedley said in the Court of Appeal: 'The law no longer needs to construct an artificial relationship of confidentiality between intruder and victim: it can recognise privacy itself as a legal principle drawn from the fundamental value of personal autonomy.'

▶ Elements of a breach of confidence

There are three elements in a breach of confidence.

The information:

- must have 'the necessary quality of confidence';
- must have been imparted in circumstances imposing an obligation of confidence; and
- there must be an unauthorised use of that information to the detriment of the party communicating it (*Coco v AN Clark (Engineers) Ltd* [1969] RPC 41 at 47).

The phrase 'the party communicating it' means the person who originally communicates the information, that is, the person to whom the confidence is owed. A patient who tells a doctor about an ailment, or allows him/her to take blood tests or conduct a pregnancy test, is communicating information. The doctor and any other staff at the surgery or hospital owe the patient a duty of confidence in respect of that information.

But, again, it should be remembered that a court enforcing the law of confidentiality does not require a direct relationship between the person who wishes to protect the information and the person who wishes to disclose it. The law of equity – explained in ch. 1 – operates on the consciences of the parties, and so the legal criterion is whether a reasonable person would understand from the nature and circumstances of a disclosure that he/she was receiving information or material in confidence. Thus, a journalist who receives a leak of someone's medical records usually has a duty not to reveal it to others, just as the doctor has. The same principle applies to other types of information ruled to be confidential.

👁 Case study

In 2000 the actors Michael Douglas and Catherine Zeta-Jones and the publishers of *OK!* magazine sued in the High Court for breach of confidence. Their lawsuit was against the rival *Hello!* magazine because it published unauthorised photographs of the couple, taken at their wedding reception in a New York hotel. The couple had an exclusive, £1 million deal for *OK!* to have pictures taken by their own photographer and for only those images they approved of to be published. But *Hello!* obtained unauthorised pictures from a paparazzi photographer who had infiltrated the hotel. *Hello!* rushed its next edition into print to spoil the impact of the *OK!* 'exclusive' pictures. Mr Justice Lindsay, ruling that *Hello!'s* publication of the unauthorised pictures had infringed the couple's privacy, ordered it to pay them £14,600 damages and pay £1 million damages to *OK!* magazine. *Hello!* appealed against the £1 million award, but in 2007 it was upheld by the House of Lords (Michael *Douglas, Catherine Zeta-Jones, Northern and Shell PLC v Hello! Ltd, Hola SA, Eduardo Sanchez Junco (4), Marquesa de Varela, Neneta Overseas Ltd and Philip Ramey* [2007] UKHL 21).

In *Douglas* it was ruled that *Hello!* magazine, when it bought the unauthorised pictures, knew that the 'information' they contained – images of the couple – was regarded as private and confidential, and was also capable of commercial exploitation, and therefore *Hello!'s* conscience was touched – it was bound by the duty of confidentiality. It was noteworthy as regards the development of privacy law, and – for some in the media, controversial – that the decision in *Douglas* was that the couple's wedding was a private occasion, although there were 350 guests and the couple were exploiting it in the picture deal with *OK!*. The ruling was that the security measures the couple took against intruders, and their insistence on approving which images were published, made it private.

The quality of confidence

The law of breach of confidence safeguards ideas and information imparted or obtained in confidential circumstances. Generally, information is not confidential if it is trivial – for example, a company's canteen menu – or is already in the public domain.

Obligation of confidence

An obligation of confidence can arise in a variety of ways: These include:

Contractual relationship Employees may have signed agreements not to disclose an employer's secrets. This applies as much to a celebrity's chauffeur, who wants to sell to the media tales of what he saw and heard in his employment, as it does to scientists employed in commercial research. Even if the written contract does not make this clear, there is an implied term in every employment relationship that an employee will not do anything detrimental to an employer's interests.

see ch. 26, p. 318, The privacy of sexual relationships

Personal relationship In 1967 the Duchess of Argyll prevented the *People* newspaper, and her former husband, from publishing marital secrets (*Argyll v Argyll* [1967] Ch 302). By the 1980s the courts had extended the protection to prevent the publication of kiss-and-tell stories originating from less formal relationships. But these stories are now generally dealt with in privacy law.

Unethical behavior It now seems to be established by case law that journalists who obtain confidential information by unethical means such as trespass, theft, listening devices or long-range cameras are usually in breach of an obligation of confidence owed to the targets of this activity – an obligation created and breached by the tactics used. If not, the case will probably be covered in privacy law, as ch. 26 explains.

Detriment

The confiding party must suffer or be at risk of suffering a detriment of some sort to be able to claim a breach of confidence, such as financial loss from exposure of commercially-sensitive information. But it could also be of another kind. In the *Spycatcher* case in the House of Lords Lord Keith of Kinkel said it would be a sufficient detriment to an individual that information he/she gave in confidence was to be disclosed to people he/she would prefer not to know it. The detriment could be the adverse effect on someone's mental well-being or physical health, caused by unauthorised publication of their confidential, personal information – for example, if it causes people to ridicule or shun them.

▶ Breach of confidence and official secrets

In 1985 the UK government used the law of breach of confidence when attempting to stop publication of information acquired by Peter Wright during his former job as senior officer of its internal security service, MI5. He planned to make money by selling his memoirs – a book called *Spycatcher*. The UK's Attorney General, on behalf of the government, sought an injunction to stop the book's publication, arguing that former members of the security services had an absolute and life-long duty not to reveal any details of their employment.

In June 1986 the *Observer* and *Guardian* newspapers carried stories which included brief details of some allegations Wright, who had retired to Australia, planned to publish. An English court then gave the Attorney General interim injunctions preventing both newspapers from disclosing any information Wright had obtained as a member of MI5. In 1988, after many legal actions involving the government and newspapers, in the UK and abroad, the House of Lords ruled that the original articles in the *Observer* and *The Guardian* in 1986 were not published in breach of confidence; that the government was not entitled to a permanent injunction preventing the newspapers from making further comments on the book and using extracts from it; and that the government was not entitled to a general injunction restraining the media from future publication of information derived from Wright.

The *Spycatcher* case showed that the government was prepared to use the civil law of breach of confidence, rather than rely on prosecutions under (controversial) official secrets law. The case also established the principle that an injunction granted against one media organisation, to stop it publishing material, could cover all of them.

 See Useful Websites at the end of this chapter for a BBC report of the House of Lords judgment, and www.mcnaes.com ch. 33 on official secrets law.

▌ Injunctions

A person or an organisation who discovers that the media intend to publish confidential information without their consent can apply to the High Court for a temporary injunction to stop it.

On many occasions, temporary injunctions which appeared to be harsh and wide-ranging in their terms have been lifted when the media organisation's case was heard. This did not mean that the judge made a mistake, legally speaking, when imposing the temporary injunction. It is intended to 'hold the ring' until the case can be fully heard on whether a breach of confidence could occur. As a condition for obtaining an interim injunction the party which applies for it has to give an undertaking to pay damages to the other side if, at the trial, it is ruled that the order should not have been made.

But a media organisation, having been injuncted, may decide the cost of fighting the injunction or the case in a full trial is not worth it.

Disobeying an injunction can result in an action for contempt of court which could lead to an unlimited fine.

Section 12 of the Human Rights Act 1998 is intended to provide some protection against injunctions in matters involving freedom of expression.

Claimants applying to the High Court for injunctions should only obtain them if they persuade the judge that they are 'likely' to establish at the trial that publication should not be allowed.

Before the 1998 Act was implemented, the application might be without notice, which meant that only one party – the claimant – was represented, and a media organisation, as the defendant, would only learn of the proceedings when it was told that an injunction had been granted. That can and still does happen. Section 12 says that if the defendant is not present when the application is made, the court must not grant an injunction unless it is satisfied either that the claimant seeking the injunction has taken all practicable steps to notify the defendant, or there are compelling reasons for not giving notice.

But these cases are generally conducted at speed, and it may not be possible to tell a defendant. Injunctions have sometimes been granted when a newspaper has been printed and is ready to go on sale, or a programme was ready for broadcast, causing great inconvenience and expense.

The journalist's dilemma

The law of confidentiality regularly presents journalists with a dilemma. Suppose a reporter learns about some newsworthy misconduct from a source who received the information confidentially. The journalist should, as a matter of ethical conduct, and because of the law of libel, approach the person alleged to have misbehaved to get their side of the story and to check facts.

For example, the BBC Editorial Guidelines tells broadcasters:

> " When our output makes allegations of wrongdoing, iniquity or incompetence or lays out a strong and damaging critique of an individual or institution the presumption is that those criticised should be given a 'right of reply', that is, given a fair opportunity to respond to the allegations. "

((•)) See Useful Websites at the end of this chapter for this part of the BBC Editorial Guidelines.

But a journalist who does make such an approach faces the risk that, as explained in the next paragraph, the subject will immediately obtain an injunction banning use of the information, killing the story before it can be published.

! Remember

You should certainly check a story if it might be defamatory – but if possible, phrase your questions so that you do not reveal that you have confidential material, to avoid laying yourself open to the risk of an injunction.

Injunction against one is against all

In 1987 the Court of Appeal ruled that when an interim injunction is in force preventing a media organisation from publishing confidential information, other media organisations in England and Wales which know of it can be guilty of contempt of court if they publish that information, even if they are not named in the injunction.

In 1989 two papers were fined £50,000 each for publishing extracts from *Spycatcher* because at the time of publication they knew that interim injunctions were in force against the *Observer* and *The Guardian* preventing them from publishing this material. The fines were later discharged, but the convictions were upheld and the ruling on the law was confirmed by the House of Lords in 1991.

This legal device for silencing the media is all the more effective because the injunction is sometimes phrased in such a way that journalists are forbidden even to mention the existence of the proceedings – a so-called super-injunction.

An injunction issued by an English court does not prevent publication in another country. In particular, it does not prevent publication in Scotland – though Scottish judges may be asked to impose their own injunction, known as an **interdict**.

see the www. mcnaes. com chapter on Scotland

→ glossary

▶ Legal remedies for breach of confidence

People or organisations who say their confidential information has been unlawfully published can, as claimants in legal action:

- ask a judge to impose an injunction to stop it being published again by that publisher or by others;
- seek an order for the confidential material, such as documents or pictures, to be 'delivered up' – that is, given back to the claimant or destroyed;
- sue the publisher for damages, or 'an account of profits';
- ask a judge to order the publisher to reveal the source of the information, if this is not known, so that the source can be sued for damages and/or to stop disclosure of more confidential information.

Damages

These are likely to be higher in a case where the breach of confidence caused commercial loss – for example, the £1 million awarded to *OK!* magazine in the *Douglas* case – rather than loss of personal privacy.

👁 Case study

The supermodel Naomi Campbell was only awarded £2,500 damages for distress and injury to her feelings in 2002 against Mirror Group Newspapers when she sued for breach of confidence and infringement of the Data Protection Act 1998. The *Daily Mirror* had published detail about her receiving therapy from Narcotics Anonymous for drug addiction. She was awarded an additional £1,000 for 'aggravated damages' as a result of an additional article published by the paper. (*Campbell v Mirror Group Newspapers* [2004] UKHL 22).

However, in 2008 Max Mosley was awarded £60,000 against the *News of the World*, in an action alleging breach of confidence and unauthorised disclosure of personal information for its exposure of his participation in a sado-masochistic orgy with prostitutes.

 Ch. 26 has more detail of the *Campbell* and *Mosley* cases, and ch. 28 explains data protection law.

Account of profits

A person misusing confidential information to make money may be asked to account for the profits to the person or organisation whose confidence was betrayed. A court may rule, after seeing this account, that the person who misused the information should pay some or all of these ill-gotten profits to the party betrayed. But for a media organisation, the order is more likely to be for damages, because of the difficulty a judge would face deciding which story led to what profit.

Order to reveal source

A court can order a journalist to reveal the name of the informant who provided the confidential information. If the journalist promised the source anonymity, the ethical position is that he/she must keep that promise – which means facing the consequences of disobeying the court. The defiance could be deemed a contempt of court which could lead to a fine or, conceivably, the journalist being jailed, though he/she may have some protection from Article 10 of the European Convention on Human Rights and the 'shield law' in section 10 of the Contempt of Court Act 1981.

 see ch. 34, The journalist's sources and neutrality

👁 Case study

In 1989 an engineering company, Tetra Ltd, obtained injunctions against *The Engineer* magazine and its trainee reporter Bill Goodwin. The company, which was in financial difficulties, had prepared a business plan for the purpose of negotiating a substantial bank loan. A copy of the draft plan 'disappeared' from the company's offices and the next day an unidentified source telephoned Mr Goodwin and gave him information about the company, including the amount of the projected loan and the company's forecast results. Goodwin phoned the company and its bankers to check the information. The company obtained a **without notice** injunction restraining the magazine from publishing information derived from the draft plan and later obtained an order requiring Goodwin and *The Engineer* to hand over notes that would disclose the source of the information. Mr Goodwin refused to comply and was fined £5,000. In 1996 the European Court of Human Rights ruled that the court order and the fine violated his right to freedom of expression under Article 10. Goodwin was supported by the National Union of Journalists (*Goodwin v United Kingdom* (1996) 22 EHRR 123).

→ glossary

▌ Defences

A media organisation sued for an alleged breach of confidence in what it has published may have a defence. Defences include:

- the information did not have 'the necessary quality of confidence' because
  - of its nature – for example, it was trivial and/or unlikely to cause much detriment;
  - or it was already in the public domain;
- it was in the public interest to publish the information – for example, to expose wrongdoing, negligence or hypocrisy.

The same arguments can be used against an application for an injunction.

Information already in the public domain

If a media organisation publishes commercially sensitive information leaked from a business, or information leaked from a public institution, a court is unlikely to grant an injunction or award damages for breach of confidence if the material was already widely in the public domain – for example, already published by other media outlets or by members of the public on internet sites and other social media.

Judges, as some have said, do not wish to make pointless orders like King Canute ordering the tide to recede.

But the scope for the public domain defence may be more limited if personal privacy has been infringed – for example, a judge might rule that embarrassing private footage improperly copied by a maid from a celebrity's computer should not – to spare the celebrity any further distress – be published by the mainstream media, even if thousands of copies are already visible on the internet.

Case study

In a 1982 case involving the *Watford Observer*, the Court of Appeal lifted an injunction which had stopped the newspaper covering developments at publisher Robert Maxwell's printing operation, Sun Printers. The paper wanted to report that the company was considering making 180 workers redundant. It had been given a copy of a report, commissioned by the company, which suggested these job cuts were needed. The court said this report could not be regarded as confidential because the company had circulated 120 copies to management and trade union officials so they could discuss it. So whoever handed a copy to the *Watford Observer* had not breached any confidence. One judge, Lord Denning, said that publishing the information would also be in the public interest, because many people in the Watford area could be affected by the job losses (*Sun Printers v Westminster Press Ltd* [1982] IRLR 292).

Publication in the public interest

Section 12 of the Human Rights Act 1998 says a court considering imposing an injunction in a matter affecting freedom of expression, where **journalistic material** is involved, must have particular regard to the extent to which it is, or would be, in the public interest for the material to be published.

→ glossary

But even before the Act was implemented, journalists have successfully argued that disclosing confidential information would be in the public interest.

👁 Case study

The Court of Appeal ruled in 1984 that it was in the public interest for the *Daily Express* to publish information from an internal memo, leaked from a company making breathalyser equipment, which cast doubt on its accuracy at a time when police were using it to clampdown on drink-driving (*Lion Laboratories v Evans* [1985] QB 526).

But the public interest argument failed in the case of *McKennitt v Ash* [2006] EMLR 10) in which the Canadian folk singer sued a former friend who had written and published a book, *Travels with Loreena McKennitt: My Life as a Friend*, which revealed a lot of information about the singer's private life. Mr Justice Eady ruled in the High Court that several references in the book were intrusive and insensitive, and there was insufficient public interest in publishing them. The Court of Appeal upheld this decision, though it said that the judge's statement that 'a very high degree of misconduct must be demonstrated' if behaviour was to trigger the public interest defence might well have gone too far, if treated as an 'entirely general statement, divorced from its context', although on the facts of this case that high test was appropriate.

Correcting 'a false public image'

In 2005 celebrities David Beckham and Victoria Beckham failed to get an injunction against the *News of the World* concerning information about the state of their marriage. The paper argued that the Beckhams had portrayed a false image about their private life, and so it was in the public interest for it to publish information from their former nanny that she had witnessed blazing rows between the couple (*Media Lawyer*, 25 April 2005).

▶ Relevance of ethical codes

Section 12 of the Human Rights Act also says a court considering a matter affecting freedom of information must have particular regard to 'any relevant privacy code'. In cases involving the media, judges will consider, depending on the media sector involved, if the journalism has conformed to either the Editors' Code of Practice (or whatever code is adopted by Ipso or press organisations who do not sign up to the Ipso system) or the Ofcom Broadcasting Code.

 see ch. 27 on the codes and ch. 2 on Ipso

If the journalism does conform, judges may be more likely to rule that any breach of confidence or privacy was justified by the public interest. The wording of the parts of each code which relate to public interest justifications are, anyway, influenced by case law.

➡ Recap of major points

- The law says that a person who has obtained information in confidence must not take unfair advantage of it.

- The three elements of a breach of confidence are:

  (1) the information must have 'the necessary quality of confidence';

  (2) the information must have been imparted in circumstances imposing an obligation of confidence; and

  (3) there must be an unauthorised use of that information to the detriment of the party who first communicated it.

- The person who believes his/her confidence is to be breached can get an injunction preventing this.

- An injunction preventing one publication from publishing confidential information prevents all the media from publishing it, if they know about it.

- Disobeying an injunction can result in an action for contempt of court.

- If confidential matter is published, the person whose confidences have been breached may be able to claim damages.

((•)) Useful Websites

http://news.bbc.co.uk/onthisday/hi/dates/stories/october/13/newsid_2532000/2532583.stm
   BBC news archive story in the *Spycatcher* saga

www.bbc.co.uk/editorialguidelines/page/guidelines-fairness-right-of-reply/
   BBC Editorial Guidelines on fairness and right of reply

26

Privacy

Chapter summary

The law of privacy developed from the action for breach of confidence. It has been used by a large number of people to prevent publication of information about their lives and activities. In 2008 it attracted widespread publicity with the case of Max Mosley, who won £60,000 in damages when he sued the *News of the World* over a story about his involvement in a sado-masochistic orgy with five prostitutes. Increasing numbers of sportsmen and celebrities sought injunctions to stop the media reporting on their activities. This chapter explains the development of privacy law, and warns that journalists who electronically snoop on people or hack into their phone messages may well be committing a crime.

Development of the law

The Human Rights Act 1998 came into force on 2 October 2000, incorporating the European Convention on Human Rights, Article 8 of which guarantees the right to respect for privacy and family life, into UK law, giving it what it previously lacked – a specific law of privacy.

As the legislation went through Parliament journalists and media organisations expressed concerns about the potential effect of the right to privacy on their freedom to publish true information of public interest. Section 12 of the Act requires courts considering granting an **injunction** banning publication of information to have 'particular regard' to the importance of freedom of expression, guaranteed by Article 10 of the Convention. The protection afforded by this provision has proved minimal.

→glossary

In the *Douglas* case, outlined in ch. 25, Lord Justice Sedley rejected the view that section 12 gave greater weight to freedom of expression than to privacy, saying: 'Everything will ultimately depend on the proper balance between privacy and publicity in the situation facing the court.'

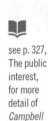

see p. 327, The public interest, for more detail of *Campbell*

In 2004, in the *Naomi Campbell* case, the House of Lords established that 'unjustified disclosure of private information' could be a cause of legal action. The Law Lords agreed that Ms Campbell was entitled to damages after the *Daily Mirror* reported that she was attending Narcotics Anonymous meetings. The paper was held to have infringed her privacy by giving details of the therapy and her reaction to it, and publishing surreptitiously taken photographs of her emerging from a session (*Campbell v Mirror Group Newspapers* [2004] UKHL 22).

In 2004 the European Court of Human Rights ruled that Princess Caroline of Monaco's privacy was breached by the publication of photographs of scenes from her daily life, shopping or on holiday with her family, in public places. An important consideration in its decision was that she had suffered years of being stalked and photographed by paparazzi and this had interfered with her human right, protected by Article 8, to enjoy social interaction with people (*von Hannover v Germany, Application no. 59320/00* of 24 June 2004, ECtHR).

In the House of Lords, in *In Re S (FC) (a child) (Appellant)* [2004] UKHL 47; [2005] 1 AC 593) Lord Steyn made it clear that neither Article 8, guaranteeing the right to respect for privacy and family life, nor the Article 10 right to freedom of expression 'has as such precedence over the other'.

This is also the view of the European Court of Human Rights – meaning that section 12 of the Human Rights Act has little effect on the courts in relation to whether they will issue an injunction, as the Act also requires, in section 3, that the courts must act in a manner compatible with the Convention, while section 2 requires them to 'take account' of the decisions of the European Court. Judges have argued that criticism of the way in which they have applied and developed the law of privacy is misguided and unreasonable, because Parliament must have known what it was doing when it passed the Act.

ch. 25 explains breach of confidence

At one point it seemed clear that, unless there was a strong public interest justification – the material in question had to contribute to a debate of general public importance – the courts would issue injunctions to prevent publication of the sort of kiss-and-tell stories which were once the standard fare of tabloid journalism. The court does not need to find that the information is published in breach of confidence – but if it is, the argument for issuing an injunction is all the stronger. However, in February 2012 the European Court eased the position somewhat, saying that media coverage of celebrities' private lives was 'acceptable if in the general interest and if in reasonable balance with the right to respect for private life' (*Axel Springer AG v Germany* Application no. 39954/08, and *Von Hannover v Germany No 2*, Applications no 40660/08 and 60641/08).

The factors a court will consider in deciding on injunctions include the degree to which the material makes a contribution to a debate of general interest – which does not just cover politics – how well known the person concerned is, the subject of the report itself, the prior conduct of the person concerned, the method of obtaining the information and its truth, the content, form and consequences of the publication, and the severity of any sanctions imposed on media organisations which published the material.

Remedies for breach of privacy

The remedies which courts will provide for a breach of privacy include damages and permanent injunctions to prevent material being published.

A person who considers his/her privacy to have been infringed can appeal to the European Court if he/she is dissatisfied by a decision in the UK courts.

In 2008, Max Mosley, then president of the Fédération Internationale de l'Automobile (FIA), which runs Formula 1 grand prix racing, sued the *News of the World* over stories, photos and video footage about his participation in sado-masochistic activities with prostitutes (*Mosley v News Group Newspapers Ltd* [2008] EWHC 1777). The case did not establish new principles of privacy but the level of damages awarded, at £60,000, was the highest yet, putting privacy on a par with other costly legal actions, such as libel.

see www. mcnaes. com for detail of *Mosley*

Injunctions and super- injunctions

The issue of injunctions and so-called super-injunctions – orders which include a clause prohibiting the media or anyone from even publicising the fact that they have been made – attracted considerable media coverage in April and May 2011, with detailed reporting on each new injunction which was issued and claims that freedom of expression was being irrevocably damaged. Footballers, actors and business people sought orders giving them anonymity and blocking publication of information about their private lives, while bloggers and Twitter users sought to undermine orders by naming those they claimed had obtained them. The uproar led Lord Neuberger, then the Master of the Rolls, to issue Practice Guidance tightening up the rules on non-publication injunctions and requiring that cases should normally proceed to trial once an interim order was made. The result was that the number of applications for privacy injunctions against the media dropped sharply, while two celebrities – broadcasters Andrew Marr and Jeremy Clarkson – withdrew injunctions they had obtained. The number of 'super-injunctions' against the media – orders which could not even be reported – dropped to zero.

The scope of Article 8

The right to privacy is guaranteed by Article 8 of the Convention on Human Rights, which says:

1. Everyone has the right to respect for his private and family life, his home and his correspondence.

2. There shall be no interference by a public authority with the exercise of this right except such as is in accordance with the law and is necessary in a democratic society
    – in the interests of national security, public safety or the economic well-being of the country,
    – for the prevention of disorder or crime,
    – for the protection of health or morals, or
    – for the protection of the rights and freedoms of others.

Article 8 gives protection for privacy against a 'public authority' and against the media or other intrusions, such as blogging.

▌ 'Reasonable expectation of privacy'

Although it sprang from the law of breach of confidence, privacy law has moved away from its roots and become established as a separate cause of action.

A claimant seeking an injunction to stop the media publishing information about his/her private life and activities must first demonstrate that he/she has a 'reasonable expectation of privacy' in relation to the information. Only after that will the court go to the second stage, balancing the right to privacy against the right to freedom of expression, and considering the proportionality of any interference with either right in a process called the parallel analysis, before conducting the 'ultimate balancing test' to reach a decision.

A court deciding if the expectation of privacy is reasonable may take into account the location of the event(s) – because the expectation may not be reasonable, for example, in respect of something done in a public place. But location may not be a key consideration. Someone who falls ill or suffers an accident in a public street has a reasonable expectation that this vulnerability gives them a right of privacy – for example, filming them in their distress would infringe it.

In Re S, see ch. 1, p. 7, Weighing competing rights

👁 Case study

In 2003 the European Court of Human Rights ruled that a British man's privacy was infringed when the media broadcast footage of his suicide attempt in the centre of Brentwood in 1994. The council released the footage to show that its installation of CCTV cameras helped save his life because police were alerted by the camera operators, and had taken a knife from him. But the man, who was mentally ill at the time, was recognisable in images broadcast, despite the council's request that he should not be (*Peck v the United Kingdom,* Application no. 44647/98). His complaints about this were upheld in 1996 by the broadcast regulators but he took a case to the European Court, because the UK courts did not in 1996 recognise what they now do – a specific right of privacy.

The courts also recognise that people have a reasonable expectation that what they say and do intimately within a personal relationship is private – whether the relationship is a marriage, co-habitation, love affair or friendship. If after the relationship ends, one person wants (often to earn money) the media to publish secrets from the relationship, the courts may injunct to protect the other person's Article 8 rights, or – if the information is already published – award damages for the infringement.

 Ch. 27 gives examples of how the Press Complaints Commission ruled on 'reasonable expectation'.

▸ Privacy versus freedom of expression

A major consideration for the courts in a privacy case is the question of whether the material which the media organisation seeks to publish contributes to a 'debate of general interest to society'. Decisions by the European Court indicate that it sees freedom of expression as being on various levels of value to society, with political expression about the conduct of politicians in public office, and including statements made at elections, having the highest value. The higher up the hierarchy, the greater the protection the courts should give freedom of expression, and vice versa, although each case will, as the European Court and UK courts consistently stress, depend on its specific facts. However, in the *Von Hannover No 2* cases the European Court court quoted Resolution 1165 (1998) of the Parliamentary Assembly of the Council of Europe on the right to privacy, including paragraph 7, which said:

> " Public figures are persons holding public office and/or using public resources and, more broadly speaking, all those who play a role in public life, whether in politics, the economy, the arts, the social sphere, sport or in any other domain. "

This greatly widened the definition of public figure from the approach taken in the first *Von Hannover* case.

◉ Case study

In February 2012 Mr Justice Tugendhat declined to continue an interim injunction obtained by the then Environment Secretary, Caroline Spelman, and her husband Mark which banned the *Daily Star Sunday* from publishing a story that their teenaged son, Jonathan, an international rugby player, had, after being injured, taken drugs to aid his recovery which, while legal, were banned under anti-doping rules. Keeping the order in place was neither proportionate nor necessary, said the judge, who also quoted Resolution 1165 of the Council of Europe which was cited by the European Court in the *Von Hannover No 2* case. In effect, he held that as Jonathan Spelman was an international rugby player he was a public figure (*Spelman v Express Newspapers* [2012] EWHC 355 (QB)).

▌ The privacy of sexual relationships

In the years immediately after the Human Rights Act came into force, courts took the view that not all sexual conduct was entitled to be viewed as confidential or, indeed, deserved legal protection. In 2002 the Court of Appeal lifted an injunction banning publication of details of the extra-marital affairs of a professional footballer, Blackburn Rovers' captain Garry Flitcroft (*A v B (A Company)* [2002] EWCA Civ 337). It said there was a significant difference between the confidentiality that attached to what was intended to be a permanent relationship and that which attached to the category of relationships with which Flitcroft was involved in this case.

Since then, however, as the *Mosley* case demonstrates, the courts have been more willing to rule that adulterous or casual sexual affairs are matters in which one or both of the people involved have a reasonable expectation of privacy, and will issue gagging orders – injunctions – unless the defendant (the party from the relationship who wishes to reveal the intimate matters) or the media can persuade the judge that there is a strong public interest in publishing the information.

In 2011 one footballer was known to have obtained two privacy injunctions banning the media from reporting on his sexual liaisons with two different prostitutes, with the court agreeing that the material was not in the public interest and that the player had a reasonable expectation that the information would remain private.

But former England football captain John Terry obtained and then lost an interim injunction which had banned the media from reporting on his relationship with a former team-mate's ex- partner after Mr Justice Tugendhat concluded that the aim of the order was to protect Terry's reputation, and sponsorship and commercial deals relying on it, rather than his privacy. This, the judge said, meant that the order was in reality a way of circumventing the rule in libel law from *Bonnard v Perryman* that a prior restraint injunction would not be granted to stop publication of an alleged libel if the defendant intended to plead that what was published was true (*LNS v Persons Unknown* [2010] EWHC 119 (QB)).

👁 Case study

In September 2012 former England soccer manager Steve McClaren lost a bid to stop *The Sun on Sunday* publishing a story about a sexual relationship he had with a woman when a judge held that he was a public figure from whom it was reasonable for the public to expect a higher standard of conduct. McClaren, who is married with three children, and was then manager of Dutch team FC Twente, applied to the High Court for an interim injunction to stop News Group Newspapers, publisher of *The Sun* and *The Sun on Sunday*, from publishing a story about a brief relationship he had with a woman referred to as SA. Mr Justice Lindblom rejected the application. Richard Spearman QC, for News Group Newspapers, had told the judge that in April 2006 McClaren had sold *The Sun* his account of a previous affair, and had chosen to talk publicly about his family in May 2010 and again in November 2012. Mr Justice Lindblom said he had applied the two-stage test a court was required to conduct, considering first whether, on the facts, McClaren's right to respect for privacy and family life under Article 8 of the European Convention on Human Rights were engaged, so that there was a reasonable expectation of privacy; and, secondly, deciding where the balance lay between his rights under Article 8 and those of the defendant under Article 10, guaranteeing the right to freedom of expression. While in principle McClaren had a reasonable expectation of privacy, in the circumstances of this case the balance 'clearly fell in favour of publication', the judge said. He added: 'As a former manager of England's football team, the claimant is in my view undoubtedly a public figure within the definition recognised by Mr Justice Tugendhat in *Spelman*.' Even allowing for the degree of difference between the position of a former manager and that of a serving captain of England's football team, McClaren was 'clearly still a prominent public figure who has held positions of responsibility in the national game' (*McClaren v News Group Newspapers Ltd* [2012] EWHC 2466 (QB)).

▌ The permanent injunction

An interim injunction is held, under the *Spycatcher* principle to bind all those on whom it is served or who are aware of it. But such an order, when made final, only binds those against whom it was obtained – meaning anyone else could then publish the information covered. The response of the courts in these circumstances has been to issue so-called *contra mundum* orders – orders of general effect which bind anyone who knows about them.

ch. 25 explains *Spycatcher*

In 2000 Dame Elizabeth Butler-Sloss, the then President of the Family Division of the High Court, issued a ground-breaking injunction banning the media from revealing the new identities and whereabouts of Robert Thompson and Jon Venables, who murdered two-year-old James Bulger. The order was justified on the grounds that disclosure of the information would infringe their rights to privacy (Article 8 of the European Convention), Article 2 (right to life) and Article 3 (prohibition of torture) following threats to their lives.

see ch. 11, p. 125, Indefinite anonymity for convicted defendants, and www. mcnaes. com ch. 11 for details of these cases

This was followed by similar injunctions to prevent disclosure of information about other notorious offenders and, as this chapter shows, *contra mundum* injunctions were used on privacy grounds to prevent the media publishing material. In April 2011 Mr Justice Eady said the court's jurisdiction to grant an injunction *contra mundum* was available, wherever necessary and proportionate, for the protection of Convention rights whether of children or adults (*OPQ v BJM and CJM* [2011] EWHC 1059 (QB)).

The way in which the privacy or other rights of those linked to a claimant will also influence the outcome of an application for an injunction was illustrated in a decision by the Court of Appeal.

👁 Case study

The Court of Appeal said a judge was wrong to refuse to grant an interim injunction to stop a newspaper publishing information about a married man in the entertainment industry who had had an affair with a woman with whom he was working. The man's wife found out about the relationship. The woman, who was also married, subsequently lost her job. The Court of Appeal held that a sexual relationship was essentially a private matter – the fact that the pair's work colleagues knew of it did not put the information into the public domain. But it said weight also had to be given not only to the man's right to respect for his privacy, but to the same rights in respect of his wife and children. Lord Justice Ward said of the children's position: 'They are bound to be harmed by immediate publicity, both because it would undermine the family as a whole and because the playground is a cruel place where the bullies feed on personal discomfort and embarrassment.' (*ETK v News Group Newspapers Ltd* [2011] EWCA Civ 439; *The Times*, 22 April 2011.)

The likelihood now is that anyone with a wife and children will seek to put their rights into the balance when applying for a privacy injunction banning publication of stories of extra-marital affairs or other questionable behaviour.

▶ Children

The media have to be careful over publicity about children, especially the children of celebrities and others in the public eye. Using paparazzi pictures taken of youngsters in the street could cause problems.

The Court of Appeal upheld the appeal by *Harry Potter* author J K Rowling and her husband against a judge's decision to strike out their claim against a photographic agency which photographed them with their son, who was in a pushchair, in a street in Edinburgh. The Court of Appeal said it was arguable that the child had a reasonable expectation of privacy. A child whose parents were not in the public eye could expect that the press would not use his photograph, and the same was true here – the photograph would not have been taken or published had he not been Ms Rowling's son. Even routine activities such as going to the shops might attract a reasonable expectation of privacy – it all depended on the circumstances. The law should protect children from intrusive media attention, the court added (*David Murray (By his litigation friends (1) Neil Murray (2) Joanne Murray) v Big Pictures (UK) Ltd* [2008] EWCA Civ 446; (2008) 3 WLR 1360).

▶ Information concerning health

Information concerning health is normally treated as of the highest confidentiality – people can usually have 'a reasonable expectation' that information about their health is private.

In 2002 the Court of Appeal banned the *Mail on Sunday* from naming a local health authority where a healthcare worker, referred to as H, had quit his job after being diagnosed HIV positive. The High Court had earlier said it could name the authority, but not the healthcare worker.

Health figured in the *Campbell* case, see p. 313, Development of the law

Lord Phillips, Master of the Rolls, said there was a public interest in preserving the confidentiality of healthcare workers who might otherwise be discouraged from reporting they were HIV positive. The *Mail on Sunday* believed H's patients were entitled to know they had been treated by someone who was HIV positive, but naming the authority would inevitably lead to the disclosure of H's identity, as only his patients would be offered HIV tests and counselling, he said. The paper could say the healthcare worker was a dentist.

But there are exceptions to the general rule. In 2006 murderer Michael Stone failed to ban the press and public from seeing an independent inquiry report into the treatment he had received from mental health, probation and social workers before he killed. A judge ruled that the report would assist public debate about treatment of the mentally ill and of those with disturbed personalities (*Michael Stone v South East SH* [2006] EWHC 1668).

▌ Can information be private if it is in the public domain?

In 2005 a judge granted an injunction restraining a newspaper from publishing the addresses of buildings acquired for housing vulnerable adolescents, although they would be known to neighbours and others living nearby and might also be available from the Land Registry (*Green Corns Ltd v Claverley Group Ltd* [2005] EMLR 31). Mr Justice Tugendhat said:

> There will be cases where personal information about a person (usually a celebrity) has been so widely published that a restraint upon repetition will serve no purpose, and an injunction will be refused on that account. It may be less likely that that will be so when the subject is not a celebrity. But in any event, it is not possible in a case about personal information simply to apply [the] test of whether the information is generally accessible, and to conclude that, if it is, then that is the end of the matter...
>
> I conclude that the information as to the addresses which is sought to be restrained is not in the public domain to the extent, or in the sense, that republication could have no significant effect, or that the information is not eligible for protection at all.

What is the position with 'widely published' photographs? The Court of Appeal in the *Douglas* case (paragraph 105) said:

> Once intimate personal information about a celebrity's private life has been widely published it may serve no useful purpose to prohibit further publication.

The same will not necessarily be true of photographs. Insofar as a photograph does more than convey information and intrudes on privacy by enabling the viewer to focus on intimate personal detail, there will be a fresh intrusion of privacy when each additional viewer sees the photograph and even when one who has seen a previous publication of the photograph is confronted by a fresh publication of it. **"**

▶ Information obtained covertly

What if the information is obtained, for example, by bugging or long-lens photography?

In 2006 the Court of Appeal referred to cases where 'confidence' arose from information having been acquired by 'unlawful or surreptitious means'. The court regarded the taking of long-distance photographs as being 'an exercise generally considered to raise privacy issues' (*Niema Ash and another v Loreena McKennitt and others* [2006] EWCA Civ 1714; [2007] 3 WLR 194).

for
Douglas,
see ch.
25, p. 303,
Elements
of a
breach of
confidence

In the *Douglas* case the wedding pictures were taken by an uninvited freelance photographer. Photographs of Naomi Campbell leaving a Narcotics Anonymous therapy session were also taken surreptitiously. In a 2006 case involving the Prince of Wales's 'Hong Kong Journal', the information was leaked by a 'disaffected secretary' (*HRH the Prince of Wales v Associated Newspapers Ltd* [2006] EWHC 522).

In 2007 former Prime Minister, Tony Blair, and his wife, Cherie won damages – which they gave to charity – from Associated Newspapers over 'long-lens' pictures taken of them while they were on holiday at Sir Cliff Richard's villa in Barbados. The Blairs said while they accepted a certain level of scrutiny, here the photographers had overstepped the mark.

▶ The public interest

Even before the Human Rights Act, journalists could plead that the disclosure of confidential information would be in the public interest. But judges, once possibly prepared to accept that a claimant's celebrity could generate a public interest in private conduct that would otherwise be protected, are now much less likely to do so.

p. 313,
Development
of the law,
outlines
Campbell

In the *Naomi Campbell* case, publication of some information was held to be in the public interest, and some not. There were five distinct 'elements' of private information:

- the fact of Ms Campbell's drug addiction;
- the fact that she was receiving therapy for it;
- the fact that she was having therapy at Narcotics Anonymous (NA);

- details of the NA therapy and her reaction to it; and,

- surreptitiously obtained photographs of her emerging from an NA session.

Because the model had publicly denied using drugs previously, the first and second facts could be published in the public interest. But the rest could not, because of the intrusiveness of the disclosure and the likelihood that it would interfere with or disrupt her treatment. Three of the judges – the majority – held that Article 10 considerations could not justify publication of the information.

Two of the judges considered that the third, fourth and fifth categories added little of significance to the disclosure of the first and second and that journalists should be given greater latitude. The difference of opinion between the judges illustrates the difficult decisions journalists might face when considering such stories.

The Data Protection Act

The *Naomi Campbell* case alerted the media to the implications for the law of privacy of the Data Protection Act (DPA) 1998. She sued the *Daily Mirror* for both breach of confidence and infringement of the DPA.

data protection law is explained in ch. 28

▌ Electronic 'snooping', intercepting and hacking into communications

Journalists who use electronic equipment to spy on other people should know that they could be committing a crime as well as running the risk of being sued for infringing privacy.

 Ch. 35 explains the risks of being charged with hacking into computers, telephone message and email systems or otherwise 'intercepting' communications – activity intrusive into privacy.

▌ What media codes say

The Editors' Code of Practice, used by the Press Complaints Commission, and which – as ch. 2 explains - will be the starting point for the Ipso code, has clauses which require newspapers, magazines and free-standing editorial websites to protect people's privacy.

The general protection of privacy provided by these clauses is explained in the next chapter, which also explains rules and 'practices' in the Ofcom Broadcasting Code concerning privacy. That code governs standards for the broadcast media.

codes are relevant in privacy lawsuits, see ch. 25, p. 311, Relevance of ethical codes

Chs. 2 and 3 explain the parts of these codes which deal with undercover work by journalists, which has potential to breach privacy, and with journalists recording the phone calls they make.

➡ Recap of major points

- The right to privacy is guaranteed by Article 8 of the Convention on Human Rights.
- The law of privacy developed from the action for breach of confidence.
- The test in a privacy claim is whether the claimant has 'a reasonable expectation of privacy'.
- The right to privacy is not necessarily lost because the activity happened in public.
- There is a defence that publication was in the public interest.
- Other remedies for breach of privacy include the Data Protection Act and, as ch. 35 explains, the Regulation of Investigatory Powers Act 2000.

((•)) Useful Websites

www.judiciary.gov.uk/Resources/JCO/Documents/Guidance/practice-guidance-civil-non-disclosure-orders-july2011.pdf
  The Master of the Rolls' Practice Guidance on privacy injunctions

News-gathering avoiding intrusion

Chapter summary

Journalists should avoid unnecessary intrusion into people's privacy, but know when it can be justified. They should combine knowledge of the legal basics with a good grasp of the codes used by media regulators. Ofcom adjudications are based on its Broadcasting Code, and those of the Press Complaints Commission were based on the Editors' Code of Practice. These adjudications provide guidance covering a far wider range of situations than is dealt with in privacy case law. Few people can afford to go to court if they feel their privacy is breached, but many complain to regulators about journalists taking photos, filming and audio-recording, and about what is published. Publishing 'user-generated' photographs or footage supplied by the public or material from social media sites can create ethical or legal problems. This chapter also explains that the codes seek to minimise intrusion into grief, and have particular rules for when children are interviewed, filmed or photographed by journalists.

▌ Civil law on privacy – photography, filming and recording

Landmark cases in privacy law have concerned publication of intrusive photographs and footage, as chs. 25 and 26 show. In these cases, judges weigh the individual's right to privacy under Article 8 of the European Convention on Human Rights against the media's Article 10 rights to freedom of expression and to impart information, and the public's right to receive it. This checklist, compiled from court judgments, is a rough guide to when civil law may be breached if people are photographed or filmed or audio-recorded without their consent (for convenience, references to filming include videoing).

ch. 1
explains the
Convention

- Was the person filmed or photographed or recorded in a location where he/she had 'a reasonable expectation of privacy'? An individual could reasonably expect privacy at home, in a secluded garden or on a private beach, but would normally have less or no expectation of it in a public place.

- Has the person been persistently harassed by the media? If so, the court might decide that his/her privacy was violated even though he/she was pictured or filmed or recorded in a public place – see the *Princess Caroline* case in ch. 26, pp. 313–315, Development of the law.

- Was the person in a condition, situation or event giving rise to a reasonable expectation of privacy, even though he/she was in or could be seen from a public place? For example, was the person mentally ill, or having medical treatment or therapy? – see the *Campbell* and *Peck* cases in ch. 26.

- Is there a 'public interest' factor in revelations in the journalism which over-rides the person's right to privacy, whatever the location or situation?

- Is the photo or footage or recording already so widely published – for example, copied worldwide on hundreds of internet sites – that banning publication is pointless?

Courts also consider the degree of harm which publication might cause, or has caused, the person, and might also consider the detail or extent of images captured – was the photograph a long shot or close-up of a face, or was the film a brief clip or lengthy footage? Covert photography, filming or recording with hidden cameras or microphones is likely to be more intrusive as the target is unaware of it and may assume the situation is private and act accordingly.

! Remember

Journalists also need to know the law on trespass, dealt with in ch. 36, p. 425, Trespass and bye-laws.

▶ Law against harassment

see also ch. 36 on the right to take photos, film and record

There is no criminal law banning photography or filming or recording in the street or other public places. But paparazzi who hound celebrities could be prosecuted under the Protection From Harassment Act 1997, which created criminal offences and civil remedies to deal with 'stalkers' – for example, men who obsessively harass ex-partners – but has also been used against paparazzi.

👁 Case study

In 2008 actress Sienna Miller accepted a settlement of £53,000 in a claim for harassment and breach of privacy against Big Pictures UK Ltd. The agency agreed that its photographers would not pursue her, and not take pictures of her leaving buildings where she had an expectation of privacy, which did not – she agreed – include restaurants, nightclubs or when she attended a red carpet event (*Media Lawyer*, 21 November 2008).

The 1997 Act says harassment can include causing alarm or distress, and is 'a course of conduct' – that is, the conduct must have occurred more than once. It was amended in 2012 to create specific 'stalking' offences. Following, watching or spying on someone could be stalking if they cause alarm or distress.

As this chapter explains, harassment would also normally breach the codes of the media regulators.

 see http://mcnaes.com ch. 27 for recent cases involving 1997 Act.

▶ The Editors' Code of Practice and Ofcom Broadcasting Code

The Editors' Code of Practice was used by the Press Complaints Commission (PCC), and is the code Ipso will use, at least initially. Ch. 2 explains that Ipso has for much of the newspaper and magazine sectors, and for their websites, replaced the PCC, and ch. 3 explains Ofcom's regulation of broadcasters. The Editors' Code and the Ofcom Broadcasting Code give guidance on when photography, filming or recording is unethical. These codes have clauses or sections on covert photography, filming or recording, explained in those chapters. This chapter mainly deals with journalists openly using cameras or microphones, though it is possible even then that people – for example, in crowds or in the chaos after an accident – might be unaware that their images or voices are being captured.

> See Appendix 2 for the full text of the Editors' Code. See Useful Websites, at the end of this chapter, for the full text of the Ofcom code.

The codes' general protection of privacy

Breaching the codes is not necessarily to breach privacy law, but complying with the codes is ethical and helps reduce the likelihood of a privacy lawsuit.

The Editors' Code clause 3 (Privacy) states:

i) Everyone is entitled to respect for his or her private and family life, home, health and correspondence, including digital communications.

ii) Editors will be expected to justify intrusions into any individual's private life without consent. Account will be taken of the complainant's own public disclosures of information.

iii) It is unacceptable to photograph individuals in private places without their consent.

Note – Private places are public or private property where there is a reasonable expectation of privacy.

The PCC made it clear that people have a reasonable expectation of privacy in a cafe even if other members of the public are present.

References to photography in the Editors' Code include filming. Neither Ipso nor Ofcom will normally adjudicate against the use of innocuous images of people in public places or in crowds. Ofcom has said that as a general rule there is no obligation to get consent to film or show images of people shown incidentally as clearly random members of the public. But Ipso and Ofcom will take account of situational factors as well as location, as do courts.

◉ Case study

In 2008 the PCC criticised a newspaper's publication of an online image of a road accident victim, part of whose face was shown, receiving emergency medical treatment at the scene. It said: 'There is a clear need for newspapers to exercise caution when publishing images that relate to a person's health and medical treatment, even if they are taken in public places.' The public interest in reporting the accident, which was not a rare or large-scale event, was not sufficient to override clause 3 (Privacy) and justify use of the image. A photo published in the paper, showing the woman at the crash scene but with her face entirely obscured, was 'just on the right side of the line' (*Kirkland v Wiltshire Gazette & Herald*, adjudication issued 23 April 2008).

The Ofcom code tends to use the phrase 'legitimate expectation of privacy' rather than 'reasonable expectation of privacy'. But most principles in its rules for broadcasters are similar to those in the Editors' Code for newspapers and magazines. Use in the Ofcom code of the term 'warranted' refers to public interest exceptions, explained later in this chapter.

Section 8 of the Ofcom code says, in rule 8.1: 'Any infringement of privacy in programmes, or in connection with obtaining material included in programmes, must be warranted'. It adds: 'Legitimate expectations of privacy will vary according to the place, and nature of the information, activity or condition in question, the extent to which it is in the public domain (if at all) and whether the individual concerned is already in the public eye. There may be circumstances where people can reasonably expect privacy even in a public place. Some activities and conditions may be of such a private nature that filming or recording, even in a public place, could involve an infringement of privacy.'

◉ Case study

In 2013 Ofcom ruled that the privacy of a woman it referred to as Ms D had been unwarrantably infringed by the inclusion of 10 seconds of footage of her with her face visible, including shots of her dancing, in an episode of Channel 4's programme *The Hotel*. It showed a 'ladies night' attended by 300 women, which featured male strippers. Ms D made clear she did not want to appear in the programme. But the footage was included because of 'human error'. Ofcom said there were elements of 'personal sensitivity' in attendance at such an event (*Ofcom Broadcast Bulletin*, Issue 236, 27 August 2013).

Ofcom guidance is that property that is privately owned but readily accessible to the public, such as a railway station or shop, can be a public place.

The Ofcom code adds in practice 8.4: 'Broadcasters should ensure that words, images or actions filmed or recorded in, or broadcast from, a public place, are not so private that prior consent is required before broadcast from the individual or organisation concerned, unless broadcasting without their consent is warranted.'

 See www.mcnaes.com for Ofcom's ruling that a programme about binge drinking did not infringe the privacy of a man shown intoxicated in a public street.

Ofcom's guidance to section 8 gives, as examples of when people can reasonably expect a *degree* of privacy even in a public place, someone with a disfiguring medical condition or CCTV footage of a suicide attempt.

 See also ch. 26, p. 316, 'Reasonable expectation of privacy', on the *Peck* case.

Practice 8.16 of the Ofcom code says: 'Broadcasters should not take or broadcast footage or audio of people caught up in emergencies, victims of accidents or those suffering a personal tragedy, even in a public place, where that results in an infringement of privacy, unless it is warranted or the people concerned have given consent.'

! Remember

Both Ipso and Ofcom will make some exception to their normal rules in respect of coverage of major incidents, such as a terrorist bombing. See p. 334 and case studies in www.mcnaes.com ch. 27.

! Remember

Practice 8.2 of the Ofcom code says that information which discloses the location of a person's home or family should not be revealed without permission, unless this is warranted.

Doorstepping

In section 8 of the Ofcom code the term 'doorstepping' means 'the filming or recording of an interview or attempted interview with someone, or announcing that a call is being filmed or recorded for broadcast purposes, without any prior warning'.

Doorstepping, then, is an ambush technique which can be used against someone unlikely to agree to an interview – for example, a crook being investigated, or a politician in a scandal – when they open the door at their home or workplace.

Practice 8.11 of the code says: 'Doorstepping for factual programmes should not take place unless a request for an interview has been refused or it has not been possible to request an interview, or there is good reason to believe that an investigation will be frustrated if the subject is approached openly, and it is warranted to doorstep.'

But the practice adds that broadcasters may normally, without prior warning, interview, film or record people in the news when they are in public places.

Also, it makes clear that vox-pops (sampling the views of random members of the public) are not considered 'doorstepping'.

The PCC made clear, in adjudications based on the Editors' Code, that a photograph taken from a public highway of someone on their threshold or in their garden does not breach the code, even if public interest considerations do not apply, if there is no 'reasonable expectation of privacy' and the picture does not show anything private (for example, *A woman v Scottish Sun*, issued 7 April 2010).

Hospitals and institutions

Clause 8 of the Editors' Code says journalists must identify themselves and obtain permission from a responsible executive before entering non-public areas of hospitals or similar institutions to pursue inquiries.

Ofcom code practice 8.8 says: 'When filming or recording in institutions, organisations or other agencies, permission should be obtained from the relevant authority or management, unless it is warranted to film or record without permission. Individual consent of employees or others whose appearance is incidental or where they are essentially anonymous members of the general public will not normally be required. However, in potentially sensitive places such as ambulances, hospitals, schools, prisons or police stations, separate consent should normally be obtained before filming or recording and for broadcast from those in sensitive situations (unless not obtaining consent is warranted). If the individual will not be identifiable in the programme then separate consent for broadcast will not be required.'

By 'separate consent', the code means there needs to be a two-stage consent – for example, consent must normally be obtained from the institution before filming/recording begins, and then further consent must be obtained from individuals for the broadcasting of footage or audio which identifies them. Broadcasters may need to ask the people filmed or recorded to sign consent forms so that, should there be a complaint, there is proof of consent.

The codes' protection against harassment

Under the Editors' and Ofcom codes, a journalist should normally respect a person's refusal to answer questions or their request to stop photographing, filming or recording them.

Clause 4 (Harassment) of the Editors' Code says:

see p. 334,
Public
interest
excep-
tions in
the codes

i) Journalists must not engage in intimidation, harassment or persistent pursuit.

ii) They must not persist in questioning, telephoning, pursuing or photographing individuals once asked to desist; nor remain on their property when asked to leave and must not follow them. If requested, they must identify themselves and whom they represent.

iii) Editors must ensure these principles are observed by those working for them and take care not to use non-compliant material from other sources.

The Ofcom code's practice 8.7 says: 'If an individual or organisation's privacy is being infringed, and they ask that the filming, recording or live broadcast be stopped, the broadcaster should do so, unless it is warranted to continue.'

👁 Case study

In 2007 the *Daily Mirror* apologised after Prince William's then girlfriend Kate Middleton – they married in 2011 – complained to the PCC. The paper had published a photo, taken by a freelance, of her walking down a street holding a cup of coffee. Her lawyers said it was taken in circumstances amounting to harassment (*Middleton v Daily Mirror*: Report 75).

Prohibitions on intrusion into grief and shock

Clause 5 (Intrusion into grief or shock) of the Editors' Code says (in part):

> In cases involving personal grief or shock, inquiries and approaches must be made with sympathy and discretion and publication handled sensitively. This should not restrict the right to report legal proceedings, such as inquests.

The PCC made clear in various adjudications that articles breaking news of violent or accidental deaths should not contain graphic detail likely to add to the distress of relatives as this breaches clause 5.

Broadcast journalists should be aware that images or descriptions of such material could, depending on the context, breach the Ofcom code's prohibitions on harm and offence explained in ch. 3.

The PCC said journalists should not break news of a death to the deceased's family or close friends, either personally or by what they publish. This would be a breach of clause 5 (adjudication in *Oliver v Manchester Evening News*, Report 43).

The PCC censured a newspaper for publishing online a photo showing, identifiably, an accident victim at a crash scene, when family members might not have been informed or would have been in a state of shock (the *Kirkland* case cited earlier).

Practice 8.18 of the Ofcom code says broadcasters should take care not to reveal the identity of a person who has died or of victims of accidents or violent crimes,

see also
p. 365,
Material
from
social
media
sites, on
the need
to avoid
aggravat-
ing grief

unless and until it is clear that the next of kin have been informed or unless it is warranted. The PCC censured newspapers for publishing photographs of funerals taken without bereaved families' consent (for example, *Rosemary MacLeod v Scottish Sun*, adjudication issued 23 April 2013). But the Editors' Code does not ban this outright.

👁 Case study

The PCC upheld a complaint by Paul McCartney against *Hello!* magazine's publication in 1998 of a photo of him and two of his children lighting a candle in a Paris cathedral for his wife Linda, who had died a month earlier. The PCC deplored publication of the photo as breaching its clauses 3 (Privacy) and 5 (Intrusion into Grief and Shock) of the Editors' Code, saying the cathedral was 'a clear example of a place where there is a reasonable expectation of privacy' (*McCartney v Hello!* Report 43, 1998).

---

ch. 3
explains
informed
consent

The Ofcom code warns broadcasters that the bereaved may need special consideration as a 'vulnerable person' who may not be able to give informed consent to be featured in a programme. Ofcom guidance is that at funerals, programme-makers should respect requests to withdraw.

Practice 8.19 of the Ofcom code says broadcasters should try to reduce the potential distress to victims and relatives when making or broadcasting programmes intended to examine past events that involve trauma to individuals (including crime) unless it is warranted to do otherwise. It adds that so far as reasonably practicable, surviving victims and the immediate families of those whose experience is to feature in a programme should be told of the plans for the programme and its intended broadcast, even if the events or material to be broadcast are already in the public domain.

Protecting children's privacy and welfare

The Editors' Code, clause 6 (Children) says:

i) Young people should be free to complete their time at school without unnecessary intrusion.

ii) A child under 16 must not be interviewed or photographed on issues involving their own or another child's welfare unless a custodial parent or similarly responsible adult consents.

iii) Pupils must not be approached or photographed at school without the permission of the school authorities.

iv) Minors must not be paid for material involving children's welfare, nor parents or guardians for material about their children or wards, unless it is clearly in the child's interest.

v) Editors must not use the fame, notoriety or position of a parent or guardian as sole justification for publishing details of a child's private life.

The code does not seek to place a general inhibition on photographing or filming children. But PCC adjudications make clear that publishing photographs in which children are identifiable and which could cause embarrassment or show them in distress – for example, in a swimsuit or after an accident – or referring to children's medical conditions, concerns their welfare and therefore should not normally be done without a parent or legal guardian's consent. Obscuring the child's identity could avoid an adverse adjudication, as long as the way in which the picture or information was obtained did not breach the code.

The PCC also said parental consent for publishing a child's image could in some instances be implied because of the context – for example if a parent has allowed the child to be a spectator at a televised sports event – and that 'innocuous' pictures of children in crowds or public places will not normally breach the code (*Quigley v Zoo magazine*, adjudication issued 23 June 2006).

see www. mcnaes. com ch. 27 for adjudications and p. 334, Public interest exceptions in the codes

 www.mcnaes.com ch. 27: 'Images of youngsters committing crime.'

 ### Case study

In 2007 the PCC criticised a Scottish newspaper for publishing on its website mobile phone footage shot by a child showing disruptive behaviour by some of her classmates. The PCC accepted it was in the public interest to show the behaviour, which the girl said contributed to her poor exam results, but criticised the paper for failing to conceal the children's identities (*Gaddis v Hamilton Advertiser*, adjudication issued 30 July 2007).

The Ofcom code says in practice 8.20: 'Broadcasters should pay particular attention to the privacy of people under 16. They do not lose their rights to privacy because, for example, of the fame or notoriety of their parents or because of events in their schools.'

Practice 8.21 adds:

ch. 3 explains the code's general protection for the under-18s

> Where a programme features an individual under 16 or a vulnerable person in a way that infringes privacy, consent must be obtained from:
>
> - a parent, guardian or other person of eighteen or over in loco parentis; and
> - wherever possible, the individual concerned;
> - unless the subject matter is trivial or uncontroversial and the participation minor, or it is warranted to proceed without consent.

The code says a vulnerable person may include those with learning difficulties, mental health problems, the bereaved, the traumatised and the sick.

The Ofcom code, like the Editors' Code, states that normally broadcasters must get a school's permission before filming pupils – see practice 8.8, cited earlier.

! Remember

Paranoia about paedophiles may prompt irrational objections by officials or the public to journalists filming or photographing children in innocuous situations. Journalists should, before photographing or filming youngsters taking part in organised events such as sports, liaise with organisers and carry a press card or similar identification. See Useful Websites at the end of this chapter for Football Association guidelines.

▶ Public interest exceptions in the codes

The Editors' Code and Ofcom code allow that some rules may be breached if the journalist is covered by 'public interest' exceptions. The exceptions cover types of valuable journalistic activity, as outlined in chs. 2 and 3, and include exposing crime or negligence imperilling people's safety and exposing deception of the public by an organisation or a hypocritical politician. If the public interest factor is sufficient, and any intrusion into privacy proportionate, Ipso and Ofcom will say that a photographer's persistent pursuit of a criminal to take his picture, or surveillance or undercover filming – even of children – was justified.

see also
chs. 2
and 3 on
subter-
fuge and
decep-
tion by
journalists

👁 Case study

In 2008 Ofcom rejected complaints by several parents whose children were filmed by the BBC during an undercover investigation into standards at a nursery as part of an inquiry into how nurseries were regulated. Ofcom said the filming was justified by the strong public interest and that the broadcast of the programme, *Whistleblower: Childcare*, in which the children's faces were blurred to obscure their identity, had not infringed their privacy. The nursery had broken glass in the garden, power tools left unattended near children and failed to check the false CV of a new member of staff (in fact, the undercover reporter) (*Ofcom Broadcast Bulletin 116*, 1 September 2008).

---

see www.
mcnaes.
com ch. 27,
'Coverage
of major
incidents'

Ipso and Ofcom are also likely to accept that after major incidents such as disasters or terrorist bombings the public interest in journalists immediately revealing the scale or effect is so strong that breaching privacy to show victims needing or receiving medical treatment may be justified, even though they have not consented to being pictured. But some parts of each code have no public interest exceptions – for example, the first part of clause 5 (Intrusion into grief and shock) of the Editors' Code.

▶ User-generated content

Pictures and footage supplied by readers and viewers – for example, mobile phone footage – frequently feature in media coverage. This is particularly the case in major events such as the aftermath of the terrorist bombings in London on 7 July 2005. Journalists handling this 'user-generated content' (UGC) – whatever the nature of the coverage – should realise it might breach the privacy of those depicted.

 See also p. 332, Protecting children's privacy and welfare, on mobile phone footage of unruly children at a school.

ch. 29 explains copyright

Some UGC pictures published have turned out to be faked, or supplied in breach of someone else's copyright.

Material from social media sites

Journalists routinely search social media sites, including Facebook, Flickr, Tumblr, Instagram and Twitter for pictures or footage of people in the news, or to find news. Again, publishing this material may breach copyright.

((•))

see Useful Websites at the end of this chapter for the Codebook

It might also be an intrusion into privacy if the person was portrayed in a private situation, and was unaware that he/she was being pictured or that the material was being posted on the social media site. The Editors' Codebook, produced by the committee of editors who oversee the Editors' Code, suggests these questions can be asked when considering when such material should be used in news coverage: How personal is it?; What is the public interest in its publication?; Has the person tried to restrict access?; Are they responsible for uploading it themselves?

👁 **Case study**

The PCC ruled that a newspaper had not breached an assault victim's privacy when it published a photo of his injured face, taken from his Facebook page, and identified him. The man did not consent to the *Farnham Herald* using the photo and police did not identify him to the paper. But the PCC noted that he himself posted the photo on to Facebook and had referred there to an attack, and that there were no privacy settings. The PCC said the *Herald* used the photo in a straightforward report, substantially corroborated by the police, of an incident which was a matter of legitimate local concern (*A man v Farnham Herald*, 27 November 2012).

Even if the person shown is the one who placed his/her own image in the public domain by uploading the material on to the website, journalists must consider if it is ethical to use the image in the context of a news story projected to a different, and probably much bigger, audience. For example, the grieving family of a teenager who has died may be even more distressed if media reports include a social website picture showing the youngster apparently drunk on a social occasion.

The PCC guidance 'Privacy and the Public Domain', issued in 2012, warned editors that they could breach clause 5 (Intrusion into grief or shock) of the Editors'

Code by publishing such a picture in a way which was insensitive to the feelings of close friends and family.

But the PCC ruled that publication of an innocuous image, obtained from a publicly-accessible website, of someone who died in shocking event – in that instance, the 2004 tsunami disaster – was not insensitive (*The family of Alice Claypoole v Daily Mirror*, Report 71, 2005).

((•))

see Useful
Websites
at the end
of this
chapter
for this
guidance

It also ruled that news media can publish statements people make on social media sites, even when access is restricted to 'friends', though generally only if in the public interest to do so. It rejected a complaint made on behalf of a police officer that his privacy was breached when a newspaper published an apparently flippant message he posted on Facebook about the death of a member of the public, Ian Tomlinson, during the G20 protest in London (*Phyllis Goble v The People*, adjudication issued 29 September 2009).

The PCC ruled that a newspaper which published remarks a civil servant 'tweeted' about her job in her Twitter account, which had 700 followers, did not breach her privacy because this was publicly-accessible information and not of an intimate nature (*Sarah Baskerville v Independent on Sunday*, adjudication issued 2 February 2011).

➡ Recap of major points

- The civil courts use the criterion of 'a reasonable expectation of privacy' when deciding if the media have breached a person's human rights by photographing or filming him or her. Intrusion into privacy can be lawful if there is a 'public interest' justification.

- People who object to being filmed or photographed or recorded by the media may complain to Ipso or Ofcom.

- Their codes require journalists to have parental consent for photographing, filming or recording a child if his/her welfare or privacy is involved.

- Journalists must take care when deciding whether to publish pictures or footage supplied by the public or copied from social media sites, as publication may breach privacy or copyright.

- Journalists should not intrude into grief, for example when filming or photographing funerals or publishing photos from social media sites.

((•)) Useful Websites

http://stakeholders.ofcom.org.uk/broadcasting/broadcast-codes/broadcast-code/
   The Ofcom Broadcasting Code

http://stakeholders.ofcom.org.uk/broadcasting/guidance/programme-guidance/bguidance/
  Ofcom's guidance on the code

www.editorscode.org.uk/the_code_book.html
  Editors' Codebook – collates PCC adjudications and provides advice on the Code

www.pcc.org.uk/news/index.html?article=ODEwNg==
  PCC guidance on 'privacy and the public domain'

www.bbc.co.uk/editorialguidelines/page/guidelines-privacy-privacy-consent
  BBC Editorial Guidelines of filming in public places, sensitive places, private property and use of social media material

www.bbc.co.uk/editorialguidelines/page/guidance-social-media-pictures
  BBC editorial guidance on use of social media pictures

www.bbc.co.uk/editorialguidelines/page/guidelines-children-introduction
  BBC Editorial Guidelines on children as contributors

www.thefa.com/~/media/Files/TheFAPortal/governance-docs/safeguarding/raising-awareness/photography-guidelines.ashx
  Football Association guidelines on photography of children

28

Data protection

Chapter summary

The privacy of personal information kept on computers and in filing systems is safeguarded by data protection law. This covers data we give about ourselves to government departments, councils, banks, telephone companies and other commercial and public institutions, and data they generate about us. The law affects journalists in three ways. First, a journalist who uses underhand methods to gain access to people's personal data may be prosecuted, unless he/she has a 'public interest' or other defence. Secondly, institutions – including police forces and schools – sometimes misunderstand data protection law when claiming it stops them releasing information to the media. Thirdly, because journalists generate and store data about people – in research, news stories, recordings, pictures and footage – media organisations and freelance journalists must be lawful in how they process and publish data, to avoid paying damages for breaching privacy or being fined by the Information Commissioner.

▎ Protection for stored data

In 2000 the Human Rights Act created a specific right of privacy. But even before then, the law recognised rights of privacy relating to the vast amount of information held in computer and manual records. It has been estimated that public and commercial institutions hold in total about 700 databases on each working adult. For personal data held on computer, these privacy rights were provided in the Data Protection Act 1984. The Data Protection Act 1998 strengthened them and extended them to information about people contained in 'structured manual files'.

This law requires personal data to be kept securely. Many news stories have highlighted lax observance by employees of public bodies or companies – for example, when huge amounts of official or commercial data about individuals, including lists of clients or customers, their dates of birth, addresses and bank account details, are found in laptops or on memory sticks left in pubs or taxis.

But in recent years Parliamentary debate has focused on what is seen as widespread breach of data protection law by some journalists – mainly those of national newspapers – when seeking and publishing information.

▶ Data protection principles

Under the 1998 Act a 'data controller' is someone or an organisation who determines the purposes for which and the manner in which any personal data are processed. Data controllers include local authorities, health trusts, government departments, commercial organisations, magistrates courts and the police – in fact, any organisation or individual keeping personal data about others in a computer or in structured filing systems.

A 'data subject' is a person about whom the information is held.

The 1998 Act says people handling personal data must comply with data protection principles. Data must, for example, be:

- fairly and lawfully processed;
- processed for limited purposes – for example, for the purpose for which a person (the data subject) provided it to the data controller; for instance, to open a bank account, claim benefits, get a mobile phone account, etc
- processed in accordance with the data subject's rights;
- secure.

▶ Crimes of procuring, gaining or disclosing personal data

Anyone who without a lawful purpose obtains or procures personal data from a data controller, or anyone who unlawfully discloses it (for example, by publishing it) commits an offence under section 55 of the 1998 Act. A conviction is punishable by a fine of up to £5,000 in a magistrates court or an unlimited amount on conviction in the Crown court.

Section 55 says:

> A person must not knowingly or recklessly, without the consent of the data controller
>
> (a) obtain or disclose personal data or the information contained in personal data, or
>
> (b) procure the disclosure to another person of the information contained in personal data.

'Blagging' by a journalist to gain someone else's personal data could be an offence under this section – for example, the journalist posing as someone else when phoning a bank to get information from that person's account. If a journalist persuaded or paid someone to leak personal data from a data controller's records, it might be an offence for both the journalist and the 'leaker'.

Defences are available to those who act in the reasonable belief that they would have obtained permission from the data controller for their actions, and to anyone who shows that obtaining, disclosing or procuring the information was 'justified in the public interest'. But the public interest is not defined. Section 55 also contains a defence that obtaining, disclosing or procuring the information was necessary for the purpose of preventing or detecting crime, so this defence might aid investigative journalists.

Although data protection law has been in force for nearly three decades, most journalists know little about it, probably because threats of prosecution against journalists have been rare. But this is changing.

▶ Increasing concern about data breaches

((•))

see Useful
Websites
at the end
of this
chapter
for these
reports

In 2006 the Information Commissioner urged Parliament to make the section 55 offence punishable by up to two years' imprisonment. In reports entitled '*What Price Privacy?*' and '*What Price Privacy Now?*' he said that his office and the police had uncovered evidence of a widespread and organised undercover market in confidential personal information, procured and sold by dishonest private detectives.

Some of the information was 'blagged', and some was obtained corruptly from dishonest individuals – including police officers – whose jobs within institutions and companies gave them routine access to personal data.

Among the 'buyers' for this information were many journalists wanting details to trace people or inquire about them.

👁 **Case study**

The Information Commissioner reported in 2006 that a criminal investigation into one private detective's agency had revealed it had committed thousands of section 55 offences. The detective's records showed he had sold information to 305 named journalists working for a range of newspapers. The data he supplied included records of people's criminal convictions, the number plates of people's cars, driving licence details, ex-directory phone numbers, mobile phone numbers and details of people's 'family and friends' phone contacts. The Commissioner said that some of those whose confidential information was violated were celebrities or public figures, but others were people who had simply 'strayed by chance into the limelight' because they had some connection with people in the news. He added that some of the disclosures of this information may have been in the public interest, but noted that this defence was not raised by those working for the agency who were prosecuted (*What Price Privacy?* and *What Price Privacy now?*).

It should be remembered that no journalists were prosecuted in this investigation, and that journalists who dealt with this agency may in many instances have had a public interest justification for seeking out such information, or for accepting it when offered.

But following publication of the Commissioner's reports, Parliament legislated to introduce jail terms of up to two years for breach of section 55. The measure is in section 77 of the Criminal Justice and Immigration Act 2008. But the new power has not yet been brought into effect.

Media lobbying led to the inclusion in the 2008 Act of a new defence for someone charged under section 55 – but it has not been brought into force. If it does come into force, it will give someone who has obtained, disclosed or procured data 'with a view to the publication by any person of any journalistic, literary or artistic material' a defence if they did so with 'the reasonable belief that in the particular circumstances' their actions were 'justified as being in the public interest'.

! Remember

The focus on how journalists gain information was intensified by the official inquiry into 'the culture, practices, and ethics of the press' by Lord Justice Leveson. Ch. 2 explains this, and that the Editors' Code of Practice normally bans accessing digitally-held private information without consent.

▶ When journalists' lawful inquiries are thwarted

When journalists ask for information organisations sometimes cite the 1998 Act to justify their refusal to give it. But the Act covers personal data, not all data, and even personal data can be lawfully released in some circumstances – for example, if the 'data subject' agrees.

Data is only personal if it can lead to a living individual being identified.

Getting information from police

Police officers who claim the Act prevents them from releasing information may have misunderstood the law. People involved in road accidents and the victims of crime may ask police not to give the media their details. Guidelines issued by the Association of Chief Police Officers say that these requests should be honoured unless police feel on a case-by-case basis that there is an exceptional reason why the details must be given, for example to help solve a crime. But police are not

see Useful
Websites
at the end
of this
chapter
for ACPO
guidelines

obliged to agree to requests from victims, witnesses or next of kin not to release information about an incident. Police, when asking for their consent to release information, should use the question format in the ACPO guidelines: 'We often find it helpful in our enquiries to pass on someone's details to the media. Do you object if we do that in your case?'

The Act does not apply to dead people, so does not prevent police naming victims who have died once they are positively identified and immediate relatives notified.

Getting information from courts

Journalists sometimes have difficulty obtaining information from courts.

Guidance for court staff prepared by H M Courts Service published in August 2013 states, on p. 14: 'The Data Protection Act must not be used as a blanket excuse for withholding information.' It also makes clear, on p. 13, that a defendant's address may be supplied to reporters even if it has not been read out in court.

> 📖 See also ch. 14, pp. 156, What information and help must criminal courts provide?

Getting information from schools

Schools have cited the Act as a reason for refusing to allow photographs of sports and activities, or – if photography has been allowed – refusing to name the children in the pictures.

Department of Education guidance is that schools and local authorities are free to decide their own policies about when photos can be taken, and on the release of associated information for publicity, but that it will require the consent of pupils' parents or legal guardians.

see Useful
Websites
at the end
of this
chapter
for the
ICO
guidance

The Information Commissioner has issued this guidance about photographs being taken by a local newspaper of a school awards ceremony: 'As long as the school has agreed to this, and the children and/or their guardians are aware that photographs of those attending the ceremony may appear in the newspaper, this will not breach the Act.'

The Commissioner's guidance is also that schools do not breach the Act by releasing exam results to the local media for publication, and that in general, because a school has a legitimate interest in publishing results, pupils or parents or guardians do not need to consent to publication.

▌ Media and journalists as 'data controllers'

Media organisations and freelance journalists are data controllers because they decide how they will use the personal data that they hold about individuals. The

Information Commissioner keeps a public register of data controllers. The registration requirement mainly affects media managements, but freelances should also register. The Act puts virtually all responsibility for data protection on the data controller.

A privacy case brought against a media organisation or journalist may include an element claiming breach of data protection law.

👁 **Case study**

In 2002 supermodel Naomi Campbell was awarded £3,500 damages for breach of confidence and infringement of data protection rights over the *Daily Mirror's* publication of details about her therapy at Narcotics Anonymous (NA), an award upheld by the House of Lords (*Campbell v Mirror Group Newspapers Ltd* [2004] UKHL 22). But the judgment did not treat the data protection element as a separate issue from the breach of confidence, and the court ruled that both elements concerned the same misuse of private information acquired (and therefore processed) by the newspaper – a photo of her leaving the therapy and some detail of it.

ch. 26 gives details of the *Campbell* case

In 2003 damages for infringement of rights under the 1998 Act were awarded to the film stars Michael Douglas and Catherine Zeta-Jones, after *Hello!* magazine published pictures covertly taken of their wedding. But they were awarded only £50 each for the infringement. Most of the damages were for breach of confidence/privacy – see ch. 25 for other detail on this case.

These cases show that a media organisation which breaches someone's privacy is also likely, in the processing of information gained, to have breached their data protection rights, but that the courts will examine the total effect on the claimant, and not differentiate between the wrong caused by each breach.

Sensitive personal data

The Act provides particular privacy protection for 'sensitive personal data', which means information about the data subject's:

- racial or ethnic origin;
- political opinions;
- religious beliefs or other beliefs of a similar nature;
- membership of a trade union;
- physical or mental health or condition;
- sexual life;
- criminal offences and any proceedings for offences committed or alleged to have been committed.

The judge in the *Naomi Campbell* case held that the information about the nature and details of the therapy she was seeking was 'sensitive personal data' in respect of her physical or mental health.

Under the law as originally enacted, sensitive personal data can usually only be processed lawfully if either of two main conditions are met, for example, the person gave 'explicit' consent or deliberately made the information public; or the use to which the information was to be put was necessary for the administration of justice.

However, as a result of media representations, the government introduced a statutory instrument that widened the grounds for any third party's lawful release of information to the media for publication by adding another 'gateway' for the lawful processing of sensitive personal data. This is the Data Protection (Processing of Sensitive Personal Data) Order 2000 (SI 2000/417).

For detail of how this order and other exemptions in the Act protect media activity which is in the public interest, and whether a 'subject access request' could threaten a journalist's protection of the identity of a confidential source, see www.mcnaes.com ch. 28. In January 2014 the Information Commissioner's Office began a consultation on draft guidance to be issued to the media on data protection law – see the Late News section and www.mcnaes.com ch. 28.

➡ Recap of major points

- Journalists seeking information should realise that it is a criminal offence to procure the disclosure of personal data, unless there is a legal defence.

- Sometimes the Act is mistakenly used as a reason to deny journalists information.

- The Act has exemptions protecting journalism which is in the public interest.

((•)) Useful Websites

www.ico.gov.uk/
   Information Commissioner's website

www.acpo.presscentre.com/content/default.aspx?NewsAreaID=19
   Association of Chief Police Officers (ACPO) Communication Advisory
   Group – Guidance 2010

www.ico.gov.uk/for_the_public/topic_specific_guides/schools/photos.aspx
   Information Commissioner's guidance for schools about photos

http://www.ico.gov.uk/for_the_public/topic_specific_guides/schools/exam_results.aspx
   Information Commissioner's guidance for schools about exam results

29

Copyright

Chapter summary

Copyright is a property right to control who can copy work created by artistic and other intellectual endeavour. Copyright protects journalism articles, website content, books, photographs, films, sound recordings and music, TV and radio broadcasts. This chapter explains how copyright law, by deterring and punishing plagiarism, protects the ability of journalists and media employers to earn profit from their output. Copyright lasts for decades. Copyright also protects work created by others which journalists may wish to copy, for example by quoting from or showing. Journalists need to know how much they can copy without infringing someone's copyright, and the legal consequences of infringement.

▎ What material does copyright protect?

The source of most UK law on copyright is the Copyright, Designs and Patents Act 1988, as amended by subsequent law.

Section 1 says copyright subsists in:

- 'original literary, dramatic, musical or artistic works' – this includes all kinds of text whether handwritten, printed or online, such as journalistic and scientific articles, poems, lyrics, books, plays, scripts, shorthand or longhand records of speeches and interviews; musical manuscripts; photographs; design documents, websites, templates and bureaucratic forms; graphic works, maps, plans, sketches, paintings, sculptures; databases and computer programs.

- 'sound recordings, films or broadcasts', including journalism in these media; files and CDs of music; home and cinema movies; TV and radio output.
- 'the typographical arrangement of published editions'.

→glossary

Unauthorised copying of all or 'any substantial part' of any work in these categories is a criminal offence and a civil **tort** unless justified by a defence or exception. More than one type of copyright, with different owners, may exist in a single product. For example, a film will have copyrights in the script, footage and music.

Who owns copyright under the 1988 Act

- The 'first owner' of copyright in a literary, dramatic, musical or artistic work is the author as creator. This definition includes the journalist as an article's writer, the photographer as creator of a photo, the artist who makes painting or sculpture, etc. If authorship is joint, each author is a 'first owner' and permission is needed from each to copy the work.

The 'first owner' has the copyright unless he/she agrees, for example for payment, to assign to another party the right to control who makes copies – see later in this chapter.

- But the Act says an employer owns the copyright in a literary, dramatic, musical or artistic work – including a journalistic article or photo – which is created by an employee in the course of his/her employment. This is usually stated in the employment contract.
- A staff journalist only has the copyright in an article or photo if the employer specifically agrees to this, for example, in the contract of employment. (1988 Act, section 11)
- Self-employed journalists, including freelance and commercial photographers, are the 'first owners' of copyright in their works.

The terms, including payment, under which freelances assign or licence copyright in their work to media publishers may be specific to each deal, or governed by custom and practice. Assign means to transfer ownership of the copyright, while licence means to permit a use of the copyright work.

- The 'first owner' of copyright in a sound recording is the producer. The Act says a producer is the person/organisation who undertook 'the arrangements necessary' for creating the work.
- The 'first owners' of copyright in a film made on or 1 July 1994, whether made for journalism or entertainment, are jointly the producer and

principal director. The producer owns the copyright in films made earlier which are covered by the Act.

- The 'first owner' of copyright in a broadcast is the person or organisation 'making the broadcast' – that is, transmitting it if responsible for content, or providing that content and arranging transmission. This is usually a broadcast company.

- The 'first owner' of copyright in 'the typographical arrangement of a published edition' is the publisher.

- The 'first owner' of copyright in 'computer-generated work', a category which the Act limits to circumstances of 'no human author', is the person who or organisation undertaking 'the arrangements necessary' for the work's creation.

▶ Commissioner's copyright

Section 4 of the Copyright Act 1956 governs who owns copyright in literary, dramatic and artistic work created before 1 August 1989 – that is, before the 1988 Act came into force. Copyright in such a work, including a journalism article, which was created in the course of employment, is owned by the employer unless the employer agreed to assign it to someone else.

But if a work was created by a freelance paid or commissioned to do it, the 1956 Act says that, in the absence of any other agreement, the copyright is owned by the commissioner – for example, a newspaper or magazine.

This difference between the two Acts decides who, as copyright holder, can successfully object to the use of an archived photo or demand payment for using it.

- Copyright in a commissioned photograph taken before 1 August 1989 is owned by the commissioner, even though the freelance or commercial photographer who took the photo may own the negatives or have digital copies of it.

- The photographer or his/her employer owns the copyright in a photo taken before 1 August 1989 which was not commissioned.

see p. 351, Assignment and licensing of copyright

This summary assumes that copyright in the photograph has not been not assigned to someone else.

A family wedding photo taken by a commercial photographer before 1 August 1989 will almost certainly have been commissioned by someone in the family, who will probably own the copyright.

- Under the 1988 Act, the copyright in a photograph taken on or after 1 August 1989 is owned by the photographer's employer, or by the photographer if he or she is self-employed, *unless* there is an agreement to the contrary.

A celebrity who hires (commissions) a photographer to take pictures of a family occasion may well insist on the copyright being assigned to them, to control their use.

▶ Private and domestic photographs and films

→ glossary Section 85 of the 1988 Act gives '**moral rights**', in essence privacy rights, to people who commission the taking of photographs or making of films for 'private and domestic purposes'.

- The rights are that no copies of the photograph or film should be published, issued to or exhibited to the public without the commissioner's agreement.

- Commissioners have these rights even if they do not own the copyright, and can sue and recover damages from anyone who publishes a commissioned photo or film of a private and domestic occasion without his/her permission.

ch. 26 explains general privacy rights

- A publisher who uses the photo or film in breach of copyright could also be sued – for example, by a photographer who holds the copyright.

Consider this hypothetical case: A woman is hurt in a train crash. A journalist traces a relative, who emails the journalist a copy of a picture of the woman, taken some years previously at her wedding. If the relative took the picture himself, and agrees for it to be published, there is no infringement of copyright. If the wedding picture was taken by a commercial photographer commissioned by the bridegroom (that is, the injured woman's husband) the photographer will probably own the copyright, and may be glad to accept a fee for media publication of the picture. But the husband may not want it published. He may sue for breach of his moral right, and win, even if he is not in the photo.

see p. 354, Legal remedies for infringement of copyright

This 'moral right' can be waived. But otherwise it lasts as long as the copyright, see later in this chapter.

> A High Court judge ruled in 2012 that photos created by a photographer as a present for his friend Carina Trimingham, who appeared in them, were not 'commissioned' because he was not obliged by any financial deal to create them, and so for these photos she had no moral rights under section 85 to control their use – see p. 359, Moral rights for creators.

see www. mcnaes. com ch. 29 for this case

When a big story breaks, the media tend to rush to get 'pick-up' pictures or family-held footage of those involved, and to adopt a 'publish first, worry later' approach. Most families know little about copyright or moral rights, so financial consequences for media organisations are rare – but they could occur.

▶ Copying from the internet, including social networking sites

The fact that material, including any photo, can be seen by all on the internet – for example, via Google Images – does not mean that anyone has the right to copy and publish it. Publishing material such as a photo or an extract of 'original' text copied from the internet infringes any copyright in the work, unless the copyright owner consents or a defence or exception applies. Downloading can itself be an infringement.

- Publishing photos copied from a social networking site – such as Facebook, Instagram, Flickr, Twitter, or Tumblr – may infringe the copyright in the site, and/or the copyright held by the person who created the picture, who might not even be aware that someone else has uploaded a copy on to the site.

see also, p. 359, 'Open content' licences

👁 **Case study**

Commercial photographer Jason Sheldon sued Daybrook House Promotions Ltd, a company running Nottingham dance venue Rock City, after he discovered it used one of his pictures in a poster campaign for its events. The picture was of popstars Ke$ha and LMFAO on their tour bus. Daybrook said the photo had been available on the Tumblr website, which it mistakenly believed meant the photograph was there to be freely used. Daybrook offered to pay Mr Sheldon £150 for its use. But in a preliminary ruling Judge Birss in the Patents County Court said that, if the case proceeded and he found copyright had been breached, he would award Mr Sheldon £5,682.37 damages, noting that for this particular photo Sheldon had exclusive access to the popstars (*Sheldon v Daybrook House Promotions Ltd* [2013] EWPCC 26). It was later reported that Daybrook settled the case – see Useful Websites at the end of this chapter. The Patents County Court is now called the Intellectual Property Enterprise Court.

 If the material was posted on a personal webpage a media organisation may need to consider too whether, apart from copyright law, ethical considerations mean it should not be used in news coverage, see ch. 27, p. 335, Material from social media sites.

Photos of TV images, and photos shown on TV

see p. 354, Defences to alleged infringement of copyright

Publishing a photo (for example, a 'screengrab') of the whole or a substantial part of a television or film image without permission can infringe copyright under section 17 of the 1988 Act. Showing a photo on a TV programme without the copyright owner's permission is also an infringement, unless a defence applies.

▌ The scope of copyright protection

Copyright is automatically in force as soon as a work is created in any permanent form. In the UK, copyright does not have to be registered.

What is 'original'?

Copyright protects an 'original literary, dramatic, musical or artistic work'. 'Literary' in this context includes any work written or spoken which exists in some form – it has no reference to a work's literary or artistic merits. The legal definition of 'original' has for some decades in UK law simply required that the work was originated by the creator(s) using some element of 'skill, labour and judgment' (see, for example, *Express Newspapers plc v News (UK) Ltd* [1990] 3 All ER 376).

The elements of skill, labour, judgment, time or expense have not needed to be great. Judges cite the rough guideline that 'anything worth copying is usually worth protecting'.

- Skill, labour and judgement spent in creating a bus or rail timetable, or tide table or a database, means that that such works have been protected by copyright, vested in the 'first owner' as creator or, if employed, his/her employer.

- Copyright could also subsist in even a fairly basic form of map, diagram, drawing or sketch, so journalists should also beware of reproducing these without permission.

But a commonplace expression such as 'Love is Blind', if used in a book title, is not protected by copyright because of lack of originality.

 See www.mcnaes.com for detail on copyright which exists in TV and radio programme listings and for the significance of a ruling in 2012 by the European Court of Justice that copyright did not exist in lists of Premier League football fixtures.

No copyright in news or in unrecorded ideas

Copyright does not protect ideas – it controls the right to copy the form or manner in which ideas are expressed or executed. The law of breach of confidence, explained in ch. 25, would apply in some circumstances if a considered 'idea' with commercial value was exploited in breach of 'confidential' discussions about it.

- There is also no copyright in facts, news or information. Copyright exists in the form – for example, sentences, a photo, footage – in which these things are expressed, and in the selection and arrangement of the material for publication.

'Lifting' stories

News organisations often include in their own coverage facts in stories such as political initiatives or a famous person's death which are 'broken' by rivals. This is known as 'lifting' a story. There is no copyright infringement in reporting in a *re-written* version the facts uncovered or published by others (*Springfield v*

Thame (1903) 89 LT 242). But there may be infringements in 'lifting' verbatim phrases and quotes from the original report, depending on the extent. See p. 354, What is 'substantial'? and p. 352, Copyright in speeches and interviews.

ch. 19 explains the defamation danger in lifting stories

👁 **Case study**

High Court judge Sir Nicolas Browne-Wilkinson said in 1990: 'For myself, I would hesitate a long time before deciding that there is copyright in a news story which would be infringed by another newspaper picking up that story and reproducing the same story in different words… That would not be in the public interest…' (*Express Newspapers plc v News (UK) Ltd* [1990] 3 All ER 376).

He also observed that as the practice among UK national newspapers of copying quotes from each other was so widespread, and rarely led to copyright disputes, it could be argued that the newspaper gave each other implied licence for the practice by 'acquiescence'.

see p. 358, Acquiescence

Changing the odd word or two when writing a news report by 'lifting' facts from a rival report will not be enough to avoid copyright infringement. But the 1988 Act's defence of 'fair dealing' for reporting current events can allow a media organisation to copy some quotes and other sentences from a rival's report, and to broadcast short extracts of film or sound footage already broadcast by a rival: see later in this chapter.

▌ Assignment and licensing of copyright

Copyright holders can 'assign' copyright, wholly or in part, to another person or organisation, either temporarily or for the copyright's duration. This transfers control to exploit the work. Or the owner can, while retaining the copyright, 'licence' another party to exploit the work in a particular deal or territory. Section 90 of the 1988 Act says an assignment of copyright is not effective unless it is in writing and is signed by or on behalf of the person assigning it – for example, the 'first owner'.

A licence need not be in writing. In journalism, licences are often agreed verbally, or implied by what has become custom and practice. For example, freelance journalists who regularly send articles or photos to newspapers know their fee rates, and whether they also want the right to use the work in magazine supplements and on websites, or possibly in overseas editions and for syndication. Any doubts on either side about licence terms should be discussed then agreed in writing before the work is published.

Material from non-journalist contributors

- A reader sending a letter for publication has by implication licensed the media organisation to publish it once, but retains the copyright.

If the organisation subsequently wants to publish a compilation of readers' letters as a book, it will need to contact each letter-writer to seek a licence to re-publish the letters.

▌ Copyright in speeches and interviews, and in notes or recordings of them

Copyright exists in spoken words such as public speech as soon as the speaker's words are recorded in some form, with or without permission. The copyright arises even if the speech is not delivered from a script, but is, for example, uttered in an improvised comedy show, or in an interview with a journalist. The speaker, as the author of a 'literary work' – that is, his/her words as recorded – owns the copyright in that work, unless he/she is speaking in the course of his/her employment, in which case the employer owns the copyright, or is reciting words in which someone else holds copyright (for example, from a play script).

As copyright protects the 'original' product of 'skill, labour and judgment', there is no copyright in casual conversational or trite remarks, short jokes already in circulation or in commonplace or ill-judged sayings.

Section 58 of the 1988 Act – a specific defence for journalism – says it is not infringement of copyright to use a record of all or part of a speaker's words for reporting current events, as long as:

(1) The record of the words – that is, as recorded on tape or digitally, or in shorthand or longhand – is a direct record of their utterance, and is not taken from a previous record or broadcast (as taking the record from such sources could infringe the copyright in them);

(2) The speaker did not forbid any note or recording being made of his/her words, and making the record of them did not infringe any pre-existing copyright (it might, if the speaker was quoting someone else's words);

(3) The use made of the record of the words, or extracts from it, is not of a kind prohibited by the speaker (or anyone else who owns copyright in words used by the speaker) before the record was made;

(4) The record is used with the authority of the person who is lawfully in possession of it – who would usually be the journalist who took notes or made a recording of the speaker's words, or his/her employer.

Journalists should not be over-concerned about infringing a speaker's copyright when reporting verbatim a speech from a note or recording they made of a speech or an interview, as usually a speaker who knows they are journalists has consented to publication, expressly or by implication. Even if a speaker withholds consent, one or both of the fair dealing defences can apply, see later in this chapter.

The first and fourth conditions listed earlier reflect the fact that, apart from the speaker's copyright in the recorded words, a separate copyright exists in the actual record – the audio-recording, shorthand or longhand note – because of the skill, labour and judgement involved in making it (*Walter v Lane* [1900] AC 539). The journalist who made the record will, if a freelance, be 'first owner' of that copyright. If the record was made in the course of his/her employment, the employer owns it.

Parliament and the courts

Section 46 of the 1988 Act says copyright is not infringed by anything done for the purposes of reporting Parliamentary and judicial proceedings. This means there is no copyright infringement in reporting what is said in proceedings of the UK and Scottish Parliaments, the Northern Ireland and Welsh Assemblies or in the proceedings of statutory public inquiries and court cases.

 See www.mcnaes.com ch. 29 for a ruling that section 46 protected the media's use, approved by a court, of photos which figured in a murder trial.

▶ How long does copyright last?

Durations of copyright, set out in section 12 to 15 of the 1988 Act, can be summarised as:

- Copyright in a literary, dramatic, musical or artistic work – including a journalism article or a photo – lasts for the author's (that is, creator's) lifetime and then a further 70 years from the end of the calendar year in which he/she dies. So an author's copyright can be bequeathed to his/her heirs. The duration is the same even if the copyright is owned by an employer or has been assigned to a company.

- Copyright in a work of computer-generated music or graphics lasts for 50 years from the end of the year in which it was made.

- Copyright in a sound recording published or communicated to the public lasts 70 years from the end of the year in which that first happened.

- Copyright in a broadcast lasts 50 years from the end of the year in which it was made.

There are different (but still lengthy) periods of copyright for various other works, such as films, works of unknown authorship and for some particular circumstances.

 See www.mcnaes.com ch. 29 for detail of provision in the Enterprise and Regulatory Reform Act 2013 about copyright in 'orphan works'.

Crown copyright

Work produced by civil servants in the course of their employment is protected by Crown copyright, which can last up to 125 years.

▶ Legal remedies for infringement of copyright

Civil law

- A copyright holder who discovers that someone plans to infringe it can get a High Court or county court **injunction** to stop it.
- If the infringement has happened, an injunction can ban any repetition. The copyright owner can also sue the infringer for damages or 'an account of profits', to claim all or some of any profit made.
- The court can also order all infringing copies of the work to be handed to the copyright owner or destroyed.

The damages awarded by a court may reflect its view that there has been a flagrant breach of copyright.

Criminal law

The 1988 Act makes infringing copyright a criminal offence, though prosecutions tend to be confined to cases of large-scale piracy, eg of DVDs of Hollywood films. Fines can be as high as £50,000.

▶ Defences to alleged infringement of copyright

What is 'substantial'?

A question regularly asked by journalists is: 'How much can we copy or quote without infringing copyright?' One consideration is whether the copyright owner, in the case of copied text or quotes, will think it worth the effort to sue – but copyright can reside in a single sentence.

Section 16 of the 1988 Act says there is an infringement of copyright if the whole or 'any substantial part' of a work is copied. 'Substantial' refers to 'the quality of the originality', including the importance of the copied material in relation to the rest of the original work, rather than merely to how much was copied (*Newspaper Licensing Agency Ltd v Meltwater Holding BV* [2010] EWHC 3009 (Ch)).

For example, a face may be a small part of a photograph but is probably more important, as regards its commercial value, than the rest of the picture. A court dealing with a 'literary work' would consider to what degree unauthorised, verbatim publication of part of it might devalue the work's copyright.

 See the *Ashdown* case study, p. 357, Defence of fair dealing for the purpose of criticism or review.

In the *Meltwater* case, cited earlier, High Court judge Mrs Justice Proudman drew on the 2009 judgment in which the European Court of Justice ruled that a single extract of 11 consecutive words from a newspaper article could be protected by copyright if the work had sufficient originality. This EJC ruling is Case C-5/08 *Infopaq International A/S v Danske Dagblades Forening* [2010] FSR 495.

Mrs Justice Proudman said 'the ECJ makes it clear that originality rather than substantiality is the test to be applied to the part extracted. As a matter of principle this is the only real test.'

see p. 350, What is 'original'?

The issue of what is a 'substantial part' is not always relevant for the news media, as documents can be paraphrased or summarised to avoid quoting verbatim. Also, editors can aim to rely on a fair dealing defence, because then the issue of how much can be copied/quoted must be assessed in terms of 'fairness' rather than substantiality, see later in the chapter.

 See www.mcnaes.com ch. 29 for more about the *Meltwater* case. In it Mrs Justice Proudman considered whether subscribers to Meltwater News, a commercial monitoring service, had infringed the copyright of UK national newspapers by receiving, via Meltwater, headlines and short text extracts electronically 'scraped' from newspapers' websites.

Fair dealing defences

The two 'fair dealing' defences in sections 30 and 178 of the 1988 Act recognise the public interest in media coverage being free of some copyright restraints.

Defence of fair dealing for the purpose of reporting current events

- Section 30 of the Act allows publication of work protected by copyright 'for the purpose of reporting current events', even if there is no consent from the copyright owner.

- But there must be 'fair dealing' by those publishing it for this purpose, and an accompanying 'sufficient acknowledgement' of the work copied.

- 'Fair dealing' means fair practice – for example, the publisher should not take unfair commercial advantage of the copyright owner by excessive publication of the copied work.

- 'Sufficient acknowledgement' means that a report, in a newspaper, magazine, website or other textual medium, must
  - cite the work's title, or include some identifying description of it, and
  - name its author/creator, unless it was published anonymously.

- Photographs are specifically excluded from the fair dealing defence of 'reporting current events', because otherwise no news photographers could earn their living by selling their pictures.

Case law suggests that a court will be less likely to uphold the defence if the work copied has been 'leaked' to the media organisation. But the defence would probably not be undermined if the leak, for example, of an internal company memo, revealed wrongdoing or a threat to public safety. In such a case, the defence may protect verbatim publication of an entire document. But if the copyright in a text or document has a legitimate, commercial value, judges will expect the media to make only limited use of verbatim extracts, so that the copyright owner's ability to exploit that value is not compromised unfairly. See the *Ashdown* case discussed later in the chapter.

Although the fair dealing defence does not cover using still photographs, it does cover media use – that is, if 'fair' – of copied film footage and sound recordings, including in digital forms.

👁 Case study

In 1991, the High Court dismissed a copyright action by the BBC against British Satellite Broadcasting over the use by the satellite company's sports programme of highlights from BBC coverage of the World Cup football finals, to which the corporation had bought exclusive rights. The court said BSB's use of short clips showing goals scored, varying from 14 to 37 seconds, and up to four times in 24 hours, with a BBC credit line included as acknowledgement, was protected by the defence of fair dealing for reporting current events (*BBC v British Satellite Broadcasting* [1991] 3 All ER 833, Ch D).

Rival broadcast organisations sometimes agree protocols for limited copying of each other's output.

The Act says sound recording, film or broadcast reports of current events do not need to acknowledge the copied work's title, or other description of it, or the identity of its author/creator 'where this would be impossible for reasons of practicality or otherwise'. This reflects the difficulty of including all such detail in a broadcast of a short piece of copied footage. But acknowledgements help prove fairness.

Defence of fair dealing for the purpose of criticism or review

Section 30 of the Act allows publication of copies of a work, even without the copyright owner's consent, 'for the purpose of criticism or review'.

- But the work must already have been 'made available to the public' *with* the copyright owner's consent – for example, published or exhibited. The defence does not protect use of leaked material.

- There must also be 'fair dealing' by those publishing it for criticism or review, and an accompanying 'sufficient acknowledgement' of the work.

See earlier in this chapter for explanation of 'fair dealing' and 'sufficient acknowledgement'. These requirements are in essence the same as those required for the defence of fair dealing in reporting current events.

Authors or creators who have released works to the public may well be happy for extracts from them to appear in criticisms or reviews, as they will receive wider publicity. But the defence applies irrespective of whether they object. The defence would, for example, cover publication of a whole photo from an exhibition or book of artistic photos.

The requirement of fairness means that in a dispute about the extent of the use of copied material a court would consider if the media organisation genuinely sought to criticise the copied work(s), or had the baser motive of taking commercial advantage.

Case study

Paddy Ashdown, when leader of the Liberal Democrats, kept a private diary. After stepping down as leader he decided to publish it. But before he did, the *Sunday Telegraph* published, from a leaked copy, verbatim quotes from a confidential minute he made of a discussion in 1997 with Labour Prime Minister Tony Blair and two other senior politicians on the idea of a coalition Cabinet. Lord Ashdown sued for breach of copyright. The *Sunday Telegraph*, which had quoted verbatim or nearly verbatim some 20 per cent of the five-page minute, attempted to use both fair dealing defences. The Court of Appeal rejected both defences, ruling that there was no criticism or review of the minute as a literary work – the criticism was of the actions of Blair and Ashdown. It also ruled that arguably the 1997 meeting could be regarded in 1999 as a current event, but that 'one or two short extracts' of verbatim quotes from the minute would have sufficed to make the paper's account authoritative. But the newspaper had extensively 'filleted' the minute, in furtherance of its commercial interests, which competed with Ashdown's plan to sell his memoirs. It was also material that the minutes were leaked in breach of confidence (*Ashdown v Telegraph Group Ltd* [2001] All ER (D) 233 (Jul)).

See www.mcnaes.com ch. 29 for more case studies of copyright disputes involving the media.

Public interest defence

The public interest defence in copyright **case law** is narrow, reflecting the fact that the 'fair dealing' defences have a public interest element. But whereas the defence of fair dealing for the purpose of reporting current events cannot protect the unauthorised copying (publication) of a still photo, the 'public interest' defence can protect publication of any copyrighted work, including a still photo, →glossary if the purpose is to expose it as an immoral work, or one damaging to public life, health, safety or the administration of justice, or as a work which incites immoral behaviour, and in some other circumstances.

 Case study

In 2010 the *Reading Post* succeeded with the public interest defence in the small claims court after being sued by the owner of copyright in several photos which it had copied from a website. Police had directed the *Post* to the site, which showed the apparent exploits of 'urban explorers' inside abandoned buildings. The *Post* said it published the pictures to highlight police concerns that these activities involved criminal damage, including graffiti, and to help identify those involved. The judge said he felt the pictures were posted on the website to encourage the activities, which could cause an accident, and the public to suffer, and were a serious social problem (*Newspaper Society* website, 28 January 2010).

See www.mcnaes.com ch. 29 for other examples of journalistic use of the 'public interest' defence.

Incidental infringement and publicly-displayed artworks

Section 31 of the Act says copyright in a work is not infringed by its incidental inclusion in a photo, sound recording, film or a broadcast. So there is no infringement if a TV news report incidentally shows, in the background, a work of art, or its sound track of coverage of a wider event incidentally includes a band playing, although deliberately including music would need to be covered by another defence or exception, for example, fair dealing.

Innocent infringement

If an infringer did not know and had no reason to believe the copied work was subject to copyright, for example he/she genuinely believed the copyright had run out, the copyright owner would be entitled to an account of profits but not to damages.

p. 354, Legal remedies for infringement of copyright, explains what 'account of profits' means.

Acquiescence

A copyright holder who encourages or allows another to make use of a work without complaining may destroy any claim for infringement.

▌ 'Open content' licences

Some creators – including some who post photographs on social media sites such as Flickr – give a general, 'open content' licence for people to copy and distribute their work free of charge, provided that attribution to the creator is included and specified conditions are honoured. The licence may be in the Creative Commons format. One condition may be that the use of the work is not commercial, which would exclude use in journalism for which consumers pay. A different licence would have to be agreed with the copyright owner to permit such journalistic use, unless a defence applied.

see Useful Websites at the end of this chapter for Creative Commons site

▌ Moral rights for creators

The 1988 Act, to comply with an international convention, gives 'moral rights' to authors (creators) of some categories of copyright work, including literary and artistic work – for example, a photo – and to the director of a film. He/she can assert the right to be identified when his/her work is published, and has the right not to have it subjected to 'derogatory' (for example, distortive) treatment. A person has a moral right not to have a work falsely attributed to him/her. This law is in sections 77 to 84 of the Act. The rights to be identified and not to have the work subject to derogatory treatment do not apply to work created in the course of employment, or for reporting current events, or to other types of content in a newspaper, magazine or periodical. But a freelance with sufficient clout can insist, as a term of the copyright licence, on being identified by a media publisher as the work's author.

▌ 'Passing off' and trade marks

Other civil law provides remedies against someone who, to gain profit, falsely 'passes off' his/her products or services as being retailed by a more prestigious organisation. A celebrity could use this to stop his/her name or image being falsely used to endorse a product. The system of registration of trademarks gives similar protection in the retail of goods and services.

➡ Recap of major points

- Copyright law controls who can commercially exploit literary, musical, dramatic and artistic works, including journalism articles and photos, as well as the exploitation of sound recordings, film, broadcast, and typographical arrangements.
- There is no copyright in news in itself, only in the form in which it is expressed.

- Defences of fair dealing are available for publication of copyrighted work, if the copying is not excessive and if the publisher honours requirement for attribution to the creator(s).

- But photographs are excluded from the fair dealing defence which covers reporting news and current events.

- A copyright owner whose rights are infringed can seek an injunction and/or damages.

((•)) Useful Websites

www.ipo.gov.uk/types/copy.htm
  Intellectual Property Office, a Government agency – see its guides to copyright and trade marks

www.londonfreelance.org/advice.html
  London freelance branch of the National Union of Journalists – advice on copyright

www.justice.gov.uk/courts/rcj-rolls-building/intellectual-property-enterprise-court
  The Intellectual Property Enterprise Court

www.epuk.org/
  The Editorial Photographers group, whose site features copyright issues

www.epuk.org/News/1039/infringer-who-originally-offered-150-forced-to-pay-20000-in-settlement
  Editorial Photographers article on the *Sheldon* case

http://creativecommons.org/licenses/
  Guide to Creative Commons copyright licences

Part 5

Information and expression

Freedom of Information Act 2000

Chapter summary

The Freedom of Information (FoI) Act 2000, which came into effect in 2005, created the UK's first general right of access to information held by government departments and public authorities. Use of the Act has produced many exclusive stories, some about the highest reaches of government. But the Act is bedevilled by bureaucratic delay and wide-ranging exemptions, and a requestor must be prepared to argue that the 'public interest' justifies disclosure of information. This chapter deals with FoI law as it applies in England, Wales and Northern Ireland, and information access rights in the Environmental Information Regulations.

▶ Introduction to the Act

The Freedom of Information Act gives people the right to require 'public authorities' to disclose information they would not otherwise publish. Authorities must supply information without charging for finding and collating it, subject to cost limits.

The Parliamentary expenses scandal in spring 2009 highlighted the Act's shortcomings. FoI requests by campaigner and journalist Heather Brooke forced House of Commons officials to disclose details of what some MPs were claiming in expenses for their second homes. But official disclosures were anodyne in comparison with the truth, which emerged when virtually every detail about MPs' expenses was leaked to the Telegraph Media Group – and showed that MPs 'flipped' their main and second homes to maximise expenses, claimed for items such as moat-clearing and duck houses, could make claims without producing receipts and had reclaimed the cost of things ranging from dog biscuits to bath plugs. None of that emerged in the official disclosures.

see p. 366, Cost limits

In July 2010 Information Commissioner Christopher Graham, who oversees the Act's workings, said it was 'completely unacceptable' that House of Commons authorities had delayed releasing embarrassing details about MPs' unpaid bar and restaurant bills until after the general election. The authorities took more than seven months to disclose the food and drink tabs of 74 MPs. The debts should have been disclosed within 20 working days of the Press Association's request in September 2009 but were kept secret until 19 May 2010, after the election, by which time many of the MPs had quit politics or lost their seats.

▶ Difficulties with FoI obligations

The Act has brought many newsworthy disclosures by national, regional and local journalists.

Although public bodies are helpful when responding to FoI requests, many authorities delay answering requests and are extremely slow when considering the 'public interest test' (discussed later in the chapter). In October 2010, the Information Commissioner put more than 30 public bodies, including the Cabinet Office, Home Office, Ministry of Defence, Metropolitan Police, British Transport Police, Department for Work and Pensions, Transport for London and Scotland Office on a list of organisations to be monitored for three months as they were taking too long to respond to FoI requests. In April 2011 he said the Cabinet Office – the government department in charge of openness – was among the worst offenders for delays in meeting FoI requests, and in August 2013 he placed the Home Office – one of the government's largest departments – on watch by the data watchdog over its poor record in responding to information requests.

Government departments and other public bodies often seek to use the Act's exemptions to thwart requests for information, and numerous requestors win appeals to the Information Commissioner and the First-tier Tribunal (Information Rights). Journalists using the Act need to be systematic and persistent. But despite the drawbacks it is a worthwhile tool for investigative journalism.

▶ What is a 'public authority' under the Act?

The Act covers about 100,000 major and minor bodies in the public sector, including:

- national government departments and ministries such as the Home Office, Foreign Office and Prime Minister's Office;
- the House of Commons, the House of Lords, the national assemblies of Northern Ireland and Wales;
- the armed forces;

- local government – metropolitan, city, county, district, and parish councils, transport executives, waste disposal agencies, police forces, fire services;
- national park authorities;
- universities, colleges, and schools in the state sector;
- the National Health Service, including primary care trusts, hospital trusts, health authorities, doctors' and dentists' practices;
- various advisory councils, and regulatory bodies with statutory powers such as Ofcom and the General Medical Council.

It does not define 'public authority', but lists, in Schedule 1, the bodies and organisations it covers. More have been added by statutory instruments.

Institutions and agencies not covered by the Act

The security and intelligence agencies – MI5, MI6 and GCHQ – are exempt, and so not required to respond to FoI requests. Courts and tribunals are not covered, though some information gathered or created in their functions will be available if a request is made to the government department holding it, such as the Ministry of Justice.

The following are not public authorities under the Act: housing associations; charities; private prisons; harbour authorities; and MPs and Peers, as individuals.

The Royal Family never came under the Act. But an amendment introduced in Section 46(1) and Schedule 7 of the Constitutional Reform and Governance Act 2010, which came into force in January 2011, gives the Queen, the Prince of Wales and Prince William absolute exemption from any application for information. This ends the situation under which FoI campaigners, requestors and the press could ask the government and other public bodies to release details about them on the grounds that there was a legitimate public interest in disclosure. Other members of the Royal Family, such as the Duke of Edinburgh and Prince Harry, remain subject to a qualified exemption – public bodies holding information relating to them should release it if there is a public interest in disclosure.

Since the coalition government took power in 2010 it has made many more bodies, including the Universities and Colleges Admissions Service (UCAS), the Association of Chief Police Officers (ACPO), the Financial Ombudsman Service (FOS) and companies entirely owned by local authorities subject to the Act. More are expected to follow.

check www. mcnaes. com for updates

▶ How the Act works

A public authority should respond to a request for information within 20 working days, either supplying the information or explaining that it cannot do so because:

- it does not hold it – in most circumstances this must be made clear;
- providing it would exceed the cost limits for free provision – see later in the chapter;
- it is exempt from disclosure.

see p. 368,
Exemptions

In the case of some exempt categories, eg information held in confidence or concerning national security, an authority does not have to say what it holds if denying or confirming the information's existence would undermine the purpose of the exemption.

Journalists should check an authority's website, if it has one, for information before making an FoI request, as it might already publish the material there. The Act says each authority must have a 'publication scheme'. If the information sought is not listed there, the journalists should ask the official who coordinates the authority's FoI matters about the types of information it holds. Section 16 of the Act says authorities must offer 'advice and assistance', including on how to frame requests to stay within the cost limits for free information – although sometimes this is not done, as this chapter explains.

A requestor's reason for wanting information plays no part in an authority's decision on providing it (unless a request is 'vexatious' – for example, from someone who repeatedly seeks the same or similar information).

An authority which has to apply the 'public interest test' (see later) to consider if information is exempt may take more than 20 working days to give its final response. It must consider, even if some information specified in a request is deemed exempt from disclosure, if the request can be met in part by releasing non-exempt information.

What is information?

Section 84 of the Act defines information as 'information recorded in any form'. An authority is not required to gather information it does not already have. The right under the Act is for *information* to be communicated to the requestor, not necessarily in the form of particular documents, though requests often refer to particular documents, which are supplied. 'Document' includes electronic documents (*Dominic Kennedy v Information Commissioner and Charity Commission* [2010] EWHC 475 (Admin); [2010] 1 WLR 1489).

see Useful
Websites
at the end
of this
chapter

The Protection of Freedoms Act 2012, by amending the 2000 Act, gave requestors greater rights to have datasets held by public authorities sent to them in electronic, re-usable form, if available under the 2000 Act.

Cost limits

A government department required to disclose requested information must do so free if it costs no more than £600. All other public authorities covered by the Act must provide such information free if doing so costs no more than £450. Cost is estimated by assessing – at £25 an hour – the staff time reasonably needed to determine whether a body holds the information, to find and retrieve it, and, if necessary, extract it from a document. If, after a *bona fide* estimating process, the cost limit is exceeded, the authority is not obliged to supply any information requested, but may *choose* to supply it without charge, or at a price which reflects the cost of providing it, if the requestor is willing to pay. An authority which can comply with part, but not all, of a request within the cost limits has a duty under section 16 to offer a requestor advice to see if he/she wishes to re-define or limit the request. If the information is to be provided on paper, the requestor can be charged a reasonable price for photocopying. Information can often be sent by e-mail.

Journalists should make requests as specific as possible. A requestor may get round a cost limit by breaking a 'large' request into several smaller ones, sent serially. But authorities may 'aggregate' the cost of two or more requests made within 60 days by the same person for the same or similar types of information – that is, treat them as being part of a single request, and refuse them, if in total they breach the cost limit for one request. Authorities should not use aggregation powers to frustrate a sequence of requests each of which, on the basis of information sent previously, digs further into a topic by asking for further, different information.

Advice and assistance

Section 16 requires a public body to give prospective or actual requestors 'advice and assistance, so far as it would be reasonable to expect the authority to do so'.

- It should, if asked, tell a requestor *before* he makes a request what information of the type sought might be available, and help frame a request.
- It should give guidance to avoid a request breaching the cost limit for providing information free.

Some staff in public bodies, particularly national government departments, are not always helpful. But the Information Tribunal has made clear that it expects the Information Commissioner, when adjudicating an appeal against a refusal to supply information, to consider the extent to which a body met its obligations under section 16, so a requestor should if necessary remind the body, in writing, of these obligations. The Act says an authority which, in relation to the duty to advise and assist, conforms to the Code of Practice issued by the Ministry of Justice is to be taken as complying with that duty.

Paragraph 8 of the Code says 'authorities should, so far as is reasonably practicable, provide assistance to the applicant to enable him or her to describe more clearly the information requested'. The Information Tribunal has said of the duty to help: 'An applicant does not have to ask for it…nothing [in the Act] restricts the duty to advise and assist only to those cases when some form of request has [already] been made…the duty must include at least one to advise and assist an applicant with regard to the formulation of an appropriate request' (Appeal number EA/2006/0046).

Section 1(3) allows a body which 'reasonably requires' further detail to identify and locate information to clarify this with the requestor, and, if such further detail is not provided, not to comply with the request. The Information Commissioner has made clear that if a public authority tells a requestor that the information is

((•))

see Useful
Websites
at the end
of this
chapter
for this
code

already in the public domain it should, to comply with section 16, indicate where it can be found.

Exemptions

Bodies may refuse to supply information on various grounds – exemptions. The Information Commissioner's Office website has guidance on these.

see Useful Websites at the end of this chapter for ICO guidance

Absolute exemptions

Some exemptions are 'absolute' – the authority does not have to give a reason for refusing disclosure beyond stating that the exemption applies because of the nature of the information. Absolute exemptions include:

Section 21 – information reasonably accessible by other means.

Section 23 – information supplied to the public authority by or relating to bodies dealing with security matters eg supplied by MI5, MI6 and GCHQ.

Section 32 – court records This exemption covers documents held by a public authority because it is a litigant or an interested party in a court case – for example, copies of material filed with a court for the purposes of proceedings.

ch. 28 explains data protection law

Section 40 – personal information The Act does not override data protection law. A public body may decide that an FoI request encompasses exempt 'personal data'. But it should consider whether deleting references which could identify an individual could allow disclosure of non-exempt information.

The Commissioner has made clear that when considering personal data issues, authorities should distinguish between 'professional personal information' such as staff job descriptions and details of their responsibilities and 'private personal information' such as sickness records.

Section 41 – information provided to the authority in confidence by another party This does not cover information which the public body has generated itself, so does not cover any contract the authority has entered into.

But the Information Tribunal, as it was, has said that the section 40 or 41 exemptions are not as absolute as they first appear, because a body should apply a public interest test under data protection law and/or the law of confidence when deciding on disclosure.

Section 44 – information the disclosure of which is forbidden by other law For example, the Information Tribunal upheld a ruling that the Independent Police Complaints Commission could not, because of a provision in the Police Act 1996, disclose under the FoI Act copies of files relating to complaints against the police.

Qualified exemptions

The other exemptions are 'qualified' – if a public body decides against supplying information in these categories it must give reasons, showing how it has applied the public interest test. The Act says information may be withheld only if the public interest in withholding it is greater than the public interest in disclosure.

It does not define 'the public interest'. But in guidance in 2013 the Information Commissioner said public interest factors which should encourage public authorities to disclose information included:

- general arguments in favour of promoting transparency, accountability and participation;
- disclosure might enhance the quality of discussions and decision making generally;
- the balance might be tipped in favour of disclosure by financial issues – if the information requested involved a large amount of public money, this might favour disclosure;
- the specific circumstances of the case and the content of the information requested in relation to those circumstances;
- the age of the information;
- the timing of a request, in respect of information relating to an investigation, may be relevant;
- the impact of disclosure upon individuals and/or the wider public.

((•))

see Useful
Websites
at the end
of this
chapter
for this
ICO
guidance

The Campaign for Freedom of Information has stressed the importance of applicants pursuing requests all the way to the First-tier Tribunal (Information Rights) if necessary, and not accepting a public authority's initial refusal. Requestors should not assume that the Information Commissioner will automatically recognise the public interest case for disclosing information, and should raise it in appeal correspondence. But appeals take time, even when authorities have clearly misapplied absolute or qualified exemptions, as the Information Commissioner's office is overworked and under-resourced.

Qualified exemptions include:

Section 24 – information which if disclosed is likely to prejudice national security This concerns information other than that already absolutely exempt under section 23.

Section 27 – information which if disclosed is likely to prejudice international relations

Section 31 – information held by an authority for law enforcement functions This is exempt if its disclosure would, or would be likely to, prejudice the prevention or detection of crime, the apprehension and prosecution of offenders, or the administration of justice. So details of when a speed camera at a particular site is active do not have to be disclosed as this would compromise the camera's effect. But more general information, such as how many drivers a particular camera caught speeding on a particular day could be published.

Section 35 – information relating to formulation or development of government policy The First-tier Tribunal (Information Rights) – formerly the Information Tribunal – has been robust in disapproving of some attempts to use this exemption, noting that there is a public interest in involuntary disclosure of information under the Act as it acts as a check on information disclosed voluntarily. The older the information, the less sensitive it is as an indication of an authority's policy options.

Section 36 – information the disclosure of which is likely to prejudice effective conduct of public affairs This exemption is controversial as it is so vague. Parliament intended it to cover material which did not fall into other categories but which, if disclosed, would damage a public body's ability to carry out its duties. Heather Brooke says a public authority relying on it 'is desperate and grasping at straws'.

Section 43 – commercial interests This covers trade secrets and information which, if disclosed, 'would, or would be likely to, prejudice the commercial interest of any person (including the public authority holding it)'.

👁 Case study

In *John Connor Press Associates v Information Commissioner* (EA/2005/0005), the Information Tribunal held that the National Maritime Museum should have disclosed financial information concerning its purchase of a set of artworks. The Museum had argued that when it received the freelance news agency's FoI request it was negotiating with another artist about another project, and its ability to ensure value for public money would have been prejudiced had financial details about the previous deal been released. The Tribunal held that no real and significant risk of such prejudice existed, partly because the deal under negotiation – which included payment for 'performance art' – differed in scope from the museum's previous deal for artworks.

Delays in the public interest test

The Act does not set public authorities a deadline for completing the 'public interest test' over an FoI request – considering it may mean the 20-day period for responding to requests instead becomes months. But a public body must tell a requestor within the 20-day limit that a qualified exemption might apply.

If the information is not supplied

If an authority takes no decision on supplying the information within the 20-day limit, or refuses to supply it because of the cost limit or an exemption, a requestor can ask for an 'internal review' of the decision, which should be conducted by an official other than the one involved in the refusal. There is no timescale for completing this review. The Information Commissioner's Office has said 20 working days (from the time a request for a review is received) is a reasonable time for a review, and that in no case should the time exceed 40 working days. A requestor dissatisfied with the result of a review can appeal to the Information Commissioner.

The Information Commissioner and the First-tier Tribunal (Information Rights)

The Freedom of Information Act is enforced by the Information Commissioner, who also oversees the Data Protection Act 1998. The current Commissioner is Christopher Graham.

The Commissioner can order a body to release information if he disagrees with a refusal to disclose it. He can question an authority's claim not to hold requested information and its estimate that disclosure would exceed the cost limit for free provision.

If a requestor claims an authority has not responded within the 20-day limit, the Commissioner can, under section 52, serve it with an enforcement notice requiring compliance with the Act. As an ultimate sanction, he can ask the High Court to punish an authority's failure to comply with the notice as contempt of court. Section 48 gives him the power to issue a 'good practice recommendation' specifying the steps an authority should take to improve compliance. FoI campaigners have criticised the Commissioner for not using his powers enough.

Requestors and public authorities dissatisfied with the Information Commissioner's decision can appeal to the First-tier Tribunal (Information Rights). Appeals should be made within 28 days of receipt of the Commissioner's decision. The Tribunal, part of the First-tier Tribunal in the administrative justice system – see ch. 17 – publishes its decisions online.

((•))

see Useful Websites at the end of this chapter for the Tribunal's site

Ministers' power of veto

Cabinet Ministers can veto notices issued by the Commissioner requiring government departments to disclose requested information. In July 2013, the High Court upheld the Attorney General's decision to block public disclosure of letters the Prince of Wales wrote to government ministers. The Lord Chief Justice, Lord Judge, sitting with Lord Justice Davis and Mr Justice Globe, refused to overturn the veto Mr Grieve issued in October 2012 banning the release of the correspondence, saying that the use of the veto was lawful, and that Mr Grieve had reasonable grounds for deciding it was 'an exceptional case meriting use of the ministerial veto to prevent disclosure and to safeguard the public interest'.

Mr Grieve had said his decision was based on his view that the correspondence was undertaken as part of the Prince's 'preparation for becoming king', and

see this book's Late News for update on this case

making it public could potentially damage the principle of the heir to the throne being politically neutral, and so undermine his ability to fulfil his duties when king.

▌ The FoI Act's coverage of media organisations

The BBC, Channel 4 and S4C – public service broadcasters – were made subject to the Act, but in a limited way as disclosure provisions only apply to information they hold 'for purposes other than those of journalism, art or literature'. It does not require these broadcasters to comply with:

(1) requests attempting to reveal journalists' confidential sources;

(2) requests by rival news organisations, or by the subjects of journalistic investigations (that is, 'data subjects'), aimed at securing, before or after broadcast, material gathered in a journalistic investigation, including any footage/audio not broadcast.

chs. 2 and 3 explain the roles of Ipso and Ofcom

The Supreme Court has ruled that that if information was held for journalistic purposes, it was exempt from disclosure even if it was also held for other purposes (*Sugar (Deceased) (Represented by Fiona Paveley) v BBC and another* [2012] UKSC 4; [2012] 1 WLR 439; [2012] 2 All ER 509). This decision marked the end of the BBC's battle over the Balen Report, an internal document which reviewed, and made recommendations about its coverage of the Middle East, including best practice on matters such as impartiality.

Ofcom is subject to the Act, but Ipso, which is not a public authority, is not.

▌ Environmental information

The Environmental Information Regulations (EIR), the latest version of which came into force in 2005 (SI 2004/3391), require public authorities to provide information about environmental matters. They implement a European Union directive and give, in the environmental field, the public – and journalists – more powerful rights of access to information than those in the FoI Act. A public authority receiving a request for information within the scope of the EIR should automatically deal with it under the EIR rather than under the Act (ideally the request should refer to the EIR). For guidance on using the EIR, see Useful Websites at the end of this chapter.

ch. 1 explains EU directives

Environmental information covers air, water, land, natural sites and living organisms – including GM crops – and discharges as well as noise and radiation. The EIR cover more bodies than the FoI Act, with fewer exemptions. For example, information about emissions cannot be withheld because of commercial confidentiality.

All bodies subject to the FoI Act are also subject to the EIR and the same 20-day deadline applies to requests for information. Privatised water and sewerage companies in England and Wales are not subject to either the Act or the EIR, although they are in Scotland.

The EIR require that public authorities must assist those requesting information.

EIR requests can be turned down on grounds of national security. But all refusals are subject to a public interest test and requests can be refused only if the public interest in non-disclosure far outweighs the public interest in disclosure. A 'reasonable' fee can be charged for EIR requests.

The EIR, which are enforced by the Information Commissioner, can be used, for example, to obtain reports of hygiene inspections at factories and restaurants as they cover information on 'the state of human health and safety, including the contamination of the food chain'.

⊙ Case study

The Times used the Scottish EIR to by-pass the exemption in the FoI Act to force local authorities north of the border to disclose details of lobbying by the Prince of Wales. The Scottish Information Commissioner held (Decision 039/2011: *Mr Dominic Kennedy of The Times and the Scottish Ministers*) that the newspaper had more right to the information than the Prince had to keep it quiet. The newspaper pointed out that the EIR, which were imposed by Brussels, had no opt-outs or exemptions for royalty.

▶ Legal issues in using FoI disclosures in stories

Publication of material disclosed under the FoI Act or the EIR brings no special protection against an action for defamation. The FoI Act and EIR do not confer statutory qualified privilege on such reports. Such reports may be protected by other defences, such as justification.

chs. 21 and 22 explain defamation defences

Material disclosed under either the Act or the EIR will be protected by copyright, which must be respected. If you have any doubts about copyright, consult the public authority about the status of information. In some cases copyright may be waived or information licensed for re-use. Copyright protects photographs, maps and diagrams, but does not protect facts as such, only the way in which they are recorded. Thus, a journalist using information from material supplied under FoI and putting it into a news story does not have to fear that factual revelations will raise copyright issues. Also, the **fair dealing** defence applies to citing some text verbatim.

ch. 29 explains copyright law

→glossary

➡ Recap of major points

- The Freedom of Information Act gives a general right of access to information held by public authorities including government departments and local authorities.

- But there are wide-ranging exemptions, and plenty of potential for delays in responding.

- The Act obliges public authorities to offer requestors advice to enable them to word their requests in such a way that they are more likely to succeed.

- The Information Commissioner hears appeals against a body's refusal to supply information. The First-tier Tribunal (Information Rights) can hear appeals against the Commissioner's decisions.

- The Environmental Information Regulations provide powerful rights of access to information in fields they cover.

((•)) Useful Websites

www.informationcommissioner.gov.uk/
  Information Commissioner

http://ico.org.uk/for_the_public/official_information
  Information Commissioner's Guidance on advice and assistance for requestors

www.ico.org.uk/~/media/documents/library/Freedom_of_Information/Detailed_special-ist_guides/the_public_interest_test.ashx
  Information Commissioner's Guidance on the public interest test

http://foia.blogspot.com/
  The Campaign's UK Freedom of Information Blog

http://heatherbrooke.org/category/freedom-of-information/
  Heather Brooke's articles on FOI

www.holdthefrontpage.co.uk/day/FoI/FoIindex.shtml
  Holdthefrontpage stories on journalists using the FoI Act

www.justice.gov.uk/information-access-rights/foi-guidance-for-practitioners/code-of-practice
  Code of Practice for public authorities on FoI requests

www.justice.gov.uk/downloads/information-access-rights/foi/code-of-practice-datasets.pdf
  Code of Practice on release of datasets

www.opsi.gov.uk/Acts/acts2000/ukpga_20000036_en_1/
  The Freedom of Information Act

www.ico.org.uk/news/blog/2013/freedom-of-information-the-next-generation
  ICO guidance on datasets

www.ico.gov.uk/what_we_cover/environmental_information_regulation/guidance.aspx/
  ICO guidance on Environmental Information Regulations

http://Folman.com
  Blog written by an FOI practitioner, and with a useful guide on making FOI requests

Other information rights and access to meetings

Chapter summary

The public and journalists have rights to information under various laws, most notably as regards the workings of local government. These rights can be used to get policy documents from public bodies, and ensure journalists can report important meetings. For some types of material the laws are better than the Freedom of Information Act (see previous chapter), as they offer quicker rights to obtain copies of or inspect documents.

▌ Local government

Local government is a major source of stories and should be subjected to rigorous scrutiny by journalists.

Authorities fall into two categories. Principal authorities include County Councils, District Councils, London boroughs, the London Assembly and fire authorities. The others – Parish Councils and Community Councils – are not principal authorities.

Access to information from principal authorities was governed by the Public Bodies (Admission to Meetings) Act 1960, the Local Government Act 1972 and the Local Government (Access to Information) Act 1985. The Local Government Act 2000, which has since been amended by the Localism Act 2011, reformed the way authorities are run, introducing new models of 'cabinet style' government, of which two survive – a leader (elected by council members) and cabinet, and a directly elected Mayor and cabinet.

see also p. 385, Police and Crime Commissioners

▍ The Local Government Act 2000

Regulations covering access to information under the 2000 Act are contained in a Statutory Instrument and apply to unitary authorities, London borough councils, county councils and district councils in England operating executive arrangements under the Act.

The full texts of the regulations – should any journalist need to cite part of them to unhelpful officials – is at www.legislation.gov.uk/uksi.

Some regulations are in the Local Government (Access to Information) (Variation) Order 2006 (SI 2006/88), and the Local Government (Access to Information) (Variation) (Wales) Order 2007 (SI 2007/969 (W86)), which was produced when the Welsh Assembly took responsibility for local government in the principality. The main regulations are now in the Local Authorities (Executive Arrangements) (Meetings and Access to Information) (England) Regulations (SI 2012/2089), which were intended to achieve greater transparency and ensure that journalists and others reporting on authorities may also do so by blogging and tweeting live from meetings. But many authorities still refuse to allow journalists and members of the public to film meetings for broadcast over the internet. The regulations define 'newspaper' as including news agencies; any organisation systematically engaged in collecting news for sound or television broadcasts; and any organisation which collects news for use in electronic or any other format to provide news to the public by means of the internet.

see p. 378 on new regulations pending

When bodies must meet in public

Meetings of decision-making bodies – local authority executives and their committees – must be open to the public (Regulation 3). Previously, authorities only had to meet in public when making 'key decisions'.

But the public may be excluded if it is likely that:

- confidential information would be disclosed in breach of the obligation of confidence;
- the decision-making body concerned passes a resolution to exclude the public during an item in which disclosure of exempt information is likely – the resolution must describe the exempt information concerned; or
- it is necessary to maintain orderly conduct or prevent misbehaviour at a meeting.

The public may only be excluded under the first two for the part or parts of the meeting when confidential or exempt information is likely to be disclosed.

Confidential information

'Confidential information' is information provided to the local authority by a government department upon terms (however expressed) forbidding its disclosure to the public, or information the disclosure of which to the public is prohibited by or under any enactment or by the order of a court.

Exempt information

Exempt information in England is information relating to:

(1) an employee, job applicant or office holder of the council, or an employee, applicant or official of the magistrates courts or probationary committee;

(2) a particular council tenant or applicant for council services or grants;

(3) the care, adoption or fostering of a child;

(4) a particular person's financial or business affairs;

(5) the supply of goods or services to or the acquisition of property by the council, if disclosing the information would place a particular person in a more favourable bargaining position or otherwise prejudice negotiations;

(6) labour relations matters between the council and its employees, if and so long as disclosing it would prejudice negotiations or discussions;

(7) instructions to and advice from counsel;

(8) the investigation and prosecution of offenders, if disclosing the information would enable the wrongdoer to evade notice being served on him.

Any part of an agenda, report or other document which contains exempt information does not have to be made available for inspection.

Exempt information in Wales is similar, but less wide-ranging.

The categories of exempt information are wider than the categories of information which an authority is not obliged to disclose under the Freedom of Information Act – so exempt material might be obtained through an FoI request.

ch. 30 explains the FOI Act

Notification of private meetings

A decision-making body planning to meet in private must give at least 28 days' clear notice of its intention by making a notification, which explains the reasons, available at its offices and publishing it on its website (Regulation 5).

It must publish a further notice about the meeting at least five clear days before it takes place, and a statement of the reasons for holding it private; details of any representations it has received about why the meeting should be open to the public; and a statement of its response to those representations.

A decision-making body which wishes to hold a meeting so quickly that it cannot comply with these time limits must obtain consent to do so from the chair or deputy chair of a relevant scrutiny committee or, in their absence, the authority's chair or deputy chair.

Notice of public meetings

A decision-making body must display a notice giving the time and place of a public meeting at its offices, and publish it on its website, at least five clear days before the meeting or, if the meeting is convened at shorter notice, at the time it is convened (Regulation 6).

Items of business may only be considered at a public meeting when a copy of the agenda or part of the agenda including them has been available for inspection by the public for at least five clear days beforehand or, if the meeting is convened at shorter notice, from the time it was convened.

 The Local Audit and Accountability Act, granted Royal Assent in 2014, enables new regulations to be made to ensure that people can film council meetings, and tweet and blog from them. See www.mcnaes. com for updates..

Access to agendas and reports for public meetings

A copy of the agenda and every report for a meeting must be available for public inspection at the authority's office and on its website (Regulation 7). Copies of reports do not have to include material relating only to matters to be dealt with in private.

Any document which has to be available for inspection by the public must be available for at least five clear days before the meeting, except when the meeting is convened at shorter notice, in which case they must be available for inspection when the meeting is convened.

If an item which would be available for public inspection is added to an agenda, copies of the revised agenda and any report relating to the item must be available for public inspection when it is added. But no documents have to be available for public inspection until a copy is available to members of the decision-making body concerned.

If all or part of a report for a public meeting is not available for public inspection, it must be marked 'not for publication', and to say that it contains confidential information, or contains exempt information, which must be described.

A reasonable number of copies of the agenda and reports must be available for the public attending the meeting.

Journalists and members of the public who ask must, on paying for postage, copying or other necessary charge for transmission, be supplied with:

- a copy of the agenda and each report for a public meeting;
- the further statements or details necessary to indicate the nature of the items in the agenda; and
- if the proper officer thinks fit, in the case of an item, a copy of any other document supplied to the executive's members in connection with it.

Regulation 20 says this does not authorise the disclosure of confidential information in breach of the obligation of confidence, or of anything likely to contain exempt information or the advice of a political adviser or assistant.

Key decisions

Special rules apply when a 'key decision' is to be made – this is covered by Regulations 9 and 10. A key decision is one which is likely:

- to result in the authority incurring spending or making savings which are significant having regard to its budget for the relevant service or function; or
- to be significant in terms of its effects on communities living or working in an area comprising two or more wards or electoral divisions.

Publicity in connection with key decisions

At least 28 days before a key decision is made, a local authority must publish, at its office and on its website, a document giving details about it. Regulation 10 says this must specify:

- that a key decision is to be made;
- the matter to be decided;
- if the decision maker is an individual, his/her name, and title, if any, and, if the decision maker is a decision-making body, its name and a list of its members;
- the date on which or period within which the decision is to be made;
- a list of the documents submitted to the decision maker for consideration in relation to it;
- the address from which copies of or extracts from any document listed is available;
- that other documents relevant to those matters may be submitted to the decision maker; and
- the procedure for requesting details of those documents (if any) as they become available.

If the public may be excluded from the meeting at which the matter is to be discussed, or documents relating to the decision do not have to be disclosed to the public, the published notification must contain particulars of the matter but cannot contain any confidential, exempt information or details of advice from a political adviser or assistant.

If the required notification period for a meeting to make a key decision is impractical, the decision may only be made five clear days after various authority members have been notified of the fact in writing, and a copy of that notification has been made available for public inspection and published on the authority's website.

As soon as reasonably practicable after this, the officer concerned must set out the reasons why compliance with Regulation 9 is impracticable in a notice made available at the authority's offices and on its website.

Similar requirements apply in cases of special urgency – those when the date by which a key decision must be made makes compliance with Regulation 10 impracticable.

Documents that must be made available after a meeting

Regulation 12 requires a written statement to be produced 'as soon as reasonably practicable' after a public or private meeting at which an executive decision is made. It must include:

(1) a record of the decision;

(2) a record of the reasons for the decision;

(3) details of any alternative options considered and rejected at the meeting;

(4) a record of any conflict of interest and, in that case, a note of any dispensation granted by the authority's standards committee.

An executive decision made by an individual or a key decision made by an officer must be recorded similarly.

The record must be made available at the council office for public inspection as soon as 'reasonably practicable', with any report considered at the meeting or by the individual member or officer making the decision.

A media organisation which requests copies of any of the documents available for public inspection must be supplied with them on payment of postage, copying 'or other necessary charge for transmission' (Regulation 14).

▮ Register of interests

The Localism Act 2011 places a duty on councillors to enter certain personal interests on a publicly available register. Failure to disclose interests is a criminal offence punishable by a fine of up to £5,000 and possible disqualification from membership of the authority for up to five years.

▮ Obstruction is an offence

A person who has custody of a document which must be available for public inspection who intentionally obstructs any person exercising a right to inspect or make a copy of it, or refuses to supply a copy of it, commits an offence punishable by a fine of up to £200 under section 100H(4) of the Local Government Act 1972 (as inserted by the Local Government (Access to Information) Act 1985 section 1), and under Regulation 22 of the Local Authorities (Executive Arrangements) (Meetings and Access to Information) (England) Regulations.

Copyright and defamation

Regulation 21(3) and (4) say that any member of the public may reproduce any document supplied to him or her, or made available for public inspection under the regulations, or provide commentary on it, in any publicly available medium. This will not infringe copyright in the document as long as the local authority is the copyright holder.

ch. 29 explains copyright

But the provision does not authorise infringement of anyone else's copyright.

On defamation, it extends the protection of qualified privilege to the publication of any defamatory matter contained in any document required by the Regulations to be open to inspection by the public and supplied to or available for inspection by members of the public; or supplied for a newspaper's benefit.

Defamation and council meetings

If a local authority holds a meeting in private under any of the legislation referred to, a defamatory media report of the discussion in such meetings, and of documents considered in them, if leaked unofficially to the media, would not be protected by qualified privilege under Schedule 1 of the Defamation Act 1996, now amended by section 7 of the Defamation Act 2013.

Media coverage of an official statement issued to journalists about a meeting held in private will be privileged under the 1996 Act if the defence's requirements are met.

Media coverage of the public proceedings of local authorities, whether in full council, committees or sub-committees, and of minutes, agendas, reports or other documents officially made available to journalists or the public, will also be privileged.

 Ch. 21, pp. 267–272, Qualified privilege, explains the requirements of this defence.

The Local Government (Access to Information) Act 1985

The Local Government (Access to Information) Act (LG(AI)A) 1985 predates the introduction of Cabinet-style councils. It amends the 1975 Act to insert these requirements.

When meetings must be in public

All meetings of principal authorities, their committees and sub-committees must be open to the public unless dealing with confidential or exempt information. The position about working parties and advisory or study groups, which may in effect act as sub-committees without the name, is unclear.

The Act says principal authorities, their committees and sub-committees must exclude the public when confidential information is likely to be disclosed.

A local authority may, by passing a resolution, exclude the public when disclosure of exempt information is likely. The resolution must state the part of the meeting to which the exclusion applies and describe the category of the exempt information.

While the meeting is open to the public, 'duly accredited representatives' of newspapers or news agencies must, under section 100(6)(c) of the 1975 Act, as inserted by the LG(AI)A 1985, be afforded reasonable facilities for taking their report.

Documents that must be made available

A newspaper or news agency must on request (and on payment of postage or other transmission charge) be supplied with (a) agendas, (b) further particulars necessary to indicate the nature of the items on the agenda, and (c) if the 'proper officer' thinks fit, copies of any other documents supplied to council members, although he/she may exclude from what he/she sends out any report, or part of a report, relating to items not likely to be discussed in public.

Late items, reports and supplementary information can be admitted at the meeting only if the chairperson regards the matter as urgent and specifies the reason for the urgency.

Copies of agendas and of any report for a meeting of a council must be open to public inspection at least five clear working days before the meeting (except for items not likely to be discussed in public). Where a meeting is called at shorter notice they must be open to inspection from the time the meeting is convened.

 See www.mcnaes.com ch. 31 for other rights to inspect council records – for example, planning applications.

Fire authorities

The 1975 Act, as amended by the LG(AI)A 1985, also applies to fire authorities, meetings of joint consultative committees of health and local authorities and to some joint boards.

Parish and community councils

It does not apply to parish, town and community councils. These are covered by the Public Bodies (Admission to Meetings) Act 1960 (PB(AM)A), which says they must admit the public to their meetings and to meetings of committees consisting of all members of the body. It also allows for the public to be excluded for all or part of a meeting 'whenever publicity would be prejudicial to the public interest because of the confidential nature of the business to be transacted or for other special reasons stated in the resolution and arising from the nature of that business or of the proceedings'.

Public notice of the time and place of a meeting must be given by posting it at the offices at least three days before the meeting, or, if the meeting is convened at shorter notice, when it is convened.

On request and on payment of postage, if required, the body must supply to any media organisation a copy of the agenda as supplied to its members, but excluding, if thought fit, items to be discussed when the meeting is not likely to be open to the public.

The PB(AM)A 1960 says that, so far as is practicable, reporters shall be afforded reasonable facilities for taking their report.

Minutes of the proceedings of a parish or community council must, under the Local Government Act 1972, as amended by the LG(AI)A 1985, be open to inspection.

Parish meetings and other public bodies

Rights to admission and to reporting facilities, agendas and telephones, see earlier, under the terms of the PB(AM)A 1960 also apply to:

see p. 385, Health authorities and NHS trusts

(1) parish meetings of rural parishes where there are fewer than 200 electors;

(2) bodies set up under the Water Act 1989 – regional and local flood defence committees, regional rivers advisory committees, salmon and freshwater fisheries advisory committees and customer service committees.

▶ Access to financial accounts

Journalists often miss golden opportunities to find local authority stories by using the Audit Commission Act (ACA) 1998 and the Accounts and Audit Regulations 2003 (SI 2003/533). 'Local authorities' includes fire and civil defence authorities.

The coalition government has announced its intention to abolish the Audit Commission. But the provisions detailed below should be retained in the new legislation, expected to come into force towards the end of 2014.

see www. mcnaes. com for updates

Section 15 of the Act says 'any persons interested' may inspect a local authority's accounts and 'all books, deeds, contracts, bills, vouchers and receipts related thereto', and make copies. Each authority in England and Wales and Northern Ireland must make the accounts and documents available for public inspection for 20 full working days before a date appointed by the auditor, or 15 days in Scotland. A public notice about this right, giving contact details for the officer responsible and the name and address of the external auditor, and the date from which he/she may be contacted by any local taxpayer or elector, must be published in at least one newspaper 14 days before the date on which the accounts and documents become available.

Lawyers differ about whether the phrase 'any persons interested' includes reporters, but if the reporter is also a local elector there is no problem. A journalist's employer who is a ratepayer is an interested party. A party's motive for wishing to see the material is irrelevant – see *R (on the application of HTV) v Bristol City Council* [2004] EWHC 1219 (Admin), [2004] 1 WLR 2717.

Section 8 says auditors must consider whether, in the public interest, they should report on any matter which came to their attention during the audit, which they do by issuing public interest reports covering everything from the mundane to major stories such as how local authorities lost local taxpayers' money when Icelandic banks collapsed in 2008. Under the Local Government Finance (Publicity for Auditors' Reports) Act 1991 a council must make available immediately any report on a matter of particular concern produced by the auditors.

Local authorities cannot use the Data Protection Act to deny access to the accounts or documents, and cannot legally blank out details on grounds in the Act – sections 34 and 35 of that Act make it clear that it does not trump local electors' and taxpayers' statutory rights to view and copy the accounts.

Journalists should deal directly with the officer identified in the public notice (see earlier), who is legally responsible for dealing with requests to view and copy the accounts.

Some journalists ask a local authority (via the press office) to send them photocopies or electronic copies of 'spending on such and such an issue'. This takes them outside the Audit Commission Act system, giving the authority the chance to delay responding until the journalist runs out of time to examine the material himself, or to treat the request as an FoI request and deny access on grounds which do not apply under the Audit Commission Act.

The Act makes it a criminal offence for any officer or councillor to obstruct local taxpayers or electors exercising their rights to view and copy the (non-exempt) material. Council press officers who try to involve themselves in the actual inspection should be warned off.

Personal expenses of councillors

There is no right to examine documents relating to personal expenses incurred by a council's officers.

But the Local Government (Allowances) Regulations 1986 (SI 1986/724) enable electors at any time of the year to demand to see a breakdown of allowances and expenses paid to councillors.

County, District and London Borough councils must, under Regulation 15 of the Local Authorities (Members' Allowances) (England) Regulations 2003 (SI 2003/1021), send the local media information about amounts paid to councillors in the previous financial year and reports on recommendations about the levels of allowances.

▎ Health authorities and NHS Trusts

Admission to meetings of local health authorities and NHS Trusts, and rights to their agendas, are subject to the Public Bodies (Admission to Meetings) Act (PB(AM)A 1960.

Department of Health guidance to these bodies in 1998 (Health Service Circular 1998/207) said the government was 'committed to ending what it sees as excessive secrecy in decision making in public bodies' and that although authorities and trusts could exclude press and public in the public interest under the terms of the PB(AM)A 1960, they were expected to conduct their business in public in as open a manner as possible.

The PB(AM)A 1960 gives the same rights of admission to any committee of a health authority consisting of all members of the authority.

The Health and Social Care Act 2001 gave new powers to overview and scrutinise committees of those local authorities with social services responsibilities (county councils, London borough councils, unitary authorities), and these are subject to similar access to information provisions as other committees covered by LG(AI)A 1985.

But extended exemptions apply – see Schedule 1 to the Health and Social Care Act 2001. These go further than the exemptions in the LG(AI)A 1985 by exempting also information on: (1) a person providing or applying to provide NHS services, (2) an employee of such a person, or (3) information relating to a person's health. Minutes, agendas and reports are open to public inspection for only three years and background papers for only two years.

▎ Police and Crime Commissioners

Police and Crime Commissioners must, under provision in sections 5 and 12 of the Police Reform and Social Responsibility Act 2011, publish a Police and Crime Plan and annual reports. Financial and other information, including a register of interests, must be published, as specified in the Elected Local Policing Bodies (Specified Information) Order 2011 (SI 2011/3050).

Police and crime panels

Much of the law on access to information referred to in this chapter also applies to the police and crime panels in each police area – see the Police and Crime Panels (Application of Local Authority Enactments) Regulations 2012 (SI 2012/2734).

((•))
see Useful
Websites at
the end of
this chap-
ter for the
Order and
Regulations

▎ Magistrates courts committees

The public must be admitted to a meeting of the magistrates courts committee at least once a year. The minutes of every meeting must be open to public inspection at the committee's office. Confidential information can be excluded, but the committee must explain why. Copies must be made available, for a fee.

▶ Quangos

Many day-to-day services to the public which were administered by bodies on which representatives of the public served have become semi-independent agencies with managing bodies staffed by appointees rather than representatives.

The term quango (quasi-autonomous non-governmental organisation) describes non-elected public bodies operating outside the civil service and funded by the taxpayer. Generally, there is no right of access to meetings of quangos, although there is a right to information to most of them under the FoI Act, explained in ch. 30.

➡ Recap of major points

- People have rights to other information from local authorities, such as annual budget figures and agendas, as well as rights to attend meetings.

- In certain circumstances authorities have the right to withhold documents or to deny public access to meetings.

- Laws giving rights to examine accounts can be a very good source of stories, provided the journalist knows where to look.

- There are rights to attend the meetings of health authorities and these bodies are required to publish each year their performance in key areas of health provision.

((•)) Useful Websites

www.communities.gov.uk/
  For guidance on the Local Government Act 2000 and exemptions from rights to access meetings

http://openlylocal.com/
  A project to develop a unified way of accessing local government information

www.orchardnews.com/accounts.htm
  Website run by journalist Richard Orange of Orchard News Bureau, who specialises in local government

www.legislation.gov.uk/uksi/2012/2089/contents/made
  Local Authorities (Executive Arrangements) (Meetings and Access to Information) (England) Regulations 2012

www.communities.gov.uk/documents/localgovernment/pdf/1850773.pdf

Letter from Government Minister urging councils to allow blogging, filming and 'tweeting' in council meetings

www.legislation.gov.uk/uksi/2012/2479/article/1/made

Elected Local Policing Bodies (Specified Information) Order 2011 and amendments

www.gov.uk/government/uploads/system/uploads/attachment_data/file/143836/publishing-information.pdf

Government guidance to Police and Crime Commissioners on publishing information

www.legislation.gov.uk/uksi/2012/2734/made

Police and Crime Panels (Application of Local Authority Enactments) Regulations 2012 and their Explanatory Notes

32

Reporting elections

Chapter summary

The Representation of the People Act 1983 makes it a criminal offence to make or publish false statements about election candidates. There are restrictions on publishing 'exit polls'. Broadcast journalists must maintain impartiality in coverage of elections and referendums.

▎ False statements about candidates

Section 106 of the Representation of the People Act 1983 makes it a criminal offence to:

- make or publish a false statement of fact about the personal character or conduct of an election candidate, if the purpose is to affect how many votes he/she will get.

To constitute such an offence, the falsity must be expressed as if it were a fact, as distinct from a statement which is clearly merely comment or an opinion about the candidate. It is a defence for someone accused of publishing such a false statement to show that he/she had reasonable grounds for believing when the statement was published that it was true, and did at that time believe it was true (even if it turns out to be untrue).

Section 106(5) makes it an offence:

- to publish a false claim that a candidate has withdrawn from the election, if the publisher knows it to be false and published it to promote or procure the election of another candidate.

Breach of section 106 is punishable by a fine of up to £5,000. If the publisher is a company, its directors can be convicted. The law is to deter 'dirty tricks' by those campaigning in elections, or by their supporters, and is not aimed specifically at the media. In 2010 Labour MP Phil Woolas lost his seat when his election was declared void after he was convicted of illegal practices under section 106 by publishing election addresses containing statements of fact about the character and conduct of a Liberal Democrat candidate Robert Elwyn Watkins – involving where he lived, his attitude to Muslim extremists and his election expenses – which he had no reasonable grounds for believing were true and did not believe were true (*Robert Elwn James Watkins v Philip James Woolas* [2010] EWHC 2702 (QB)).

This ban in criminal law on such false statements applies from the time formal notice is given that an election is to take place until the election ends. For local government elections, this period is about five weeks. For national Parliamentary elections, the period begins with the date of the dissolution of Parliament or any earlier time at which Her Majesty's intention to dissolve Parliament is announced.

If the false statement is defamatory, the publisher may – of course – also face a libel action. But the criminal sanction in the 1983 Act enables quicker remedial action, in that a candidate who can prove a **prima facie** case that he/she has been traduced by such a false statement can obtain a court **injunction** preventing its repetition, whereas the legal rule against **prior restraint** means it is harder to get an injunction in a libel action, which could take months to be settled or resolved at trial. The 1983 Act also prohibits such false statements even if they are not defamatory. A journalist who in 1997 published false allegations on the internet that an election candidate was a homosexual was fined £250 under the Act. A statement which inaccurately states that someone is homosexual is not, in itself, defamatory. But in the context of an election, it could cost a candidate votes if, for example, voters with anti-gay religious beliefs decide because of the false statement not to support that candidate.

→ glossary

→ glossary

→ glossary

 see ch. 19, p. 241, Changing standards

▌ Defamation dangers during elections

Election candidates and their supporters may make defamatory allegations about rivals, using, for example, terms such 'racist', 'fascist' and 'liar'.

A media organisation which publishes them may be successfully sued for libel if it has no defence. There is no specific statutory privilege for the media to publish election material produced by candidates, or what they say. But qualified privilege protects fair and accurate reports of public meetings and of press conferences, if all requirements of that defence are met.

 Ch. 19 has definitions of **defamatory statements** and ch. 21 explains **qualified privilege**.

! Remember

Journalists reporting speeches by extremist candidates should remember that such speakers, and reports of their speeches, are subject to the laws against stirring up hatred, including on racial and religious grounds.

 see the www. mcnaes. com chapter on hate crimes

▶ Election advertisements

In election law, only an election candidate or his/her agent may incur any expenses relating to their campaign, including for publication of an advertisement. It is an offence for anyone else to pay for such an advertisement unless the election agent authorise him/her to do so, in writing. This stops well-wishers from putting advertisements in newspapers on behalf of candidates without their express authority.

▶ Broadcasters' duty to be impartial

Section 6 of the Ofcom Broadcasting Code has detailed rules on how broadcast output must be impartial in election and referendum periods. Ofcom has fined several radio stations after presenters or others made partial declarations of support for political candidates or parties. The BBC is not subject to this section but has similar provision in its Editorial Guidelines.

> See also ch. 3 on impartiality, and Useful Websites at the end of this chapter.

👁 Case study

In 2008 Ofcom fined Talksport radio £20,000 for breach of the impartiality requirement, after presenter James Whale directly encouraged listeners to vote for Conservative candidate Boris Johnson in the London mayoral elections and criticised Labour candidate Ken Livingstone (*Ofcom Broadcast Bulletin*, No. 123, 8 December 2008).

Among the rules in section 6 of the Ofcom code are that:

- due weight must be given to the coverage of major parties during the election period, and broadcasters must also consider giving appropriate coverage to other parties and independent candidates with significant views and perspectives (rule 6.2);

- if a candidate takes part in an item about his/her particular constituency, or electoral area, then candidates of each of the major parties must be offered the opportunity to take part (rule 6.9);

- broadcasters must offer the opportunity to take part in constituency or electoral area reports and discussions, to all candidates within the constituency or electoral area representing parties with previous significant electoral support or where there is evidence of significant current support, including any such independent candidate (rule 6.10); and

- any constituency or electoral area report or discussion after the close of nominations must include a list of all candidates standing, giving first names, surnames and the name of the party they represent or, if they are standing independently, the fact that they are an independent candidate. This must be conveyed in sound and/or vision. Where a constituency report on a radio service is repeated on several occasions in the same day, the full list need only be broadcast on one occasion, but the audience should be directed to where the list can be seen – for example, a website (rule 6.11).

▶ Exit polls

The term 'exit poll' describes any kind of survey in which people who have voted are asked which candidate and/or political party they voted for. When conducted scientifically, such survey of people leaving polling stations can often produce data which accurately predict an election result, hours before it is officially declared. A number of democratic nations, including the UK, have imposed legal restrictions on when such data/predictions can be published. The rationale, disputed by some, is that publishing such data, or predictions based on them, at a time when some members of the electorate have yet to vote could skew the election result. The concern is that telling people who have yet to vote which candidate/party is apparently due to win, with that information being apparently soundly based on votes already cast, could cause people to change their original voting intentions. Some, for example, might switch to support another candidate who appears – from the exit poll data – to have a better chance of victory, while others might decide not to vote at all, believing, for example, that the exit poll data show either that their favoured candidate cannot win, or will win so easily that no further votes are needed. These possible effects are seen as potential contamination of the democratic process, in that: (a) the later group of voters will have made choices on data not available to those who voted earlier; and (b) those data, and any prediction apparently based on them, might be inaccurate or, in the worst cases, might have been falsified to influence voting.

Section 66A of the Representation of the People Act 1983, as inserted by the 2000 Act of the same title, makes it a criminal offence to:

- publish, before a poll is closed, any statement about the way in which voters have voted in that election which is or might reasonably be taken to be, based on information given by voters after they have voted; and to
- publish, before a poll is closed, any forecast – including any estimate – of that election result, if the forecast is based on exit poll information from voters, or might reasonably be taken to be based on it.

So, for example, it would be illegal to broadcast, or put on a website, before polling stations closed, the statement: 'Fifty-five per cent of the people we have questioned say they have voted today for Labour'.

This law applies to Parliamentary and council elections, to those for the Welsh Assembly, and to by-elections. It applies in respect of exit polls conducted to focus on an individual constituency or ward, or on voting nationally. Publication of material in breach of section 66A leaves the publisher liable to a fine of up to £5,000 or a jail term of up to six months. Publication of exit polls during polling for European Parliamentary elections is also prohibited (SI 2004/293).

It is perfectly legal to publish, at any time, opinion poll data on voting intentions which was gathered before voting began, because the information was not based on how people say they actually voted. Also, it is legal to report the results of exit polls, and any forecast based on them, as soon as polling has finally closed, as TV programmes frequently do. But it is not always accurate now to talk of 'an election day'. For example, experiments to encourage more people to vote may mean that in some places voting takes place over several days. It will be an offence to publish an exit poll, or forecast apparently based on it, during any of the polling days, until the polls close on the final day.

👁 Case study

During elections for the European Parliament in June 2004, *The Times* published an opinion poll which had asked people how they had voted in areas using all-postal ballots. The Electoral Commission, the independent elections watchdog, said this amounted to an exit poll and referred the matter to the Crown Prosecution Service, but later reported that the CPS had concluded that it would not be appropriate to take any further action (Electoral Commission report on European Parliamentary elections, 21 December 2004).

Regulatory codes for broadcast journalists have, for some time, placed similar controls on the publication of exit polls, and indeed go further. Rule 6.5 of the Ofcom Broadcasting Code states: 'Broadcasters may not publish the results of any opinion poll on polling day itself until the election or referendum poll closes. (For European Parliamentary elections, this applies until all polls throughout the European Union have closed.).' Rule 6.4 bans discussion and analysis of election and referendum issues during polling, a period which begins when polling stations open. This rule does not apply to any poll conducted entirely by post.

BBC Editorial Guidelines take the same approach.

▌ Election counts

Journalists, including photographers and TV crews, attend election counts so declarations of the result can be quickly aired. There is no statutory right to attend a count – admission is at the discretion of the Returning Officer, who has legal responsibility for security and procedures at the count. The Electoral Commission's media handbook for the 2010 General Election said members of the media wishing to attend a count had to apply to the Returning Officer, and should abide by any direction he gave. Returning Officers' decisions were final, it said, adding: 'They do not have to allow any member of the press into the count (unless they are also a candidate, candidate's agent, counting agent or an accredited observer etc).'

👁 **Case study**

In the 2010 General Election, the media were initially banned from the count at Staffordshire Moorlands, and told by council officials running it that they had to stay in a separate room, apparently because of fears that their presence in the counting hall would be disruptive. The ban was lifted after lawyers for the *Staffordshire Sentinel*, *Leek Post and Times* and the BBC wrote to the acting Returning Officer protesting that it was undemocratic and a breach of the right to freedom of expression under Article 10 of the European Convention on Human Rights. The *Sentinel* also planned to get round the ban by having three staff members accredited as 'observers' at the count (*Media Lawyer*, 6 May 2010).

Registering as an observer takes 10 days, and it seems observers cannot be barred from a count – see Useful Websites at the end of this chapter.

The Returning Officer at the high-profile by-election at Oldham East and Saddleworth in January 2011, which followed Phil Woolas's removal as MP, referred to earlier, refused to allow journalists into the count, despite protests from the BBC and Press Association, saying there would be too many of them to accommodate comfortably. Journalists had to stay on a balcony overlooking the hall, with any communication with candidates, agents and others being 'facilitated' by Oldham Council press officers.

➡ **Recap of major points**

- Once an election has been called it is a criminal offence to publish a false statement about the personal character or conduct of a candidate for the purpose of affecting the number of votes he/she gets.

- It is an offence to publish before the end of polling any data obtained in exit polls on how people have voted, or any prediction of the election result based on such data.

- The Ofcom Broadcasting Code and the BBC Editorial Guidelines require broadcasters to follow certain practices to ensure impartiality in coverage of elections and referendums, and restrict use of opinion (including exit) polls.

((•)) **Useful Websites**

http://stakeholders.ofcom.org.uk/broadcasting/broadcast-codes/broadcast-code/elections/
Section 6 of the Ofcom Broadcasting Code, on elections and referendums

http://stakeholders.ofcom.org.uk/binaries/broadcast/guidance/831193/section6.pdf
  Ofcom's guidance on section 6 of the code

www.bbc.co.uk/guidelines/editorialguidelines/page/guidelines-politics-practices-elections/
  Section 10 of BBC Editorial Guidelines on 'Politics, Public Policy and Polls'

www.bbc.co.uk/guidelines/editorialguidelines/page/guidance-polls-surveys-full
  BBC Editorial Guidance on opinion polls, surveys, questionnaires, votes and straw
  polls

www.electoralcommission.org.uk/
  Electoral Commission

www.electoralcommission.org.uk/elections/electoral_observers
  Electoral Commission guidance on observers

Official secrets

Chapter summary

Official secrets legislation protects national security. It has not been used in recent years to prosecute journalists, but has been used to jail civil servants and others who have given journalists sensitive information. Police could search the home and news-room of a journalist who is thought to have breached this law, seize their records, and make sustained efforts to discover the source's identity. There is no public interest defence for anyone facing prosecution.

◗ Introduction

The Official Secrets Acts of 1911 and 1989 protect national security and can be used to enforce the duty of confidentiality owed to the UK state by Crown serv-ants or employees of companies doing military and other sensitive work. Crown servants include civil servants, members of the armed services, the police and civilians working for them. The Act imposes a similar duty on members of the security and intelligence services.

Part of the legislation was designed to punish those spying on the UK for foreign powers, and those who plan to do this.

👁 Case study

Royal Navy Petty Officer Edward Devenney, 30, was jailed for eight years in 2012 after he admitted breaching the Official Secrets Act 1911. Aggrieved by failure to gain pro-motion, he secretly took photographs on a Trident nuclear submarine of code material which enabled NATO communications to remain secret. He rang the Russian embassy, intending to pass this information to Russian agents. He was arrested after meeting two men he thought would be the agents. They were from MI5, the UK's security service (Metropolitan Police press release, 12 December 2012).

Official secrets legislation can also punish the leaking of sensitive information to a journalist or a member of the public. Publishing such material makes it available to hostile powers, terrorists and criminals, and can embarrass the UK's allies, for example by disclosing diplomatic correspondence.

ch. 1, p. 9, High offices in law, explains the Attorney General's role

Using the law to punish leaks is controversial. Attorney Generals have approved prosecutions of Crown servants and others who, on grounds of conscience, leaked information to the media to throw light on controversial government policies. In such cases the media and others have questioned whether the prosecution was intended to protect vital state secrets or stifle debate about matters which embarrassed the government. A journalist seen as being an accomplice to a leak could be prosecuted. Journalists and their editors could also be prosecuted for circulating or publishing such information. As the law is complex, there is a longer version of this chapter on www.mcnaes.com.

▌ The law's consequences for journalists

As this book went to press no journalist had been successfully prosecuted, let alone jailed, under official secrets legislation for many years.

👁 Case study

In 2013 Edward Snowden leaked to journalists material he copied when he was a contractor with the USA's National Security Agency. After travelling to Hong Kong Snowden publicly revealed he was the leaker, saying he wanted to expose the extent of the USA and UK's secret surveillance of the world's communications systems. *The Guardian*, drawing on this material, revealed some detail of the UK's secret cooperation with the USA in this surveillance, including emails. A former head of the UK's surveillance base GCHQ was quoted in *The Times* as saying that it had to be assumed that Snowden's travels meant UK intelligence files had been hacked from his computer by China and Russia, and that this was 'the most catastrophic loss to British intelligence ever'. But by late 2013 *The Guardian* had not been charged with breaching official secrets law for receiving or publishing some of Snowden's material, although a threat of legal action meant that the newspaper complied with a demand by government officials that they should destroy computer hard drives containing files he leaked (*The Guardian*, 10 June, 19 and 20 August 2013, *The Times*, 11 October 2013).

---

 see the chapter on terrorism law on www.mcnaes.com for David Miranda's detention

But although officialdom is reluctant to use official secrets law to prosecute journalists, for reasons discussed later, journalists must know about this law to be ready to protect the identities of confidential sources of information. The journalist might not be jailed for his/her story. The source might be. Police seeking to identify the source of leaked information could raid a journalist's newsroom, office or home. The journalist might be arrested and threatened with prosecution.

ch. 34 explains police powers to search

👁 Case study

In 2003 armed police raided the home of Liam Clarke, Northern Ireland editor of the *Sunday Times*, and arrested him and his wife, Kathryn Johnston, following publication of an updated version of their book *From Guns to Government*. This contained transcripts of tape-recordings, made in a joint police/MI5 surveillance operation, which detailed bugged telephone conversations acutely embarrassing to the UK government. The couple were detained at their home for five hours. Later the police admitted the raid was unlawful because although a search warrant was issued under the Police and Criminal Evidence Act 1984 it was only authorised by a magistrate, not by a circuit judge. In 2006 the two journalists reportedly received a 'five-figure' sum from police in settlement of a claim for false imprisonment (*Press Gazette*, 20 September 2006).

see ch. 34, pp. 406–409, The Police and Criminal Evidence Act 1984 (PACE)

The fate of sources

Sources are generally dealt with more severely than journalists. For example, a former civil servant, David Keogh, and Leo O'Connor, who had worked as an MP's researcher, were jailed in 2007 for six months and three months respectively for leaking a memo, received by the *Daily Mirror*, about a conversation US President George Bush and UK Prime Minister Tony Blair had about the Iraq war.

 The version of this chapter on www.mcnaes.com provides detail of this case and others in which sources were jailed.

▌ Reluctance to prosecute journalists

The reluctance of officialdom to use official secrets law against UK journalists is partly an effect of the legislation. The 1989 Act contains defences which journalists can use, but sources cannot. For example, a journalist has a defence that disclosure of the information was not 'damaging' to state interests.

John Wadham, former director of the civil rights organisation Liberty, has said of the lack of prosecutions of journalists:

> It is partly because governments don't like to be seen to be trying to put journalists in prison and partly because juries are less sympathetic to civil servants – who are employed to keep their mouths shut, who are aware of the rules but break them,

and who breach the trust with employers and colleagues – compared with journalists, who are paid to find things out and publish them. **"**

▶ The use of injunctions

From the 1980s onwards UK governments used injunctions to stop publication of leaked 'official secrets', to silence the media without a criminal prosecution and the accompanying danger of serious political embarrassment if a jury decided the publication was lawful. Injunctions are granted by judges sitting alone.

> See ch. 25, p. 305, Breach of confidence and official secrets, which outlines the *Spycatcher* case, and www.mcnaes.com ch. 33 for more detail on such injunctions.

▶ The 1911 Act

Section 1 of the 1911 Act is concerned with spying, but journalists need to know about it. Section 1 makes it an arrestable offence, carrying a penalty of up to 14 years' imprisonment, to do any of the following 'for any purpose prejudicial to the safety or interests of the state':

(a) approach, inspect, pass over, be in the neighbourhood of, or enter any prohibited place (see below);

(b) make any sketch, plan, model, or note that might be or is intended to be useful to an enemy;

(c) obtain, collect, record or communicate to any person any information that might be or is intended to be useful to an enemy.

Offences under (c) are most relevant for journalists. Section 3 of the 1911 Act gives a lengthy and wide-ranging definition of a 'prohibited place' as including 'any work or defence, arsenal, naval or air force establishment or station, factory, dockyard, mine, minefield, camp, ship, or aircraft' as well as 'any telegraph, telephone, wireless or signal station, or office' when any such property is used by the state. Statutory instruments added British Nuclear Fuels plc and Atomic Energy Authority sites to the list of prohibited places.

The media must remember that taking photos or gathering information outside or near prohibited places, even for routine news coverage of events such as peace protests, could be held to be a breach of the Act, for example if material gathered and published jeopardises security at a defence base.

▶ The 1989 Act: the journalist's position

The Act defines offences of disclosure by reference to various classes of information. These include information about security and intelligence; defence;

international relations; official investigations into crime, for example, by the police or other agencies; official phone-tapping and the official interception of letters or other communications; prison and custody facilities; and matters entrusted in confidence to other states or international organisations.

Section 5 of the Act says a person – for our purposes, a journalist – commits an offence if he/she discloses without lawful authority information protected by the Act, knowing or having reasonable cause to believe that it is thus protected against disclosure, if he/she received it from a Crown servant or government contractor either without lawful authority or in confidence, or received it from someone else who received it in confidence from such a person.

see www. mcnaes. com ch. 33 for more detail of what must be proved

Damage test but no public interest defence

Though the 1989 Act can catch journalists and members of the public, it is directed particularly at security services members, other Crown servants and government contractors. The degree of damage (by disclosure) to state interests necessary for conviction under the Act varies according to the class of information and the category of person accused. The damage alleged to have occurred could be, for example, to the capacity of the armed forces to carry out certain duties, or to British relations with another state.

There is no public interest defence in official secrets cases – and information can be classed as secret even if it has been published previously.

Breaching the 1989 Act is punishable by a jail term of up to two years and/or a fine.

▌ The public and media may be excluded from secrets trials

Section 8 of the Official Secrets Act 1920 allows the public and media to be excluded from secrets trials when publishing evidence would be 'prejudicial to the national safety'.

▌ Defence Advisory Notices

The Defence Press and Broadcasting Advisory Committee, a joint government/ media body, gives the media guidance on national security and defence issues through Defence Advisory Notices (DA-Notices, formerly known as D-Notices) and other correspondence.

((•))

see Useful Websites at the end of this chapter about the Notices

The five DA-Notices in force cover:

(1) military operations, plans and capabilities;

(2) nuclear and non-nuclear weapons and operational equipment;

(3) cyphers and secure communications;

(4) identification of specific installations and home addresses;

(5) UK security and intelligence services, and special forces.

The system is, in effect, voluntary self-censorship by the media. Editors who consult the DA-notice secretary sometimes decide to limit what is published, and sometimes publish information that they might otherwise have left out. The committee has no statutory enforcement powers.

 See www.mcnaes.com ch. 33 for further details about the DA-notice system, including how it was used after *The Guardian* published material leaked by Edward Snowden.

➡ Recap of major points

- Official secrets law is complex and frequently controversial. There is longer version of this chapter on www.mcnaes.com.

- This law protects national security and the safety of citizens, and can be used against foreign spies, terrorists or other criminals.

- But journalists say it is sometimes used to punish those who leak information which is politically embarrassing for the government, and to deter the media from revealing such information.

((•)) Useful Websites

www.dnotice.org.uk/
   The Defence, Press and Broadcasting Advisory Committee website

www.parliament.uk/briefing-papers/SN02023
   House of Commons Library, Note on Official Secrecy

The journalist's sources and neutrality

Chapter summary

It is an ethical principle that journalists do not disclose sources of confidential information. Journalists often have to rely on information from people whose safety or careers would be at risk if they were known as the sources. If disclosing such sources became commonplace, journalists' jobs would be much harder as fewer people would be willing to speak to them, and many important stories would not be revealed. Various bodies have legal powers to demand that journalists reveal where they got a story. This chapter explains those powers and how journalists can protect confidential sources, and warns that investigative journalists suspected of receiving leaks of sensitive, official information may be placed under secret surveillance. On some occasions when journalists refuse voluntarily to hand over material or give evidence, their object is not to protect an individual source but to maintain a reputation for neutrality.

▌ Protecting your source: the ethical imperative

Clause 14 of the Editors' Code of Practice says simply: 'Journalists have a moral obligation to protect confidential sources of information.' This clause is not subject to the code's 'public interest' exceptions, and does not give any circumstance which justifies breaching it. The Editors' Code is explained in ch. 2.

The National Union of Journalists code of conduct has a similar clause. It too has no exception to this principle.

Journalists' codes in nations all round the world state the same principle. If confidential sources were not sure that journalists would not betray their identities, many stories of great public interest would never be published.

((•))
see Useful
Websites
at the end
of this
chapter
for NUJ
Code

All journalists and their employers should do everything they can to protect the identity of a source who needs confidentiality. This would include ensuring that if a source is paid, the payment is untraceable, and that a source's details are not kept anywhere where they might be found or accessed, including on computers or devices such as memory sticks, or in a manner which might link them to stories done as a result of information or material they provided. Sources who offered or sold leaked information were prosecuted after their identities were uncovered by the Metropolitan police investigation into the *News of the World* phone-hacking scandal.

see ch. 35
for more
on this
investiga-
tion

If a court orders a journalist to identify a source, the journalist or his/her editor may well decide it is ethical to defy the order. But they must be prepared to face the legal consequences – which could be a substantial fine, or even a jail sentence for contempt of court, though in the last four decades no UK journalist has been jailed for such a contempt.

The Ofcom Broadcasting Code, explained in ch. 3, says in practice 7.7: 'Guarantees given to contributors, for example relating to the content of a programme, confidentiality or anonymity, should normally be honoured.'

Journalists have needed to protect the identities of sources from companies or public agencies which resorted to court action when attempting to discover who leaked information. It should be remembered that, even in routine stories, failure to protect a source's identity can have life-changing consequences for that person.

👁 Case study

In 2007 the Press Complaints Commission ruled that a newspaper breached clause 14 in an article about the possible closure of Burnley mortuary. A man who spoke to the paper on condition he was not identified was referred to in the article as 'a worker at Burnley's mortuary'. As he was one of only two people who worked there – the other was his boss – his employers identified him as the paper's source, and he was sacked for gross misconduct. The paper said the reporter had not known, and had no reason to know, that the man was one of only two employees. But the PCC said it should have established with the man how he should be described (*A man v Lancashire Telegraph*, adjudication issued 31 October 2007).

▶ Who might ask you to divulge your source?

ch. 25
explains
breach of
confidence

In law the term 'wrongdoer' may include a person who breaches a duty of confidence – for example, owed by an employee to a government department or company – by leaking sensitive information gained in that employment to the media.

Judges

In **common law** judges have the power to order disclosure of the identities of → glossary wrongdoers (*Norwich Pharmacal Co v Customs and Excise Comrs* [1974] AC 133).

Until fairly recently, UK judges – for example, in the *Goodwin* case, explained below – tended not to place much weight on the idea that there is a general public interest in journalists protecting sources who want to remain anonymous. But judgments in the European Court of Human Rights (ECtHR) and the UK's adoption of the European Convention on Human Rights have improved the legal climate. Journalists can point to their, and the public's, rights under the Convention's Article 10, guaranteeing freedom of expression and the right to impart and receive information.

ch. 1 explains Convention rights

◉ Case study

In 1989 a High Court judge ordered Bill Goodwin, a trainee reporter on The Engineer magazine, to disclose his source of information for a story about an engineering company's financial difficulties. He refused, and was fined £5,000 for contempt of court (*X Ltd v Morgan-Grampian (Publishers) Ltd* [1991] 1 AC 1).

The Court of Appeal and House of Lords upheld the High Court's decision, saying that disclosure was 'necessary in the interests of justice' because the company had a right to know who was leaking information about it. Mr Goodwin went to the ECtHR which in 1996 agreed that the UK courts had breached his Article 10 rights (*Goodwin v United Kingdom* (1996) EHRR 123). It said protection of journalistic sources was a basic condition for press freedom, and a court order to disclose a source could not be compatible with Article 10 unless it was justified by an overriding requirement in the public interest.

see ch. 25, p. 309, Order to reveal source, for more detail on the *Goodwin* case

---

In some circumstances a journalist may need to rely on another Convention right – Article 2, the right to life.

◉ Case study

In 2009 a judge accepted that the Article 2 rights of Suzanne Breen, the then Northern Editor of Ireland's *Sunday Tribune* newspaper, meant that she should not be compelled to produce to the police notes and records of a phone call she received from a spokesperson for the Real IRA terrorist group in which it claimed responsibility for two murders. A judge ruled that her life would be at 'real and immediate' risk from the Real IRA if she was forced to produce this information. She has condemned terrorist violence.

A recent European Court case

A decision by the fifth section chamber of the ECtHR in 2013 illustrates that its judges continue to recognise that it is necessary to protect journalists' sources to uphold human rights and freedoms.

It ruled that a warrant for a search of a newspaper's office issued by a Luxembourg court breached both Article 8, covering the right to respect for privacy and family life, and Article 10, guaranteeing the right to freedom of expression (Case No 26419/10 *Case of Saint Paul Luxembourg SA v Luxembourg*). *Contacto Semanário*, a Portuguese language newspaper, had in December 2008 carried an article about families losing custody of their children. This sparked a defamation complaint and criminal investigation, and in March 2009 a search warrant was issued to obtain documents relating to these offences, including identification of the article's author. The warrant was executed and the journalist gave police the relevant documents. In its judgment the ECtHR rejected the notion that Article 8 only protected individuals' 'homes', saying the term 'home' should be interpreted 'as also including the official office of a company run by an individual, and the official office of a legal person, including subsidiaries and other business premises'. It was clear that the search was an interference with the applicant's Article 8 rights, and were unnecessary as less restrictive steps could have been taken, the judgment said.

Tribunals of inquiry

Lord Saville, chairman of the inquiry established in 1998 under the Tribunals of Inquiry (Evidence) Act 1921 to investigate the 1972 Bloody Sunday killings in Northern Ireland, threatened three journalists with actions for contempt of court after they refused to name the sources of stories about the killings. The Act, now repealed, gave tribunals wide powers to send for and examine witnesses. In 2000 one journalist, Toby Harnden, of the *Daily Telegraph*, was 'placed in contempt' of the inquiry and told the matter was being referred to the High Court. But contempt proceedings were dropped in 2004.

Requests by a police officer

Journalists, like other citizens, have no general obligation to give police information.

If police want journalistic material to assist investigations they normally have to apply to a judge. They also generally need a judge's consent before searching a journalist's premises for it. See this chapter's explanation of the Police and Criminal Evidence Act 1984 and other statutes.

▌ Be ready for a long battle

A journalist protecting a source's identity must be ready for a long and tortuous legal battle. In 2000 Ashworth High Security Hospital obtained an order that the *Daily Mirror* should disclose the source of a story on Moors murderer Ian Brady, concerning his treatment at the hospital, starting a legal case which lasted six years. The Court of Appeal upheld the order, as did the House of Lords, saying in 2002 that while disclosing sources had a 'chilling effect' on freedom of the press it was 'necessary and proportionate and justified' in this case (*Ashworth Security Hospital v MGN Ltd* [2002] UKHL 29; [2002] 4 All ER 193). Freelance journalist Robin Ackroyd then said he was the source of the *Mirror* story – but refused to identify his own source. The High Court ordered him to do so – but in May 2003 the Court of Appeal upheld his appeal against the order and ruled there should be a full trial of the issue, saying he had an arguable defence – the court now knew, as the earlier court had not, that the person who gave Mr Ackroyd the information for his story was not paid for it. If that individual had a public interest defence to any breach of confidence or contract claim by the hospital, a claim could not succeed against Mr Ackroyd. The Court of Appeal also said it did not automatically follow that the public interest in non-disclosure of medical records should override the public interest in maintaining the confidentiality of his source (*Mersey Care NHS Trust v Robin Ackroyd* [2003] EWCA Civ 663). At the High Court trial, in February 2006, Mr Justice Tugendhat rejected Ashworth Hospital's argument that the need to protect the confidentiality of medical records overrode the public interest in protecting a journalist's sources. (*Mersey Care NHS Trust v Robin Ackroyd* [2006] EWHC 107 (QB)). The NHS Trust appealed but the Court of Appeal found for Mr Ackroyd in February 2007 (*Mersey Care NHS Trust v Robin Ackroyd* [2007] EWCA Civ 101). The House of Lords rejected the Trust's petition to appeal against that decision.

▶ The 'shield law' has not always shielded

In section 10 of the Contempt of Court Act 1981 Parliament created what is sometimes referred to as a 'shield law' to protect journalistic activity, though – some UK journalists would argue – other democracies have better shield laws.

Section 10 says: 'No court may require a person to disclose, nor is any person guilty of contempt of court for refusing to disclose, the source of information contained in a publication for which he is responsible, unless it is established to the satisfaction of the court that disclosure is necessary in the interests of justice or national security, or for the prevention of disorder or crime.'

Journalists hoped the section would lead judges to create a high threshold of 'necessity' in cases involving corporate or official attempts to flush out the identities of a journalist's source. But two cases show that the protection the section gives journalists has not proved to be as great as many had hoped.

The first concerned the scope of the phrase 'national security'. In 1983 *The Guardian* was ordered to return to the government a leaked photocopy of a Ministry of Defence document revealing the strategy for handling the controversial arrival of US Cruise nuclear missiles, due to be based in the UK. *The Guardian* did not know the informant's identity, but, realising that it might be revealed by examination of the document, argued that section 10 meant it did not have to hand it over. The House of Lords said the interests of national security required disclosure of the informant's identity – publishing this document posed no threat to national security, but the person who leaked it might leak another. *The Guardian* handed over the document, and consequently the informant, Foreign Office clerk Sarah Tisdall, was convicted under the Official Secrets Act and jailed for six months (*Secretary of State for Defence v Guardian Newspapers Ltd* [1985] AC 339).

! Remember

Had *The Guardian* destroyed the document after using it to prepare the article and before being ordered to hand it over, Ms Tisdall's identity might have remained secret.

The second case, involving City journalist Jeremy Warner, showed what the courts understood by the word 'necessary' and the phrase 'prevention of crime'.

Inspectors investigating 'insider dealings' in shares sought a court order that Warner, then on *The Independent*, should reveal his sources for a business story he wrote in 1988. Lord Griffiths said in the House of Lords that 'necessary' in section 10 of the Contempt of Court Act 1981 had a meaning which lay somewhere between 'indispensable' on the one hand and 'useful' or 'expedient' on the other. The House of Lords ruled against Warner's appeal, but he continued to refuse to reveal who his source was, and was fined £20,000 (*In Re An Inquiry under the Company Securities (Insider Dealing) Act 1985* [1988] AC 660, *The Times* 27 January 1988).

ch. 33 deals with official secrets law

However, the jurisprudence of the European Court of Human Rights, outlined earlier, and Article 10 of the European Convention have, since these cases about the scope of section 10 of the 1981 Act, improved the legal climate for UK journalists' protection of sources.

▶ Statutory powers of investigators

Various statutes have provision for the police and other official investigators, when investigating crime, to get a court order requiring a person to surrender material, or in some circumstances to search premises without warning to seize it. In the case of a journalist, this could be notes of interviews, computers or phones, etc which could reveal the identity of a source of published stories about the crime being investigated.

The Police and Criminal Evidence Act 1984 (PACE)

Police, if they wish someone to be compelled to surrender documents or other material, need a court order in most circumstances. PACE is the legislation they use most when applying for these orders.

Special procedure material

In PACE, special protection is given to 'journalistic material', defined as 'material acquired or created for the purposes of journalism'. When seeking to compel journalists or media organisations to surrender such material, police investigating a crime must use PACE's 'special procedure', which means they must apply to a High Court judge, a **recorder** or a **circuit judge**. If the application succeeds the judge makes a 'production order' – that is, an order requiring the person or organisation holding the material to produce it to the police.

→ glossary
→ glossary

The application is normally 'on notice', so the holder of the material has the chance to attend the hearing to argue against the order being granted.

Before making the order a judge must be satisfied that there are reasonable grounds for believing that a serious offence has been committed; that the material the police want would be admissible evidence at a trial for that offence and of substantial value to the investigation; that other methods of obtaining it have been tried without success, or have not been tried because it appears they would be bound to fail; and that production of the material to the police would be in the public interest, having regard to:

see this Book's Late News for PACE case

(1) the benefit likely to accrue to the investigation if the material is obtained; and

(2) the circumstances under which the person in possession of the material holds it.

The Act's 'special procedure' appears to give journalistic material useful protection. But judges have interpreted it in a way which makes the protection less valuable than was hoped.

In several cases, applications by the police for production orders have concerned photographs or film taken during rioting and other public disturbances. Although such material does not reveal the identity of any sources promised anonymity, there is another principle involved for the media, that of maintaining neutrality.

see also, p. 412, Maintaining a reputation for neutrality, on this principle

Most editors and journalists take the view that they should hand over such material only after careful consideration, and generally only after a court order, arguing that if it becomes routine for police to obtain unpublished photographs or film, journalists, photographers and camera operators will be seen as an arm of the state. This could increase the danger that they will be attacked when covering such events. For example, untransmitted footage of the riots in London in August 2011 was handed to the police by BBC, ITN and Sky News only after police obtained production orders.

A judge may reject the application for a production order if, among other things, he/she does not consider it in the public interest to grant it. Media lawyers have argued that it is not in the public interest to prevent the media doing their job. In nearly every case judges have found that the police's need for evidence outweighed that argument, though the case described below was a welcome exception.

👁 Case study

In 2012 the High Court overturned an order made by a judge at Chelmsford Crown court for broadcasters to hand over more than 100 hours of footage of evictions from the Dale Farm travellers' site. The High Court said there were no reasonable grounds to believe that the footage included material likely to be of substantial value to the police investigation. Applicants for such an order had to produce 'clear and compelling' evidence that it was necessary. A judge facing such an application also had to exercise his discretion in a manner compatible with Article 10, even if the conditions for having the material were satisfied, said Lord Justice Moses, who added: 'First, the objective must be sufficiently important to justify the inhibition such orders inflict on the exercise of the fundamental right to disseminate information. Second, the means chosen to limit the right must be rational, fair and not arbitrary, and third, the means used must impair the right as little as is reasonably possible' (*R (on the application of BSkyB, the BBC, ITN, Hardcash productions Ltd and Jason Parkinson) v Chelmsford Crown Court* [2012] EWHC 1295 (Admin); [2012] 2 Cr App R 33; [2012] EMLR 30).

Excluded material

→ glossary

Under PACE, **excluded material** is exempt from compulsory surrender. It includes journalistic material which a person holds in confidence – for example, from a source promised confidentiality by a journalist.

But material which was already liable to search and seizure under the previous law is not protected. For example, a stolen document acquired by a journalist, even from a confidential source, would not be 'excluded material' because it would already be liable to seizure under a warrant issued under the Theft Act 1968.

Expect your premises to be searched

Increasingly authorities with powers to demand information also have powers to search the premises of the person they believe has it. But freedom from an oppressive search is an important civil liberty, safeguarded as early as 1765 in a case concerning a clerk called Entick whose house was entered and papers seized by 'the king's messengers' on the authority of a warrant from the Secretary of State (*Entick v Carrington* (1765) 19 State Tr 1029). In that case, a court condemned the action as unlawful.

That ruling was referred to and endorsed in the Queen's Bench Divisional Court in 2000 when the court rejected a police application for an order that *The Guardian* and *Observer* should hand over all files, documents and records they had relating to a letter in *The Guardian* from former M15 officer David Shayler and an article in the *Observer* by reporter Martin Bright repeating allegations that M16 officers were involved in a failed attempt to assassinate the Libyan leader, Colonel Gaddafi. The police particularly wanted an email letter sent by Shayler so they could discover his email address (*R v Central Criminal Court, ex p Martin Bright* [2001] 2 All ER 244)

Lord Justice Judge said that the principle that an Englishman's home was his castle was linked to freedom of speech and continued:

see www. mcnaes. com ch. 33. for detail about Shayler

> " Premises are not to be entered by the forces of authority or the state to deter or diminish, inhibit or stifle the exercise of an individual's right to free speech or the press of its freedom to investigate and inform, and orders should not be made which might have that effect unless a circuit judge is personally satisfied that the statutory preconditions to the making of an order are established, and, as the final safeguard of basic freedoms, that in the particular circumstances it is indeed appropriate for an order to be made. "

Search warrants under PACE

Instead of asking for an order for a journalist or media organisation to produce (surrender) material, police can apply to a circuit judge for a search warrant under PACE to obtain either non-confidential or confidential material. The person or media organisation does not have to be told of the application, and has no right to be heard by the judge.

Before granting a warrant, a judge must be satisfied that the criteria for ordering the production of the material are satisfied, and that one of the following circumstances applies:

- it is not practicable to communicate with anyone entitled to grant entry to the premises;
- it is not practicable to communicate with anyone entitled to grant access to the material;
- the material contains information which is subject to an obligation of secrecy or a restriction on disclosure imposed by statute (for example, material subject to the Official Secrets Act) and is likely to be disclosed in breach of that obligation if a warrant is not issued; or
- giving notice of an application for an order may seriously prejudice the investigation.

The Serious Organised Crime and Police Act 2005

The Serious Organised Crime and Police Act 2005 allows police, subject to the PACE procedure for search warrants for journalistic material (described earlier), to obtain a warrant to search all property occupied or controlled by the person named in the warrant and not merely specific premises.

see ch. 33 on official secrets law

But before issuing an all-premises warrant a judge must be satisfied that:

(1) there are reasonable grounds for believing that it is necessary to search premises occupied or controlled by the person in question which are not specified in the application, as well as those which are, in order to find the material in question; and

(2) it is not reasonably practicable to specify all the premises which he/she occupies or controls which might need to be searched.

See www.mcnaes.com ch. 34 for further detail of the 2005 Act.

Official Secrets Acts

The Official Secrets Act 1920 operates where a chief officer of police is satisfied that there is reasonable ground for suspecting that an offence under section 1, covering espionage, has been committed and for believing that any person is able to furnish information about the offence.

ch. 33 explains official secrets law

The officer may ask the Home Secretary for permission to authorise a senior police officer to require the person to divulge that information. Failing to comply is an offence.

A chief officer of police who has reasonable grounds to believe that the case is an emergency and that immediate action is necessary in the interests of the state may demand the information without the Home Secretary's consent.

Section 9 of the Official Secrets Act 1911 gives police powers to make searches, subject to PACE as regards journalistic material.

Counter-terrorism legislation

Counter-terrorism legislation includes a number of offences which could relate to journalist's sources, and gives police powers to seize a journalist's research material.

The Terrorism Act 2000 enables a court to issue a warrant for police investigating a terrorist offence to search premises.

 See www.mcnaes.com for the online chapter: 'Terrorism and the effect of counter-terrorism law'.

Other statutes

Various other statutes could affect journalists by placing them under a legal obligation to disclose information, for example to an official investigation into fraud or share-dealings. See www.mcnaes.com ch. 34 for further detail.

! Remember

The Data Protection Act does not require journalists to disclose material, which could help reveal a source's identity.

The Information Commissioner's Office (ICO) ruled in 2012 that a weekly newspaper, when refusing a request made under the Data Protection Act for a document, had been correct to cite the exemptions in the Act's section 32, relating to information held for the purposes of journalism. Cullompton Town Council and former councillor Ashley Wilce had asked the *Mid Devon Gazette* series for a copy of a leaked email on which it based a story that the authority had been holding finance committee meetings in secret, contrary to the rules.

ch. 28,
p. 338,
Protection
for stored
data,
explains
the Act

▶ You may be put under surveillance

Journalists in touch with secret sources yielding information on crime or what the state considers should be secret should realise that various statutes give police and other agencies the right to carry out surveillance of them personally, their correspondence including emails and phone calls.

👁 Case study

In 2008 *Milton Keynes Citizen* reporter Sally Murrer and Mark Kearney, a former detective accused of leaking information to her, walked free after a court ruled that prosecution evidence gathered by police bugging Mr Kearney's car was inadmissible. Mr Kearney faced charges of misconduct in a public office and Ms Murrer was charged with aiding and abetting misconduct in a public office. At Kingston Crown court Judge Richard Southwell said gathering evidence by using the listening device was an unjustifiable violation of the freedom of expression rights of both, and of Ms Murrer's rights to protect her sources. The information allegedly leaked was not sensitive, let alone 'highly sensitive' and the police action could not be justified. Ms Murrer's counsel, Gavin Millar, QC, told the court: 'One of the protections of the Strasbourg [European Court] law is a practical one ... It is the right to be brought before a court and have a court decide whether you are required to disclose your source. What they did here was a no-no in Strasbourg terms – and a pretty big no-no' (*R v Kearney and Murrer* ; *Media Lawyer*, 28 November 2008).

The Police Act 1997

Journalists in touch with secret sources yielding information on crime should know that the Police Act 1997 enables police to put them under electronic surveillance. The Act allows police to authorise themselves to break into premises and place bugs if they believe doing so will help them investigate serious crime. Sections 92 to 98 make entering or interfering with property or 'wireless telegraphy' lawful when a chief constable or, in urgent cases, an assistant chief constable, 'thinks it necessary ... on the ground that it is likely to be of substantial value in the prevention or detection of serious crime'.

Under the Act, the government appoints a small number of Commissioners, current or former High Court judges. Police must obtain a Commissioner's prior approval for bugging homes, offices and hotel bedrooms, and in respect of doctors, lawyers, and 'confidential journalistic material'. Prior approval is not necessary in urgent cases, but the chief officer must apply for approval as soon as reasonably practicable and say why he/she could not do so before.

The Regulation of Investigatory Powers Act 2000

Journalists remain concerned about many aspects of this Act, fearing in particular that the ability of the police to gain information about phone calls and access to their emails could stop them assuring contacts that their confidentiality will be protected. Had the Act been in force when police were attempting to access the email David Shayler sent *The Guardian* (see earlier), there would have been no need for the authorities to ask a judge for an order; they could simply have obtained a warrant from the Home Secretary. The Act also gives official agencies extensive powers of surveillance. A journalist who needs to protect a source's identity should be aware these powers may be deployed and so avoid using emails if possible, and only use untraceable pay-as-you-go mobile phones.

 See www.mcnaes.com ch. 34 for details of how police and other official agencies can use RIPA.

▌ Maintaining a reputation for neutrality

Reporters who cover events which lead to prosecutions of those involved or civil lawsuits may be asked – for example, by prosecution or defence – to give evidence of what they themselves have seen. Most journalists in this situation will wish to retain their reputation for neutrality and will agree to be a witness only after → glossary   receiving a **subpoena** (in civil cases) or witness summons (in criminal cases).

➡ Recap of major points

- It is a matter of professional principle that a reporter does not reveal his/her source of confidential information.

- The European Court of Human Rights has said that an order to disclose the source of information cannot be compatible with Article 10 of the Convention (freedom of expression) unless it is justified by an overriding requirement in the public interest.

- Section 10 of the Contempt of Court Act 1981 says that a disclosure order must not be made 'unless it is established to the satisfaction of the court that disclosure is necessary in the interests of justice or national security, or for the prevention of disorder or crime'.

- Various laws allow the authorities to put journalists and others under surveillance.

((•)) Useful Websites

www.nuj.org.uk/about/nuj-code/
National Union of Journalists Code of conduct

35

The risks of being charged with bribery, misconduct, hacking or intercepting

Chapter summary

The way journalists gain information may leave them and their sources at risk of prosecution. Journalists offering or paying money to sources may be accused of conspiring with the source to commit 'misconduct in a public office', or of bribery. Hacking into a computer, a phone voicemail or email system, or intercepting communications may also be prosecuted as an offence. Few of the relevant statutes contain a public interest defence. But the Director of Public Prosecutions has said in guidance to prosecutors that the public interest should always be considered when decisions are taken on whether to prosecute journalists in cases arising from their work. Journalists who realise they may be suspected of such offences should consider whether there is a sufficient public interest to justify what they plan to do – and remember that some offences may also leave them open to being sued in the civil courts for damages. This chapter details the main risks.

▌ More than 20 journalists charged

In 2011 the Metropolitan police re-opened inquiries into the hacking scandal at the *News of the World*, after media revelations suggested that the police's original investigation, which led to a reporter and a private detective being jailed in 2007, had failed to result in all those responsible being prosecuted.

 See p. 419, Regulation of Investigatory Powers Act (RIPA) 2000, for this 2007 case.

The police investigations encompassed other alleged offences. By September 2013 *Press Gazette* had reported that some 26 journalists who had worked or were

see Useful
Websites
at the end
of this
chapter
for the
list

working for London-based national newspapers each faced one or more charges. The offences alleged including hacking into mobile phone messages, hacking into emails and making corrupt payments to police officers and other public servants. Police investigations continue.

The Crown Prosecution Service has issued a list of offences 'most likely to be committed' in cases involving journalists.

The consent of the Director of Public Prosecutions or Attorney General is needed before proceedings can be launched for some of these offences. Some are outlined later in this chapter.

Guidance for prosecutors on whether a journalist should be prosecuted

see Useful
Websites
at the end
of this
chapter
for this
guidance

The DPP has published guidance for prosecutors on the factors to be considered when they are deciding whether journalists – or sources of information who interact with journalists – should be charged with criminal offences that may have been committed in the course of journalists' work.

The guidance acknowledges that prosecuting journalists may have an impact on the rights of the media and public to freedom of expression and to receive and impart information, both at common law and under the European Convention on Human Rights. The guidance points out that it is important at the outset to distinguish between the public interest served by these rights and the separate question of whether a prosecution is in the public interest – for example, the public interest in punishing criminality. In general terms, it says that once prosecutors have decided that there is sufficient evidence to continue with a case, they must consider whether it is in the public interest to go ahead with a prosecution.

ch. 1
explains
the Article
10 rights

The guidance indicates that this decision involves considering a variety of factors. The nature of the information gained or sought by the journalist would be one factor. For example, is the information that a crime has been, is being or is likely to be committed by someone; or does it show that someone has failed or is likely to fail to comply with any legal obligation; or that conduct capable of disclosing a miscarriage of justice has occurred, is occurring or is likely to occur, or is the conduct capable of raising or contributing to an important matter of public debate?

see also
ch. 34 on
journal-
ists
protecting
sources

The guidance indicates that if the journalist gained or sought information in these categories, the public interest in such information coming to light weighs against the public interest in prosecuting the journalist for alleged criminality in his or her news-gathering methods.

On the other side, prosecutors also have to consider the overall criminality of the activity in question – including its effects, the vulnerability of any of its victims, and whether the behaviour was repeated or involved corruption.

▌ Misconduct in a public office

This is a common law offence with which public officials will be charged when accused of disclosing to the media (or others) information which is not specifically protected by legislation such as the Data Protection Act or Official Secrets Act.

 Ch. 28 deals with data protection law affecting journalism and ch. 33 with official secrets law.

The 'misconduct' may be by an act, or an omission, but must be wilful, and the offender must be a public officer acting as such. Public officials include police and prison officers, magistrates, judges, registrars, and council and court officials. The offence can be committed even if no money changes hands. Lord Justice Pill, in the Court of Appeal in *Attorney General's Reference No. 3 of 2003* [2004] EWCA Crim 868; [2005] QB 73) said that there must be:

> a serious departure from proper standards before the criminal offence is committed; and a departure not merely negligent but amounting to an affront to the standing of the public office held. The threshold is a high one requiring conduct so far below acceptable standards as to amount to an abuse of the public's trust in the office holder. A mistake, even a serious one, will not suffice.

The associated charge for a journalist would be conspiring to commit the misconduct – for example, an alleged plot involving the public official and/or another person for information to be supplied in breach of this law – or aiding and abetting the offence. This law was used in a controversial and discredited prosecution of a journalist in 2008.

No journalist had been convicted of such an offence by late 2013. But cases were pending.

see the *Murrer* case, ch. 34, p. 411, You may be put under surveillance

---

👁 Case studies

On 27 March 2013, prison officer Richard Trunkfield was jailed at the Old Bailey for 16 months after admitting misconduct in public office by selling *The Sun* information about Jon Venables, one of the killers of James Bulger, who was being held at Woodhill Prison, where he worked. On the same day former Surrey police officer Alan Tierney was jailed for 10 months for selling *The Sun* details of the separate arrests of footballer John Terry's mother and Rolling Stone Ronnie Wood. Another officer who sold information was jailed for two years (*Media Lawyer*, 27 March 2013).

▌ Bribery Act 2010

A journalist who pays a source for information could in some circumstances be charged under the Bribery Act 2010. A source could also be charged under the Act if he/she could be accused by another party – for example, his/her employer – of acting improperly by giving the journalist information. Offences under the Act can be committed by anyone, not just public officials.

When the Act first came into force it was described as the toughest bribery legislation in the world, and there were fears that it could mean that journalists, particularly those working on investigations, would be breaking the law by paying confidential sources.

By late 2013 no journalist had been charged under the Act. But this legislation, and the 'misconduct' cases, have caused media organisations to review procedures about paying or otherwise rewarding sources of information, to avoid breaching these laws.

The bribery offences

The Act creates four main offences – bribing someone, accepting bribes, bribing foreign officials and failing, as a commercial organisation, to prevent bribery. All four can only be prosecuted with the consent of the Director of Public Prosecutions. There is no public interest defence in the Act itself.

It is an offence to offer, promise or give someone else a financial or other advantage to get someone 'improperly to perform a relevant function or activity', or to reward someone for such improper performance, or to do so knowing or believing that accepting the inducement would itself be improper performance.

It is irrelevant whether the person to whom the advantage is offered, promised or given is the same person who performs the function or activity concerned, and it does not matter whether the offer is made directly or through a third party.

The offence of being bribed is covered by four sets of circumstances:

- where someone requests, agrees to receive or accepts a financial or other advantage – a bribe – intending that as a result he/she or someone else will improperly perform a relevant function or activity;

- where someone seeks or accepts a bribe when doing so constitutes improper performance of a relevant function or activity;

- where someone seeks or accepts a bribe as a reward for his/her own or someone else's improper performance of an activity;

- where someone improperly performs an activity in anticipation of or as a consequence of him/herself or someone else having sought or accepted a bribe.

The Act states that in all four of these cases it does not matter whether a bribe is accepted directly or through a third party; or whether it is, or is to be, for the benefit of that person or another person.

In the second, third and fourth cases it is irrelevant whether the person receiving the bribe knows or believes that the performance of the function or activity is improper. In the final case, if the function or activity is being performed by someone other than the person receiving the bribe it does not matter whether that other person knows or believes that the performance is improper.

Section 3 says the Act covers:

- any function of a public nature;
- activities connected with a business, trade or profession;
- things done in the course of employment;
- activities performed by or on behalf of a body, whether corporate or unincorporated

as long as a person performing it is expected to do so in good faith, or impartially, or is in a position of trust by virtue of what they are doing. They are covered by the Act even if they have no connection with the UK and acts are performed outside the UK.

The penalties on summary conviction are up to six months in prison and/or a fine of up to £5,000, and on conviction on indictment up to 10 years in jail and an unlimited fine.

Section 6 creates the offence of bribing a foreign public official if the person paying intends to influence the official in his/her capacity as a public official and also intends to obtain or retain business or an advantage in the conduct of business.

A company is guilty of the section 7 offence of failing to prevent bribery if someone associated with it bribes someone with the intention of obtaining or keeping business for the company, or getting or keeping an advantage in the conduct of the company's business.

This is a strict liability offence – meaning the prosecution does not have to prove any intention to commit it – but it is a defence for a company to prove that it had adequate procedures in place intended to stop people associated with it from bribing others. This offence is punishable by an unlimited fine.

▶ Cases in which the public interest was clear

There are clear examples of when a possible breach by journalists of the law of 'misconduct in a public office' or of the Bribery Act might be considered to be justified as being in the public interest.

One is the exposure by the *Daily Telegraph* of the scandal of MPs' unjustifiable and inflated expenses claims, in that the newspaper had paid a considerable amount of money for the information on which its exposés were based. This was before the Bribery Act came into force. However, it was later made clear that prosecutors would not have brought a case.

see also ch. 30, p. 363, Introduction to the Act, on the expenses story

The first criminal conviction under the Bribery Act came after *The Sun*, in the public interest, risked being prosecuted itself under the Act by paying Redbridge Magistrates' Court office worker Munir Yakub Patel a £500 bribe – which it secretly filmed him accepting – to stand up a story that he was taking bribes to keep details of a traffic offence summons off a court database. Patel was jailed for six months in November 2011.

 See www.mcnaes.com ch. 35 for hypothetical cases studies on whether a journalist paying for showbiz gossip or for information about a Minister could be deemed to breach the Bribery Act.

▶ Computer Misuse Act 1990

This Act creates computer hacking offences of unauthorised access to a computer with the intention of:

- getting to any program or information it holds; or
- committing or facilitating the commission of an offence; or
- impairing a computer so as to stop or hinder access to any program or data held in any computer; or
- impairing or intending to impair the operation of any such program or the reliability of any such data.

It is also an offence to make, adapt, supply or offer to supply any article intending or believing that it will be used to commit, or help the commission of one of these offences.

Penalties range from six months in prison and a fine of up to £5,000 on summary conviction to up to 10 years in prison and/or an unlimited fine if convicted on indictment.

These offences clearly cover computer hacking activities, such as hacking into someone's emails. The unauthorised access offences require that the defendant must have known that the intended access was unauthorised – which will generally not be an issue if a journalist has accessed someone else's computer.

The Act itself does not contain a public interest defence, but acting in the public interest will help protect journalists.

👁 Case study

ch. 3 explains Ofcom's role, and ch. 26 explains the code's privacy section.

The Crown Prosecution Service announced in March 2013 that Sky News reporter Gerald Tubb would not be prosecuted for hacking into the emails of back-from-the-dead canoeist John Darwin and his wife Anne, who were jailed in 2008 after staging his 'death' to make a fraudulent life insurance claim.

Malcolm McHaffie, CPS deputy head of special crime said a prosecution would not be in the public interest. It was also unclear whether the material in question was accessed from the UK or the United States.

In July 2013 Ofcom cleared Sky News of having breached the Broadcasting Code, saying that it had concluded that the 'exceptional circumstances of this case outweighed Mr and Mrs Darwin's expectation of privacy', and that while the company's conduct was 'at the boundaries of what is appropriate' it was 'warranted in the particular circumstances of this case'.

Sky News had earlier said that it stood by its actions as being editorially justified and in the public interest. (*Media Lawyer*, 29 March and 1 July 2013).

▌ Regulation of Investigatory Powers Act (RIPA) 2000

This Act creates a series of offences which could affect journalists, all of which can be prosecuted only with the consent of the DPP. There is no public interest defence in the Act itself.

Section 1 creates the offences of unlawfully intercepting any communication being transmitted through a public postal service or through a public or private telecommunication system.

Private investigator Glenn Mulcaire, who hacked phone messages for *News of the World* Royal Correspondent Clive Goodman, admitted five offences under this Act when the two men were jailed in January 2007. Mulcaire was given a six-month sentence, and Goodman received four months.

The two men had also admitted the Criminal Law Act 1977 offence of conspiring to intercept communications without lawful authority.

Penalties for the RIPA offences are a fine of up to £5,000 (the current statutory maximum) on summary conviction or two years' imprisonment and/or an unlimited fine on conviction on indictment.

The case came to light when Prince William began to fear aides' mobile phone voicemail messages were being intercepted after a story about his knee injury, of which few people were aware, appeared in the *News of the World* in November 2005.

Section 2(7) of RIPA classifies messages stored for later retrieval as still being 'in the course of transmission', thus putting voicemail within the scope of 'interception'.

The scandal set off by disclosures about the amount of phone-hacking at the *News of the World*, and revelations that it had hacked into the voicemails on a murdered schoolgirl's phone, led to the newspaper's closure in June 2011. As this book went to press, a number of people, including former News International chief executive Rebekah Brooks and former *News of the World* editor Andy Coulson were on trial on phone-hacking charges and charges connected with allegedly corrupt payments to police and other public officials for information.

! Remember

As ch. 2 explains, the Editors' Code of Practice specifically protects the privacy of 'digital communications' and bans the interception of private or mobile telephone calls, messages or emails.

Recording phone calls

Journalists frequently record the calls they themselves make or receive. Under RIPA, interception occurs in the course of transmission, so recording telephone conversations by a device at either end of the communication is not interception and is lawful and not a breach of the Editors' Code of Practice – see ch. 2, p. 18, Recording phone calls, and, ch. 3, p. 33, Recording phone conversations, for Ofcom's rules.

▶ Wireless Telegraphy Act 2006

The Act prohibits the use without authority of wireless apparatus with intent to obtain information about the contents, sender or addressee of any message, and prohibits the disclosure of any such information.

▶ Perverting the course of justice

This is a common law offence. It includes falsifying, concealing or destroying evidence or potential evidence, such as emails, records or files, and so on. Criminal proceedings do not have to be in progress when the act is done for an offence to be committed. Police who reopened inquiries into allegations of widespread phone-hacking by the *News of the World*, have arrested a number of people in connection with allegations of perverting the course of justice in relation to the inquiry.

▶ Serious Crime Act 2007

Sections 44 to 46 of this Act make it an offence intentionally to encourage or assist an offence, or to do so believing the offence will be committed, or to do so believing that that offence or another will be committed.

The penalty for each offence is any penalty the offender would be liable to face if he were convicted of the anticipated offence.

These offences would cover, for example, the position of a journalist or editor who commissions a private investigator or someone else to hack into someone's emails.

 Ch. 27 deals with the risk of journalists being charged with harassment. The risk of journalists being charged under counter-terrorism law is discussed in the www.mcnaes.com chapter: 'Terrorism and the affect of counter-terrorism law. See too ch. 5, pp. 49–53, Definitions of crimes, on what is theft.

➡ Recap of major points

- News-gathering activities may leave journalists at risk of being charged with criminal offences such as conspiracy to commit misconduct in public office, or with bribery.

- Public officials – police, prison officers and others – who sell information to the media may also face criminal prosecution for misconduct in public office.

- Hacking into computers, emails and voicemail messages is a criminal offence.

- The DPP has issued guidance saying that the issue of public interest must be considered before journalists are prosecuted in connection with news-gathering activities.

((•)) Useful Websites

www.cps.gov.uk/legal/assets/uploads/files/media_guidelines_annex_a.pdf
   Crown Prosecution Service (CPS) list of offences which journalists are most likely to be accused of

www.cps.gov.uk/news/latest_news/dpp_launches_final_guidelines_for_prosecutors_on_cases_affecting_the_media_following_public_consultation/index.html
   CPS guidelines for prosecutors assessing whether journalists should be charged

www.sfo.gov.uk/media/167348/bribery_act_2010_joint_prosecution_guidance_of_the_director_of_the_serious_fraud_office_and_the_director_of_public_prosecutions.pdf
   Serious Fraud Office and Director of Public Prosecutions guidance on the Bribery Act

36

The right to take photographs, film and record

Chapter summary

Journalists should know their rights when gathering visual images or making recordings in the streets or countryside. There is no criminal law restricting photography or filming or recording in public places. As this chapter explains, concern has grown in the media that over-zealous police officers, security guards and members of the public raise invalid objections to journalists using cameras. Photographers have been wrongly arrested. This chapter covers laws which are sometimes officiously cited or used against journalists, and the civil law of trespass.

▶ Introduction

Many police officers and members of the public offer help to the media. But some do not, and become officious or hostile to journalists going about their lawful business to gather material. In tense situations, journalists may find laws being invalidly used or cited against them. They need good legal knowledge to make decisions on how to handle events.

Guidance to police issued by the Association of Chief Police Officers says: 'There are no powers prohibiting the taking of photographs, film or digital images in a public place. Therefore, members of the public and press should not be prevented from doing so.'

Some 'public places' such as shopping malls are private property, and security staff may intervene unless journalists get permission to take pictures, film or record there.

▶ Trouble with the police in public places

A reporter using a notebook to cover incidents in a public place, including a demonstration, protest or riot, can choose when to blend into the background. But a photographer, radio reporter, video-journalist or film crew cannot – they must get in close for their pictures and/or sound. They may be attacked by disorderly people and – even during a small-scale event – be improperly arrested by police as tension rises.

👁 Case study

In 2010 the Metropolitan Police paid photojournalists Marc Vallée and Jason Parkinson £3,500 each in damages after armed officers stopped them from taking video footage and photos at a protest outside the Greek Embassy. Diplomatic Protection Group officers, claiming the pair were not allowed to film them, pulled Marc's camera away from his face and covered the lens of Jason's camera (*Media Lawyer*, 28 June 2010).

Police guidelines on media photography and filming

In 2010 the Association of Chief Police Officers (ACPO) issued updated guidelines for the police on how to deal with the media.

The guidelines remind police that the media have a duty to report from accident and crime scenes, and say that if police cordon off a scene it is best practice to give the media a good vantage point.

((•))

see Useful Websites at the end of this chapter for these guidelines in full

The guidelines also say that if a distressed or bereaved person asks the police to stop the media taking pictures or filming, officers can pass on the request but have no power to prevent or restrict such activity.

The guidance also points out: 'Once an image has been recorded, police can only seize the film or camera at the scene on the strictly limited grounds that it is suspected to contain evidence of a crime. Once the photographer has left the scene, police can only seize images with a court order. In the case of the media, the usual practice is to apply for a court order under the Police and Criminal Evidence Act for production of the photograph or film footage.'

! Remember

If police want to view or seize journalistic material, including photographs they must first get a court order under the Police and Criminal Evidence Act, explained in ch. 34. Police at the scene of an incident have no power to insist that a journalist deletes images.

False imprisonment

A journalist who is subject to unlawful physical restraint – such as being locked in the cells, or physically restrained by a police officer might be able to sue for false imprisonment. Movement must be completely restricted; barring a photographer from going in one particular direction – for example, towards the scene of a crash – is not false imprisonment.

👁 Case study

Wiltshire police paid compensation to photojournalist Robert Naylor after an incident in 2009 when he went to a canal to report on a death in a boat fire. A police sergeant told him he could not take photos because of 'respect for the deceased'. Soon afterwards, as he started back to this car, he was dragged to the ground, arrested and handcuffed for allegedly 'breaching the peace'. Wiltshire police later accepted he was unlawfully detained, and apologised (*Media Lawyer*, 30 March 2011).

▌ Public order offences

((•))

see Useful
Websites
at the end
of this
chapter
for further
guidance
on public
order
offences

Police officers sometimes warn media photographers or video-journalists that they may be arrested. The arrest would probably be under common law for breach of the peace, or under section 5 of the Public Order Act 1986. Arrest for breach of the peace is only justified if harm has been done or is likely to be done to a person or their property in their presence, or when a person is in fear of being harmed. Section 5 allows arrest if anyone's behaviour is disorderly and likely to cause 'harassment, alarm or distress' to another person. Though the journalist is not intending to cause distress, etc, in some situations the mere fact that he/she is taking pictures or shooting footage, perhaps of someone or a group who object to this, may prompt an arrest.

▌ Obstructing the highway

Section 137 of the Highways Act 1980 makes it an offence for someone 'without lawful authority or excuse' to obstruct free passage along a highway in any way. This power allows police to arrest journalists in a public place who fail to move on when asked to do so.

▌ Obstructing the police

Section 89 of the Police Act 1996 says that a person commits an offence if he/she 'resists or wilfully obstructs a constable in the execution of his duty, or a person assisting a constable in the execution of his duty'. The obstruction does not have to be a physical act – it may occur, for example, if someone makes it more difficult for the constable to perform his/her duty. A journalist who persists in taking photographs or shooting footage, and engages in argument with a police officer, therefore runs the risk of arrest.

👁 **Case study**

A freelance photographer was arrested in 2007 as he tried to take pictures of a man threatening to jump from the Tyne Bridge in Newcastle. He was later charged with obstructing the police. A district judge at the city's magistrates courts acquitted the photographer, saying he had acted 'professionally' (*Media Lawyer*, 15 October 2007).

---

for an outline of the polices' general powers of arrest, see ch. 4, p. 39, Arrest

▌ 'Stop and search' under the Terrorism Act 2000

Complaints by photographers of excessive use by police of 'stop and search' powers under the Terrorism Act 2000 – for example, if a photographer was taking pictures of buildings – have decreased since the government amended the law to produce a more tightly defined 'stop and search' power in the Act's section 47A. This change is primarily concerned with the criteria police can use to designate areas as being at risk of terrorist attack. Police in such areas are still permitted to stop and search an individual without 'reasonable suspicion'. A revised code of practice issued to police makes clear that they have no power under the 2000 Act to stop filming or photography of incidents or of police officers, and that it is not an offence to film/photograph a public building or in public places. Police retain power under section 43 of the Act to stop and search, and to seize equipment, if they reasonably suspect someone is a terrorist.

 See Useful Websites at the end of this chapter for the code of practice in full. See the www.mcnaes. com chapter 'Terrorism and the effect counter-terrorism law' for other counter-terrorism laws which could affect journalists.

▌ Trespass and bye-laws

Property and land owners who object to photography or filming or recording on their sites may decide to enforce objections by using the civil law of trespass, which forbids unlawful entry to land or buildings. Because trespass is a **tort**, the remedy is an action in the civil courts which could result in an injunction to prevent further trespass, and/or damages. Also, the occupier of property or land may use reasonable force to eject the trespasser. Police may lawfully assist, though they have no duty to do so.

 →glossary

see ch. 27, News-gathering avoiding intrusion.

There is no trespass if a journalist photographs, films or records an event on adjoining private land from a site where he/she has permission or a right to be – for example, on a public highway. But such media activity might lead to a subject suing for intrusion into privacy or complaining to Ipso or Ofcom. Trespass can also include 'trespass to the person' – for example, compelling a person to be filmed by stopping him/her from entering home or a workplace. Trespass to goods means, for instance, picking up a document without permission and photographing it.

ch. 33, p. 398, the 1911 Act, explains official secrets law on 'prohibited places'

Trespass is not usually a criminal offence, and so a police officer threatening an arrest for civil trespass is wrong in law. However, there are trespass offences for certain sites for example, Ministry of Defence (MoD) land and railway property, and there is a specific offence of aggravated trespass. Also, bye-laws ban photography in and of MoD establishments.

▌ Aggravated trespass

see Useful Websites at the end of this chapter for Crown Prosecution Service guidelines on this offence

Section 68 of the Criminal Justice and Public Order Act 1994 created the offence of aggravated trespass. It has been used against protesters – for example, those who, demonstrating about alleged tax evasion by the rich, occupied Fortnum and Masons store in London in 2011. A journalist covering such an event could be accused of the offence. A person commits aggravated trespass if he/she trespasses and, in relation to any lawful activity which other persons are engaged in on that or adjoining property, does anything intended to have the effect of:

- intimidating any of them so as to deter them from engaging in that activity; or
- obstructing that activity; or
- disrupting that activity.

The penalty for aggravated trespass is up to three months' imprisonment or a fine.

Section 69 of the Act says a senior police officer present at the scene has power to order any person believed to be involved in aggravated trespass to leave the property. Failure to leave, or returning within three months, is an offence. A journalist who fails to leave may have a defence under the Act that he/she had 'a reasonable excuse' to stay.

 Ch. 27, Newsgathering avoiding intrusion, covers privacy issues in photography, filming and recording, including when a child is the subject. That chapter also covers intrusion into grief, and explains that paparazzi who stalk celebrities could be sued or prosecuted for harassment.

➡ Recap of major points

- There is no law against photography, filming or recording in public places.
- But journalists need to be familiar with the law on trespass, and general powers police have to arrest those 'obstructing' them or the highway.
- Police have been issued with guidelines that they should help the media take photos and gain footage, but individual officers may need reminding of these.

((•)) Useful Websites

www.acpo.presscentre.com/content/default.aspx?NewsAreaID=19
   Association of Chief Police Officers (ACPO) Communication Advisory Group – Guidance 2010

http://content.met.police.uk/Site/photographyadvice
   Metropolitan Police 'Photography Advice'

www.cps.gov.uk/legal/p_to_r/public_order_offences/
   Crown Prosecution Service guidance on public order offences

www.gov.uk/government/uploads/system/uploads/attachment_data/file/97944/
stop-search-code-of-practice.pdf
   Code of practice for police 'stop and search' powers under Terrorism Act 2000

www.cps.gov.uk/legal/s_to_u/trespass_and_nuisance_on_land/
   Crown Prosecution Service guidance on trespass offences

www.epuk.org/Resources/958/police-photographers-and-the-law
   Editorial Photographers website guide to photographers and the law

http://media.gn.apc.org/photo/index.html
   National Union of Journalists London Freelance branch advice for photographers

www.digitalcameraworld.com/2012/04/14/photographers-rights-the-ultimate-guide/
   Digital Camera World guide to the law

37

Northern Ireland

Chapter summary

Media law in Northern Ireland is, with some exceptions, particularly in defamation law, the same as that in England and Wales. In the few important cases involving the media which have gone to the High Court, cases in England have been freely cited. The Supreme Court in London is the final court of appeal for criminal and civil cases. Restrictions on reports of preliminary hearings before magistrates, prior to committal to Crown court, follow Northern Ireland law but restrictions on reports of criminal proceedings involving juveniles are along the lines of those on the mainland. Victims or alleged victims of sexual offences must remain anonymous. It is an offence to disclose the identity of a juror who is serving or has served on a trial in Northern Ireland, or of a person who is on the jury list there.

▌ The law is broadly the same as in England and Wales

see the www. mcnaes. com chapter on Scotland

The law in Northern Ireland, including the courts structure, is broadly the same as that in England and Wales. Scotland has its own system.

Many of the laws applicable in England and Wales extend to Northern Ireland by means of Orders made by the Secretary of State.

The Lord Chief Justice of Northern Ireland is assisted by High Court judges and circuit judges who try cases in the Crown court, which also hears appeals from magistrates courts. Civil cases are heard by High Court judges sitting in the Northern Ireland High Court, or circuit judges sitting in the county court. Three Lords Justices of Appeal, sometimes sitting with other High Court judges, hear appeals from the Crown court, county court or High Court in the Court of Appeal in Belfast.

Most cases in magistrates courts are heard by a **district judge**.   → glossary

The UK Supreme Court is the final court of appeal for criminal and civil cases.

▶ Defamation

Defamation law in Northern Ireland and England diverged when the Westminster Parliament passed the Defamation Act 2013 to reform the law, and Northern Ireland's government, the Executive, decided against adopting the legislation. The result is that reforms in the 2013 Act have no effect and Northern Ireland continues to operate under the Defamation Act (Northern Ireland) 1955 and the relevant parts of the Defamation Act 1996. Thus, there will be no requirement in Northern Ireland for claimants to show that they have suffered serious harm when suing for defamation, while website operators will have fewer defences in relation to user-generated content. Even if such a website publisher has procedures to enable complaints to be remedied, it can be sued in Northern Ireland much more easily than in England or Wales. Also the new statutory defences in England and Wales of responsible publication on matters of public interest, truth, and honest opinion do not apply. Instead defendants in Northern Ireland have to rely on the often difficult to prove common law defences of justification and honest comment.

 The 'justification' and 'honest' comment defences are explained on www.mcnaes.com in the additional material for this chapter. For general principles of defamation law, see chs. 19 to 24, where some explanation is in the context of the law in England and Wales.

▶ Contempt of court

The Contempt of Court Act 1981 is effective in Northern Ireland and the many contempt decisions by the High Court in London are equally applicable there.

The only significant difference is the reporting of courts unique to Northern Ireland known as 'Diplock courts'. These were introduced during the Troubles to allow terrorists charged with scheduled offences to be tried by a judge sitting without a jury. The reduction in terrorist activity with the peace process now means these sit extremely rarely. It has been argued that the absence of a jury means that reporting on 'Diplock' involves a much reduced risk of contempt through creating a substantial risk of serious prejudice to the proceedings. But the danger remains that the evidence of witnesses might be coloured by accounts given by others.

 ch. 18 explains contempt law

▶ Reporting restrictions

Guidelines on reporting restrictions issued in 2008 by the Judicial Studies Board for Northern Ireland, say courts are encouraged to exercise their discretion to hear media representations when considering discretionary reporting restrictions. See Useful Websites at the end of this chapter for this guidance.

ch. 8,
p. 81,
Appeals
against
rulings
by judge:
reporting
restrictions,
explains
these
appeals

▶ Preliminary hearings

Committal proceedings must be in open court except where it appears to the court that the ends of justice would not be served by reports of the whole or part of the hearing. The Magistrates' Courts (Northern Ireland) Order 1981 (SI 1981/1675) prohibits publication of a report of any opening statement made by the prosecution. There is no automatic ban on reporting evidence, but the Act allows a court to prohibit publication of any evidence if it is satisfied that publication would prejudice the defendant's trial. The court may impose additional restrictions where objection is taken to the admissibility of evidence. The court may, if satisfied that the objection is made in good faith, order that such evidence and any discussion on it shall not be published.

▶ Crown courts

Restrictions under the Criminal Justice Act 2003 on reporting prosecution appeals against the termination of a trial by a judge, or against an acquittal, were extended to Ulster under the Criminal Justice (Northern Ireland) Order 2004 (SI 2004/1500).

The Court of Appeal in Belfast ruled in 1995 that hearing plea bargaining submissions in open court could inhibit rather than secure the achievement of justice.

▶ Juveniles in court

A child under 10 cannot be charged with a criminal offence in Northern Ireland. Youth courts deal with offences committed by those below the age of 18. The Criminal Justice (Children) (Northern Ireland) Order 1998 (SI 1998/1504), as amended, makes it an offence in reporting the proceedings to publish the name, address or school, or any particulars likely to lead to the identification of anyone under 18 involved in youth court proceedings, or in an appeal from a youth court, as defendant, witness or alleged victim/victim. It is also an offence to publish a picture of or including anyone under 18 so involved. A youth court may lift the restrictions on a convicted young offender in the public interest but must first afford parties to the proceedings an opportunity to make representations.

Under article 22 of the 1998 Order, an adult court may order that nothing should be published which would identify those under 18 involved in the proceedings as a defendant, witness or party. An order is not effective if the person has reached 18.

 See ch. 9, Juveniles, which explains law applying to media reports of youth court cases in England and Wales, which is similar to that in Northern Ireland, and explains too the 'section 39' orders used in England and Wales which are comparable to article 22 orders.

The 1998 Order empowers a court in any criminal proceedings to exclude – everyone not concerned in the case, where it considers the evidence of a child is likely to involve matter of an indecent or immoral nature. There is no specific provision for the press to remain, unlike the position in England and Wales under section 37 of the Children and Young Persons Act 1933.

ch. 14. pp. 152–154, Statute law on open and private hearings, explains section 37

Domestic proceedings

Representatives of newspapers and news agencies may attend domestic proceedings but reports must be confined to four points, as is the case for family and domestic proceedings in England and Wales. The court may, under the Children (Northern Ireland) Order 1995 (SI 1995/755), direct that any report of non-criminal proceedings must not lead to the identification of any person under 18 as being involved where any power is being exercised under that order, except to the extent which the court may allow. The court has power to sit **in private** when exercising any power under the 1995 Order.

→ glossary

Sexual offences

The Sexual Offences Act 2003 and the Youth Justice and Criminal Evidence Act 1999 amended the Sexual Offences (Amendment) Act 1992 and the Criminal Justice (Northern Ireland) Order 1994 (SI 2004/2795) in relation to media reports of sexual offences in Northern Ireland. This law, which provides anonymity in media reports for victims/alleged victims of sexual offences, is essentially the same as in England and Wales – explained in ch. 10.

see also ch. 13 and www. mcnaes. com ch. 13 on family cases

Identifying defendants in sexual offence cases

There is nothing in the 1994 Order giving a court discretionary powers, in addition to the automatic restrictions protecting victims/alleged victims, to impose further restrictions such as prohibiting identification of the defendant.

A number of Crown courts and magistrates courts have attempted to make orders banning the naming of a defendant, citing the 1994 Order, on the grounds that publishing his/her name would either lead to the identification of the complainant or be detrimental to the complainant's well-being. Such purported orders would seem to be *ultra vires*. The Order's article 19 prohibits publication of particulars which would lead to the identification of the complainant, but there is no provision in the article for a court to determine which particulars they might be.

See also ch. 15, p. 172, Is anonymity necessary for justice to be done? for the judgment in *R v Newtownabbey Magistrates' Court, ex p Belfast Telegraph Newspapers Ltd* (1997), and ch. 15, p. 186, Sexual offence law does *not* give anonymity to defendants.

In 1999 at Newtownabbey Magistrates' Court in the case of a police officer accused of indecently assaulting a child, the prosecution and defence made a joint application for the press to be excluded. Mr Phillip Mateer, a deputy resident magistrate, refused the application, referring to *R v Newtownabbey Magistrates' Court*, cited earlier.

see also
ch. 11, pp. 118–119, Contempt risk in identifying or approaching jurors

▶ Identifying jurors

It is an offence to identify someone as being or having been a juror in Northern Ireland, or as being listed as a juror or selected for inclusion on the jury list. The offence is contained in the Juries (Northern Ireland) Order 1996 (SI 1996/1141), as amended, which provides a defence that there was reasonable belief that disclosure of the juror's identity was lawful.

ch. 11 explains the 1925 Act and also covers the ban on audio-recording in courts

▶ Photography, filming and recording at court

The Criminal Justice (Northern Ireland) Act 1945, operating in a similar way to the mainland Criminal Justice Act 1925, prohibits photography, filming or sketching in a court or its precincts. Guidelines from the Judicial Studies Board say the court can issue guidance, by way of a map, on the extent of the precincts.

! Remember

www.mcnaes.com has a chapter outlining Scottish media law.

➡ Recap of major points

- The law in Northern Ireland, including the courts structure, is broadly the same as in England and Wales, with minor variations.

- It is easier to sue for defamation in Northern Ireland than in England and Wales as a claimant does not have to prove any damage and the defences are weaker.

- Reporting restrictions in Northern Ireland broadly follow those in England and Wales but many of them are contained in Orders made by the Secretary of State rather than in Acts of Parliament.

- When a child is giving evidence involving indecent or immoral matters the court may exclude everyone not concerned in the proceedings.

((•)) Useful Websites

www.jsbni.com/Publications/reporting-restrictions/Pages/default.aspx
   Judicial Studies Board for Northern Ireland guide to reporting restrictions

www.courtsni.gov.uk
   Northern Ireland Courts and Tribunals Service

Part 6

Online chapters

38

The incitement of hate

Chapter summary

Freedom of expression has boundaries. One boundary is that making or publishing some kinds of threatening statement is a crime. As this chapter explains, it is an offence to stir up hatred against people because of their race, religious beliefs or their sexual orientation.

Full chapter available at www.mcnaes.com.

39

Scotland

Chapter summary

The law of Scotland affects journalism in different ways from that in England and Wales. This chapter briefly outlines the Scottish legal system and its judiciary and shows how reporting restrictions affect coverage of criminal proceedings, especially cases involving children. Media organisations based in other parts of the UK may need to pay special consideration to what they publish in Scotland, because contempt laws are interpreted differently.

Full chapter available at www.mcnaes.com.

Terrorism and the effect of counter-terrorism law

Chapter summary

The heightened threat of terrorism in recent years has led to more counter-terrorism laws in the UK, some controversial because of their actual or potential interference with journalists' work. These laws ban the gathering of certain information, and restrict what can be published. As this chapter shows, the wide scope of counter-terrorism law has the potential to deter journalistic investigation of the causes and control of terrorism.

Full chapter available at www.mcnaes.com.

Appendix 1
Extracts from the European Convention for the Protection of Human Rights and Fundamental Freedoms (known as the European Convention on Human Rights)

Article 2: Right to life

1) Everyone's right to life shall be protected by law. No one shall be deprived of his life intentionally save in the execution of a sentence of a court following his conviction of a crime for which this penalty is provided by law. [*see also * at the end of this Appendix*]

2) Deprivation of life shall not be regarded as inflicted in contravention of this Article when it results from the use of force which is no more than absolutely necessary:
   (a) in defence of any person from unlawful violence;
   (b) in order to effect a lawful arrest or to prevent the escape of a person lawfully detained;
   (c) in action lawfully taken for the purpose of quelling a riot or insurrection.

Article 3: Prohibition of torture

No one shall be subjected to torture or to inhuman or degrading treatment or punishment.

Article 6: Right to a fair trial [the article is quoted in part]

1) In the determination of his civil rights and obligations or of any criminal charge against him, everyone is entitled to a fair and public hearing within a reasonable time by an independent and impartial tribunal established by law. Judgment shall be pronounced publicly but the press and public may be excluded from all or part of the trial in the interest of morals, public order or national security in a democratic society, where the interests of juveniles or the protection of the private life of the parties so require, or to the extent strictly necessary in the opinion of the court in special circumstances where publicity would prejudice the interests of justice.

2) Everyone charged with a criminal offence shall be presumed innocent until proved guilty according to law.

Article 8: Right to respect for private and family life

1) Everyone has the right to respect for his private and family life, his home and his correspondence.

2) There shall be no interference by a public authority with the exercise of this right except such as is in accordance with the law and is necessary in a democratic society in the interests of national security, public safety or the economic well-being of the country, for the prevention of disorder or crime, for the protection of health or morals, or for the protection of the rights and freedoms of others.

Article 10: Freedom of expression

1) Everyone has the right to freedom of expression. This right shall include freedom to hold opinions and to receive and impart information and ideas without interference by public authority and regardless of frontiers. This Article shall not prevent States from requiring the licensing of broadcasting, television or cinema enterprises.

2) The exercise of these freedoms, since it carries with it duties and responsibilities, may be subject to such formalities, conditions, restrictions or penalties as are prescribed by law and are necessary in a democratic society, in the interests of national security, territorial integrity or public safety, for the prevention of disorder or crime, for the protection of health or morals, for the protection of the reputation or rights of others, for preventing the disclosure of information received in confidence, or for maintaining the authority and impartiality of the judiciary.

* Article 1 of the Thirteenth Protocol of the Convention, which was adopted into UK law in 2004, stated: 'The death penalty shall be abolished'. It had already been abolished in the UK.

For the Convention's full text see www.echr.coe.int/Documents/Convention_ENG.pdf

Appendix 2
The Editors' Code of Practice

The Press Complaints Commission was charged with enforcing the following Code of Practice which was framed by the newspaper and periodical industry and was ratified by the PCC in December 2011. Clauses marked* are covered by exceptions relating to the public interest. This code is to be the starting point for the code to be adopted by the Independent Press Standards Organisation, and therefore references to the PCC should be read as referring to Ipso.

THE CODE

All members of the press have a duty to maintain the highest professional standards. The Code, which includes this preamble and the public interest exceptions below, sets the benchmark for those ethical standards, protecting both the rights of the individual and the public's right to know. It is the cornerstone of the system of self-regulation to which the industry has made a binding commitment.

It is essential that an agreed code be honoured not only to the letter but in the full spirit. It should not be interpreted so narrowly as to compromise its commitment to respect the rights of the individual, nor so broadly that it constitutes an unnecessary interference with freedom of expression or prevents publication in the public interest.

It is the responsibility of editors and publishers to apply the Code to editorial material in both printed and online versions of publications. They should take care to ensure it is observed rigorously by all editorial staff and external contributors, including non-journalists, in printed and online versions of publications.

Editors should co-operate swiftly with the PCC in the resolution of complaints. Any publication judged to have breached the Code must print the adjudication in full and with due prominence agreed by the Commission's Director, including headline reference to the PCC.

1 **Accuracy**
   i) The Press must take care not to publish inaccurate, misleading or distorted information, including pictures.
   ii) A significant inaccuracy, misleading statement or distortion once recognised must be corrected, promptly and with due prominence, and – where appropriate – an apology published. In cases involving the Commission, prominence should be agreed with the PCC in advance.
   iii) The Press, whilst free to be partisan, must distinguish clearly between comment, conjecture and fact.

iv) A publication must report fairly and accurately the outcome of an action for defamation to which it has been a party, unless an agreed settlement states otherwise, or an agreed statement is published.

2 **Opportunity to reply**

A fair opportunity for reply to inaccuracies must be given when reasonably called for.

3 *****Privacy**
   i) Everyone is entitled to respect for his or her private and family life, home, health and correspondence, including digital communications.
   ii) Editors will be expected to justify intrusions into any individual's private life without consent. Account will be taken of the complainant's own public disclosures of information.
   iii) It is unacceptable to photograph individuals in private places without their consent.

Note – Private places are public or private property where there is a reasonable expectation of privacy.

4 *****Harassment**
   i) Journalists must not engage in intimidation, harassment or persistent pursuit.
   ii) They must not persist in questioning, telephoning, pursuing or photographing individuals once asked to desist; nor remain on their property when asked to leave and must not follow them. If requested, they must identify themselves and whom they represent.
   iii) Editors must ensure these principles are observed by those working for them and take care not to use non-compliant material from other sources.

5 **Intrusion into grief or shock**
   i) In cases involving personal grief or shock, enquiries and approaches must be made with sympathy and discretion and publication handled sensitively. This should not restrict the right to report legal proceedings, such as inquests.
   *ii) When reporting suicide, care should be taken to avoid excessive detail about the method used.

6 *****Children**
   i) Young people should be free to complete their time at school without unnecessary intrusion.
   ii) A child under 16 must not be interviewed or photographed on issues involving their own or another child's welfare unless a custodial parent or similarly responsible adult consents.
   iii) Pupils must not be approached or photographed at school without the permission of the school authorities.

iv) Minors must not be paid for material involving children's welfare, nor parents or guardians for material about their children or wards, unless it is clearly in the child's interest.

v) Editors must not use the fame, notoriety or position of a parent or guardian as sole justification for publishing details of a child's private life.

7 *Children in sex cases

1. The press must not, even if legally free to do so, identify children under 16 who are victims or witnesses in cases involving sex offences.

2. In any press report of a case involving a sexual offence against a child –

   i)   The child must not be identified.

   ii) The adult may be identified.

   iii) The word 'incest' must not be used where a child victim might be identified.

   iv) Care must be taken that nothing in the report implies the relationship between the accused and the child.

8 *Hospitals

i) Journalists must identify themselves and obtain permission from a responsible executive before entering non-public areas of hospitals or similar institutions to pursue enquiries.

ii) The restrictions on intruding into privacy are particularly relevant to enquiries about individuals in hospitals or similar institutions.

9 *Reporting of Crime

(i) Relatives or friends of persons convicted or accused of crime should not generally be identified without their consent, unless they are genuinely relevant to the story.

(ii) Particular regard should be paid to the potentially vulnerable position of children who witness, or are victims of, crime. This should not restrict the right to report legal proceedings.

10 *Clandestine devices and subterfuge

i) The press must not seek to obtain or publish material acquired by using hidden cameras or clandestine listening devices; or by intercepting private or mobile telephone calls, messages or emails; or by the unauthorised removal of documents or photographs; or by accessing digitally-held private information without consent.

ii) Engaging in misrepresentation or subterfuge, including by agents or intermediaries, can generally be justified only in the public interest and then only when the material cannot be obtained by other means.

11 Victims of sexual assault

The press must not identify victims of sexual assault or publish material likely to contribute to such identification unless there is adequate justification and they are legally free to do so.

12 Discrimination

i)   The press must avoid prejudicial or pejorative reference to an individual's race, colour, religion, gender, sexual orientation or to any physical or mental illness or disability.

ii) Details of an individual's race, colour, religion, sexual orientation, physical or mental illness or disability must be avoided unless genuinely relevant to the story.

13 Financial journalism

i)   Even where the law does not prohibit it, journalists must not use for their own profit financial information they receive in advance of its general publication, nor should they pass such information to others.

ii) They must not write about shares or securities in whose performance they know that they or their close families have a significant financial interest without disclosing the interest to the editor or financial editor.

iii) They must not buy or sell, either directly or through nominees or agents, shares or securities about which they have written recently or about which they intend to write in the near future.

14 Confidential sources

Journalists have a moral obligation to protect confidential sources of information.

15 Witness payments in criminal trials

i)   No payment or offer of payment to a witness – or any person who may reasonably be expected to be called as a witness – should be made in any case once proceedings are active as defined by the Contempt of Court Act 1981.

This prohibition lasts until the suspect has been freed unconditionally by police without charge or bail or the proceedings are otherwise discontinued; or has entered a guilty plea to the court; or, in the event of a not guilty plea, the court has announced its verdict.

*ii) Where proceedings are not yet active but are likely and foreseeable, editors must not make or offer payment to any person who may reasonably be expected to be called as a witness, unless the information concerned ought demonstrably to be published in the public interest and there is an over-riding need to make or promise payment for this to be done; and all reasonable steps have been taken to ensure no financial dealings influence the evidence those witnesses give. In no circumstances should such payment be conditional on the outcome of a trial.

*iii) Any payment or offer of payment made to a person later cited to give evidence in proceedings must be disclosed to the prosecution and defence. The witness must be advised of this requirement.

16 *Payment to criminals

i)   Payment or offers of payment for stories, pictures or information, which seek to exploit a particular crime or to glorify or glamorise crime in general, must not be made directly or via agents to convicted or confessed criminals or to their associates – who may include family, friends and colleagues.

ii) Editors invoking the public interest to justify payment or offers would need to demonstrate that there was good reason to believe the public interest would be served. If, despite payment, no public interest emerged, then the material should not be published.

The public interest

There may be exceptions to the clauses marked * where they can be demonstrated to be in the public interest.

1. The public interest includes, but is not confined to:
   i) Detecting or exposing crime or serious impropriety.
   ii) Protecting public health and safety.
   iii) Preventing the public from being misled by an action or statement of an individual or organisation.
2. There is a public interest in freedom of expression itself.
3. Whenever the public interest is invoked, the PCC will require editors to demonstrate fully that they reasonably believed that publication, or journalistic activity undertaken with a view to publication, would be in the public interest and how, and with whom, that was established at the time.
4. The PCC will consider the extent to which material is already in the public domain, or will become so.
5. In cases involving children under 16, editors must demonstrate an exceptional public interest to over-ride the normally paramount interest of the child.

Appendix 3
Schedule 1 to the Defamation Act 1996

Statements having qualified privilege (see chapter 21, pp. 267–272)

This is the text of Parts 1 and 2 of Schedule 1 to the 1996 Act, paras 1–16, as amended by section the Defamation Act 2013.

Part 1: Statements privileged without explanation or contradiction

1. A fair and accurate report of proceedings in public of a legislature anywhere in the world.

for definition of 'court', see p. 452

2. A fair and accurate report of proceedings in public before a court anywhere in the world. [*para. 17 makes clear that this includes the European Court of Justice, the European Court of Human Rights, and any international criminal tribunal established by the United Nations or by an international agreement to which the UK is a party*]

3. A fair and accurate report of proceedings in public of a person appointed to hold a public inquiry by a government or legislature anywhere in the world.

4. A fair and accurate report of proceedings in public anywhere in the world of an international organisation or an international conference. [*para. 17 limits these definitions to a conference attended by representatives of two or more governments or an organisation of which two or more governments are members, including any committee or other subordinate body of such an organisation*]

5. A fair and accurate copy of or extract from any register or other document required by law to be open to public inspection.

6. A notice or advertisement published by or on the authority of a court, or of a judge or officer of a court, anywhere in the world.

7. A fair and accurate copy of or extract from matter published by or on the authority of a government or legislature anywhere in the world.

8. A fair and accurate copy of or extract from matter published anywhere in the world by an international organisation or an international conference. [*same definitions as for para. 4*]

Part 2: Statements privileged subject to explanation or contradiction

9. (1) A fair and accurate copy of, extract from or summary of a notice or other matter issued for the information of the public by or on behalf of—

    (a) a legislature or government anywhere in the world;

    (b) an authority anywhere in the world performing governmental functions;

    (c) an international organisation or international conference.

  (2) In this paragraph 'governmental functions' includes police functions.

10. A fair and accurate copy of, extract from or summary of a document made available by a court anywhere in the world, or by a judge or officer of such a court.

11. (1) A fair and accurate report of proceedings at any public meeting or sitting in the United Kingdom of –

    (a) a local authority or local authority committee;

    (aa) in the case of a local authority which are operating executive arrangements, the executive of that authority or a committee of that executive;

    (b) a justice or justices of the peace acting otherwise than as a court exercising judicial authority;

    (c) a commission, tribunal, committee or person appointed for the purposes of any inquiry by any statutory provision, by Her Majesty or by a Minister of the Crown, a member of the Scottish Executive, the Welsh Ministers or the Counsel General to the Welsh Assembly Government, or a Northern Ireland Department;

    (d) a person appointed by a local authority to hold a local inquiry in pursuance of any statutory provision;

    (e) any other tribunal, board, committee or body constituted by or under, and exercising functions under, any statutory provision.

  (1A) In the case of a local authority which are operating executive arrangements, a fair and accurate record of any decision made by any member of the executive where that record is required to be made and available for public inspection by virtue of section 22 of the Local Government Act 2000 or of any provision in regulations made under that section.

  (2) In sub-paragraphs (1)(a), (1)(aa) and (1A) 'local authority' means—

    (a) in relation to England and Wales, a principal council within the meaning of the Local Government Act 1972, any body falling within any paragraph of section 100J(1) of that Act or an authority or body to which the Public Bodies (Admission to Meetings) Act 1960 applies,

(b) in relation to Scotland, a council constituted under section 2 of the Local Government etc (Scotland) Act 1994 or an authority or body to which the Public Bodies (Admission to Meetings) Act 1960 applies,

(c) in relation to Northern Ireland, any authority or body to which sections 23 to 27 of the Local Government Act (Northern Ireland) 1972 apply; and

'local authority committee' means any committee of a local authority or of local authorities, and includes –

(a) any committee or sub-committee in relation to which sections 100A to 100D of the Local Government Act 1972 apply by virtue of section 100E of that Act (whether or not also by virtue of section 100J of that Act), and

(b) any committee or sub-committee in relation to which sections 50A to 50D of the Local Government (Scotland) Act 1973 apply by virtue of section 50E of that Act.

(2a) In sub-paragraphs (1) and (1A) 'executive' and 'executive arrangements' have the same meaning as in Part II of the Local Government Act 2000.

(3) A fair and accurate report of any corresponding proceedings in any of the Channel Islands or the Isle of Man or in another member state.

11a A fair and accurate report of proceedings at a press conference held anywhere in the world for the discussion of a matter of public interest.

12 (1) A fair and accurate report of proceedings at any public meeting held anywhere in the world.

(2) In this paragraph a 'public meeting' means a meeting bona fide and lawfully held for a lawful purpose and for the furtherance or discussion of a matter of public interest, whether admission to the meeting is general or restricted.

13 (1) A fair and accurate report of proceedings at a general meeting of a UK public company.

(2) A fair and accurate copy of, extract from or summary of any document circulated to members of a listed company—

(a) by or with the authority of the board of directors of the company,

(b) by the auditors of the company, or

(c) by any member of the company in pursuance of a right conferred by any statutory provision.

(3) A fair and accurate copy of, extract from or summary of any document circulated to members of a listed company which relates to the

appointment, resignation, retirement or dismissal of directors of the company or its auditors.

(4) In this paragraph 'listed company' has the same meaning as in Part 12 of the Corporation Tax Act 2009 (see section 1005 of that Act).'

14. A fair and accurate report of any finding or decision of any of the following descriptions of association formed anywhere in the world or of any committee or governing body of such an association –

(a) an association formed for the purpose of promoting or encouraging the exercise of or interest in any art, science, religion or learning, and empowered by its constitution to exercise control over or adjudicate on matters of interest or concern to the association, or the actions or conduct of any persons subject to such control or adjudication;

(b) an association formed for the purpose of promoting or safeguarding the interests of any trade, business, industry or profession, or of the persons carrying on or engaged in any trade, business, industry or profession, and empowered by its constitution to exercise control over or adjudicate upon matters connected with the trade, business, industry or profession, or the actions or conduct of those persons;

(c) an association formed for the purpose of promoting or safeguarding the interests of a game, sport or pastime to the playing or exercise of which members of the public are invited or admitted, and empowered by its constitution to exercise control over or adjudicate upon persons connected with or taking part in the game, sport or pastime;

(d) an association formed for the purpose of promoting charitable objects or other objects beneficial to the community and empowered by its constitution to exercise control over or to adjudicate on matters of interest or concern to the association, or the actions or conduct of any person subject to such control or adjudication.

14A A fair and accurate—

(a) report of proceedings of a scientific or academic conference held anywhere in the world, or

(b) copy of, extract from or summary of matter published by such a conference.

15 (1) A fair and accurate report or summary of, copy of or extract from, any adjudication, report, statement or notice issued by a body, officer or other person designated for the purposes of this paragraph by order of the Lord Chancellor.

(2) An order under this paragraph shall be made by statutory instrument which shall be subject to annulment in pursuance of a resolution of either House of Parliament.

16   In this Schedule—'court' includes—

(a)   any tribunal or body established under the law of any country or territory exercising the judicial power of the State;

(b)   any international tribunal established by the Security Council of the United Nations or by an international agreement;

(c)   any international tribunal deciding matters in dispute between States;'international conference' means a conference attended by representatives of two or more governments;'international organisation' means an organisation of which two or more governments are members, and includes any committee or other subordinate body of such an organisation;'legislature' includes a local legislature; and'member State' includes any European dependent territory of a member State.

Glossary

Absolute discharge A decision by a court after conviction that the defendant should not be punished for the offence.

Affidavit A statement given on oath to be used in court proceedings.

Alibi The defence case of an accused who asserts that he/she was not at the scene of a crime when it occurred and that he/she is therefore innocent.

Allocation The procedure at magistrates courts which determines whether an **either-way** criminal case is dealt with by magistrates or by a Crown court, also known as the **mode of trial hearing**.

Arraignment The procedure at Crown courts in which charges are put to defendants for them to plead guilty or not guilty.

Automatic, automatically Terms used for reporting restrictions which ban publication of certain information if no court order is needed to put them into effect in respect of a particular case or individual. Statute specifies the circumstances when it operates.

Bail The system by which a person awaiting trial, or appeal, may be freed by a court pending the next hearing. *See also* Police bail.

Bailiff A court official who enforces its orders.

Case law The system by which reports of previous cases and the judges' interpretations of the common law are used as precedents where the legally material facts are similar.

Circuit judge Judge who has been appointed to sit at a Crown court or county court within a circuit – one of the regions of England and Wales into which court administration is divided. Unlike High Court judges, circuit judges do not go on circuit, that is travel to various large centres dispensing justice.

Claim form *Previously known as* writ or default summons. A document that begins many forms of civil action.

Claimant *Previously known as* plaintiff. The person who takes an action to enforce a claim in the civil court.

Committal for sentence, committed for sentence When a defendant at a magistrates court who has admitted an offence or been convicted in a trial is then sent to Crown court to be sentenced because the magistrates decide their powers of punishment are insufficient. (There are no reporting restrictions on committals for sentence.)

Common Law Law based on the custom of the realm and the decisions of judges through the centuries rather than on an Act of Parliament.

Community punishment An order that an offender must carry out unpaid work in the community under a probation officer's supervision.

Concurrent sentences Two or more sentences of imprisonment imposed for different offences; the longest one is the sentence actually served.

Conditional discharge A decision by a court that a convicted defendant should not be punished unless he/she re-offends: that is, a condition is imposed that if he/she commits another crime within a specified period, eg a year, he/she can be punished for the original offence as well as for the re-offending.

Conditional fee agreements (CFAs) No win, no fee agreements – their use was extended to defamation cases in 1998 under the Conditional Fee Agreements Order 1998 (SI 1998/1860).

Counsel Barrister (singular or plural), not solicitor.

Disclosure and inspection *Previously known as* discovery. The process whereby each side in a court action serves relevant documents on the other, which has the right to inspect them.

Discovery *See* Disclosure.

District judge An official of the county court who also adjudicates in smaller cases, presides at public examinations in bankruptcy, and deals with cases under the informal arbitration procedure.

District judge (magistrates courts) The title given to full-time, legally qualified magistrates, *formerly known as* Stipendiary magistrates.

Editors' Code of Practice Code of ethics which was used by the Press Complaints Commission to adjudicate on complaints against newspapers, magazines and website-only publications. It will be the starting point for the code to be adopted by the Independent Press Standards Organisation.

Either-way offence One triable either summarily at magistrates court or before a jury at Crown court. In an either-way case a defendant who has indicated a plea of not guilty has the right to opt for jury trial at Crown court. But if he/she chooses to be tried by the magistrates court, it may overrule him by deciding the Crown court should deal with his case – *see* also **allocation**, and **mode of trial hearing**.

Evidence-in-chief The main evidence given by a witness before he/she is cross-examined.

Ex parte *See* **without notice**.

Excluded material Such material is exempt from compulsory disclosure under the Police and Criminal Evidence Act 1984 (PACE). It includes **journalistic material** (*see later*) that a person holds in confidence and that consists of documents or records.

Fair dealing A defence to breach of copyright for use of extracts of a copyrighted work, properly attributed to its author.

Hearsay Evidence of what a witness is told, rather than what they actually saw or heard for themselves.

Honest opinion A defence to a libel action, *formerly known as* honest comment or fair comment; the defendant does not have to show the words were fair, but must show they were an honestly-held opinion.

In camera Proceedings in a courtroom which are heard in secret, with the media and public excluded (for example in Official Secrets Act cases).

In chambers Used to describe the hearing of an application which takes place in the judge's room. If there is no legal reason for such a hearing to be held **in private** (*see next term*), journalists who want to report it should be admitted if 'practicable'.

In private A term used of a court hearing **In camera** (*see earlier*), or one **In chambers** (*see previous term*) which the press and public are not entitled to attend.

Indictable offence A charge which may be tried by a jury at Crown court, which will therefore be either an **indictable-only offence** (*see later*) or an **either-way offence** (*see earlier*).

Indictable-only offence One that can only be tried by a jury at Crown court.

Indictment A written statement of the charge(s) which is put to the defendant at the **arraignment** (*see earlier*) at Crown court.

Information A written statement alleging an offence, that is presented or laid before a magistrate who is then asked to issue a summons or warrant for arrest.

Inherent jurisdiction The powers of a court which derive from common law rather than statute. The inherent jurisdiction of lower courts, for example magistrates courts, is more limited than that of the higher courts, for example the High Court.

Injunction A court order requiring someone, or an organisation, to do something specified by the court, or forbidding a specific activity or act.

Interdict In Scottish law, an **injunction** (*see earlier*).

Journalistic material Material acquired and created for the purposes of journalism. Special protection is given to journalistic material in the sections of the Police and Criminal Evidence Act 1984 that lay down the procedure whereby the police may search premises for evidence of serious arrestable offences.

Judicial review A review by the Queen's Bench Divisional Court, part of the High Court, of decisions taken by a lower court, tribunal, public body or public official.

Legal aid Public money provided to pay for legal advice and legal representation in court for a party in a civil case or a defendant in a criminal case, if their income is low enough to qualify for such aid.

Malice In law not only spite or ill-will but also dishonest or improper motive. Proof of malice can be used by a **claimant** (*see earlier*) in a libel action to deprive the defendant of the defence of qualified privilege.

Mitigation A plea for leniency in the sentence due to be imposed, citing extenuating circumstances, which is made in court or on behalf of a convicted defendant.

Mode of trial hearing The hearing at a magistrates court which determines whether an **either-way case** (*see earlier*) is dealt with by that court or proceeds to a Crown court. Also known as the **allocation** procedure

Moral rights The rights of an author of a work, in addition to copyright, to be correctly identified as the author and the right to object to derogatory treatment of that work.

Narrative verdict/narrative conclusion The system of allowing a coroner or inquest jury to make a short statement of the circumstances of a person's death, rather than the traditional 'short-form' verdicts.

Newton hearing A hearing in which, after a defendant is convicted, the court hears evidence to help it decide on sentence because the prosecution version of the circumstances of the offence differs substantially from the defence version. Newton was the defendant's name in the relevant, precedent case.

Ofcom Broadcasting Code Code of ethics used by Ofcom to adjudicate on complaints against broadcasters.

Police bail The system administered by police whereby a person under ongoing investigation can be released from arrest on conditions, including that they return to a police station on a later date, at which time they may be questioned again, charged, or be told there will be no charge. They can be arrested if they breach the conditions. After being charged, they can be bailed by police to attend court, or may be taken there in custody.

Preliminary hearing A hearing at magistrates or Crown court before any trial.

Prima facie Literally, 'at first sight'. In criminal law a 'prima facie case' is one in which a preliminary examination by a court has established that there is sufficient prosecution evidence for it to proceed to trial. In journalism ethics, the term prima facie grounds means that preliminary inquiries have established there is sufficient evidence or sufficient ground of suspicion to justify use of deception or undercover tactics in an investigation.

Prior restraint The power which courts have to stop material being published. The UK's tradition of a free media means there is a general rule against prior restraint in defamation law, making judges very reluctant to ban publication of material which the media argue can be successfully defended in any future libel trial. However, in privacy cases judges are more likely to grant injunctions.

Privilege A defence, absolute or qualified, against an action for libel which attaches to reports produced from certain events, documents, or statements.

Public interest The phrase 'in the public interest' is used by judges to define when an individual's rights, for example to privacy, can legally be infringed if this produces a sufficiently major benefit to society, for example from investigative journalism. But judges may also decide that a general 'public interest', for example in the confidentiality of medical records, needs to be upheld against media activity. Code of ethics use the phrase too, to indicate when journalists may be justified in infringing people's rights.

Recorder An assistant judge at Crown court who is usually appointed to sit part-time (for example for spells of a fortnight). Solicitors and barristers are both eligible for appointment as a recorder.

Remand An individual awaiting trial can be remanded on bail, or in custody.

Robbery Theft (*see later*) by force, or threat of force. The word robbery is often used, wrongly, to describe simple theft.

Sending for trial The procedure by which an **indictable-only offence** (*see earlier*) and, in the **allocation** procedure, some **either-way offences** are sent from the magistrates court to a Crown court

Skeleton arguments The documents in which each side in civil or criminal court proceedings sets out the basis of their case. Journalists should normally be allowed to see them to assist the reporting of the proceedings.

Spent conviction A conviction that is no longer recognised after the time (varying according to sentence) specified in the Rehabilitation of Offenders Act 1974. After this time, a media organisation referring to the

conviction may not have available some of the normal defences in the law of libel.

Statements of case Documents including the **claim form** (*see earlier*), particulars of claim, defence, counterclaims, reply to the defence and 'further information documents' in a civil action – reports of which are now protected by **privilege** (*see earlier*).

Statute An Act of Parliament – that is, primary legislation created by Parliament.

Statutory instrument Secondary legislation which can be enacted without parliamentary debate by a Minister to make detailed law (for example rules and regulations) or amendment to the law, under powers given earlier by a statute (an Act of Parliament, the primary legislation). Statutory instruments are also used to phase in gradually, for administrative convenience, legal changes brought about by Acts.

Strict liability A strict liability offence does not require the prosecution to show intent on the part of the accused. Statutory contempt of court is a strict liability offence.

Sub judice Literally 'under law'. Often applied to the risk which may arise in reporting forthcoming legal proceedings. Frequently used by authority as a reason for not disclosing information. But this is not the test for strict liability under the Contempt of Court Act 1981.

Subpoena A court order compelling a person to attend court to give evidence.

Summary offence A comparatively minor offence which can usually only be dealt with by magistrates.

Summary proceedings Cases dealt with by magistrates. At the end of a summary trial of an **either-way offence** (*see earlier*), however, magistrates can, if they consider their powers of sentence insufficient, **commit for sentence** (*see earlier*).

Summary trial A trial at a magistrates court.

Supreme Court The name originally given to the Court of Appeal, the High Court, and the Crown court as a combined system. However, from October 2009 the House of Lords appellate committee (the court commonly referred to merely as 'the House of Lords') became the UK Supreme Court.

Surety A person, usually a friend or relative of the defendant, to whom a court entrusts the responsibility to ensure that the defendant, having been given **bail** (*see earlier*), returns to court on the due date. The surety may pledge a sum of money as guarantee that the defendant will answer bail, and risks losing it if the defendant fails to do so.

Taken into consideration The system under which a defendant admits to having committed offences with which he has not been charged, enabling him to clear the slate and avoid the risk of subsequent prosecution for those offences.

Theft Dishonest appropriation of another's property with the intention of permanently depriving the other of it.

Tort A civil wrong for which monetary damages may be awarded if the person affected sues in civil law, for example defamation, medical negligence.

Truth The defence in defamation actions that the words complained of are proved as true.

Warranted Term used in the **Ofcom Broadcasting Code** (*see earlier*) to indicate that an ethical norm can be breached if there is a public interest justification, or some other exceptional justification.

Without notice *Previously known as* ex parte, of the one part. An injunction without notice is one granted after a court has heard only one side of the case.

Book list

Chapter 1, Introduction

Free Speech, E M Barendt (Oxford University Press, 2nd edition, 2007)

Chapter 2, The Editors' Code of Practice

A Press Free and Responsible: Self Regulation and the Press Complaints Commission, 1991-2001, Richard Shannon (John Murray, 2001)

Chapter 14, Open justice and access to court information

Media Law, Geoffrey Robertson and Andrew Nicol (Penguin, 5th edition, 2008)

Chapter 18, Contempt of court

Arlidge, Eady and Smith on Contempt, Sir David Eady and Professor A T H Smith (Sweet & Maxwell, 4th edition, 2011)

Chapter 19, Defamation – definitions and dangers

Blackstone's Guide to the Defamation Act, James Price QC and Felicity McMahon, (Oxford University Press, 2013)

Carter-Ruck on Libel and Privacy, Alastair Mullis and Cameron Dole (eds) (LexisNexis Butterworths, 6th edition, 2010)

Defamation and Freedom of Speech, Dario Milo (Oxford University Press, 2008)

Defamation: Law, Procedure and Practice, David Price, Nicola Cain and Korieh Duodu (Sweet & Maxwell, 4th edition, 2009)

Gatley on Libel and Slander, Richard Parkes, (Alastair Mullis and Godwin Busuttil (authors), Patrick Milmo and W V H Rogers (eds) (Sweet & Maxwell, 12th edition, 2013)

Chapter 25, Breach of confidence

Confidentiality, Charles Phipps and Roger Toulson (Sweet & Maxwell, 3rd edition, 2012)

Chapter 26, Privacy

Privacy and Media Freedom, Raymond Wacks (Oxford University Press, 2013)

The Law of Privacy and the Media, Mark Warby QC, Nicole Moreham and Iain Christie (eds) (Oxford University Press, 2nd edition, 2011)

Privacy and Freedom of Expression, Richard Clayton QC and Hugh Tomlinson QC (Oxford University Press, 2nd edition, 2010)

Chapter 28, Data Protection Law

Data Protection Law and Practice, Rosemary Jay (Sweet and Maxwell, 4th edition, 2012)

Data Protection: A Guide to UK and EU Law, Peter Carey (Oxford University Press, 3rd edition, 2009)

Chapter 29, Copyright

Copinger and Skone James on Copyright, Nicholas Caddick QC, Gillian Davies and
  Gwilym Harbottle (Sweet and Maxwell, 16th edition, 2010)

Chapter 30, Freedom of Information Act 2000

Your Right to Know, Heather Brooke (Pluto Press, 2nd edition, 2006)
Freedom of Information: The Law, the Practice and the Ideal, Patrick Birkinshaw
  (Cambridge University Press, 2010)

Chapter 33, Official secrets

Media Law, Geoffrey Robertson and Andrew Nicol (Penguin, 5th edition, 2008)
National Security and the D-Notice System, Pauline Sadler (Dartmouth Publishing Co
  Ltd, 2001)
Official Secrets: The Use and Abuse of the Act, David Hooper (Coronet Books, 1988)
Secrecy and the Media: The official History of the D-notice System, Nicholas John
  Wilkinson (Routledge, 2009)

www.mcnaes.com online chapter, Terrorism and the effect of counter-terrorism law

Terrorism and the Law, Clive Walker (Oxford University Press, 2011)

Table of Cases

Table of Statutes

The European Convention on Human Rights is tabled under Sch 1 of the Human Rights Act 1998

Table of Statutory Instruments

Index